PRAISE FOR

WEALTH BY
STEALTH

THE BOOK IS JUST SUPERB. In clear, limpid prose the author, a noted corporate law scholar, demystifies corporate law. He dissects the complex legal apparatus that corporations and their supporters ("cheerleaders", in Harry Glasbeek's words) have used to secure and maintain the political, legal, and ideological dominance they now enjoy, in Canada and increasingly throughout the world. The book shows why corporations are persistent and chronic offenders against every kind of law (with lots of great examples), and why they tend to escape punishment, or get off very lightly. Most important of all, the book shows how corporate dominance can be contested, setting out numerous strategies that democratic activists can employ.

— *Laureen Snider*, *Department of Sociology, Queen's University*

HARRY GLASBEEK PROVIDES the evidence to those of us who always suspected that there was something profoundly undemocratic about corporate capitalism. This is a rare analysis that examines not only corporate behaviour but also how our legal systems let the real actors hide behind their actions. I recommend this book as a work of genuine legal education.

— *Mary Marrone*, *Former Executive Director,*
Community Legal Education Ontario

HOW DO YOU LIKE THE ARGUMENT offered by Philip Morris to Czech Republic authorities that they ought not to interfere with a free market in cigarettes because the resulting deaths of more people at an earlier age would save the government enormous sums that otherwise would have to be spent to provide medical care for these people in their old age? If you find this view morally obnoxious, as I do, you will be further outraged by the information and analysis offered by Professor Harry Glasbeek of the way corporations prey upon the public because they are driven by greed and emboldened by capitalistic laws that shield them from the retribution they so richly deserve. *Wealth by Stealth* is a book for every reader. It is written in straightforward language, richly documented, and profoundly disturbing.

—*Gilbert Geis, Professor Emeritus, Department of Criminology,*
Law and Society, University of California, Irvine;
Past President, American Society of Criminology

GLOBALIZATION HAS MEANT the universalization of the limited liability capitalist business corporation. Here, at last, is an accessible book written by a lawyer that shows the relationship between this legal form and the uses to which it is put. Harry Glasbeek clearly explains the nature of that piece of social engineering, the corporation, and shows how it provides a shield behind which the deep irresponsibility of all capitalist production is multiplied many times.

—*Frank Pearce, co-author of* Toxic Capitalism: Corporate
Crime and the Chemical Industry

WEALTH BY STEALTH

STEALTH

Corporate Crime, Corporate Law,
and the Perversion of Democracy

Harry Glasbeek

Between the Lines
Toronto, Canada

Wealth by Stealth

First published in Canada in 2002 by
Between the Lines
720 Bathurst Street, Suite #404
Toronto, Ontario
M5S 2R4

National Library of Canada Cataloguing in Publication Data

Glasbeek, H.J.
  Wealth by Stealth : corporate crime, corporate law, and the
perversion of democracy / Harry Glasbeek.

Includes bibliographical references and index.
ISBN 1-896357-41-5

  1. Corporations—Corrupt practices. 2. Corporate power.
3.Business and politics. 4. Social responsibility of business.
I. Title.

HV6768.G52 2002   174'.4   C2002-903384-5

Cartoons and cover art by Phillipe Maurais
Cover and text design by Jennifer Tiberio

Printed in Canada

Between the Lines gratefully acknowledges assistance for its publishing activities from the Canada Council for the Arts, the Ontario Arts Council, and the Government of Canada through the Book Publishing Industry Development Program.

THE CANADA COUNCIL LE CONSEIL DES ARTS
FOR THE ARTS DU CANADA
SINCE 1957 DEPUIS 1957

Canada

ONTARIO ARTS COUNCIL
CONSEIL DES ARTS DE L'ONTARIO

Contents

Acknowledgements

I was a legal academic for a long time, and for most of my career my obsession was labour relations law. Because law in a liberal-capitalist society emphasizes the centrality of the individual, the place of the collective always needs justifying. Most of labour law teaching and writing, therefore, concentrates on how to deal with workers' evident need and desire to collectivize, to build some countervailing power to offset the economic clout of the much wealthier employing classes. We, labour law scholars, concentrate on trade unions and the scope of legitimacy they should be granted, on the scope that their collective actions—bargaining, strikes, picketing—should be given. The employer, like the employee, is considered to be legally unproblematic. Employers are seen to be acting as individuals, requiring no special licence for their activities.

One day, while presenting materials on occupational health and safety issues to my class, I became angry at the numbers: workers were being maimed and killed in droves. Why, I exclaimed, should not the employers who profited from this mayhem be held criminally accountable? My students, being law students, were appalled. They forced me—as good students should do—to support my claim. I researched the issue and wrote about the feasibility of criminalizing harmful conduct in workplaces. The technical arguments made appeared to meet with scholarly approval, but yielded no concrete results: employers were still rarely prosecuted and even more rarely convicted. I pondered and eventually came to understand that one of the ingredients in the mix that makes for this gap between theory and practice is the nature of the dominant employers. They are corporations. Scales fell off my eyes.

There might be something about how some enterprises are organized as corporations that has an impact on law and other institutions of our liberal democracy. It does matter, therefore, who the employer is—not just for the purposes of labour law but, indeed, for all sorts of other purposes. Once I began to think about these questions, I came to the conclusion that it would be worthwhile to determine what it is about corporate structure that might be occluding the normal operation of the criminal law when the alleged wrongdoers had adopted a corporate guise. I commenced teaching a course I entitled "The Corporation as Criminal," and I wrote about the subject-matter in the usual academic way whilst I made myself more familiar with standard corporate law and became a corporate lawyer. This book is an outcome of these reflections and the many discussions and debates with my students and colleagues that these new—to me—lines of inquiry opened up.

Clearly, then, I owe a debt to the experiences and knowledge of countless others, known and unknown to me. Having lived my professional life in a university law school—one unusually friendly to alternative and critical approaches—I found it to be more obvious than is perhaps usually the case that I was drawing on socially developed knowledge and experience. Colleagues and students are all participating in a common exercise, one that, to thrive, does not rely on each and everyone of us to get ahead regardless of the common enterprise's good. This is an important point for me to make, because it is one of my hopes that this book will contribute to an understanding that it is more likely that we can enrich our sense of community and reciprocity by doing things together in a public, collective setting, in a circumstance in which private profit-making is not central to our thinking.

This work sets out to demonstrate how the uses of the corporate form distort various beliefs and ideals that many of us claim are dear to us. It is intended, through an exposition of a number of features of corporate life that are rarely discussed in this kind of setting, to make readers question what they are asked to accept as normal and "natural" as they live out their everyday lives.

To acknowledge the debt owed to the multitudes whose understandings and actions contribute to our own understandings and actions does not gainsay the need to thank people who were directly and personally supportive and helpful. While even such a personal list would be a long one, too long to offer, I would be remiss if I did not express my gratitude to my spouse, Sandra Glasbeek, whose tolerance and indulgence with my intense preoccupations define loving patience; my daughters, Amanda and Denise, whose commitment to the plight of the more vulnerable, and to the truth, fill me with respect and imbue me with sentiments that I hope to have conveyed in these pages; and Phil Maurais, whose political art graces these pages and whose well-developed sense of right and wrong is manifest in everything he says and does. I also want to thank Rob Clarke, who had the tiresome task of editing the manuscript and did so, elegantly; and all at Between the Lines, who were uncompromisingly courteous and supportive.

Introduction

This is a book about democracy in Canada or, more accurately, about the lack of democracy in Canada. It is written by a lawyer—worse, by a corporate lawyer. Clearly, for many people this particular mix of subject and authorship will require justification.

The conventional characterization of Canadian governance is that of a mature liberal democracy, a country in which the people are sovereign. The wishes of the majority are to prevail, provided implementation of those formally expressed wishes is respectful of the rights of the minority. Somehow, though, this characterization does not work out in practice. Indeed, in contemporary Canada, the majority of the alleged sovereign people get the opposite of what they want. Opinion polls tell us, for instance, that Canadians want security in employment and in old age.* Time and again the polls show that most Canadians want equal access to quality education and health services and a stable social welfare system that permits the vulnerable amongst them to live decently. Canadians also show a strong preference for

---

* My purpose in writing *Wealth by Stealth* has been to offer a no-nonsense description of corporations and the world they inhabit. For those who may find the presentation too plain, the notes and sources beginning on p. 285 provide nuances, and enrich the arguments made. The reader will quickly see that these notes are more substantial than conventional endnotes.

the maintenance of a cultural environment that they can call their own and a physical environment that they can respect and enjoy.

Even allowing for the nuances of interpretation—these preferences can mean different things to different observers—it is obvious that Canadian governance blatantly ignores the majority's wishes. For the last decade or more there has been less and less security in employment. For more than twenty years the rate of unemployment has remained historically high. Real wages have been dropping; people who are employed have to work longer hours to maintain the living standards that were achieved during the 1950s. Contingent, precarious, insecure work is on the rise as full-time work decreases proportionally. Unsurprisingly—but no less obscenely for that— more and more people, including employed people, are driven to the indignity of having to rely on food banks; more and more people in this bountiful land are forced to live on the streets; more and more children live below the poverty line—all at the very same time as governments of all stripes are making access to (the even more) needed educational and health services less easily available. These trends have been complemented by savage cuts in the social welfare systems. Canadian cultural institutions have been sold to the highest bidder and the degradation of the environment continues apace. Women, whose labour is still largely underpaid—or not paid for at all— remain disproportionately excluded from the dominant economic and political institutions.

Does this dismal record mean that, after all, Canada is not a real democracy? The only way that this clear negation of the well-known wishes of Canadians might be explained away is that, although we are members of a true democracy, there is something that we refer to as "the economy" that does not permit all of us to have what we so badly want. Now, because "the economy" is a capitalist economy, the only interpretation we can draw from this failure is that capitalism cannot deliver what people want. This conclusion signifies that what so many pundits have been calling the triumph of capitalism over socialism also heralds the end of contentment. Those pundits are not anxious to draw that conclusion; they prefer instead to see the present parlous circumstance as just a temporary downturn.

Of course, this is not the first time in history that the pursuit of riches by the few has brought hardship or even worse to the many. In relatively recent history, wealth-seekers, supported by European nations such as England, France, Germany, Spain, Portugal, and the Netherlands, as well as, even more recently, the United States, have enslaved populations and bought and sold human beings as if they were baubles. Our Western predecessors dispossessed indigenous people who lived in territories that they, the Westerners, felt the need to exploit; they slaughtered the people and destroyed their ancient cultures in the unabated search for material wealth. They pillaged and ravaged natural resources and animal life as if there would be no tomorrow.

Those events are now said to be ancient history, a tale of days gone by. Further, those early phases of capitalism, ugly though they seem to our modern eyes, did bring economic abundance to many—if not all—people. They are often seen as somewhat regrettable, but necessary, stages in the evolution of capitalist relations of production. We have left the state-supported capitalist phases of imperialism and colonialism behind; capitalism has matured and, in the process, become more civilized. Capitalists no longer need to rely directly on the military and economic might of their own nation-states. The traditional uses made of national power, namely to protect capitalists from rivals from another country and to help them subjugate local populations, are no longer required. A worldwide commitment to the free movement of goods and people is rapidly emerging and eventually this phenomenon will turn the world into one integrated market. Although we are not quite there yet, the conventional view is that this perfected phase of capitalism is around the corner. It will be a world in which the neutral market, rather than political power with its potential for tyranny, will determine people's well-being, even if this well-being seems a little out of reach just now.

It is this set of beliefs that allows so many pundits to feel good when they trumpet the triumph of capitalism. It is in this sense that some intelligent observers have come up with the logically absurd idea that we have reached the end of history, that we have mounted the highest possible plateau of political and economic development. This new, allegedly more civilized, stage of capitalism is called globalization. In essence, the idea is that capitalism's principal actors are liberated (or soon will be) from state-created shackles and are free to roam the globe in search of resources, labour, and markets. Capitalism's principal actors are corporations. Sometimes, therefore, this latest manifestation of capitalism is referred to as "corporate capitalism," while those who disparage its outcomes will attribute them to the workings of what they refer to (with anger) as "corporate rule" or "the corporate agenda."

But, after thus implicitly acknowledging the centrality of the corporation, both proponents and antagonists of the "new" capitalism tend to ignore the significance of this legal creation, which is seen simply as a tool, a device. In a general way, this view is accurate enough: we would still have capitalism if there were no corporations involved. But it might well be a very different kind of capitalism. Both scholars inquiring into the scope and character of the new capitalism and activists who want to resist its forward march ignore the nature of the corporation at their peril.

That is why, as a corporate lawyer, I might be able to make a contribution to the consideration of these questions. This book sets out to describe, accurately but plainly, what a corporation actually is and how it has become such a useful tool in furthering the drive to accumulate the wealth that lies at the heart of the political-economic system we call capitalism. As the narrative unfolds, the tensions created, both for the political and the economic legitimacy of the corporation, will be teased out. This will be done to show that, *in principle*, the legal architecture of capitalism's favourite device—the legal corporation-for-profit—undermines the political and economic justificatory scheme essential to the acceptability, maintenance, and perpetuation of capitalism.

Once we recognize the existence of this underlying contradiction, we should find it easier to force through corporate law reforms. That change could reduce, somewhat, the disproportionate political and economic power wielded by some very few rich people, hidden from view by corporations. That is, wealth-owners would face increased pressure to find ways of assuring the people that Canada remains wedded to the ideals of a liberal democracy. But still, any ensuing concessions in that regard will make only a marginal difference. To make a crushing impact on the disproportionate power bestowed by the corporate form on a privileged minority, we need more than a demonstration that the *theoretical* underpinnings of the corporation are challengeable. To delegitimate the existing regime, we have to complement the theoretical exercise with an examination of the *actual practices* of corporations.

Part of my approach here is to demonstrate the extent to which anti-social and criminal behaviour are endemic to the very structure of the corporation-for-profit. This conceptual exposition is in turn related to the clear inability and/or unwillingness of the state to treat the very large number of instances of serious corporate wrongdoing as crimes. That position is in turn connected to the Canadian state's political and economic dependence on what is called the corporate sector, a dependency that, to an alarming extent, dilutes the democratic rights of Canadians.

This book, then, is not a book about corporate law for lawyers and their clients. It is about how the law has stepped in to make "capitalist" the most important word in the much-invoked term "liberal-capitalist democracy." Correspondingly, this emphasis has marginalized the ideals contained in the words "liberal" and "democracy." Law has helped this process along by a sleight of hand: its agenda is hidden by its pretence that, in the corporation, it has invented a mere instrument, a tool, an entity that does not favour some particular political goals over others. But the resulting constraints on democratic rights and entitlements are not "natural" and, therefore, unavoidable. Rather, they are the result of legal and political manipulations that underpin the corporate way of doing business. If the limits on democratic practices arise out of legal and political machinations, those same limits can be removed by informed legal and political activists.

After introducing the legalized nature of this thing that we call a corporation, I take up, first (in chapters 3 and 4), the matter of how corporations and corporate law function in the small-business setting. My hope is that the distortion of the market model by the corporation's involvement will quickly become apparent. This should tend to undermine the legitimacy that corporate capitalism derives from its supposed association with market values and practices. The remainder of the book then turns to the structure and machinations of large, publicly traded corporations. Once again, it will be demonstrated that adherence to the idealized market model by corporate actors is the exception rather than the rule. This should reinforce the contention that corporate capitalism cannot be justified by reference to the market model. In addition, the structure and workings of these corporate behemoths will be shown to be antithetical to the political values of liberal democracy with which capitalism seeks to ally itself.

Bob Sass, an occupational health and safety activist and scholar, once told me, "Knowledge is not power, power is power." The dissemination of knowledge, then, is a first, but necessary, step to changing things; and things need to be changed. As part of that important first step I want this book to be informative and interesting; but, somewhat immodestly, I want more. I want to show what it means to say that today's version of capitalism is characterized by corporate rule, and in particular to show how anti-human that rule is. I want this to be a political book as well as a source of information for anyone who reads it. While my work cannot hope to attain the quality of his scholarship, I am inspired by Samir Amin, who wrote:

> My stand . . . demands that I avoid a narrowly academic approach to writing. . . . I regard writing as a significant social act. Unlike many academics, I do not try to produce a definitive work, but rather a piece of writing that is one step in an endless development process carried on by a collective of oneself and others. . . . When I write I always have in mind a more attractive public from my point of view, an audience of committed militant intellectuals.

With these words in mind, then, let us now move to the task of demonstrating how the corporation, under colour of law, favours the few at the expense of the many, and how it imposes costs on the non-wealthy and limits the responsibility of the rich.

The Corporation as an Invisible Friend

Wherein we first learn that our captains of industry, finance, retail, and everything else are irresponsible hypocrites.

Sometimes when children are young they make certain they have companions by inventing friends. They talk and play with them as if they really exist. A girl might ape her parents and invite them to join her and her invisible friend Kim to take afternoon tea. The amused parents will nod gravely when they are introduced to Kim and may help set a place at the table for the invisible visitor. But the parents will stop the play-acting when their child tries to blame Kim for a broken plate. They are likely to tell their flesh and blood daughter, "Now, stop that nonsense. *You* broke that plate. *You* clean it up. Let that be a lesson to you to be more careful in the future."

Conrad Black has an invisible friend. So does Lord Thomson of Fleet, and so do Wallace and Harrison McCain, Kenneth Irving, Paul Desmarais, Frank Stronach, Galen Weston—as do all other captains of Canadian industry, finance, retail, and everything else. But, unlike our little kid, they are not asked to shoulder the responsibility for any havoc they may cause. They are allowed to blame their "Kim." They are allowed to hide behind their invisible friends. Conrad Black's invisible friend is called Hollinger Inc. Lord

Thomson's invisible friend is known as Thomson Corp. One McCain's play-mate is McCain Foods, the other's is Maple Leaf Foods. Kenneth Irving's is Irving Co. Paul Desmarais hid behind Power Corporation of Canada for years, as now do his sons Paul Jr. and André. Magna International is Frank Stronach's greatest pal, and Galen Weston's are George Weston and Loblaws Companies Ltd.

These invisible friends are corporations. We "hear" corporations talk. They "tell" us, "We are good corporate citizens." They say, "People are our most important product" and "We do it all for you." In turn we speak about them as if they have a real existence, as if they were living, tangible beings. It is more common for workers in a dispute with their employer to say "the company is unfair" than "the boss is nasty." This is so because, for many peo-ple, there is no visible human boss to be angry with but only an invisible employer—a corporation. In short, it is a commonplace to acknowledge the reality and existence of corporations and their significance to our lives.

And yet . . . corporations are constructs of law; they are not natural phenomena. No one has ever seen a corporation, smelled a corporation, touched a corporation, lifted a corporation, or made love to a corporation. Conrad Black's best friend is just as invisible and, in human terms, no more real than Kim, our inventive kid's creation. But in reality the invention of Kim is a mere psychological and passing stage in a child's life, whereas cor-porations are the primary, permanent, and very concrete tools that wealth-owners use to satisfy their never-ending drive to accumulate more riches and power at the expense of the rest of us, the majority.

The Essential Characteristics of the Invisible Friend: The Corporation-for-Profit

One of the more astonishing things about this legal creation (and there are many) is that there are virtually no legal barriers to hurdle for any individual who wants to form a corporation. Individuals need not give any reason to anyone as to why they want to form a corporation. Nor does an individual need any money, over and beyond the wherewithal to pay a derisory registra-tion fee, to form a corporation. Every sane, non-bankrupt adult has the right to form a corporation by meeting a few minor procedural requirements to the satisfaction of a government bureaucracy. Evidently, the law is eager to help us to create corporations. Also, the law's largesse does not end once it has helped a real, live, human being establish a corporation. When a busi-ness takes on a corporate form, a number of truly wondrous things happen.

First, upon registration—that is, upon birth—the corporation is instantly mature. There is no childhood or discombobulating adolescence to go through, phases through which we, mere mortals, have to suffer. Until we humans become adults, we are not trusted with the full legal rights and privileges, nor are we encumbered by the legal obligations, of social and political citizenship. Unlike us mere humans, a corporation does not have to go through a maturing, proving-itself-worthy period. From the moment it is registered—and, remember, that is no trick at all—it has all the legal capacities it is ever going to have.

This brings us to the second facet of its instant attributes. In some important ways, the legal capacities of corporations are greater than those of human beings. A corporation can buy, sell, lease, and own property, just like any adult Canadian. But, unlike us, a corporation can do so for ever. It has perpetual life; it does not age. To die, it must be killed (say, by a forced liquidation), eaten by another predator (say, by a successful takeover bidder), or commit suicide (say, by a voluntary liquidation). Being born fully mature, a corporation can instantly give birth to another corporation, or even thousands of others, by registering new entities as soon as it begins to "breathe." In turn these offspring can do the same at the very instant of their birth, that is, upon being registered. There is no pesky gestation period, nor are there any natural/biological limits on reproduction. Real live people imaginatively use this power to create family members at will to obscure corporate doings and to manipulate taxation and other laws.

This creative process is carried out in conjunction with the third characteristic of the corporation, one that is just as fantastical as the first two. Given that, upon birth, the corporation instantly acquires a whole range of capacities to engage in legal transactions—in lawyers' terms, it is endowed with some form of legal personality—what does it mean to say that something or someone has a legal personality? And what is the importance of noting that a corporation has it?

Each nation-state endows its citizens with a set of rights and duties that create a legal envelope within which the people of that nation-state can conduct themselves. Every political entity, then, bestows on its citizens a political and economic autonomy reflecting the scope of sovereignty of the human members of that polity. The content of this sphere of freedom of decision-making and action is termed the legal personality—as opposed to the psychological personality or the biological makeup—of a nation's citizens. In Canada we pride ourselves on having given ourselves a great deal of scope to make our own decisions; and, therefore, we boast that freedom reigns in Canada. We believe that this country grants its citizens the respect they should be accorded as sentient human beings. As it turns out, we accord very much the same level of respect to non-human beings, to non-sentient beings. Canadian law grants corporations, the invisible friends of our various captains of industry and everything else, the same kind of legal personality that it grants to you and me. Section 15 of the *Canada Business Corporations Act* unequivocally states, "A corporation has the capacity and . . . the rights, powers and privileges of a natural person." It could not be plainer: the law treats corporations as if they were real people. This gives corporations unexpected, indeed extraordinary, attributes.

Of course, there are some human things that a corporation obviously cannot do despite having been granted a form of personhood. A corporation, being an abstraction, obviously cannot think or have a belief, and therefore it cannot vote as if it were a flesh and blood citizen. Even this logic, though, is coming under attack. In Sydney, Australia, corporations are permitted to vote in municipal elections if they own, lease, or occupy rateable property; but that is the exception to the rule. Still, it turns out that the mere lack of human attributes does not always disqualify a corporation from claiming rights that we think of as rights that belong to human beings because, well, they are human rights in the sense of being rights associated with social relations between living persons.

A corporation *legally* can engage in speech, base claims on human beings' religious or political beliefs, or even claim protection for its need for privacy, as if it were a man or woman who craves private space for intimate thoughts, feelings, and beliefs. All scientific logic, it seems, is thrown out the window when it comes to corporations. We are to apply corporate law logic, and that logic is weird. To enable them to ward off the impact of some government regulation they do not like, corporate persons frequently claim to have what an ordinary person might think of as peculiarly human moral and political attributes. In addition—and most importantly—the grant of a legal personality allows corporations to own property, just as you and I do.

This right draws attention to the fourth major characteristic of this particular invisible friend: it has something lawyers call limited liability. The new legal person, the corporation, owns the property invested in it and borrowed by it to carry on business. It is this feature that enables it to buy, sell, lease, assign, or mortgage property and things, just as any free, adult Canadian can. This ability makes the corporation truly separate and distinct from its investors. The separate legal personality and its other capacities come as part of a package that includes limited liability—a truly stunning attribute.

For example, let's say a certain investor—we'll call her Mary Worth—makes a contribution of capital to a corporation on the understanding that she will share in the profits (if any) of the business carried on by the corporation. The value of her entitlement is related to the proportion that her contribution bears to the total of such contributions. As evidence of that interest, the corporation issues Mary a certificate describing the extent of her interest. This is a share certificate and Mary, the investor, is now called a shareholder. A shareholder can sell the certificate, the piece of paper. There is a market that attaches values to these pieces of paper—the stock or share market. The shareholders, therefore, can be said to have legal title to the value of that paper. But the investor no longer has legal title to the capital she contributed to the corporation. The legal owner of that capital is now the corporation.

No longer being the legal owner of the invested capital, and not being the legal person who enters into the corporation's business transactions, the investor/shareholder is not held personally responsible for any obligations incurred by the corporation. The only thing Mary Worth has on the line is her initial investment, which might be lost by the corporation. Her personal wealth is not available to anyone to whom the corporation owes money, even if the corporation cannot meet obligations that it incurred because of its efforts to return profits to Mary Worth as an investor/shareholder. This, of course, is what makes it attractive for owners of disposable wealth to invest in incorporated businesses as opposed to other kinds of businesses. Investors, who pride themselves on being called risk-takers, like to shift the risks they have had created on their behalf to others. This is what is called limited liability: the cat's out of the bag.

The very logic of the legal corporation, then, requires us to throw out our usual way of speaking and thinking about such things. Everything is upside down. What is apparent is that when people say a corporation has limited liability, they mean the opposite. The corporation's liability, like yours and mine, is only limited by its physical ability (that is, by the extent of its assets) to honour that liability. Its legal obligation, like yours and mine, is not limited. It is the investor/shareholder whose liability is limited. What is carefully hidden by saying that a corporation has limited liability—that is, hidden by the perverse use of language—is that it is *people* who, if they were not shaded from legal view by the veil of corporate personality, have limited liability. It is not Hollinger Inc., Thomson Corp., McCain Foods, Maple Leaf Foods, Irving Co., Power Corporation, Magna International, and George Weston and Loblaws that have limited liability, but it is Conrad Black, Lord Thomson, the McCain brothers, Kenneth Irving, the Desmarais brothers, Frank Stronach, and Galen Weston who are so blessed by corporate law. They are only responsible to the extent of their actual investment for the obligations incurred by their corporation as it pursued wealth for their benefit. The magic of corporate law has made them less responsible than you and I. We are legally responsible for *all* the harm we cause and for *all* the debts we have incurred in our pursuit of profits.

It is, of course, the same "hidden behind the veil" corporate captains of industry, finance, retail, and everything else, and their mouthpieces, who continuously urge the rest of us, unincorporated human beings, to stand on our own two feet, to take responsibility for our own actions. We are told that we should not rely on artificial protections and, especially, that we should not accept handouts from governments just to shield us from the operation of the market. We should participate in market activities and take our lumps, as sovereign beings are expected to do.

This clamour for self-reliance, for taking responsibility for one's actions, orchestrated by the leaders of our corporate world, provides us with a new definition of "chutzpah," the Yiddish word for cheekiness or unmitigated gall. Chutzpah is often defined as the characteristic of a man who, having been convicted for killing his parents, throws himself upon the mercy of the court on the grounds that he is now an orphan. This is much like the rich people who, having used their corporate vehicles to further enrich them-selves, doing harm to others and leaving unpaid debts in the process, now throw up their hands and ask their victims disingenuously, "Why did *you* not take steps to protect yourself from *our* corporation's acts? Tough luck; you only have yourself to blame."

The Story So Far

Everyone knows that the corporation Hollinger Inc. does the bidding of Conrad Black. Everyone knows it does so because Conrad Black is both a major investor and decision-maker in the corporation. But when the pressure is on, should there ever come a moment when Hollinger has inflicted harm on others that it cannot afford to redress or if it has incurred debts that it can-not afford to repay, Conrad Black will be able to rely on the corporate law that has made Hollinger legally speaking—not functionally, not morally, but *legally*—a person totally distinct from Conrad Black. Legal logic—and no other—will permit Black to say that, in a society based on individual respon-sibility, he cannot be made responsible for the acts of a truly discrete, separate person, Hollinger, the corporation.

This is particularly offensive, for no matter how often lawyers repeat the mantra that a corporation is a legal person, just like you and me and Conrad Black, it is not. It does not have flesh and blood or a mind like you and me and Conrad Black. It cannot act; it cannot think. It can only do so when some real people, with flesh and blood and a mind, do so on its behalf. How, then, can a corporation be said to be a person in its own right, making it appropriate to attach responsibilities to it and to no one else? To counter this dangerous line of argumentation and questioning, (dangerous to the legitimacy of the corporation), corporate law has had to concoct yet other myths.

Some of the corporation's senior managers—those designated as directors, officers, or executives—are treated as if they were the corporation. The thoughts and acts of these flesh and blood functionaries are deemed to be the thoughts and acts of the corporation. They are the acting will and mind of the corporation. This condition papers over the obvious inability of an inanimate being to exercise a will and to do acts. By identifying the corporate person as being the same as the real persons who are appointed to act on its behalf, those concerned find it possible to pretend that a corporation can think and act. But this is only a pretence, and it causes problems in the real world. Law has to engage in some more contortions to avert the inevitable difficulties that ensue. As some more weird corporate law kicks in, new and unappetizing outcomes emerge.

As the thoughts and acts of the very real human beings who are the directors and officers of the corporation are treated as if they were the thoughts and acts of the corporation, they are—legally speaking only, of course—not the thoughts and acts of the directors and officers as people. It follows that the corporation, and not the directors and officers, should be held legally responsible for those thoughts and acts. As a consequence, investors in the corporation are not the only ones blessed with limited liability for risks created by their wealth-seeking activities through the corporation. Directors and officers and executives have a form of limited responsibility as well.

This embarrassing state of the law is based on the mythology that the corporation is a separate person, an artificiality that we are all expected to condone because of the market conveniences it bestows. The state of the law is embarrassing, because it contradicts our elites' frequently intoned claims of belief in the social, political, and economic value of the personal responsibility that each of us supposedly has as a sovereign individual. To this contradiction is added another: it is the elites of the corporate world themselves who are exempted from the norms of personal responsibility by corporate law. Inevitably, there is pressure on those charged with justifying the status quo to offset the impression that our supposedly even-handed legal system supports such unequal treatment. Thus, in recent times, as the public has become more conscious of the many unredressed harms done by, and through, corporations, legislators have felt themselves obliged to impose *some* responsibility for corporate behaviour on real people—on directors and officers. These attempts have met with a storm of protest.

The reasoning behind the resistance to what we might call corporate legal reform has two main strands. The first warns that corporate law, with all its benefits, will be undone by this kind of development. According to this reasoning, because the essence of corporate law is that the corporation is a full legal person in its own right, logic requires the corporation to be *the* responsible person for corporate activities. If politicians truly want to offset the ill effects of a corporation's behaviour, they should do so directly by finding efficient ways of holding the corporation itself more legally accountable as a legal person. This change would leave corporate logic and, therefore, corporate legitimacy, intact. This ignores the fact that any new legislation imposing new responsibilities on directors and officers has been aimed at helping the corporation maintain its standing as capitalism's principal wealth-creating device. If some redress can be had from, or some retribution inflicted on, real people for the harm caused by corporate conduct, citizens may be more accepting of a corporate regime that limits the responsibility of investors. But many individual capitalists/directors/investors (and many people fall into all of these categories simultaneously) do not see this need to appease the public because they are—as they are meant to be—self-serving actors who do not care about the fate of capitalism when their own well-being is on the line.

The second reason for opposition to the recent spate of impositions of new legal duties on directors and officers is similar, but it is even more obviously self-serving than the first. Indeed, it is touched by arrogance. There is unconcealed anger that law-makers are seeking to make directors and officers of corporations, that is, corporate actors, answerable as if they were ordinary mortals like you and me. There are vehement (unsupported) claims that the best and the brightest will no longer make themselves available to serve corporations. Then we—the rest of us—would truly be sorry. And, the argument continues, where is all this ripping away of the corporate veil going to stop? Next, misguided politicians might pass laws to make investors/shareholders in corporations personally responsible for all of the legal liabilities of the corporations in which they invest. This has not happened yet, but, say the lobbyists hired to advocate personal irresponsibility, if it did, it would surely kill the goose that lays the golden eggs. This possibility fills the investing classes with horror. Legislators, they say, should not be permitted to continue on this slippery slope. The corporate sector has had lawyers and legal scholars work overtime to dilute the scope of the new responsibilities imposed on directors and officers and to invent new and better protections for these previously legally and largely irresponsible people. Our self-styled pro-enterprise lobbyists want the profit-seeking corporation, not profit-seeking people, to bear the bulk of the costs of the harms done, and debts left, by corporate profit-seeking conduct.

Clearly, not only have the development and practices of corporate law permitted Conrad Black and his kind to have invisible friends, but they have also let these invisible friends take most of the rap for the broken promises, crushed bodies, and torn environments they leave behind in their pursuit of profits on behalf of investors/shareholders. This legally supported passing of the buck tends to bring law into disrepute. This development is dangerous to the very people who gain from the existing system, because it is one of law's functions to maintain that regime. If the legal fabric is not respected because it treats people unequally, its defence of the status quo will not be effective. To counter these pressures, those involved fashion a whole series of arguments: (i) it is appropriate for law to help individuals pursue profits by forming corporations; and (ii) this course may lead to some apparent inconsistencies in the application of laws; but (iii) these inconsistencies are tolerable given the overall value of profit-seeking via the corporate form. We now turn to the strengths and weaknesses of these arguments.

An Ill-Assorted Trio: Capitalism, the Market, and the Corporation

Wherein we learn how greed and all sorts of inequalities are successfully portrayed as virtues, but also find out that there is something of a fly in the ointment.

The corporation measures up best when we assess its value to capitalism, rather than to liberal-democratic values. This is so because what lies at the heart of capitalism is its maxim that, all other things being equal, human beings *naturally* believe that more is better than less. In economic terms, this belief about the instincts of human beings means that the drive to accumulate wealth is both insatiable and a good thing. Any tool that increases the capacity to accumulate wealth is valuable.

The legal corporation has a number of attributes that make it valuable in this sense. The first such attribute is that, because investors in a business carried on in a corporate form can limit their risk to the amount invested, they can divide up their capital into various lots and direct these to a number and a variety of enterprises. Losses from one investment do not mean personal ruin because the investor's other investments and savings are not at risk. Further, losses from one investment are likely to be offset by gains from others. In these ways, the corporate vehicle furnishes incentives for investors to take more risks—that is, invest in more enterprises—than they otherwise might. There is an enhanced potential for more creative uses of talents and resources and, thereby, more efficient accumulation of wealth.

Second, the same logic permits a larger number of investors to join in a particular enterprise. They need not know each other; their links with the other investors in the corporation are through money only. Each investor puts in capital, and the corporation, in effect the corporation's management, runs the business. Investors have no need for personal relations with the other investors. This practice enlarges the pool of potential contributors of capital and makes it easier to get large amounts together. By contrast, entrepreneurs working alone have only their own resources and credit-ratings to rely on when setting up a business, but they also risk their personal fortunes. Clearly, from an investor's—from a capitalist's—point of view, the corporation is a privileged way of doing business when compared with a sole entrepreneurship.

As a business form, the corporate vehicle is also superior to a partnership. A partnership is created when a group of people form an association to carry on business for profit without incorporating. Because there is no incorporation, each of the partners is personally responsible for all the obligations incurred by the firm, just as if they were sole entrepreneurs. Because each of the partners can participate in the conduct of the business, it matters a whole lot to each of them who the others are. In a partnership, the relations between the investors are personal; there are real ties between real human beings. In capitalism, such touchy-feely sentiments are an encumbrance: they get in the way of the drive to accumulate as much wealth as possible, as quickly as possible.

Working, then, through the synergies obtained by the creation of a separate legal person responsible for its own acts and by the extension of limited liability to those who contribute capital to that corporation in order to profit from its business activities, corporate law provides incentives for more investment—and more varied and more innovative investments—than do other legal ways of doing business.

In addition, the corporate form is capable of yielding considerable cost-savings. Any business needs to obtain materials, component parts, and replacements, store its inventory, and distribute and market its product, among other activities. Often it makes sense to hire independent businesses to carry out some of these functions. It will make such sense when the business does not have the resources, physical facilities, or expertise to carry out these tasks and when it is cheaper to buy these services than to develop in-house capacities. But this means that such services and suppliers must be found and new contracts negotiated, again and again. Doing business in this way carries significant transaction costs. These kinds of transaction costs can be reduced in the corporate form, which can aggregate greater resources and therefore is technically more capable of housing experts and specialized departments for the long haul. This capability diminishes the need for repeat transactions. Of course, the corporation will only house skill, equipment, and resource suppliers when they are cheaper than outside suppliers. With the lowering of trade barriers and growth of new technologies comes an increased tendency to contract-out work that was previously done within the corporation. As well, there is an increasing reliance on out-sourcing for necessary materials. In principle, though, the corporate form does have the potential to reduce transaction costs, and therefore to advance the project of wealth accumulation, capitalism's central project.

These features of the corporation make it well-suited to the accumulation of wealth and, therefore, make it perhaps the most valuable tool of contemporary capitalism. This distinction ought to ensure the corporation's legitimacy. But it does not, because capitalism itself needs to fight for its legitimacy all the time. Capitalism's strongest argument is that the accumulation of wealth for its own sake is a worthwhile economic and, therefore, meritorious social and political goal. The reasoning is that the pursuit of continuous increases in overall wealth enures to the good of all members of that economy. But in economies such as Canada's, because only the few are capitalists, the majority of the population does not automatically get the benefits of the growth in aggregate wealth. The distribution of the augmenting wealth is of enormous importance to this larger group. Distributional issues are related to the sensitive issues of equity and justice; they are political issues. The mere accumulation of wealth by the few is not self-evidently a good from those perspectives. The satisfaction of greed is not an uncontested moral value in a society in which values such as compassion, altruism, and sharing also have historical claims on the collective mindset that makes up the polity.

As a consequence, capitalism's adherents seek to justify its inevitable outcome—the accumulation of wealth by the few—by reference to the machinery of capitalism, namely, the institution that we call the market. They try to establish the political neutrality of the capitalist exercise; they attempt to characterize capitalism as a mere *economic* regime, not one that is about both economic welfare creation and political control. They seek to legitimate capitalism by hiding its *political* aspects, and by equating it with a technocratic institution, the market.

The idea of the competitive market provides technical justifications for greed as a way of life and, simultaneously, a justification for the uneven distribution of the wealth generated by the greed system, by capitalism. Equating capitalism with the economic tool that we call the market thus serves to gain acceptance for capitalism. There is, however, a fly in the ointment. The very market tenets that justify greed and unequal outcomes run counter to the established functional justifications for the corporation. By the light of the unalloyed capitalist goal to generate as much wealth as possible, the way in which corporations function makes them highly acceptable creations. But by the light of the market's *raison d'être*, the way in which corporations function to accumulate wealth for the few creates tensions. As the market's precepts are treated as sacrosanct, the legitimacy of capitalism's principal vehicle—the corporation—and of the legal system that creates it should come under pressure. To those who want to bring a critical perspective to capitalism, the ways in which the market and the corporation interact are, therefore, of great importance.

The Market and Its Justifications for Greed and Inequality

The market model's starting position is that we will be making the most efficient use of our resources and talents if each of us, as *individuals*, uses personal resources and talents to the best of our abilities to meet the demands of all the other individuals who, as individuals, decide what they want and need. The assumption is that, left alone, we will behave as the model wants us to do because, market-modellers believe, greed is an innate and dominant human characteristic. Here the overlap with the tenets of capitalism is obvious.

From this it follows that, as the greed of those individuals who use their resources and talents efficiently to meet other people's demands is satisfied— that is, as they make profits that they can use to satisfy their wants and needs and to engage in more profit-making activities to meet yet more wants and needs—others will be spurred on to compete. These others, to satisfy their greed, will try to become the ones to meet the existing demands and, thereby, to reap the profits. This competition will reward the individuals who can meet a demand at the lowest cost. When all the demand for a particular product or service is met, people with resources and talents will be forced to deploy them to meet different wants and needs.

This never-ending cycle of individual decision-making in respect of the use of one's own assets and of what personal needs should be met by relying on other individuals' productive activities will lead us, the market-modellers say, to make the most efficient uses of the aggregate of our resources and talents. While this efficiency is achieved by the promotion of acquisitiveness, a capitalist goal, it also provides a justification for unequal outcomes. After all, healthy competition will *naturally* produce winners and losers. In this sense, the market model is congruent with the "accumulation of wealth by the few" agenda that is the heart and soul of capitalism.

The market, then, justifies greed and inequality on the basis that it leads to overall *economic* efficiency and, therefore, not only to the overall good, but also to a proper distribution of economic welfare as each market participant will get what she or he deserves. It is very useful for capitalism—a *political* economic system that promotes the satisfaction of the greed of the few by permitting the exploitation of the many—to be able to legitimate itself by claiming its congruence with the market. The market transforms greed from a dubious moral value into a useful technical catalyst. Greed—the ugly engine of capitalism—becomes a valuable ally to the pro-market capitalism policy-makers who claim to be pursuing the overall economic welfare of the nation. It can be advocated as a good thing. A nice example is provided by the occasion when Barbara McDougall, as minister of state for finance, addressed a conference on Native Canadian business and expressed her government's support for Native-owned businesses: "There is one underlying motive in business shared by all—it is greed. We support it wherever it happens."

The equation of capitalism, a political-economic regime, with the market, portrayed as a piece of machinery designed to promote economic efficiency, has another significant benefit. The market also provides support for an ideology and a set of political ideas that bolster the *political* aspect of the political economic regime we call capitalism. What are these ideological and political messages embedded in the market model that are so useful to the legitimacy of capitalism?

The Market and the Public/Private, Political/Economic Distinctions

The market model posits that private market activities should be the principal method by which we should create economic welfare for our citizenry. The public or social goal of providing the greatest amount of good for the greatest number of people is not to be left to an authority charged with the social planning of production and distribution of goods and services. This task is given to all individuals in society and they are to discharge it by acting as uncoordinated individuals, selfishly, to satisfy their private interests and no other. This is captured in a truly famous dictum proffered by the most important theorist of a private market economy, Adam Smith: "It is not from the benevolence of the butcher, the brewer, or the baker, that we expect our dinner, but from their regard to their own interest."

The first point, then, is that, in the name of economic efficiency, the economic sphere is to be primarily a private sphere. A remarkable set of *political* premises flow out of this *economic* starting position.

The more decisions to formulate demands and how to meet those demands that self-seeking individuals make, the smaller is the number of decisions that planners acting on behalf of the collective good have to make. There is less need for government. The closer we can get to full implementation of the efficiency-oriented market model, then, the less need there will be for a government to decide what we should want and how we are to behave to get it. The larger the domain of the *private individual economic ordering* sphere, the smaller the domain of the *public collective political ordering* sphere has to be. From this perspective, the market model is not only an institution aimed at attaining economic efficiency, but also one with an important political role. Indeed, this may well be its most significant attribute.

Milton Friedman, one of the gurus of the market model, has said as much. He argues that the untrammelled market produces economic efficiency. But, he acknowledges, the efficiency achieved will not, as a matter of logic, be superior to that which may be attained by a planned economy. He doubts whether planners, in fact, would ever do as well as the market. However, because it is possible that they might do so, Friedman—who, after all, is not just a shill for the wealthy classes everywhere but also a respected Nobel Prize winner—does not rest his case for preferring the market to government planning on an unscientific assertion. Rather he reasons that, unlike the planned economy, which subjects individuals to the decisions of elected delegates or despotic tyrants, the market model permits individuals to make their own decisions, as true sovereigns. This freedom to choose—to use Friedman's most famous phrase—makes the market model superior to a planned economy. It is this political aspect of the private economic model that makes it more desirable than a publicly run economy.

The market, an economic tool, is said to be the key to political freedom. In this equation of capitalism with the market, therefore, capitalism and freedom become synonymous. This useful line of reasoning is reinforced by another political value supported by the premises of the idealized economic market model.

The emphasis of the model is that each of us is to act as a Rational Economic Man (regardless of our gender). The use of this kind of emotive language to describe selfish economic behaviour is an indication of how truly unscientific most of the economic market modellers are. They are into manipulation, big time. According to this line of thought, there cannot be an equal division of individual biological and personal character traits. The differences among us make us individuals, and it is the individual optimization of talents and resources that makes a difference. Just this inequality, without more, would lead to inequality in the fierce competitive battles envisioned by Friedman and his ilk. Apparently they do not see this as a detraction from the arguments for efficiency and political freedom they make in support of the market model, which, to them, is synonymous with capitalism. Different talents should yield different results, they say. Unequal outcomes reflect unequal merit. Nothing could be more natural. These shallow, indeed silly, premises equate the blind biological fortuity of being strong or intelligent or particularly athletic or dexterous with personal merit and worth.

Even more thoughtless is the other major premise of market modellers. There is nothing in the market model theory that requires that there should be something like an equal division of non-personal resources among the countless individuals who are to act as Rational Economic Men. An objective observer might think that, if Milton Friedman and his friends were desirous of being taken seriously by thinking people, they would want there to be something like an egalitarian division of resources to ensure that, when individuals make decisions about how to use their resources and what goods and services they want to purchase in the market, they will do so from similar starting positions. While their model does not actually require an unequal division of resources, they do not advocate that historic inequalities be redressed before the model is given free rein. Indeed, their nostrums are conspicuously silent on this issue. Their market model requires no more than that everyone be given the same opportunity to play the market economic game. This approach to the economic model they favour dovetails nicely— and not coincidentally—with the tenets of the political philosophy that we claim to have embraced: liberalism.

As a political philosophy, liberalism does not demand that governments guarantee citizens substantive equality. This is why quintessentially liberal institutions, such as our Human Rights Codes and our Charter of Rights and Freedoms, do not have anything to say about discrimination on the basis of wealth. What they do is to stipulate that people should not be deprived of *opportunities* to apply for jobs and accommodation, to retain jobs, to be paid a wage, or to gain a benefit or entitlement because of their sex, sexual orientation, age, ethnic or national origin, race, religious or political conviction, or physical or emotional well-being. Our political system has matured to the stage at which it will interfere with the market only to the extent that it might be unwilling to tolerate inequalities arising out of certain ineradicable differences or out of differences in religious or political belief. But our political system continues to countenance, with astonishing equanimity, the egregious inequality that stems from the disparity in the ownership of resources that prevails in any capitalist economy.

Politicians, Capitalism, and the Market Modellers

While no one claims that the idealized market exists in practice, those asking us to adhere to its principles send out powerful economic and political ideological messages. These messages are that individuals, maximizing their opportunities, free from interventions by the state, will produce an efficient economy and the greatest political freedom imaginable. These messages are sent with fervour. University of Guelph philosopher John McMurtry has noted that the ardour of the market model's proponents endow it with all the trappings of a religion. Their demand is that its teachings be followed as if they constituted a fundamental text. Increasingly, this demand for unthinking adherence is meeting with success, with unhappy results for most people, both economically and politically.

More and more, politicians of all major electoral parties run on platforms proclaiming that it is the private, not the public, sector, that is to bear the primary responsibility for the creation of economic welfare—just as market dogma would have it be. More and more, politicians of all major electoral parties run on platforms stipulating that government should be leaner, meaner, and smaller and get out of the business of providing services whenever possible. The argument is that, if a particular service is really wanted, people will be willing to pay for it, and therefore private profit-seekers will use their talents and resources to provide these demanded services. That is precisely what a properly functioning market economy is supposed to do and, even more importantly, will do better than any government. More and more, politicians of all major electoral parties run on platforms calling for people to be more self-reliant, to be more flexible, to be more willing to accept the discipline of the market, and to re-tool themselves to deal with its spontaneously generated demands.

All of this leads to an increasing marginalization of the functions of governments as the direct creators of welfare. There is something bizarre about politicians fighting tooth and nail to be elected on the basis that they are the ones who can be trusted most not to use the power to plan and control that they are so strenuously seeking. They ask for the levers of power at the same time as they commit themselves not to use that power, except to enlarge the domain of private-sector economic activity. Often, this "enlargement" can only be carried out by coercing those who are not eager market actors. The politicians then use power, but only to help the private economic sector to function according to the market model. They and their supporters can only explain this priority by arguing that the *economic* values of the market model have gained widespread acceptance; and this is because those values are in harmony with the *political* values of what we call our liberal-democratic polity. In short, the values of the market are seen as being at one with our shared political values. Inasmuch as capitalism, a class-based political-economic regime, is equated with its legitimated tool, the market and its ideology, it too is legitimated; it too is an emanation of our liberal-democratic value system.

Of course, many critics of the market model have disputed its verities, particularly its claim to be an instrument for the enhancement of political freedoms and democracy. One of the most telling—indeed, to my mind, incontrovertible—critiques was provided by the great Canadian political philosopher C.B. Macpherson. In a 1968 essay, "Elegant Tombstones: A Note on Friedman's Freedom," Macpherson pointed out how Friedman equated a family able to provide for its own subsistence if it so desired with a single worker who could not. This elision permitted Friedman to pretend that individual workers, like a family, can provide for themselves and, there-fore, when they participate in the market, they may be deemed to be doing so voluntarily, as sovereign individuals. MacPherson's critique of Friedman is that workers are compelled participants in labour markets, not voluntary ones. This insight into Friedman's reasoning undermines it completely. There are many other persuasive critiques of market modelling. While these critiques are logically compellable, they tend to have little effect on public perception and, therefore, on policy-makers. Moreover, corporations, politi-cians, mainstream media, and other institutions send out a constant barrage of signals that reinforce the long-established impression of the market model as the natural order of things—something, therefore, not to be questioned. The critiques come more intermittently, get less air play, and often seem abstract—partly because they seem to come from on high at the same time as people concretely experience market forces and their ideological baggage in their daily lives.

What we need to recognize is that the corporation facilitates the very opposite of what market modellers claim to be their goals. Remember that capitalism gets legitimacy by allying itself with the market, but that corpora-tions are capitalists' favourite vehicle for participating in that market. Any evidence that corporate behaviour is antagonistic to the ideals of competition, individual sovereignty, the equality of all persons, and democratic principles will align capitalist behaviour with monopoly, hierarchy, and oppression rather than with economic competitiveness or political equality and freedom, the values said to be promoted by the market model. An exposé of how corporations are structured and how they actually behave when notionally engaged in market activities, has great political potential. It is not too hard to mount such a persuasive exposé.

The utility of the corporation to capitalism's accumulation-of-wealth project rests in the condition that, functionally, it is a collective of capitals, of inorganic and human resources. But, as a market actor, it needs to be treated as an individual—and that is because individualistic, sovereign decision-making and the taking of responsibility by selfish individuals lie at the heart of the market model's claims to be the institution capable of achieving the most economically efficient behaviour and of enhancing political freedoms. Law, by a sleight of hand, treats a corporation as an individual, as an economic actor in harmony with the idealized market model. This feature permits this *collective* to take advantage of the legal and political rights and privileges of flesh and blood *individuals*, such as you and me. It also enables the human captains of industry, finance, retail, and everything else, who hide behind their corporations, to get more protection from economic failure than the rest of us and to have more political sway than the liberal model should give them. But the legal pretence that the corporation is an individual is just that: a pretence. It creates inevitable tensions because of its objective falsity. When the tensions are confronted, the myriad of ways in which privileged corporate actors profit from the collectivist corporate form will reveal uglinesses and evils that cry out for fundamental reform, if not transformation, of our political economic system.

AFTER THE HOSTILE TAKE-OVER, PRINCE CHARMING INC. BUSTED THE UNION AND FIRED ALL THE DWARVES.

THREE

The "Small Is Beautiful" Campaign

Wherein we learn why small business is touted to be the healthy backbone of the nation.

We will begin here by considering an imaginary problem. It has an obvious solution because it is not complicated by corporate law.

Percy Dean is an employee of Henry Browne and Son Ltd., a corporation that makes nautical instruments. Robin Smith has a boat, the *Diahla*. He enters into an agreement with Percy Dean to buy an automatic helmsman for the *Diahla* from Henry Browne and Son Ltd. Henry Browne and Son Ltd. supplies the automatic helmsman and fits it in the *Diahla*. The device works as it should. Pursuant to the terms of the contract, Henry Browne and Son Ltd. now presents its bill to Robin Smith. Robin Smith does not want to pay it. The question is: can he escape his obligation to do so?

The answer is: of course not. In legal terms, a formal offer to buy something at a given price was made and that offer was equally formally accepted. One of the parties had done exactly what it solemnly had promised to do. The other party, Robin Smith, however, did not do what he had sincerely promised to do, and the law now will force him to fulfil his promise, or else.

In both liberal political philosophy and market economic terms, the answer yielded is exactly the same as the one forged by law. As a sovereign, autonomous individual, Robin Smith had voluntarily undertaken an obligation to pay for a product and a service. In liberal political terms, a sovereign, freely made choice is held to be sacrosanct and, for each such choice to be validated, all must be enforceable. From the economic perspective, for the market to work, Robin Smith also is not to be allowed to shirk his solemnly, freely assumed responsibilities. The certainty and predictability needed for the efficient working of the market would evaporate if actors could whimsically change their position after they had induced others to act in a particular way. To permit such capriciousness would throw commerce into confusion.

Now, let us change the imaginary problem slightly so that it becomes a real problem—one that was presented to a court. The court found the problem far more intractable than we found our imaginary problem, because this real-life situation was complicated by the use of corporate law. In the result, the court's solution was counterintuitive; it was not what the lay person would expect from the law; it was not what a proponent of the idealized market would want; it was not what an advocate of liberal political philosophy would like to see.

In the actual case, which took place in England, everything was virtually the same as in the hypothetical case. Henry Browne and Son Ltd. was a firm making nautical instruments; its employee Percy Dean entered into a contract to sell an automatic helmsman to be fitted on the *Diahla*, and the firm met its solemnly undertaken promise. The major difference was that Robin Smith had the contract for the sale made out in the name of a company called Ocean Charters Ltd. When Robin Smith negotiated the contract with Percy Dean, he told him that he was using the yacht *Diahla* for a chartering business he ran through that associated company, Ocean Charters Ltd., and Robin Smith entered the name and address of Ocean Charters Ltd. on the formal contract he signed. When Henry Browne and Son Ltd. sued for the amount owed it, it sued the company that appeared as the contracting party on the documentation, that is, Ocean Charters Ltd. It turned out that the company had no money at all. Its only capital had been raised by a contribution of £1 each from Robin Smith and his spouse. In return for this less than munificent funding, the company had issued a certificate for one share to each of these contributors who, thereby, were in a position to control the company. The company had raised no other capital by way of borrowing money from anyone else or by issuing shares to anyone else. The directors of Ocean Charters Ltd.—that is, those responsible for running it—were its only shareholders: Mr. and Mrs. Smith. There were no employees. After issuing the writ against Ocean Charters Ltd., Henry Browne and Son found out that Ocean Charters could not pay the contractual debt. In legal jargon, it was judgment proof.

Henry Browne and Son Ltd., therefore, sued Robin Smith, claiming that he was the real purchaser of the automatic helmsman and the real person operating the chartering business for which it had been bought. From a real-world perspective, this argument made sense. In legal terms, the supplier of the automatic helmsman was saying that Robin Smith made a formal offer to buy something at a given price, and that Henry Browne and Son equally formally accepted this offer and then carried out its end of the bargain in full. The court did not deny the truth of any of these facts, but found that Henry Browne and Son Ltd. knew that it was dealing, in formal terms, with Ocean Charters Ltd., a company, even though it was Robin Smith who had done the negotiating. In the eyes of the law the company was a real person, one totally separate from Robin Smith, who had created it and functionally controlled it. Therefore, the court held, only the company, Ocean Charters Ltd., could be held responsible for the debt owed to Henry Browne and Son. That the company could not pay the money it owed was just a fact of economic life, one that was legally irrelevant, even though it was clear that it had no money because Robin Smith had not given it any.

In market terms, Robin Smith had obtained a benefit for which it would have appeared to most objective observers he had promised to pay. From the idealized market perspective, therefore, he should have been legally responsible. If market actors do not have to meet solemnly undertaken obligations, the market system cannot function. The market depends on costs being allocated as individual private actors, exchanging promises in good faith, have agreed to distribute them. In moral terms, the court's decision meant that an individual was allowed to shift his losses to an innocent party, one who had acted in the good faith belief that the party with whom it was contracting was a person able and willing to accept the responsibility for that contract. Such an outcome undermines the trust necessary for the efficient functioning of a private enterprise economy.

The Myth of the Small-Business Love-In

Something is rotten in corporate law land. When used by small business, as it was in this case, the corporate form is apt to screw up the market system in all its aspects. This failure should be troubling to market proponents, because they tend to promote the idea of small business as the flagship of a market economy. Small business is what legitimates this kind of economy. Not at all surprisingly, numbers and slogans are cleverly used to present a picture of our economy as being constituted by individuals behaving like Adam Smith's self-seeking butcher, brewer, and baker. Such selfish behaviour, we have been taught to believe, is bound to enrich all of us. It follows that politicians cannot go wrong by supporting the idea that small-business actors such as butchers, brewers, and bakers should be promoted and by promising that governments will do so. Not only will they be expounding an ideology with a great deal of resonance, they will be speaking in support of what is, numerically, the majority of enterprisers. Most people in business are small-business people.

Industry Canada tells us that small businesses, large enough to employ workers for wages, numbered 922,182 in 1993. Some 97 per cent of these businesses had fewer than fifty employees, and 99 per cent of them had fewer than one hundred employees. As the argument to be made in this chapter is that the boosting of small business is something of a Trojan Horse, note that Industry Canada defines small business as including enterprises that have up to ninety-nine employees and also those that have an annual revenue of less than $25 million. Thus, although the title of the Industry Canada report is "Small Business in Canada," the actual statistical analysis refers to SMEs— that is, to Small and Medium Enterprises. The inclusion of "medium" enterprises in the category of small business reflects the existence of a deliberate campaign to convince us that truly small business—entrepreneurialism in the Adam Smithian sense—is at the hub of our economy. The idea of a sole entrepreneur using a basement both as a factory and an office and individualistically, bravely, chasing a pot of gold is an image put before us every day. The image-makers do not stress how some of the enterprises they talk about might have as many as one hundred employees or $25 million in annual revenues, hardly the "Mom and Pop" operations we are meant to idolize.

The image-makers' campaign has been successful. Politicians fall over themselves to support both the ideology and the actual workings of small business. To cite just one instance amongst literally hundreds of its kind, in October 1997 Al Palladini, as minister for economic development, trade, and tourism of Ontario, launched a project to be called Small Business Enterprise Centres, a network that would help small businesses gather information and be provided with guidance by large business mentors. The larger partners would help small-business owners gain managerial and marketing skills and provide advice on how to deal with technological innovation and financing problems. Palladini justified the setting up of these centres by noting that "small businesses create up to 80 per cent of Ontario's new jobs." The press release announcing these centres was entitled "Small Business—Big Result."

Governments everywhere repeatedly pump out views to the effect that "small business employs nearly 60 per cent of all Canadians" or "that firms with fewer than five employees create more jobs, both during economic downturns and economic expansions than do any other form of business." Newspapers are full of stories about how bad the chartered banks have been about lending to small enterprises, thereby inhibiting risk-takers in the one sector of the economy that really matters. The story being told, then, is about the beauty and dynamism of small business. It has a great deal of resonance in a polity that claims that freedom is associated with the market—so much so that big business feels the need to show that it, too, favours the economic activity of millions of small businesses. There is a never-ending show of concern for those who are the so-called heart of free enterprise by those who really are the heart of the economy. It might be the Toronto Dominion Bank introducing "More Business for Your Business: A Marketing Workbook for Small Business," the Royal Bank of Canada offering a series of books intended to be guides to answer questions frequently asked by small-business entrepreneurs, or the Canadian Imperial Bank of Commerce setting up a website to provide small business with information and exchanges. Schemes of this kind are always in the works, just as big businesses are regularly being co-opted by politicians in the setting up of centres, networks, and mentoring institutions.

These efforts to support small business are symbiotic with actual developments in the larger economy. There has been an impressive growth in the numbers of small businesses, and especially in the number of individuals who conduct their own business employing no one but themselves. Between 1983 and 1993, self-employment grew at twice the rate of overall employment until, by 1993, there were nearly two million self-employed persons in Canada, comprising 15.4 per cent of the total workforce. This represented an increase of about 2 per cent in just ten years. Since then the pace of growth has only accelerated. By 1996 the same group had increased to over two and a half million people. Self-employment accounted for 46 per cent of all new jobs created between the second quarter of 1996 and the second quarter of 1997.

The invigoration of the spirit of enterprise this growth seems to suggest is celebrated, even if it is "corporate downsizing and government belt-tightening [which] have had the effect of pushing thousands of Canadians into entrepreneurship," as Rick Spence, the editor of *Profit, The Magazine for Canadian Entrepreneurs*, wrote in September 1995. Entrepreneurship is welcome, no matter how it arises. The same Rick Spence quoted Michelle Gahagan, a Vancouver lawyer specializing in small-business law, as saying:

"More than being a different way to get paid, the experience transforms you. . . . The choice of entrepreneurship is actually an act of self-actualization."

This growth in truly small-business endeavours has been pushed not only by economic restructuring but also by massive propaganda campaigns. Horatio Algers such as Microsoft's Bill Gates, Magna's Frank Stronach, and the Body Shop's Anita Roddick are treated as heroes by the press. Television programs, like the CBC's *Venture*, often concentrate on individual entrepreneurs who make good against all odds. Even *The Globe and Mail*, still big business's favourite newspaper, runs a weekly page on small-business entrepreneurship. Governments set up agencies and programs (such as the Federal Business Development Bank of Canada) to create incentives for, and to help, small business. Even the supposedly worker-friendly Ontario NDP government favoured using the tax system in 1992 to set up pools of venture capital for small businesses (which included businesses with annual revenues of $50 million and employing up to two hundred employees). Ernst & Young, a large accounting and business consulting firm, got some of its big-business clients to support what is now the well-publicized Entrepreneur of the Year award. The Governor-General of Canada, no less, presents this annual trophy at a black-tie dinner.

And so it goes. Yet, despite the huge love-in, small business is not central to the Canadian economy. Indeed, the most conservative of observers document just the opposite, and therefore it must be assumed to be well-known by them. We therefore ought to be suspicious of their declarations that small business is the engine of the economy. As the record shows, they know better.

One piece of evidence came when an attempted merger between Argus and Power corporations in the early 1970s led to the establishment of an inquiry that resulted in the 1978 *Report of the Royal Commission on Corporate Concentration*, known after its chairman as the Bryce Commission Report. In its general conclusions, this Commission wrote:

> We looked at corporate concentration in terms of both aggregate concentration (the proportion of overall economic activity accounted for by the largest firms) and industrial concentration (the proportion of the activity in particular industry accounted for by the largest firms in that industry). By both measures, concentration is higher in Canada than it is elsewhere.

In 1984 the *Corporate and Labour Union Reporting Act Report* noted that the leading five hundred non-financial actors had 54 per cent of sales, 67.7 per cent of assets, and 70.4 per cent of all profits. Some 1,905 large non-financial corporations had assets of $25 million dollars or more, and they accounted for 73.3 per cent of all assets, 55.5 per cent of all sales, and 72.6 per cent of all profits made in Canada. Even when the analysis was refined by breaking the economy down into its various sectors, the domination of a few large corporations over each of those sectors emerged as the quintessential characteristic of the Canadian economy. Thus the same 1984 study showed that, in the mining sector, 5.12 per cent of corporations controlled 91.74 per cent of the assets and 91.25 per cent of equity. They made 91.28 per cent of all the sales and 98.78 per cent of all the profits. In manufacturing, 1.92 per cent of corporations had 79.29 per cent of the assets and 83.58 per cent of the equity. They made 72.89 per cent of the sales and earned 76.79 per cent of the profits.

Even in what are conventionally supposed to be highly competitive sectors because of the visible presence of many small businesses, a similar picture emerges. In 1984, for example, 0.11 per cent of the corporations in the retail sector had 41.05 per cent of the assets and 53.43 per cent of the equity. They made 35.59 per cent of the sales and earned 52.46 per cent of all the profits. In 1989, two researchers, relying on data collected in the immediate aftermath of the 1988 free-trade elections, reported that concentration had intensified. Similarly, in 1990, Statistics Canada reported that, by 1987, the top 1 per cent of all enterprises controlled 86 per cent of Canada's assets and made 75 per cent of all profits. This left the remaining 14 per cent of assets in the control of 99 per cent of all enterprises, and that 99 per cent of all enterprises shared a derisory 25 per cent of all the profits made in Canada.

For some time, then, the Canadian economy has been dominated by giant firms, more often than not in oligopolistic or monopolistic positions—an interesting feature, to say the least, of a liberal democracy said to be wedded to the competitive market model, designed to enhance efficiency and political freedoms. On the face of it, the Canadian economy is not at all like the one championed by market modellers—not at all one in which millions of individuals acting anarchically and selfishly are disciplined only by the invisible hand of the market. It is not at all an economic set-up that denies a relatively few individuals the power to dictate the terms and conditions of economic or political life to any of us. As the Bryce Commission noted as early as 1978:

> Many people have become increasingly uneasy over the economic, political and social impact of large firms in Canada. The sheer size of many of the firms in concentrated industries, the impact on their employees and communities and their potential economic power to administer prices and the quantity and quality of their output have caused apprehension among the

public and governments, since this impact is seen to run counter to the economic and political philosophy of the free market system. This free market so eloquently espoused by Adam Smith in the 18th century had promised a competitive stimulus to efficiency, low and flexible prices and competition that would direct productive activity in such a way as to maximize the national income. *Free markets composed by many small firms, which cannot influence the price at which their output is sold, have probably never existed in a modern, industrial economy. The Canadian economy, though widely thought to be a free enterprise one, has always been composed of large firms and oligopolistic markets in many industries and has been characterized by extensive government involvement.* [Emphasis added.]

But dykes, built out of such concrete facts, have not been able to stem the flood of falsifying propaganda let loose by the elite. The small-business ideology, the rugged individual entrepreneur model, is still proclaimed to be at the heart of the Canadian economy.

The Effects of the Small-Business Ideology

The advantages to the elites and the powerful of the portrayal of small business as the fulcrum of the Canadian economy are enormous. In particular:

i)   The portrayal reinforces the conventional wisdom that Canada is a polity in which individuals take responsibility for their own welfare and in which governmental interventions should be limited to measures that facilitate this natural and virtuous inclination. This is why newspaper editors and pontificating politicians are willing to read the Riot Act to risk-averse bankers who shun small business.

ii) The approach reinforces the notion of the value of the privatization of government services as (small) individual profit-seekers are bound to deliver these services more efficiently by fiercely competing with each other.

iii) It makes unemployment less of a political problem than it ought to be. If you believe that any rugged self-reliant individual can set up a business, then it will also appear not to be anything like a major crisis if the economy, as a whole, does not create enough work-for-wages jobs. "Get out there and compete! Others do!" is the not so implicit message. It is a successful message, as the growth in self-employment shows. Associated with this message is another bromide: "You will feel better." Studies are trotted out to show that the self-employed are happier than employed persons even though, on average, they do less well than employed people do. Self-exploitation is more satisfying, it seems, than being exploited by employers. This, too, fits neatly with the private-market-model image.

iv) The portrayal reinforces the idea that failure in business is not a bad thing. After all, the incentive to participate in an untrammelled market is the allure of material success and all the prestige that goes with it. But, for some to succeed, others must lose. Those failures, though difficult for those involved, are the price that an efficient and freedom-enhanced political economy must be willing, indeed happy, to pay. A market economy will necessarily have its ups and downs. To take just one example, in 1986–87—a boom year for the economy—161,285 businesses began life and another 127,085 dropped out of the economy, creating a net of 34,200 new businesses. In 1991–92—a bad year for the economy—140,711 businesses were born and 139,429 died, leaving a net of 1,282 new businesses. The amazing rise in bankruptcies in the small-business sector is not portrayed as a sign of failure of the economic system but, rather, as a reflection both of its dynamism and of the regrettable failure of governments and banks to facilitate the prosperity of small business. In this context, policies enhancing competition by privatization, deregulation, tax incentives, and cheap loans for small business are not only just sensible, but are also mandated, even if these efforts have to be made at the expense of the social contract provided by the welfare state.

v) The approach reinforces the idea that the more competition there is, the better it is for all of us. Thus, it legitimates free-trade policies. The tearing down of tariff walls and other artificial barriers becomes a laudable goal in a political milieu in which competition is the mantra. As we increasingly internationalize competition, the oligopolistic or monopolistic nature of some of our large businesses becomes less troublesome. The argument, as the Bryce Report had already concluded in 1978, is that the dominant positions and large size of some corporations are necessary for efficient competition on the international scene. Hence, there is no need to have a vigorous local competition-promoting law.

The already powerful stand to gain a great deal, then, by endorsing the idea that, despite data to the contrary, Canada is an economy composed of millions of small actors competing fiercely with each other, disciplined and guided by Adam Smith's invisible hand of the market. It helps big business to dominate and to get rid of pesky regulation. Politicians proselytizing the virtues of small business and untrammelled competition on the hustings are really acting as "advance men" of big business and wealth-owners. They are encouraged, by the opinion-moulders in the major presses and by the big-business think-tanks and intellectual gatekeepers, to *pretend* that small business is the backbone of the nation. Politicians also do their thing. For instance, in the late 1990s, when launching yet another agency to help small business, John Manley, a minister in a Liberal Party government, was heard to say, "Small businesses are the key to jobs and economic growth." At the same public relations event, Barbara Hall, the mayor of Toronto, a politician of a supposedly different political stripe, said, "Small business plays a vital part in our economy, and the City of Toronto places a high priority on working with small businesses to help them grow and prosper."

Still, despite the success of portraying Canada as a small-business economy, governments are continuously forced to acknowledge that many small businesses are as dependent on large business, if not more so, as employees of large employers are. For instance, various employment standards acts around the country provide minimum conditions for workers, including terms such as a guaranteed minimum wage, minimum vacation time, and limits on the number of hours per day that any employer can demand of an employee. In short, this is legislation that interferes with the market, because some employees have such little bargaining power that their privately arranged conditions of work, if not regulated by public legislation, would be unacceptable to our society. It turns out that many people operating small businesses—people who think of themselves as being self-employed or as running a business employing a small number of people (usually family members), such as franchisees who operate variety stores or pizza outlets— are forced to come to employment standards tribunals to have themselves classified as employees. Only in that way can they ensure that they will make at least as much as the most vulnerable employees in the economy. Similarly, people who distribute newspapers to households (and who may even employ some young people or family members to help them with the task) often seek to place themselves in the category of employee in order to get minimum employment conditions. Otherwise, as independent, unprotected small-business owners, they could not reach society's lowest acceptable standards of living set for employees by law. Others may own their own trucks or taxis or other equipment and think of themselves as being self-employed, as running their own businesses, but they rely on one customer, a larger enterprise. In order to make sure they can get a reasonable return on their "independent" efforts, they seek to get themselves categorized as dependent contractors, a classification that permits them to bargain collectively. That is, they seek to be treated by collective bargaining law as if they were employees of their one customer, rather than as owners of a self-standing business. They seek some of the unionizing privileges that vulnerable employees have had to win to protect themselves from superexploitation.

Despite the overwhelming amount of concrete evidence that small business is not the backbone of the nation's economy, the beat goes on. Waving the flag on behalf of small business promotes the kind of political climate that makes it easier for politicians to push for—and for us, the people, harder to resist—an agenda that denies us the things we really want. Goals such as the attainment and maintenance of full and secure employment, security in old age, good health-care and education systems, protection of our national and cultural symbols and artifacts, and a decent physical environment are put on the political back burner. The trumpeting of small business as the principal engine of growth necessary to the attainment of these shared goals is more than the huffing and puffing of hot air merchants. It is directly instrumental in creating a political climate in which it becomes easier for politicians to accept, and to say that the rest of us should accept, the reduction of the role of governments. Governments are there to facilitate business, which demands the dismantling of social welfare institutions and the selling of government-run monopolies, such as electricity and gas utilities, airlines, and postal services, which allows more private business to be done. The only positive thing for governments to do in such a climate is to help small business directly (with cheap money, the cutting of red tape—read: the cutting of safety and quality controls) and to maintain law and order. In short, the boosting of small business has a detrimental effect on our formal democratic institutions and a dampening effect on the expectations of a great many people.

The wonder of it all is that the propaganda is so effective, given that both the numbers and our everyday experiences directly contradict the claim that small business is the backbone of the economy. Not only are there only a few (three or four) dominant businesses in each economic sector, this is a reality that is publicly acknowledged all the time. The 1978 Bryce Commission Report was necessitated because two huge firms, the Argus and Power corporations, were trying to swallow each other. The elites were afraid that, if this merger took place, it would become obvious to everyone that the market model did not operate in Canada. Similarly, in 1999, the country was watching two proposed bank mergers with alarm. Once again, onlookers feared that consummation of the deal would give a couple of firms the power to dictate prices to all others, despite oft-repeated claims about the existence of competition amongst financial institutions. The highly visible and increasing concentration of ownership of the media leads to a great deal of caterwauling in the media themselves.

Not to put too fine a point on it, Canadians do know that, at any one time, a few major economic actors in any one sector are close to being in full control of that sector. Rogers, Bell Canada, McCain Foods, a handful of oil companies and banks, Inco and Falconbridge, and American Barrick, as well as other corporations, are commonly thought of in this vein. Yet none of this appears to discredit the notion that small business and its ideology character-ize our political economy. Small business is "in," and it is "in" because of the legitimacy it confers on the "liberate-the-market" agenda that serves large capitalists so well.

Still, a dark cloud hangs over this vast propaganda campaign: small busi-ness frequently uses the corporation as its own vehicle. As in the Henry Browne and Son case, the way in which small business uses the corporate vehicle has the potential to give the market—that is, the private ordering of our political economy, which supposedly comprises hundreds of thousands of competing actors—a bad name. Indeed, small, incorporated business appears to be a blight on the system, not its flag carrier. That blight, though, has to be considered before we turn to the real danger to our democracy: big business carried on through huge corporations.

FOUR

The Small and the Ugly

Wherein we learn that the corporate form turns small business into the cancerous spine of the economy.

ere is the problem. When a small business, typically constituted by one or two entrepreneurs, a family, or a small group of friends, uses the corporate vehicle to carry on its business, none of the economic benefits that justify the use of the corporation exist. Obviously, there is no pooling of lots of little capitals to yield a synergy that otherwise could not be obtained. Similarly, the business will be too small to yield considerable savings on transaction costs. Such a firm will have to continue to negotiate with suppliers, distributors, and financial institutions. The obvious question is: why, then, do small-business enterprises use the corporate vehicle?

The immediate answer is equally obvious. They do it to avoid personal responsibility for the harms they may inflict on others, and they do it to evade obligations to governments they would otherwise incur as unincorporated entrepreneurs.

These small ventures are able to act in an anti-social manner by exploiting the very characteristics that the law has bestowed on corporations to make them efficient wealth-creating vehicles: namely, a separate legal personality and limited liability. Together, these two legal privileges throw a veil over the real profit-seekers, the flesh and blood people who created the corporation that is used to carry on business activities. They are shielded from public view and from many of the responsibilities that unincorporated market actors must confront. The corporate veil makes risk-shifting easy. The set-up is rendered even more efficient for these purposes than it used to be by the ready availability of two corporate law features that were granted only reluctantly, precisely because it was understood that they were likely to be abused. These added features are the right for one person to form a corporation and the abandonment of an old requirement that a corporation should have a certain amount of capital contributed to it before it would be entitled to be treated as a separate legal person. We apparently no longer harbour the same fears, or, more likely, we no longer care as much about the abuse of the corporate vehicle. Today it is common for one person to form a corporation, and it is perfectly legal, and not at all unusual, for those who set up corporations not to contribute any capital to it. The ensuing potential for unredressed harms to be inflicted by small business's manipulation of the corporate form has led to continuous calls for courts to pull aside the corporate veil, to pierce the corporate shield. When this is appropriate and when it is not are central problems in corporate law scholarship, and the questions give lawyers in practice much remunerative work to do.

This is not a book on the intricacies of law, and I will not engage here in any fancy display of veil-lifting and shield-piercing. But the legal fights do provide evidence of the political frailty of the contentions that the corporation is a legitimated means of economic activity. Here I will content myself with providing a number of examples illustrating some of the many ways in which individuals use the corporate form to avoid their responsibilities as human beings. These examples, I hope, will demonstrate that when small business—the supposed paradigm of the idealized market actor—uses the corporate form, it is enabled to distort the marketplace. This activity casts a shadow over profit-seeking endeavours by private, self-serving activities, the very kinds of activities that legitimate capitalism.

The story about the boat owner who got himself an automatic helmsman for nothing from an unsuspecting vendor (chapter 3) revealed how the ability to make a corporation the legal purchaser from a technical point of view can lead to an unhappy result. A seller of a product trusted the individual he was bargaining with but was left holding the (empty) bag. The cunning purchaser used the corporation so that his own wealth would be untouched by his default. All corporate law had to say about this flummery was "Let unsuspecting, trusting people carry the can." So encouraged, so-called entrepreneurs may well often think and act ignobly. The few illustrations that follow are standard fodder in basic corporate law courses. That is, they are not aberrations; they do not depict events that rarely occur.

Fraud and the Corporate Veil

A lawyer had created a number of corporations. He made his partner and an office clerk directors of these corporations, along with himself. But he held all the shares in the corporation; he was the only person who could benefit from the corporations' activities. From time to time he got one of these corporations to purchase a piece of land as a business investment. Although the corporations had little to no capital, apparently he would arrange to have the necessary capital supplied when the corporation had to meet its obligations. But, of course, it was he who decided whether the corporation would meet its obligations. On one occasion he decided that the purchase deal he had entered into, while hiding behind the veil of one of his corporations, was a poor one. In due course a court settled the ensuing dispute between the lawyer's purchasing corporation and the vendor, in the vendor's favour. The vendor sought to recover his costs, incurred as a result of the unnecessary legal action it had to take. Of course, the purchasing corporation liable for these costs had no money. So then the frustrated vendor sued the lawyer/entrepreneur. "No," said the court. "The lawyer did not contract with you, the corporation did. You are out of luck."

That decision relates to a rather important feature of the legal system: courts are reluctant to find that commercial actors have committed fraud. This reluctance is the result of the inexorable logic of a political economy whose values are posited on greed. All of us, as individuals, are supposed to maximize every opportunity we get to make a buck within the law. Because we can make more by going to the outer limits of what the law permits, a premium is placed on getting as close to the boundaries of legality as possible. Lawyers who help clients use the corporate vehicle to push the legal envelope as far as it can go are considered to be doing their job very well. Indeed, they are said to be clever. As one judge of the British Columbia Court of Appeal put it: "It has long been settled that a contract may be avoided if it can be done so legally even if ethically it may be wrong." This finding is not surprising, given that for the most part courts are staffed by persons who during their legal careers most often served the rich and the commercially active. These judges are tolerant of people who use commercial devices in imaginative and logically permissible ways. It is hard for them to find fault with devices and schemes that they themselves once employed. The ordinary person in the street might think of the Smiths who ordered the automatic helmsman and the lawyer who did not go on with his real estate contract as being engaged in somewhat problematic, even shady, actions. But the courts treated them as normal, ordinary business persons whose bona fides were not in question.

Another B.C. judge summed-up this tendency rather nicely in a case involving a dispute between a vendor and purchaser of land. The vendor of land, when asked by the would-be purchaser about the nature of waste material on the land, had replied that it was good landfill material. The vendor had omitted to say that, as he well knew, it was radioactive waste. The purchaser later used the toxic material as landfill on his own property, which, consequently, lost a great deal of its value. He sued the vendor. He recovered damages for the loss of value. This was contentious in law. But he also asked the court to award him punitive damages. He argued that he had been deceived and that the law required some form of punishment, over and above the restitution that the sneaky vendor had to pay. There is, in fact, a special cause of action that allows punitive damages to be awarded for deceitful practices. The judge agreed that the purchaser had been deceived but did not award the punitive damages. The deception, this (all-too-frank) judge said, was not the kind of deception that "would characterize the conduct of the defendant otherwise than as ordinary commercial dishonesty."

This notion that people in business can live up to a lesser standard than the rest of us are expected to do in our non-commercial dealings provides a useful security blanket for small business when it uses the corporate vehicle. Entrepreneurs are given legal and ideological support for pushing the device to its legal limits, enabling them to pass on risks to a heedless public that expects better behaviour from its fellow citizens.

A well-known U.S. case provides another example. Under the then existing law, anyone who operated a taxi as a business was required to provide the vehicle with insurance of up to a minimum of $10,000 in case the taxi caused damage to another person. One such taxi business, run by a single entrepreneur, had twenty taxis on the road. Obviously, the entrepreneur must have been a person of means or, at the very least, have been considered a good credit risk. While not a huge business by General Motors' standards, running twenty taxicabs would require substantial assets. But, as corporate law permits, the entrepreneur hid himself and, more importantly, whatever personal assets he possessed and had not put into the business. He divided up the twenty-taxicab concern so that it was run as ten different corporations, each of them constituting one taxicab business. Each of these separate corpo-

rations owned two cabs and mortgaged these assets, its only assets, very heavily. The only shareholder of each of these ten corporations was the individual
who had established the business. He had contributed very little capital to
any one of these corporations. Each corporation had insured each of its cabs
for any liability their use might incur up to the legal minimum of $10,000.
The inevitable happened: one taxicab was involved in an accident, causing
serious physical injury to an innocent person. The only monies available to
the taxi-owning corporation to pay the damages incurred by the victim were
the proceeds of the statutorily compelled insurance policy, namely, $10,000.
This was far too little to make good the actual losses suffered by the victim
and to which he was legally entitled.

When you or I hurt another as the result of our legally culpable negligence, we will be held responsible to make good on all the damage we
caused. Whether or not we are insured is of no legal consequence: our personal assets can be tapped until the full damages have been paid—or at least
as much of those damages as the total of our personal assets can redress. The
central idea of the law is that wrongdoers be made to pay, which punishes
them and deters them, as well as others, from engaging in unacceptable
behaviour. At the same time the law wants to ensure that victims are compensated as fully as possible by wrongdoers. Compensation, deterrence, and
retribution are firmly established goals of a legal system that is posited on
rules and principles flowing from the implications of a legal/political system
in which the central principle is that sovereign individuals are to be responsible for their conduct.

In our taxicab case, the person—that is, *the individual*—legally responsible for the damages inflicted was the corporation. It did not have sufficient
assets to make good the considerable difference between the $10,000 avail-
able from the insurance policy and the actual amount of harm suffered by
the victim. Not only had the corporation been created so as to have no assets,
but it had also been managed so as to ensure that it would not accumulate
any assets. As each corporation in the group made some money from the running of the taxis it owned, the real decision-maker in each of those corporations, the person who was the only significant shareholder, caused these
profits to be paid out to the person entitled to them in law, himself. The victim of the careless operation of the taxicab, therefore, now asked the court to
disregard the corporations that shielded the entrepreneur with assets from his
legal liability. What the victim argued was that the court should treat the ten-
corporation structure as a sham in that it was there solely to disguise the role
of the one human being who ran all of them and profited from their business
activities. The corporate veil should be lifted to reveal the owner and make

him accountable as if he had never been cloaked in corporate garb; the corporate shield should be pierced, taking away the legal armoury that wrongfully protected him from meeting his full obligations.

The court hemmed and hawed, but in the end it held that, in the absence of fraud (which had been alleged but, as is the norm, not found), it would undermine the utility of corporate law if the veil were lifted as the plaintiff had requested. While the circumstances elicited sympathy for the injured victim now confronted by a virtually asset-less wrongdoing corporation, corporate law had evolved to permit the use made of it by the taxi owner precisely because, on balance, this created incentives for investors. The attraction of the corporate form includes its capacity to allow the evasion of responsibilities. Judges had frequently acknowledged this reality. For instance, in the taxicab case itself, one of the judges who wrote the majority opinion noted that the "law permits the incorporation of a business *for the very purpose* of enabling its proprietors to escape personal liability." And in *Salomon v. Salomon & Co.*, a case that helped the English House of Lords lay down the doctrine of separate legal personality and limited liability for so-called one-man corporations, it was noted that when one judge had stated that it would be lamentable if corporate law permitted the avoidance of personal responsibility by using the expedience of incorporation, a higher court had shrugged off this revulsion. It actually was the very "policy of the Companies Act to enable this [the avoidance of responsibility] to be done."

The decision in *Walkovszky v. Carlton*, the New York State taxicab case, is extremely well-known and is taught in every corporate law class in the common-law world because the result was so unpalatable and yet so much in line with precedent. It was a very strong statement to the effect that the logic of corporate law is to be protected, even if that protection leads to outcomes that are contrary to the people's expectations and to legally endorsed goals. But there will be circumstances in which adherence to the purity of corporate law will be too offensive and embarrassing. Then the courts may have to lift the corporate veil or pierce the corporate shield. But they do this only in truly exceptional situations (and the taxicab case, obviously, was not considered exceptional).

One circumstance in which courts will be persuaded to ignore the corporation in order to make the individuals who hide behind it responsible will exist when the court is satisfied that the corporate vehicle was used fraudulently. The taxicab case and the earlier noted general reluctance of courts to find fraud indicate that facts will have to be egregious before fraud is relied upon to lift a corporate veil. But sometimes these facts do present themselves to a horrified court.

In one complicated land deal, an owner of valuable land in Vancouver was approached by two entrepreneurs (we will call them A and B) who wanted to purchase the land in question. Negotiations began, and the would-be vendor was told that, should the deal be consummated, the legal purchaser would be a corporation named BSD Ltd., a corporation in which A and B were senior decision-makers. Accordingly, the would-be vendor did a credit check on BSD Ltd. and found that this corporation would be able to meet any obligations incurred in a purchase of land. Negotiations continued between the vendor and A and B. Whilst they did, however, A and B took steps to be able to avoid any obligations arising out of any purchase contract. They transferred all the assets of BSD to another corporation with a different name and then formally dissolved BSD, now asset-less. In legal terms, this action meant that BSD Ltd. ceased to exist as a person. If it had been a human being, it would have been pronounced dead.

A and B then went back to the corporation registration office and incorporated a brand new corporation with the name, once again, of BSD Ltd. This name was available again because the old person with that name had died and gone to corporate heaven. The new BSD had none of the assets that had given the old BSD its creditworthiness. A and B now decided they could complete the contract for the purchase of land. The owner of the land signed the contract as vendor; the new BSD Ltd. signed as purchaser. For reasons not given in the report of the case, A and B decided that they did not want the land and, as they could make BSD do what they wanted it to do, they caused the company not to pay the purchase price owing under the signed contract. When the vendor went to court to enforce the contract, the court had no trouble finding that BSD Ltd., as a legal person with the same capacity to enter into binding contracts as you and I have, was responsible to pay the vendor the purchase price owing under the contract it had signed. Of course, this was the most pyrrhic of legal victories: the new BSD Ltd. had no assets, by design. The vendor had to ask the court to let it get at A and B, responsible miscreants if ever there were any. The court let it. It held that A and B had committed the tort of deceit, a civil action for damages. This meant that they were liable, just as ordinary confidence tricksters would be. Their argument that they had been acting as managers of corporations, that is, not on their own behalf, was of no avail to them. Although not done explicitly by the court, the corporate veil had been effectively lifted to reveal the villains who had drawn it over themselves.

This same case also reveals some salient facts of corporate life. All the transactions engineered by A and B were paper transactions. They required no physical effort; they could not be seen to be happening by anyone; they were relatively costless. They changed a commercial fact on which the world at large reasonably relied; indeed A and B counted on that reliance to make their scheme effective. Yet not one of those actions was illegal in its own right. Worse: they were—and are—commonplace. As is usually the case, the wrongdoers did not have the technical know-how to carry off their trickery. All that they knew is that they wanted an escape route to be available should things not pan out for them. They needed professional help and got it. They used a lawyer who set in train the corporate skulduggery, which, seemingly, left everything intact while changing the very basis on which an innocent person, the vendor/owner, had been induced into solemn negotiations. And this lawyer, according to the official report of the case, told A and B when they came to him seeking a way to make themselves irresponsible, that yes, he knew of a cute scheme that would enable them to avoid any liabilities they might want to duck. The lawyer knew of this scheme, the court noted somewhat wistfully, because it was commonly used by lawyers advising land dealers in Vancouver at that time. Here a major legitimacy problem comes into view.

Tax Evasion: The Logic of Corporate Law

The manipulation of the feature of separate personality, the right to form a corporation/separate person without providing it even with a soupçon of capital to meet contingencies and the ability to spin off numerous other corporations to thicken the obscuring veil behind which flesh and blood humans hide, is routine. Inevitably, judges are all too aware that too tight an adherence to the logic of corporate law can—and often does—produce unjust, ugly results, especially in the case of a small business that uses the elasticities of corporate law to its fullest extent. In such a case the judiciary, as an institution that garners its legitimacy from its portrayal as a neutral defender of individual private market activities and individual liberty, faces a dilemma. Courts should surely not tolerate results that flagrantly violate the basic precepts of market economics and liberal political values, such as the centrality of personal responsibility and good faith in private dealings. But to reject those outcomes may require courts to ditch the principles of corporate law that they themselves have helped to develop, which they have endorsed. As much of the prestige of the judiciary and a good deal of the credibility of its claim of being a neutral arbitrator stem from its contention that it follows precedent, to overtly disregard well-established corporate law precedents is an exercise that endangers it almost as much as does the acceptance of blatantly unjust results arising out of corporate law manipulations. The anxiety so created is exacerbated because it is also the legal profession's job (aided by accountants) to take advantage of the logic of corporate law to shift risks away from their clients onto innocent others. The courts are often pushed to the wall by the functionaries of the system that they administer.

In the case of *Covert v. Nova Scotia*, for instance, a wealthy man living in Nova Scotia wanted to make sure that his grandchildren would not have to pay the province taxes on the money he intended to leave them under his will. He—or, more likely, he, after advice from his lawyers/accountants— devised a bizarre corporate scheme. First he created a corporation. This was easy and virtually costless. Let us call it Corporation I. Each of the twelve grandchildren named as beneficiaries under the will became a shareholder of Corporation I by subscribing $100. With the same flick of the (legal) wrist, grandfather created another corporation, Corporation II. All the shares in Corporation II were awarded to Corporation I. After all, as soon as a corporation is registered—that is, as soon as it is born—it can do what any mature Canadian human being can do, and can, therefore, own shares in another corporation. The arrangement here meant that, upon the dissolution, that is, upon the death, of Corporation II, all of its residual property would go to its only shareholder, namely, Corporation I. And, of course, the decision-makers in Corporation I would be able to disgorge this windfall to its legal share-holders, the grandchildren.

Neither Corporation I nor Corporation II was intended to—and never did—enter into any kind of business enterprise or activity. They were not intended to seek profits or to incur liabilities.

Not satisfied with all this feverish (legal) activity, grandfather created yet another corporation, Corporation III. Grandfather put *one dollar* into the newly created corporate coffers. This was Corporation III's only working cap-ital when it commenced life. In return for this bounty, it issued one share to grandfather. This was the only share Corporation III ever issued to anyone. As soon as these onerous tasks were completed, Corporation III determined (through its decision-makers, guess who?) that it needed more capital, although there was no plan to engage in any business activity. To get more capital, Corporation III *borrowed* about $4 million from grandfather. This turned out to be the amount grandfather wished to bequeath to his grand-children. Being a careful business person, grandfather wanted some security for the loan he was about to make to the separate person known to the world as Corporation III. Corporation III satisfied this need by issuing a bond—a fancy term for a legally enforceable IOU—to the lending grandfather.

Now grandfather was ready. He changed his will and disinherited his beloved grandchildren. His new heir was to be Corporation II: a legal fiction was now the beneficiary. Corporation II stood, then, to inherit the IOU for $4 million held by the grandfather. Corporation II was in a position to ask Corporation III to pay the debt owed to the estate of the grandfather upon his death. As everything owned by Corporation II could eventually become the property of Corporation I (the only shareholder Corporation II had) and, via Corporation I, be allotted to the grandchildren (its only shareholders), the grandchildren would get the inheritance. But there was one further, key element, in this arrangement: all the corporations created by grandfather had been born as Alberta corporations. Now, simply by registering their incorporation under Alberta law, the money would be coming to the grandchildren from an Alberta source. They would not have to pay estate taxes on this money, which they would have had to do if the money came to them under a will ruled by Nova Scotia law.

This diabolically cunning scheme, devised to beat the Nova Scotia taxpayers and their democratically elected representatives, is a rather simple version of the many sophisticated tax-avoidance schemes developed by lawyers and accountants to ensure that rich people pay less tax than working people. Those with money do this despite the lip service paid by everyone who is anyone that taxes should be levied on a progressive basis—that is, those with more income should pay a higher rate of taxation. These corporate advisors work very hard, and are handsomely paid, to undermine widely accepted public policy objectives. They use countless clever machinations and variations, and here I can only offer a crude sketch of the essence of the games played. The point is that the fundamental elements of corporate law are used not to enhance market activities in their idealized form, but rather to maintain the accumulation of wealth by the few, regardless of whether this improves the production of aggregate wealth.

Tax avoidance is furthered by making the most of the ease with which corporations can be formed. Corporations capitalized to earn profits by engaging in productive activities can spin off a series of non-productive subsidiaries and affiliates, children, grandchildren (as in the Nova Scotia case), and brothers and sisters (as in the Vancouver land-dealing case). These corporations can operate in differing jurisdictions with different taxation regimes, perhaps even a no-taxation policy. Transfers of monies made within the corporate family from one place to another (sometimes supported by formal paper transactions between related corporations) can be used to declare profits where taxes are low and losses where taxes are high. All of this activity is facilitated by the pretence that this family of related corporations is constituted by discrete legal persons, sovereign entities, independent from one another and from the human directors, managers, and shareholders who have been the initiators. Each of the decisions made, even if implemented by the same people who act as directors/managers of a bunch of these related corporations, is treated as if it were made for the particular corporation's purposes, rather than for those of the group. The law, frequently embarrassed by these pretences—which only the law purports as representing reality—is slowly introducing mechanisms to treat related corporate activity as something that ought to be dealt with as integrated activity for some purposes. But it has not proved difficult for the army of lawyers and accountants employed by the corporate sector to exploit the corporate persona and all of its facilities to avert the impact of taxation and other legal obligations. This is why they get the big bucks, very big bucks: they save the wealthy an even larger amount of money at the expense of the unincorporated taxpayers.

Certainly, these tax avoidance schemes are largely stratagems employed by the bigger, publicly traded corporations rather than by small businesses using corporate structures. But the techniques are also available to small business, as the *Covert v. Nova Scotia* case shows. When the arrangements are used to avert the impact of taxation by flipping monies around the world, governments try to react in two ways. First they seek to close some of the loopholes: for instance, by attempts to get other governments to agree not to provide tax havens or by creating new domestic taxation rulings that would treat income earned and taxed elsewhere differently. Given that some foreign governments thrive on being tax havens and that lawyers and accountants can form fierce lobbying phalanxes, these government ripostes tend to meet with limited success. Therefore governments may turn back to the courts and ask them to lift veils, or they themselves will pass laws to reconstruct a family of legally disparate corporations so that, at least for tax purposes, if no other, the group will be treated as one taxpaying entity.

From time to time the courts will co-operate with government demands for a reconsideration of the strict application of pure corporate law principles. But they always do so reluctantly. This may be gleaned from the way in which they dealt with the Nova Scotia grandfather's ingenious use of corporate law. The matter went all the way to the Supreme Court of Canada, the highest court in the land. There the judges could not reach agreement, even though the case might have seemed like a "lay down *misère*" from a layperson's or the ordinary taxpayer's perspective. But lay people do not have as high a regard for the sanctity of the legal personality of the corporation as do judges, who have had so much to do with the development of its legitimacy. In the end the Supreme Court did decide that the scheme was invalid and could not shield the benefiting grandchildren from having to pay Nova Scotia inheritance taxes. But the vote was four to three. The narrowness of this victory for such an obviously right result speaks volumes about how the law, and especially the courts applying the law, has become boxed in by its own logic.

The Courts and Corporate Abuse

From a judicial point of view, lifting the corporate veil or piercing its shield — and this is a good occasion to note the male testosterone language accompanying corporate law — is fraught with danger. Because of that, courts will try to finesse the issue in efforts to avoid an obviously abusive employment of the corporate form. From their perspective, if there is a line of reasoning that allows them, when necessary, to get at the people behind the veil, while not having to find fraud or having to deny the sacrosanct nature of the separate personality of the corporation, they can have their cake and eat it. The circumstances that allow them this pleasure are rare, but defenders of the corporate law schema make a great deal of these few cases — precisely because the results in these scarce cases show that courts are not as hidebound as their normal reading of corporate law make them out to be.

The case of the Belzbergs provides a good example of one of these occasions. In Saskatchewan the Belzbergs, using a corporation they controlled, arranged to buy an expensive piece of property through a real estate agent. After the agent successfully negotiated the deal on behalf of the corporation, the company owed that agent a fee. Before the fee was paid, the Belzbergs, as decision-makers within the corporation, had the just-bought property transferred to yet another corporation that they controlled. As they had only put enough capital into the first corporation to allow for the purchase of the property, that corporation was now asset-less. It could not pay the fee owed to the agent. The sheer effrontery of this (mis)use of corporate personality offended the court. It held the Belzbergs responsible to pay the fee. But, while the court used the rhetoric of fraud, many scholars analyse the decision as one that did not require a finding of fraud or the lifting of the corporate veil. Instead, the critics contend, the same result could have been — and should have been — reached by the employment of a special *cause of action*, one usually brought against trade unions. This cause of action is known as the tort of inducement of a breach of contract.

The tort is made out when one person induces another to breach an existing contract with another. Typically, a trade union will ask its members and/or sympathetic people not to fulfil or to enter into contracts with the employer with whom the trade union is in dispute. The common-law courts, charged as they are with the defence of private property and private contract, will give the aggrieved employer a cause of action against the trade union that interferes with contractual relations. The contention was that, in this case, the Belzbergs, by dint of their position within the corporation, caused it—a person separate from the Belzbergs—to breach its contract with the real estate agent. In this way they could be held liable for having committed a tortious (a civilly unlawful) act. The agent could be paid the fee it was owed by the people who should be made to honour this obligation. The corporate veil did not need to be lifted. Indeed, it was respected because, in order to find the Belzbergs liable as inducers of a breach of contract between a separate person and the agent, the corporate person had to be acknowledged to be a discrete contracting party, one separate from the controlling Belzbergs.

But life is rarely as accommodating as this. More often than not, courts will not be presented with facts that allow them to finesse the problem and get the manifestly right result while being able to avoid calling all-too common commercial behaviour fraud or having to lift the corporate veil. Occasionally, therefore, some judges will abandon the corporate ship and simply state that they cannot accept an entrepreneur's use of the corporation to avoid personal responsibility for what are, in the end, personal actions. The taxicab case saw a strong dissenting judgment to this effect. The argument underpinning this kind of approach fastens on the need to be fair, to do equity, even if that means piercing the corporate shield. But this approach bothers most thoughtful judges.

After all, appeals to fairness do not provide precise decision-making criteria. Different judges have different views of what is fair and what is not. If judges' subjective notions of justice were openly allowed free rein, judicially made law would lose the credibility gained from the claim that it is applied evenhandedly and scientifically by politically indifferent judges. Indeed, entrepreneurs would never be certain that the corporate vehicles and structures they have used would yield the commercial advantages that corporate law is supposed to further. This uncertainty would dramatically reduce the utility of the corporation as a business form. Unsurprisingly, the legal profession lets the judiciary know its displeasure whenever a corporate veil is lifted by some court trying to set aside an unappetizing consequence of the use of the corporate veil by a small business. These protestations have an obviously self-serving nature, but apart from that, the legal profession tends to share— strongly share—the ideological preference for small business.

All of these pressures led the Supreme Court's Madam Justice Bertha Wilson, a senior jurist famed for her frequent demands for fairness in law, to say, in a much-cited passage, that lifting of the corporate veil, in the absence of fraud, would lead to disrepute for law and chaos for the business world. She made these remarks in a case involving a truly small business; it involved one man, a Mr. Kosmopoulos, who, on the advice of a lawyer, incorporated his business. Because of the apparent incompetence of his lawyer and insurance agent, he stood to lose his livelihood when his premises burned down. It turned out that the insurance coverage was still in his name and that, as the corporation now owned the property of the business, the property was not insured. He had continued to pay for a policy that no longer covered any property he personally owned. By contrast, the corporation, which he had created as a separate person, had no insurance policy covering the property, which it now owned. All of this made for a very strong case for piercing the veil, because in this case the aggrieved person was not seeking to hide behind the veil to avoid his obligations to others; others were trying to use his veil to avoid their responsibility to him. One wing of the Supreme Court of Canada was willing to lift the veil on the basis that to do so in this rare situation was not likely to alter corporate law in general. Madam Justice Wilson, however, spoke fiercely against this lax approach to corporate logic:

> The law on when a court may disregard this principle by "lifting the corporate veil" and regarding the company as a mere "agent" or "puppet" of its controlling shareholder or parent corporation follows no consistent principle. The best that can be said is that the "separate entities" principle is not enforced when it would yield a result "too flagrantly opposed to justice, convenience or the interests of the Revenue Department." . . . If the corporate veil were to be lifted in this case, then a very arbitrary and, in my view, indefensible distinction might emerge between companies with more than one shareholder and companies with only one shareholder.

While Madam Justice Wilson found (a *very* controversial) way to give Mr. Kosmopoulos what he sought without lifting the corporate veil, her strongly expressed concern, which carries a great deal of precedential weight, has helped ensure that the lifting of that veil to get at the "real" actors has been confined to a few exceptional circumstances. The judicial awe for corporate structures and for their clever manipulators remains relatively undented.

This state of affairs has a very real potential for undermining social policies pursued by the legislative wings of government. When this potential is exploited by clever lawyers and the scheme gets judicial acceptance, governments are forced to pass legislation to set things right again. The ensuing statutory restraints limit the ability to use corporations to avoid obligations to people considered vulnerable by governments and, therefore, in need of protection. Legislators have resorted to this kind of legislative measure when they are forced to protect the integrity of their revenue-collecting laws from corporate three-card tricks. Another well-known instance of this play and counterplay between judges and entrepreneurs, on the one hand, and legislators, on the other hand, arises when the entitlements of employees are attacked by corporate manipulation.

Statutes, usually called something like the *Employment Standards Act,* provide that there will be a maximum number of hours an employer can force an employee to work, that there will be a minimum rate of pay below which no one can be asked to work, that any hours worked over some specified number must be paid for at premium or overtime rates, that a certain number of public holidays must be non-working days, that a minimum amount of notice is to be given if the employment contract is to be terminated without cause, that a minimum amount of vacation time is to be available to every worker covered by the statute, and so on. These well-known protections are provided because history teaches us that, in the absence of such legislation, the imbalance in economic bargaining power between employers and employees will result in some workers "voluntarily" agreeing to conditions of employment that offend our collective sensibilities. These statutes, then, are minimal interventions amidst the natural workings of the market in an economy in which wealth is unequally distributed A standard clause in these pieces of legislation is that individual covered workers must demonstrate that they had a certain amount of continuity of employment with one employer before they become entitled to the minimum guaranteed by the statute. This type of clause gives corporate manipulators an opportunity to manoeuvre.

Any individuals or corporations employing workers could, by transferring their business to another person, cause there to be an interruption in employment, denying the workers some of their entitlements under the protective legislation. The new employer would claim not to owe any obligations that arose by dint of employment with another distinct legal person. It would be difficult to make the old employer, if a corporation and no longer in business, accountable to the entitled employees. Because an employer can so easily create a new corporation to transfer the business to, it becomes possible to avoid obligations imposed by statute for the benefit of employees who have earned them. Indeed, it would be logically possible for the same real employer to continue to benefit from the same employees' productivity now rendered to this employer in a new corporate garb. While all this seems absurd and somewhat tawdry, corporate law, as interpreted by courts, would not doom this kind of manipulation to automatic failure.

All too often, an abuse being available, business people, especially small-business people, have been bent on exploiting it. Mindful of the importance that conventional wisdom places on the inviolability of the sanctity of the separate legal personality of the corporation, legislators, forced to pass laws to stop such abuses, have done so in a manner that preserves corporate law. The remedial statutory measures taken state that, although for all other purposes they remain separate, distinct persons, any one of the members of a group of human beings and corporations adjudged to be engaged in related and/or affiliated business activities may be treated as the employer of the workers employed by the group whenever they claim entitlement to one of the employment conditions provided for by the protective statutes. In that way, mere paper transactions that shift assets from one corporate actor to another without any functional change in real ownership and control of the business will not automatically rob the workers of their entitlements at law. Similarly, when unionized workers are confronted by the sale of the business within which they achieved their union bargaining rights and conditions of employ-ment, the supervising labour relations boards may determine that the new owner has to assume the obligations incurred by the seller of the business. Again, this safeguarding of employee conditions is to be done without ques-tioning the legitimacy of the new corporate owner as a distinct person when it is not involved in this kind of labour relations' wrangle .

That such elaborate measures have had to be devised tells us much about the pervasiveness of the intent of so-called risk-takers to avoid their solemnly undertaken and legally enforceable obligations. It tells us, very loudly if only we listen, that legislators and policy-makers acknowledge that many business people, particularly small-business people, are satisfied that their only obligation is to stay within the letter of the law. They believe that staying within the letter of the law means that they have met all of their moral and social obligations. The spirit of the law—the sense that business persons, like other people, should support publicly determined and sup-ported values and policies—does not imbue their profit-seeking psyches. For such people the corporation is a heaven-sent vehicle. The proof is in the eat-ing of the pudding. Even though legislatures have sent clear messages to the effect that they do not like the malleability of corporate law being used to undo their labour relations policies, employers continue to use the corporate veil and the complexities of corporate structuring to hide themselves and to shaft their employees.

A good example, amongst many available, is furnished by a case called *Bilt-Rite*, which illustrates the lengths to which small-business entrepreneurs (aided by their lawyers and accountants, of course) will go to evade their contractual and statutory obligations. The case also demonstrates the complexity of corporate law as applied to business organizations, a complexity that helps to hide integrity-challenged human beings from public and regulatory sight.

In the *Bilt-Rite* case, two persons, ordinary human beings like you and me, had owned and managed a furniture manufacturing and selling business. They were Martin Silver and his mother, Sylvia Silver. The firm had a number of divisions—manufacture, sales, and distribution—and employed some four hundred people. But the operation fell on hard times. Under the Ontario protective statute as it was then, a mass termination arising out of insolvency entitled the workers employed continuously for a stipulated length of time to a lump sum payment, known as severance pay, in addition to any monies owed at that time in respect of unpaid wages or unused vacation time. These payments could amount to a large sum. In the *Bilt-Rite* situation, the firm was adjudged to owe $3.5 million to its employees when it became insolvent.

While the firm had become insolvent, the same was not true of Martin and Sylvia Silver. If the principles of a liberal polity and an idealized market could have been applied, they would have been made personally responsible to pay the monies owed to the workers, who had satisfied all their contractual obligations. But the Silvers had run their enterprise through an intricate web of corporations, and when corporate law jumps into action, weird consequences follow. Normal aspirations are defeated; standard expectations are not met. The Silvers' network was intricate indeed (see Diagram 1). Martin and Sylvia Silver had functional control of all of the corporations. They could make them do whatever they wanted, and they could distribute gains and losses as it suited them. They used these powers cleverly.

The corporation named Bilt-Rite did the manufacturing. Its main shareholders were two other corporations, the holding corporations of Martin and Sylvia Silver. "Holding corporation" is the name given to corporations through which the real owners of a corporate group exercise control over the whole of the enterprise. The manufacturing corporation, Bilt-Rite, received wooden frames from National Chesterfields Frames Limited and Kings-Wood Frames Manufacturing Corporation. The eventual controlling shareholders in these two corporations were Martin and Sylvia Silver. A corporation called Bauhaus America sold the manufactured products in Canada, and Bauhaus South conducted sales to the U.S. market. The Silvers controlled both of these retailing outlets. The manufacturing corporation Bilt-Rite did

Diagram 1   The Silvers' Network

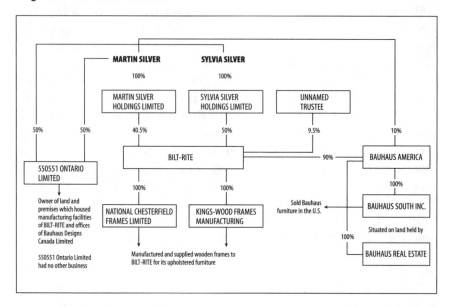

its manufacturing in premises situated on land owned by another registered corporation, 550551 Ontario Limited, completely controlled by the Silvers. When 550551 Ontario Limited had bought the land, its decision-makers had organized for it to borrow more money than it needed for the purchase price. It loaned the surplus money to Bilt-Rite on very favourable terms. Bilt-Rite, the manufacturing corporation, was the physical employer of most of the workers who were owed severance pay upon insolvency. Bilt-Rite's insolvency meant that it did not have the wherewithal to meet the severance payment obligations. The workers, therefore, went in search for anyone in this tightly integrated group of business actors who might have the needed assets. They sought to rely on the affiliated/related employer provisions of the *Employment Standards Act*. Remember that, but for the existence of these provisions, the separate legal person doctrine would have left the former employees completely without remedy, because it would have been most unlikely that a court would have lifted any of the corporate veils spun by the Silvers (and their lawyers and accountants).

At the behest of the workers, the Employment Standards Branch conducted an investigation to determine whether and how the various actors in the group were related. It found that the numbered land-owning corporation, as well as both Silvers, should be treated as related employers and that, there-fore, each of them could be made liable as *the* employer for the purposes of the owed severance payments. Now, the Employment Standards Branch did not come to this decision quickly or easily. Given the complexity of the inter-connections, the government agency had to hire a consultant forensic accounting firm to sort out who was what and how they were related to each other. This not only cost money, but also took time. After the Employment Standards Branch made its finding, the Silvers demanded that they be given a right to respond to the experts' conclusions about the legal relationships between the various members of the furniture production and selling nest of firms. They, too, wanted the right to produce expert evidence. That stage would take time. There was an adjournment.

During the adjournment the land-owning corporation "decided" to bor-row money. The inverted commas are there to remind us that a corporation only makes decisions via human beings, and the question always is: who made this corporate decision and why? The control of the land-owning corporation by the Silvers assumes significance here. In the event, the land-owning corporation borrowed $7 million from Martin and Sylvia Silver. This transaction meant that, after the land-owning corporation paid the money owed on the initial mortgage and the debt now owed to the Silvers and had foregone the monies lent on favourable terms to the now insolvent Bilt-Rite, the land-owning corporation would not have sufficient funds to make the severance payments that the Employment Standards Branch had decided it owed as a related employer. It now became imperative for the workers to get a legal holding that one of the humans, one of the Silvers, be held responsi-ble for the monies owed to them. They were known to have assets, including a debt of $7 million owed to them. The Silvers went to court to have them-selves ruled out as employers. They won.

That the Silvers were sufficiently related to the formal employer, Bilt-Rite, would not have been doubted by any person not handicapped by legal knowledge. Prior to the insolvency, those who did business with the Bilt-Rite/Bauhaus complex probably thought that they were doing business with the Silvers' firm. Most likely the Silvers themselves, if they had been asked what they did, would have said they manufactured and sold furniture. Almost certainly their reply would not have been, "We have some links with some autonomous legal persons who manufacture and sell furniture. We have no control over how they do it. We take little interest. Our links are purely finan-cial ones." So how did a court make a finding that, in essence, said just that?

The court had to accept the provisions of the *Employment Standards Act*, and it ruled that some people who were not direct employers could be treated as such, even if they were distinct and separate persons in terms of corporate law. In this case, the court agreed with the government agency that the land-owning corporation could be held responsible for severance pay as a related employer. After the court identified one asset-less corporation as a responsible employer, it ruled that the Silvers had acted as individuals. The section of the Act specifically provided that an individual could be a related employer but the court read this as meaning that an individual could only be so characterized if that person had acted as a business rather than as an individual. It was a distinction no one had ever thought of before, and one that made no legal sense. It was, "with respect," as we lawyers say with our forked tongue in both our cheeks, nonsense on stilts. Without entering into the legal nitpicking that this silly decision invites, let us simply note the outcome: a court, having been told by legislators that, in some circumstances, corporate law logic should take a back seat, had managed to give that law its usual front seat and upheld a flagrant bit of flim-flam by professionally advised risk-shifters. What message does this send out to anyone interested in the law and its workings, and justice in general, in this country?

At this point it might be useful to summarize this lengthy Bilt-Rite story and its implications.

1. A small business took on corporate form;
2. The corporate vehicles employed were not meant to, and did not, lead to the aggregation of many little capitals from a large number of investors, thereby enhancing the more efficient use of capital.
3. The corporate vehicles were used to avoid contractual and statutorily imposed obligations.
4. The corporate vehicles used made it difficult to identify the real market actors.
5. These kinds of abuses of the corporate form—properly so characterized because the uses made of the vehicle did not advance any of the productive economic goals for which the corporation was designed—are in such common use amongst small businesses that legislators have had to pass legislation to circumvent the application of pure corporate law as much as they dare.

Shifting Risk—Limited Liability

It is not only workers who need to be protected from the risk-takers who employ the corporate device to avoid the duties and responsibilities that supposedly go with the taking of risks. Third-party creditors also need to beware. As in the case of Bilt-Rite, controlling entrepreneurs can make themselves preferred creditors of the corporation, putting themselves ahead of third-party creditors who are owed a debt by the corporation. Unless such a corporate "decision" is set aside as a fraud, unsecured creditors may be left high and dry.

There is also another variant of manipulation of the corporation that has nothing to do with productivity and everything to do with the shifting of risk to others and with the avoidance of what should be binding legal obligations. This one is provided by manifestations of the many available methods of paying out monies that the corporation decides to distribute. As revenues come into the corporation, its directors and managers have a good deal of discretion as to what to do with them: retain them for future investment, invest them, pay increased salaries to worthy employees, or pay dividends to shareholders, for example. In the small-business setting, the directors, managers, shareholders, and workers are frequently the same set of people (sometimes even one person). Depending on how the payout from the corporation is characterized, its tax status will differ. For instance, dividends to a shareholder will be taxed differently than the same amount paid out as salary; more, if the payout is made to one member of the small-business group whose income from other sources is less than other people's in the group, the taxation impost on the whole of the group will be lessened. If the small business is run by, say, a family, this permits a lowering of the taxation due by the group as an entity, even as the corporate monies are going into a pot in which all members of the group share. In a widely held corporation, shareholders unconnected to the manipulators and their intended beneficiaries could, and most likely would, challenge this tax-shifting by manipulation of the categories of payouts. In the small-business setting, the only watchdog is a harassed taxation department, inhibited by the routinization of this kind of advantage-taking and by the judicially supported belief that legislators should be wary of monkeying with the doctrine of separate corporate personality. As a consequence, the ability to pay some of the spoils to someone close to the incorporator and who is taxed at a lower rate has become one of the chief motivations behind the use of corporations by truly small firms. Incorporation is not undertaken to aggregate disparate capitals; it is not undertaken to diminish transaction costs. It is undertaken for the totally unproductive and anti-social purpose of splitting incomes.

This kind of manipulation has as many variants as lawyers and accountants can devise; and, because those lawyers and accountants get paid for, and earn their prestige from, their ability to push the corporate envelope, many types of "clever" business arrangements and schemes proliferate, too many to catalogue. The very malleability of the doctrine of corporate person-ality has broad effects. When a corporation's activities violate regulatory standards, such as those relating to the already parlous state of workers' occu-pational health and safety, or to the environment, consumer protection, and advertising, corporate law doctrine mandates that the corporation, as *the* active person, should be held responsible. Shareholders are immune from prosecution for these violations. Their only potential losses are the diminu-tion of their shares' value as a consequence of any fines payable by the corpo-ration, or loss of corporate profits as a result of the corporation's damaged reputation. These risks are secondary and, for the most part, theoretical in that they materialize rarely—and, if they do materialize, it is only much later. Employees of the corporation may be liable as individuals for violations of the regulations, but not necessarily if they were acting as the guiding mind and will of the corporation. Certainly, too, it is the senior employees who should be held accountable, not the minions who do their bidding. But they will only be responsible if they made the violating act their personal act, rather than that of the corporation.

All of this means that when small business is incorporated and violates these types of public welfare-protecting regulations, the very people who set up the corporation, remain as its shareholders, and, more often than not, act as its senior managers have large areas of near immunity from legal retribu-tion for the violations. This is a disincentive to cause them to have the corpo-ration take the kinds of costly precautions prescribed by these regulatory schemes. It makes it difficult for government agencies to ensure compliance with their regulations. This endangers workers, the environment, and con-sumers. Small business, when incorporated, has the opportunity to shift costs onto others and to undermine public policy. Small business, when incorpo-rated, frequently exploits this opportunity. This ought to be a problem for those who defend market capitalism on the grounds that it encourages, and rewards, rugged, risk-taking small businesses.

There are many indications that this problem is recognized. For instance, when a small-business owner who has decided to conduct his activities through a corporation goes to a bank to raise capital for the venture, the bank managers will treat him as if he were unincorporated—that is, they will seek the same undertaking of personal responsibility for the debt that they would obtain from any individual customer. Before banks will lend to a small incor-porated business, they will obtain security for the loan by binding the real person behind the corporate veil to repay the debt. Typically, they will require him to be a personal guarantor for any loan that, in formal legal terms, is extended to the corporation. If the individual does not have the assets to meet this requirement, the bank will not advance a loan to the corporation. The bank will be making the judgement that this borrower is only a risk-taker to the extent of imposing the costs of any materialized risk on someone else. No self-respecting bank would agree to that proposition. In large part, the banks' hard-nosed, but essentially logical, stance towards small business, whether incorporated or not, is what gives them a reputation for being unkind to small business. Yet often they are only defending themselves against an attempted, or potential, abuse of the corporate vehicle.

Undoubtedly, other lenders to the small incorporated business wish they had the same ability to avert corporate law-supported irresponsibility. Trade creditors, who are often small businesses themselves and bona fide suppliers of goods and services to undercapitalized corporations (like workers who have rendered services), are often left to fight over a corporate bag emptied by preferred creditors—a category that includes banks and may include shareholders, as in the *Bilt-Rite* case. They are the victims of the abuse of the corporate veil precisely because they cannot bargain effectively before they extend credit to a small incorporated business.

Legislators have also had to limit the ability of corporate law abuses to maintain some of the protections they believe must be available to the more vulnerable amongst us. In addition, they have had to act to counter the impression that, by the clever use of corporate law, wealth-owners or major shareholders, and directors or managers acting for the companies, can flout public welfare laws with relative impunity. The failure to hold any real, live person accountable for violations delivers a message that governments are not serious about the enforcement of their much-publicized laws and that they are content to treat corporate owners and managers as being above the law. Legislators have responded to this pressure by attempting to impose at least some duties on corporate directors and senior executives. Notionally at least, not just the corporate entity but also its directors and executives may be held personally responsible to pay fines. In some instances the people responsible might even be jailed. In short, the decision-makers may be held responsible for their actions, despite the corporate veil. But these developments have met with fierce resistance.

As well, a few (a very few) courts have set aside ugly results simply because they are ugly, while others have engaged in some fancy legal dipsy-doodling to get rid of some of the more transparent abuses of the combination of legal personality, limited liability, and undercapitalization. While these occasions remain exceptions to the rule, the very fact that the judiciary, the bastion of conservatism, feels itself pushed in these directions indicates a pervasive awareness of how anti-social behaviour on the part of small business, when swathed in corporate clothing, can menace the hold of market capitalism on our collective mind.

What market capitalism's theorists and cheerleaders fear most is that the mounting evidence of abuses by small incorporated business will induce legislators to revisit the concept of limited liability—the very feature that makes attractive the investment in truly large corporations. One scheme— much talked about, but never acted upon—suggests that limited liability should only be made available to very large corporations. The advocates do not specify how legislators might draw the line between large, meritorious corporations and the others. Another strategy proposes that incorporators should guarantee a certain amount of capital before a corporation is granted the right to be registered as a legal person. Again, the difficulty of specifying what kind of capital funding should be required and how to balance such a requirement against the need to facilitate enterprise and enterprisers of all kinds makes it unlikely that this proposal will gain much political support. The prescriptions for change have had little impact outside academic circles.

In any case, the goal of these would-be reformers, all proponents of market capitalism, is to preserve the corporation as the primary vehicle for furthering the capitalist project. They seem to be sanguine that large, publicly traded corporations will not be used as often, and certainly not as blatantly, to avoid personal responsibilities and that the general legitimacy of the corporate form will be safer after the removal of some of the temptations for abuse by small business. They don't want the baby—the very large corporate baby— thrown out with the bathwater dirtied by small business. It is a good plan. Large, publicly traded corporations use the malleability of corporate law much less often than small businesses do. But sometimes they do, and we turn first to one very well-known example before going on to examine the quite different villainies and evils perpetrated by the large publicly-traded corporations.

The Westray Story

Wherein we learn that when big business actors use their invisible friends in the way that small-business actors do, they really can do as much harm as serial killers. Yet they may still be treated as lost, perhaps misguided, souls unfortunately caught in the web of a corporate veil.

On May 9, 1992, an explosion at the Westray coal mine in Pictou County, Nova Scotia, killed twenty-six coal miners. Fifteen bodies were recovered; those of the other eleven men will never be returned to their loved ones. They remain interred in the now-flooded mine. In the months and years after the explosion the Westray saga attracted a huge amount of public attention. It did so not just because the outcome was a tragedy, but also because the behaviour of the central actors was sleazy beyond belief. For our purposes what we find is that, once again, the enterprise involved used the corporate form to avoid legal and moral responsibilities. But this time the enterprise was a major player rather than the fly-by-nights that preoccupied us in the previous two chapters.

The circumstances that led to this tragedy were not unusual in our political economy. Craven politicians, pursuing their ambitious career plans and following their ideological predilections, swaddled themselves in the clothing of would-be job creators and offered huge handouts to private-sector actors. The goal was to encourage the private profit-seekers to open a mine in an area that was not only known to be rich in coal but also known to have an equally rich history of accidents and deaths. The politicians deployed tax-payers' money and infrastructure utilities to make the opening of a coal mine by private profiteers a virtually risk-free undertaking. The governmental actors, therefore, had a great stake in the success of the mining operations, and as a result they made no serious efforts to ensure the maintenance of basic health and safety precautions. After all, demands for compliance might require spending money or slow down operations, lessening the profitability of the enterprise and thereby the prestige of the supporting politicians.

The commission of inquiry set up afterwards to fathom what had happened found that the operators had been heedless of, and reckless in respect of, health and safety requirements. The finding did not surprise anyone, because by the time the commission began its hearings it had been revealed that, in its short period of operation, the mine had suffered a series of cave-ins and technicians had recorded a large number of above-acceptable levels of methane gas readings (methane being a very explosive gas). As well, it was known that the coal-mine owners had been found to have committed fifty-two violations of the provincial safety regulations prior to the explosion. The government had dispatched inspectors, as its health and safety law required, but, while the Department of Labour had dutifully recorded the violations, it had not seen fit to bring any charges against the mine-owners and/or its managers. From this perspective, the explosion was a totally predictable event. It would be misleading to characterize such a predictable outcome as an "accident," yet that is how it is conventionally viewed. The obscenity of that characterization is exacerbated by another feature of the story: after public monies had been funnelled into private actors' pockets, those actors had drawn a corporate veil over their heads and simply disappeared from *legal* sight when authorities and others concerned sought to pin down responsibility for this predictable event. What follows is an account of how the conditions for the "accident" were created—or, in my view, designed—and how responsibility was avoided.

A trio of entrepreneurs by the names of Frame, Sultan, and Hunt had formed a partnership, named Curragh Partnership, to buy a business formerly owned by Dome. The name of the business thus acquired was Cyprus Anvil Mining. As a partner, each of the trio was entitled to share in the profits of this venture, but each was also personally responsible for all the obligations incurred by the partnership. Like sensible business people, they determined to rid themselves of these risks. They had themselves bought out by a corporation registered in Ontario under the name of 715914 Ontario Inc. This corporation borrowed money to buy out Curragh Partnership's interest in

Cyprus Anvil Mining, and it now owed that money to its lenders. Frame, Sultan, and Hunt, the vendors, had money in their pocket and were no longer personally at risk for any liabilities incurred by Cyprus Anvil Mining's operations. Shortly thereafter 715914 Ontario Inc. changed its name to Curragh Resources Inc. Its chief executive officer, at a salary of over $200,000 per year, was C.H. Frame.

Frame was developing other interests. In particular, he won the right to develop the Westray mine site in Pictou County. He had won this after some serious negotiations with the provincial and federal governments. His argument—via well-connected political lobbyists—was that he would require government concessions to undertake mining at this site because several, much more prestigious, enterprises (such as Suncor and Placer Dome) with a great deal more mining experience than his own firm had turned down the opportunity. Those companies had decided that, given the difficulty of the coal extraction (because of the nature of the terrain, as reflected in its catastrophic history) and given the uncertain market outlook for any coal extracted, a mine at the Westray site was not a good proposition.

Frame got a deal that took these risks out of play. He convinced the Nova Scotia government to become a purchaser of the mine's yield in order to fuel a nearby government-operated power plant. The price to be paid by the power plant would be well above the expected extraction cost. The government even agreed to pay for a certain amount of coal each year, even if it was not produced. None of these risk-saving "gimmes" had been in place when Suncor and Placer Dome did their feasibility studies.

But Frame was not through. He wanted even more help, and he got it. The federal government agreed to guarantee 85 per cent of the $100 million that Frame wanted to borrow to start up operations. The loan was to come from the Bank of Nova Scotia. That careful institution had refused Frame's application for this loan—despite the favourable deal he had squeezed out of the Nova Scotia government. The bank wanted someone on the hook who would be capable to meet any liabilities incurred by the risk-taking Frame and colleagues. Now the federal government's willingness to be a guarantor meant that Canadian taxpayers would be the people on the hook should Frame and his colleagues fail, which the Bank of Nova Scotia apparently thought was entirely possible. But the bank was now happy to lend Frame the money he needed.

Some additional handouts sweetened this sugared pot. The federal government kicked in about $8 million by way of interest-offsetting credits and subsidies routinely made to miners. The Nova Scotia government added a loan for $12 million, on which no interest was to be payable for ten years.

When news of the spectacular explosion hit the public airwaves and presses, Frame came to the site and expressed his deep sympathies and regrets. He noted that, as a person long involved with mining, he had a profound understanding of the depth of the disaster. Afterwards this man, who had become something of a media darling and celebrity, featured in articles with photographs depicting him as a pioneer, adopted a low profile—a very low profile. He was virtually not seen again in public. The Nova Scotia Department of Labour was investigated and the commission of inquiry probed into the conduct of politicians, the management of the mine, and the behaviour of workers. It had not much to say about Frame in its report, because he had used a legal technicality to justify his refusal to come before the commission to give evidence to it, although the commission had wanted him to do so. Frame (and his lawyers) exploited the legally defensible, but morally repugnant, point that the Nova Scotia-appointed commission had no legal jurisdiction to force out-of-province persons to appear before it. Frame successfully stayed in Ontario, withholding from public gaze what he, as CEO and major everything-to-do-with-the-mine, knew about its setting up, the understandings between the mine operators and governments, and the mine's operations. The notion that he should feel morally obliged to help people understand what had happened clearly did not play a dominant role in his thinking.

It is not as if Frame, until then, had been a shrinking violet, someone not deeply involved in the undertaking. Frame owned 70 per cent of the shares of a corporation called Westray Mining Corporation. This corporation, in turn, owned 74 per cent of the shares of a corporation registered with the name Frame Mining Corporation, which was the only shareholder—that is, the complete owner—of a corporation called 630902 Ontario Inc. That corporation in turn was the registered owner of the lease and licences of the Westray Coal Project. C.H. Frame was *the* human being in control of Westray.

In December 1989, 630902 Ontario Inc. had sold 90 per cent of its interest in the lease and licences of the Westray Coal Project. The purchaser was Curragh Resources Inc., the very same corporation that had bought the Frame, Sultan, and Hunt interests in Cyprus Anvil Mining. Curragh Resources Inc. became the legal owner of the operation known as the Westray Mine. It had paid the vendor 630902 Ontario Inc., and assumed all of its remaining debts. Effectively, therefore, Frame had recouped whatever he had invested via his controlled corporations and was off the hook for any leftover liabilities.

But this did not mean that Frame stopped being involved in the tangled, government-supported affairs of the Westray Mine. After all, as an individual rather than a shareholder, Frame had assumed the mantle of chief executive officer of Curragh Resources. He had been the chief executive when Curragh Resources made its decision to buy the mining interest, which he had done so much to bring into existence and that he had effectively owned and controlled. After Curragh Resources' acquisition of the Westray Coal Project, all that had changed was the formal legal title. Functionally, not much had happened. Frame, through Westray Mining Corporation, Frame Mining Corporation, and 630902 Ontario Inc., held all the shares with voting rights in Curragh Resources Inc. This gave him control over the management of Curragh Resources, because he was in a position to determine who should be on the board of directors. As CEO, he was to report to that board of directors. He was hardly a bit player in the enterprise that was legally responsible for the operation of the Westray Mine.

Adding a little spice to this tale of the byzantine structuring of control over the mining operations by means of corporate law manipulation, Curragh Resources appointed a consultant to advise it on how to develop the Westray Coal Project. While we know little about this consultancy firm, we do know that it was a corporation that went by the name of C.H. Frame Consulting Services. Undoubtedly, the firm was hired to assist the CEO, Frame himself. The contract between Curragh Resources Inc. and C.H. Frame Consulting Services was for $6 million. Eventually, when Curragh Resources had to meet its obligations, this contract was bought out for $1.5 million, saving some $4.5 million. The $1.5 million had to be paid to the consultancy firm.

In the end, Frame did not get off scot-free. Curragh Resources Inc. became insolvent, and eventually its assets were sold and some of the debts paid. It is most likely that Frame, as a major shareholder, lost some of his investment. But he could only lose as much as he had actually invested; his personal assets could not be tapped for the payment of liabilities that he had helped to engineer and from which he had sought to profit. He would not have had to repay what he earned as a senior employee.

More significantly, these "clever" uses of corporate law permitted Frame to control an operation that ended in disaster, while denying the human victims of his operation the opportunity to satisfy the very human desire of confronting him, as a human being. On the face of it, he had a great deal to atone for, a great deal of personal influence that altered their lives forever. The (eventually dropped) attempts to charge two of the site managers — employees, as opposed to controllers of the operation — with criminal negligence were the closest they came to any kind of closure.

The Westray story is just another story of abuse of the corporate form. It does tell us, however, that, in a big business setting the risk-avoidance techniques employed by small incorporated businesses not only can lead to even greater economic harm, but they can also, as in Westray, cause death and destruction. An added malignant edge is thus added to the way in which the separate legal personality and limited liability features can be deployed. But the Westray story also provides a sharp glimpse into how large business, shielded from public gaze by the corporate veil, can manipulate—perhaps to the point of corruption—our politicians and political institutions. This singular case provides something of a conceptual bridge between the economic distortion in the legal use of the corporation and its political impacts. I believe we are ready to cross this bridge and begin the work of showing that the corporation in the large business setting is inimical to our notions of liberal democracy.

Diagram 2   The Play and the Principal Players

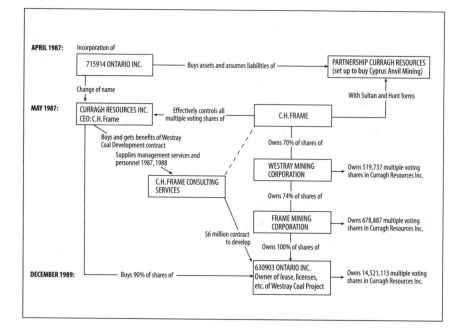

The Undemocratic Innards of the Large Corporation

Wherein we learn how the law structures our great corporations so as to enable them to avert the dangers and perils of democratic rule.

The legal (contrast: real) owner of the ill-fated Westray Mine was "someone" called Curragh Resources Inc. It was a publicly traded corporation. What this meant was that it had asked the general public to contribute capital so that it could engage in its ventures. The investors were to get shares in the corporation in return for their contribution. Their purchase of those shares entitled them to participate in any profits made.

This kind of buying and selling of shares with a view to potentially unlimited profits, while limiting the buyers' and sellers' risks, is done in marketplaces called share or stock exchanges. To get wealth-owners to invest in their enterprises, many of our largest, most famous corporations have had themselves listed on major stock exchanges. There they parade their wares before budding capitalists, hoping to inveigle them into investing in their undertakings.

While not all major corporations seek to capitalize themselves in this way, most do. Such firms go by various names: offering corporations (they offer their shares for sale to the public); issuing corporations (they issue shares to the public); distributing corporations (their shares are widely distributed); widely held corporations (their shares finish up being held by a great number of people); or finally (and the term I will use here), publicly traded corporations (their shares are freely available to be sold and bought by the public). Corporations that do not ask the general public to invest in them—mostly small- and medium-sized enterprises, although some very large ones also refrain from going to the public for capital—are known as non-offering corporations, non-issuing corporations, non-distributing corporations, non-trading corporations, or closely held corporations. I will use the last of these terms to describe these kinds of corporations.

As we've seen (chapters 3 and 4), the use of the corporate vehicle as a legal form for a small- or medium-sized enterprise is difficult to justify, either in market-economic terms or in liberal-political ones. But the pivotal features of a legal corporation—limited liability for investors and the separate personality of the corporation—will enhance economic efficiency. These features directly help the pooling of lots of little capitals. The aggregated capital is then deployed by a co-ordinating management that is likely to make better use of it than the contributors could have done as discrete, atomized owners of smaller sums. Most likely transaction costs will be reduced as a great number of human and non-human resources are brought together to be managed and co-ordinated under one giant umbrella.

It is something of a paradox, then, that when the public does show its resentment of the corporate sector, more often than not it will be because the conduct of large, immense, publicly traded corporations has offended it. This is so because, while unquestionably good at what they are supposed to do, namely to be efficient vehicles for the private accumulation of wealth, these large, publicly traded corporations violate many social and political tenets held dear. More—and this is the crunch—they do so very frequently, all too often with impunity, coupled with a display of arrogance, with an ugly, in-your-face, machismo. This is very hard to take. The truth is that publicly traded corporations (i) legally, are structured as feudal institutions; (ii) commit crimes—over and over again; and (iii) wield massive, disproportionate, and therefore unacceptable, political power in our supposed democratic polity. This chapter deals with the first of these problems, namely how the legal governance of corporations—corporate law—favours inequality and a stunted version of democracy. The following two scenarios, I hope, will provide some evidence for this statement.

Scenario I

In February 1978 the people running Westinghouse Canada were privately debating whether they should have productive work, then being done at their unionized Hamilton plant, transferred to some other smaller, more modern plants. Most of the new plants would be built nearby, in a less unionized district; and some of the operations would be transferred to faraway Ireland to take advantage of tax relief offered by that country. These plans, if carried to fruition, would lead to the closure of the whole, or a large part, of the unionized plant in Hamilton.

At the same time as the board of directors at Westinghouse headquarters was considering these operational questions, the people running Westinghouse Canada were negotiating with the United Electrical Workers union, which represented the Hamilton plant's employees. The union had initiated these negotiations to renew a collective agreement that was coming to an end. Neither Westinghouse Canada's board of directors nor the company's negotiating team bothered to tell the union about the continuing high-level deliberations about the Hamilton plant's future or lack of it.

In this vacuum, Westinghouse Canada's local negotiating team and the United Electrical Workers reached an agreement. The union recommended its acceptance to the workers. The same day that the workers ratified the agreement, the directors of Westinghouse Canada—at a separate meeting, undoubtedly conducted in comfortable surroundings—agreed to set aside funds to initiate the Hamilton's plant's closure and the relocation of its operations. They had decided to give effect to their secret deliberations. Then, and only then, was the union told of this employer decision. The union leaders, understandably upset, sought to have the corporate decision set aside and initiated a legal challenge. As a result of that litigation, based in labour law, the trade union and the workers at the Hamilton plant were granted some minor remedies. Corporate law provided no remedy: indeed, the labour law remedy available was limited because of the legal imperative to keep corporate logic intact. As a legal matter the corporate employer's decision to close the Hamilton plant was allowed to stand, and many of the workers lost their jobs.

Scenario II

In our second scenario, a run-of-the-mill takeover battle, one corporation tries to swallow another that does not want to be eaten. The people who run the corporation targeted for the takeover bid recommend to their shareholders that they should refuse the bid being made for their shares. One of the reasons they give for that recommendation is their concern for the corporation's employees, who, they say, will lose their jobs when the new owners have to repay the debt incurred in borrowing money to buy the shares needed to gain control over the target corporation. The new owners, they argue, will have to "restructure" the corporation—that is, they will have to sell some of its assets and operations, retrenching workers in the process. The directors also tell the workers about the impending danger, hoping that the workers' vigorous demonstrations of their anxieties will influence the shareholders to heed the target management's recommendation to reject the bid for their shares. The turmoil raised might also have an effect on the bidder.

Such a manifestation of the deep concern of directors for the plight of workers might well be viewed with suspicion. Workers' interests are demonstrably not usually in the forefront of directors' minds, nor do they need to be there legally. What this scenario shows, however, is that directors *can* share information with workers—and they do so when it suits them. But they have no such choice when it comes to shareholders.

When the members of a board of directors sit down to make a major corporate decision, such as what to do about a takeover, they cannot act unilaterally. They cannot reject a bid for a change of control over the corporation they are running without getting the shareholders' approval. Those who run the corporation are under a *legal* duty to their shareholders to give them every opportunity to make up their own minds as to whether or not a bid for a change of ownership should be accepted. The law imposes this duty to inform shareholders fully because the interests of the shareholders will be significantly changed by the success or failure of the takeover bid. It is seen as axiomatic that shareholders, as people likely to be affected, should be asked what they want and be given an opportunity to make a properly informed decision. In the eyes of corporate law, the shareholders' views, unlike those of the workers who also are likely to be affected (as were the workers at Westinghouse), *must* count with, and be counted, by the directors.

What is wrong with this picture? Why, and how, does the law justify preferential treatment of a corporation's shareholders and the derisory treatment of the same corporation's workers? Why, and how, does corporate law, which is meant to be part and parcel of liberal law, justify the unequal treatment of supposedly equal sovereign citizens? When directly confronted, these questions lead to replies that demonstrate that liberal legal tenets cannot be given full sway in a capitalist political economy. If liberal law truly reigned, it would rein in a corporation's ability to deliver on capitalism's goals, namely, rule by the few, exploitation of the many. Inevitably, much effort is expended to avert the direct, frontal attack that might be launched if these troubling questions had to be confronted.

The Governance of the Corporation

Efficiency dictates that, once the investors have given up their capital to a corporation to have it managed by a co-ordinating set of managers, the management team should have control over deployment of the assets. Canadian legislatures have written this efficiency principle into corporate law.

The corporate law statutes provide that shareholders are to appoint a board of directors whose legal duty it is to manage and supervise the corporation. The law defines the board's duty as being the exercise of an appropriate standard of care in the pursuit of the best interests of the corporation. In actual practice, of course, boards of directors of large, publicly traded corporations delegate the daily tasks of the management of the corporate assets and the pursuit of the corporation's interests to executives and officers, some of whom may also be members of the board of directors. Non-executive directors are not meant to be full-time, hands-on, governors of the corporation. They are not full-time employees. They are broad policy-setters. This means that, while the responsibility to look after the best interests of the corporation, as a matter of law, always remains with the board of directors, the actual implementing, managing, and administering of the policies designed to serve the best interests of the corporation are carried on by a number of professionals: executive directors, senior executives, and managers. They are relatively few in number and co-ordinate the activities of many, sometimes hundreds, sometimes thousands, of employees. Functionally, if not legally, they are the people in charge.

Logically, this particular structure does not present any kind of *legal* problem. Once investors have contributed property of their own, that property becomes the legal possession of the corporation, an entity (or "person") legally distinct from those investors. No eyebrows should be raised just because the initial investors no longer exercise immediate control over what had once been their property. This is what the law, which sets out to facilitate efficient investment, intends. Yet a problem does exist. It is a problem of *political* legitimacy. It arises because those who justify the use of the corporate vehicle do so on the basis that it is a nice fit with the idealized market's working principles.

The ideal of market efficiency is posited on the notion that each individual is to maximize her or his own resources. This approach will lead to an optimal allocation of resources in our economy, because each individual is deemed to be obsessively self-interested; no one else could possibly be as interested in that person's welfare. From this perspective, the real wants and desires of individuals will be pursued most efficiently by individuals acting for themselves. If they leave control over their resources to others, they run the danger that their goals will be diluted, thereby diminishing the efficient operation of the market economy. A scheme of private wealth generation that is justified by market criteria will, therefore, lose some of its lustre if individuals give up their right to act as grasping self-seeking market actors. On the face of it, this is precisely what happens when corporations come into play. Corporate law grants the right to manage the corporate assets to directors and managers. Shareholders—that is, the contributors of those assets—do not have any directly, legally enforceable right to manage the assets. This apparent separation between ownership and control when doing business by means of a corporation undermines the legitimacy of profit-seeking activities otherwise justified by the tenets of the idealized market.

This is no academic problem: it is a political nightmare for those who want to justify individual self-seeking and greed as the engines of economic welfare and political freedom. As early as 1776, Adam Smith, the patron saint of marketeers, wrote that the government should be loath to allow people to incorporate their businesses. Incorporation should be restricted to exceptional economic undertakings; it should be permitted only when the management team's exercise of discretion is so limited that it cannot help but coincide with the investors' interest. Smith stated:

> The only trades which it seems possible for a joint stock company to carry on successfully are those, of which all the operations are capable of being reduced to what is called a routine, or to such an uniformity of method as admits of little or no variation. Of this kind is, first, the banking trade; secondly, the trade of insurance from fire, and from sea risk and capture in time of war; thirdly, the trade of making and maintaining a navigable cut or canal; and, fourthly, the similar trade of bringing water for the supply of a great city.

It is amusing, of course, to note that the founding intellectual of market ideology believed that businesses such as banking and insurance required very little by way of special management skills. It might be nice to confront the highly paid executives of those industries with that statement from time to time. While the response of Matthew Barrett, formerly the very well-paid CEO of the Bank of Montreal and now the even better paid CEO of Barclay's Bank, undoubtedly would be that since 1776 banking and insurance have become very complicated and now require expert managers with a great deal of discretion, he also would most likely claim—as indeed all corporate leaders and capitalism's cheerleaders must claim to maintain their own and the system's political legitimacy—to be living, roughly, by the edicts of Adam Smith. While they may quibble with Smith's views on major financial institutions, his views remain central to free-market ideologues and practitioners who seek to justify capitalism. Smith's central point—about the dangers of incorporation for the efficient workings of the market created by the legal separation of ownership and control—remains unchallenged.

Indeed, almost two centuries after Smith, in a major U.S. scholarly work published in 1932, authors A.A. Berle and G.C. Means re-identified this same point as the core problem in corporate law. Berle and Means studied the leading corporations in the United States and came to the conclusion that the greatest difficulty facing American capitalism was that ownership without control and control without ownership had become the norm in U.S. corporations. The potential for inefficiency and for the misuse of resources identified by Smith was, they believed, exacerbated because there were now far more thriving and efficient stock markets (in which shareholders' interests could be bought and sold) than there had been during Smith's life. Investors could now get rid of investment risks created by managerial decisions they did not like much more easily than they could have done in the eighteenth century. This meant that they had even more economic incentive not to pay much attention to the adequacy of any one corporation's management than Smith feared they might have. By the 1930s, if they did not like a corporation's performance or outlook, shareholders could switch their allegiance, rather than discipline their managers directly. Plenty of other corporations had shares trading on the market and might be more attractive to them. The scheme, then, Berle and Means said, was producing increasingly passive investors—the very opposite of the economic actors in the idealized market model posited by Adam Smith.

The conceptual and political difficulty (then and now) is not that the corporation, especially the publicly traded corporation, has not been an efficient means of accumulating wealth. To the contrary: it has been very efficient as a *capitalist* tool. The point is that it does not generate wealth in a manner consonant with the working principles of the *idealized market*. That this is perceived as a problem is reflected by the apparent failure of the publicly traded corporation to fit in with the nostrums of the market model—because of the apparent gap between ownership and control—a failure that has been the main impetus for most efforts at reform in corporate law. It has also remained the predominant topic of the intellectual debates found in learned academic journals since Berle and Means's study.

On the one side of these debates are the liberal social engineers, who say that the inevitable gap between ownership and control means that the corporation, not being a true market institution, should be regulated and used for purposes other than profiteering. More specifically, the corporation could, and should, be used for social purposes. Because managers are not bound by shareholders' wishes, they could be required to pursue socially worthwhile goals with the vast assets they control. On the other side of the debate are the freebooting capitalists and marketeers, who are horrified by the notion that a vehicle designed to advance private, self-serving interests should be used directly to attain social and public goals. They respond vehemently to the liberal social engineers. Their counter-arguments are aimed at restoring the legitimacy of the corporation as a single-purpose institution, one dedicated to the pursuit of profits and only profits. To help them make their case, they argue that the contentions of the social do-gooders are based on a false premise.

These cheerleaders for unadulterated capitalism carried on through publicly traded corporations rely on the teachings and writings of an intellectual stream known as the school of law and economics. The members of this school are wedded, religiously so, to the principles of individualism and a market economy. They simply cannot afford to admit that the corporate vehicle, capitalism's primary piece of machinery, is anti-market in structure. If that were true, the economic centrality of the corporation would suggest that, effectively, there is no market economy. Hence they assert that, despite Smith, despite Berle and Means, despite a mountain of empirical evidence that shows law as echoing those observers' views, there is no loss of control by the owners of capital who invest in publicly traded corporations. They argue that those who point to such a gap do not understand what happens when a corporation is formed.

These apologists for the corporation argue that what really happens is that the investors/owners of capital *contractually* agree with other investors/owners of capital to give their combined capitals to others to manage. As a group of contracting owners they also contract with these managers, and therefore it is up to them, as contracting owners, to determine the terms of the contract for the management of the aggregated capitals: that is, they do, or could, control what these managers are to do. Even though it is the norm for the board of directors and the management team to have their duties on how to manage the corporation spelled out by law, rather than by any actual contract between the owners and managers, that is said not to be the point. While owners/shareholders could be (and sometimes are) specific about the objectives they want the corporation to pursue and how those goals should be pursued, inasmuch as they do not do this it is to be *assumed* that the statutory provisions covering these matters accurately reflect what these investors/owners would have put into any contract with the other investors/owners if it had been practical for them to do so. Inasmuch as they do not, the statutes should be changed. The statutory terms are (or should be) merely reflections of the result that would have been produced by complicated contract-making between a huge number of people. In short, the defenders of the corporation's legitimacy are in denial. Their line of reasoning rejects any contention that there are investors/owners without control and non-property owners with control. Their *assumption* that the concrete state of the law reflects the implicit contracts made by investors/owners and their managers enables them to assume that investors/owners continue to act as individuals, as proper market actors. There is no evidence that this assumption is warranted.

This line of argument need not detain us, for even if their fantastical assumption about the real world is accepted, these scholars are not out of the woods. The very starting position of these knight-defenders of the corporate vehicle creates another, and even more serious, set of problems for them. Their starting position is that there is nothing more innate to human beings than the search for *more*—nothing more natural and important to humans than the satisfaction of greed. It is this (profoundly superficial) understanding of human nature that makes them true believers in the market and in capitalism. But this view of human nature means that they must acknowledge that the directors and managers hired to look after other selfish people's property will also be self-seeking people; and, given the skills needed to maximize corporate profits (which is what they are supposed to do for those others), they should be amongst the sharpest, most accomplished of self-serving individuals. Indeed, this is how their extraordinary salaries are often justified. These directors and managers, then, are individuals who not only would want to put their interests at the top of any list of priorities guiding their decision-making, but also should be expected to be cunning and determined when doing so.

Just as Adam Smith argued, investors/owners should fear being short-changed by the directors and managers to whom they have entrusted their property. Their worst fears are likely to be justified if the directors and their management teams have wide discretionary powers. The management team's members may be able to pretend to be exercising these widely framed powers on behalf of the investors/owners while they are actually looking after themselves. And this is precisely the kind of leeway that the law gives to boards of directors and managers.

The legal artifice of creating a separate corporate person that owns the property invested in it puts delegated decision-making at the centre of the enterprise. There is little point in giving management of the aggregated capitals—now owned as one glob by the corporation—detailed instructions on how to deploy the assets. Hence, it is logical for the law to provide no such detailed instructions. In fact, all that the law does is to furnish a set of hortatory instructions to directors and managers. Basically, it says: "You have a duty to take reasonable care and act in the best interests of the corporation." The potential dangers created by leaving managers to be guided by such a vague direction should be obvious.

In general capitalist terms, the goal of the corporation is to maximize profit. But over what time period is profit-maximization to be measured? For some investors/owners, what is most desirable is making profits now, to enable them to cash in their shares profitably. Other investors/owners in the same corporations want to hold onto their shares because they are looking for long-term capital gains. Adding to the complications is the continuously changing identity of investors/owners capable of holding shares. This permits arguments to be made by directors and managers that they must have wide discretion to take the interests of future, unknown shareholders into account, as well as those of existing shareholders. All this, plus the corporation's notionally immortal existence, renders it equally justifiable for management to see the corporation's maximization of profits as a short-term or a long-term exercise or as aiming for an indeterminable balance between these two extremes.

Directors and managers, charged with pursuing "the best interests of the corporation," find it legally easy to justify almost any choice they make on how to use the capital put in their hands. Indeed, courts are at pains to say that they will try to respect their judgement, provided that it appears to have been exercised honestly. Now, if human beings are believed to be essentially egoistic, it is to be expected that, with the wealth of choices available, many decisions will be made that make it possible for directors and managers to shirk work, while giving them more prestige and pay—even if this comes at the expense of investors/owners. In short, believers in selfishness must acknowledge that problems will arise out of any gap between original ownership and functional control. To dilute such a critique, which is peculiarly effective because it is based on their own premises, they try to prove that the difficulties raised are due to the technical workings of the market, problems that can be overcome rather easily—that is, that they are not problems arising out of the nature of the legal corporation. They argue, then, that if the market is allowed to function as it should, the problems will disappear, as if by magic.

They contend that, if directors and managers shirk or loot—this is the language of corporate law, itself indicative of the pervasiveness of these problems—that is, if they do not work hard and honestly, if they do not put their own interests second (as the duty directly imposed by law and/or the implicit contracts between investors/owners and managers demand), the value of the shares of the corporation will reflect this failure. Poor profitability, or goods and services that become too costly, will lead to market share losses; decisions to establish or to terminate production lines in the wrong place, or at the wrong time, should also lead to lower share values, as well as to a diminution in the prestige of the management team and, hence, its professional opportunities. Inasmuch as managers' compensation depends on the value of the shares, they will suffer immediate financial losses. The argument, then, is that any difficulties arising out of the gap between ownership and control will be rectified if the markets for managers, goods and services, and shares work as they should.

But in practice these potential market incentives and disincentives do not work very well. For one thing, it is difficult for investors/owners to know what a non-abused corporation's best results would be and, therefore, how to discount the value of shares accurately for past or future bad managerial behaviour. For another, investors/owners cannot easily judge the extent to which the decision-making by the directors and managers alters a corporation's performance. This problem reduces to guesswork any market discipline to be exercised by changes in share valuation. The defenders of the faith, therefore, are forced to turn for help to the increasing number of large institutional investors who buy shares in corporations. The hope is that pension funds, mutual funds, and insurance and trust companies, among others, will use their professional acumen and control over large pools of investment funds to discipline corporate managers. They will be able to monitor the performance of corporations better than the mom-and-pop investor. As major, market-wise shareholders, if they do not like the policy and/or management, they could use their legal voting rights to appoint different people to the board of directors. But, empirically, there is no conclusive evidence that institutional investors exercise this disciplinary role very often. It would be surprising if they did.

A major reason for the institutional investors' virtual non-use of their supposed market power to discipline managers is that, in respect of any one corporation, that power is usually not that great. While institutional investors do manage large sums, their investment in any one corporation is often not significant enough to give them an incentive to monitor that corporation's management closely. If they do so act, they will be incurring costs from which other investors will benefit. Tellingly, this situation is referred to as the free-rider problem. It goes against the self-centred grain of all serious capitalists to let other non-paying parties benefit from their efforts. More: institutional investors are themselves corporations with similar "agency" problems—that is, they have managers who control other people's capital, managers who may be "opportunistic." The managers may have their eyes on their own personal interests rather than on their principals' interests. These professional fund managers have more in common with the professional managers of the corporations they are supposed to monitor than with their own investors. Like the people they are supposed to monitor, they do not like the prospect of outside interference with their discretion, and they do not like to encourage the idea that such participation should be rampant in anal-ogous situations. Finally, in this catalogue as to why institutional investors and market forces are unlikely to inhibit shirking and looting by directors and managers, note that, while, in absolute terms, the amounts that directors and managers extract for themselves at the expense of the investors/owners/shareholders are often huge, relative to the assets, revenues, and profits of large publicly traded corporations, those amounts are still often too small to have an appreciable effect on the corporation's (and shareholders') bottom line for any reaction to be triggered.

Even though the corporation's defenders deny, then, that a delegitimat-ing gap exists between owners and control, they are still forced to acknowl-edge that the self-interest of investors can lead them to become passive "owners." Inasmuch as this could happen, they are pushed on to argue, it will be offset by active professional, institutional investors, by the general dis-cipline exercised by the market, and by appropriate legislative measures that accurately reflect the kinds of contractual terms that would be entered into it if it were practicable to do so. Hence it is that they point to the safeguards that the owners/investors would try to establish if they could and, if they can-not, to those that the law already provides.

They note that, although the corporation is the legal owner of the invested capitals, the investors/owners are treated as residual owners by the law when the corporation is liquidated and its assets distributed. Eventually, then, the law does treat the contributors of capital as the real property owners, even though that same law pretends that, during the life of the corporation, the corporation is the legal owner. Further, the law has given shareholders a limited right to set into motion a derivative action when they can show that management is not appropriately pursuing the corporation's best interests. They can get the corporation to sue abusing or neglectful directors and managers. Despite their lack of legal title to the property that they entrusted to the management of the corporation's directors, on occasion, then, they can exercise the kind of control over management that principals normally exercise over their agents. They have also been given a legal right to be bought out for a "fair price" when they dissent from directors' decisions that displeases some individual investors/owners, even though the directors of the legal property owner—the corporation—may be able to argue plausibly that their disputed decisions were taken to serve the corporation's best interests. Most importantly, investors/owners can claim redress by demonstrating that they have been unfairly treated or discriminated against, or prejudiced, by directors, managers, or the corporation (possibly acting under the influence of other shareholders). This remedy is called the oppression remedy. Its availability also suggests that the law acknowledges that investors/owners retain some right to have their property dealt with as they, the investors/owners, would have wanted to deal with it if they had not given up legal title to it. In addition to all this, directors, managers, and officers are said to stand in a fiduciary relationship to the corporation and/or the shareholders: that is, the law expects them to behave better than it would if they were self-standing property-owning, self-interested, maximizing individuals. The law requires them, as any sensible contract engineered between property owners and their agents would do, to put their own interests on the back burner.

These legal rules protecting owners/investors are vague and flexible, which ensures that they will enrich the legal profession while not overly curtailing the self-serving goals of managers. But the very existence of these legal rules does suggest that, whatever the pitfalls created by a separation of control from initial ownership, there have been serious attempts to overcome them by a set of technical corporate governance rules. Inasmuch as these legal remedies are not as effective as they could, or should, be—in the sense that they do not reflect accurately what individual property owners would have done to protect their interests by enforceable private contractual arrangements if it had been efficient for them to enter into such time-consuming and costly deal-making—they can be improved, at least, in theory.

What all of this means is that, while it is not easy to fit the large publicly traded corporation within the conceptual confines of the idealized market model, those who seek to do so have done it by recasting any logical problems as difficulties that require technical solutions, rather than committing themselves to a basic rethinking of the acceptability of the corporate vehicle. This choice enables them to maintain the argument that the legal corporation merely provides an umbrella under which individuals, acting as individual market actors and individual members of a liberal polity, are pursuing their own selfish interests, just as Adam Smith would have them do. It is important to them to argue that the normal operations of corporations do not distort the market model.

Milton Friedman made this clear when he wrote, "We have introduced enterprises [read: corporations] which are intermediaries between individuals in their capacities as suppliers of services and purchasers of goods." But, he went on, just as in a simple exchange economy—that is, just as in an idealized market economy in which neither enterprises nor money complicate the picture—the economy "will remain strictly individual and voluntary *provided* (i) that enterprises are private, so that the ultimate contracting parties are individuals and (ii) that individuals are effectively free to enter or not to enter into any particular exchange, so that every transaction is strictly voluntary." Not to put too fine a point on it, the marketeers concede that, to justify capitalism, they must show that it can be equated with the free market. Hence, if the corporation can be made to appear as a market actor, just as if it were an individual flesh and blood human being, all will be hunky-dory in market-capitalism land.

The reasons offered to the effect that the corporation does not distort the market model, then, stretch credibility to the breaking point. The facts are in: it is a collective of people and inorganic capital; functionally, a potential gap exists between ownership and control, and corporate law reform and debate are forced to centre on this gap because of the conceptual difficulties it generates; so many instances of managerial self-serving abuses occur that daily newspapers fairly bristle with them; such empirical work as there is tells us that the market does not provide appropriate responses to these abuses. But, despite the mountain of evidence that contradicts it, even if the reasoning of the proponents of corporate law and economics is taken at face value, their recasting of the problem still leaves large unanswered questions lying about. They are serious questions, questions that trouble corporate cheerleaders whenever they can be made to confront them. One such question can be formulated as follows: is it really true that everyone who, according to the contract-based justifying logic of the system, *should* be allowed to participate in the control and deployment of the assets has been given a significant participatory role?

"What about the Workers, Then?"

In the case of Westray, the one group that had no say at all in whether or not there should be a mine established and, if so, who was to run it, for how long, and what equipment and production methods were to be used consisted of the workers; and workers were the only ones who died as a result of these decisions.

In the Westinghouse Canada case, the decision-makers who determined what work would be done and where did not include workers. The workers who lost jobs paid the price for these decisions. The decision-makers reaped the profits.

Why do workers not have more of a legally protected right to have a say in the decision-making of the corporation? This question raises difficulties for the defenders of the faith. This is why they tend not to address it willingly and, when forced to do so, are driven into making absurd arguments. The very absurdity of the responses can be used by those of us who want to devise ways of changing the political world in which we live.

Workers explicitly contract with the corporation when they become its employees, and the workers' welfare depends on how well or how badly the corporation does, and on its priorities. For instance, decisions on the processes, substances, and technologies to be used, the closure of one line of production, the moving of part of the business, the hiring of more workers, or the buying of more technology all have an impact on workers directly and vitally. Equally important to workers are decisions by their employers to take over another business, or the decision of their employer's managers to resist a bid for a takeover initiated by another corporation. Similarly, a decision to turn a publicly traded corporation into a closely held corporation could have a direct impact on their livelihoods. Yet the law gives workers nothing like the right to have a say in corporate governance that is akin to the rights given to investors/owners of capital. Why is that?

The answer given by the defenders of the corporate law status quo is that workers, as sovereign individuals, explicitly contract with their employer (in our case, a corporation), and the law, therefore, need do nothing for them. But these contracts are not contracts between equals. Workers enter into these contracts because they have to do so, not because they have been able to make a choice about how to deploy their spare capital. While some workers may be able to decide which employer they contract with—because various employers may be competing for their special skills—they must in the end enter into a contract with some employer. A worker does not enjoy the kind of choice envisaged by the idealized market, the kind of voluntary choice without which, as Milton Friedman says, the market cannot exist.

The difference between a capitalist (a would-be employer) and a worker (a would-be employee) is that workers have no property to invest except their own labour power. Thus, what workers invest in an employing corporation when they contract with it is their intellectual and physical abilities. The corporation needs to translate that potential into actual value; it must make individual workers apply as much of their intellectual and physical skills as possible for as little as possible. To help employers, the law implies a most peculiar term into every contract of employment: the worker is required to obey all reasonable commands by the employer. I say "peculiar" because there is no other contract known to law in which one contracting party is made legally subject to the other's right to command and to that other's right to punish her or him for disobedience of those commands.

The employment contract, then, aims at the maintenance of a superior/ inferior nexus between property and non-property owners. This harsh-sounding language is not hyperbole. The prestigious Task Force on Canadian Industrial Relations (1968) described the machinery of collective bargaining as being designed to keep the superior-inferior nexus in place. It argued that this kind of unequal relationship was crucial to the efficient deployment of capital by its managers. This understanding of capital-labour relations explains why there is a residual managerial clause in every collective agreement (and, by definition, in every individual contract of employment as well). If it is not there as a result of a specific contractual agreement, it will be imposed by law. It is there to make it clear that, unless workers have extracted some specific concessions from their employer as to how their labour is to be deployed and as to how the employer's inorganic assets are to be used, it is up to management to make those decisions. More often than not this residual decision-making power is referred to as the prerogative of management. The *Oxford Dictionary* defines the word "prerogative" as "the right of the sovereign, theoretically subject to no restriction; peculiar right or privilege; natural or divinely given advantage, privilege or faculty; privileged, enjoyed by privilege . . ." What more needs be said about the respective rights of employers and employees?

These propositions about the nature of the employment contract are equally true whether the employment contract is one between an individual employer and an individual employee or one between a corporation and an individual employee. But the corporate situation has the capacity for making the subjugation inherent in the employment contract far more transparent and, therefore, has the potential to be radicalizing. It offers this promise because of how the corporate cheerleaders, the followers of Milton Friedman, justify the legally enforceable rights of shareholders—that is, of investors/ owners who have given up the legal title to their contributed property—to participate in corporate governance. Only the functionally coercive nature of the employment contract is a satisfactory explanation as to why workers do not have the same rights as investors/owners to participate in corporate deci- sion-making. Seeing the employment contract for what it truly is—one that legally subjugates the worker—satisfactorily explains why, in the corporate sector, workers are not treated as the legal, and substantive, equals of investors/owners. This explanation, logical though it is, is rejected by law and economics scholars and market modellers. After all, it is an explanation that tells us that, in law, not all individuals are equal.

The explanation challenges the much vaunted liberal-economic and political principles that claim that all individuals are equal sovereigns and that, therefore, their voluntary decisions as to what goods and services to exchange will yield economic efficiency, at the same time as the freedom to decide what to make and to buy enriches political freedoms. To explain the different corporate governance rights of shareholders and employees of a cor- poration on the basis that workers are inferior, coerced beings, is anathema to free-market proponents. It would be an admission that the sale of workers' talents and resources is not voluntary. As a consequence, law and economic scholars have to explain the huge gap in the participatory rights in corporate governance of workers and of investors/owners in some different way. They are forced to twist and turn.

They offer a rationalizing argument that has two strands. To begin with, they claim—quite unbelievably to anybody who lives in this world—that workers are in a better position to deal with managers of corporations as equals than are shareholders. It follows that workers do not need the assis- tance of legally imposed corporate governance rights, and this is so because they are allowed to unionize. The factual feebleness of this argument is plain. Only a minority of workers have any kind of collective bargaining power. In the United States, where the law and economic scholars rule the roost, only 15 per cent of workers are unionized; in Canada, less than one- third of workers are unionized. Only a minority of all workers, then, have the potential to exploit this theoretical alternative to obtain direct, legally enforceable participation in corporate decision-making by contract-making. Further, this law and economics argument necessarily requires these propo- nents of individualism to accept the effective use of collective force as a means of overcoming individual economic weakness. Yet in other settings this very same school of lawyers and economists denounces trade unionism as a pestilence, as a perverter of the idealized market and a menace to the credo of individualism. Has anyone in Canada ever seen or heard Michael Walker of the Fraser Institute or Catherine Swift of the Independent Federation of Business show anything but a severe distaste for the role of unions? Yet for the sake of pretending that all is well in capitalism, these theoreticians are forced to argue that a distortion of the market, which their belief system and logic abhors, has set things right. The opportunistic and desperate nature of the stance of these propagandists is plain.

Continuing on the first strand of argument, some law and economics scholars are willing to acknowledge that not enough workers have been unionized to make this a viable response. These more "in-the-world" apologists argue that workers should be looked after by the state to offset their lack of participatory rights in corporate decision-making when that corporate decision-making undermines their job security, incomes, career paths, or very lives. These more pragmatic corporate propagandists, like their less worldly fellow-travellers, are also unwilling to offer workers legally enforceable rights to participate in corporate governance. They, too, understand that workers are not, and should not be treated as, the equals of property-owning investors. Still, their recommendation might have been welcomed as a useful, even democratic, response to the ravages of unmediated capitalism if it had come from a different source. But the scholars who offer this resolution believe fervently in the primacy of the independent individual. This means that a central goal of all their other writing and lobbying—following the lead of their gurus, Milton Friedman and Friedrich von Hayek—is to get the state to butt out of private wealth-seeking activities. For them—for the Michael Walkers, Catherine Swifts, and their associates—individualistic decision-making in a free-market setting is to prevail whenever possible. They contend that the setting of minimum standards by state intervention invariably will lead to distortions of the market, yielding inefficiencies and, eventually, harming workers' security and lives. The solution they offer, then—to have the state intervene to offset workers' lack of participatory decision-making rights in their employing corporations—smacks of desperation, if not hypocrisy. They resort to an argument that, normally, would be anathema to them. They do so because the denial of workers' rights in respect of corporate governance threatens to make class divisions transparent. They equate capitalism with a free market, an economic tool that, given equality of opportunity, negates class antagonism. Class divisions tolerated within the market system need to be hidden if the market is to retain its ability to legitimate capitalism. This is why they offer a resolution that, in their other work, they seek to ensure will never be implemented: turning and twisting.

The second main strand of reasoning offered by people trying to avoid the logic of an explanation for the differential treatment of workers and investors/owners in respect of governance is that owners/investors *deserve* better treatment. The notion is that, because shareholders put their property at risk by giving it over to be managed by others who may lose it, they are entitled not only to its yield but also to a decision-making role in how the managers use "their" at-risk assets. This is why, it is argued, a board of directors must get shareholders' approval to resist a takeover or to make any decision that might alter the fundamental nature of the corporation. From the perspective of a private property-based polity, from a capitalistic perspective, this argument is logical enough. But what if this logic were to be applied to workers? What if workers were characterized as investors in the same way as shareholders are?

Workers, too, invest. What they invest is the only kind of property they have. Their property is their bodies and their minds. This property is put to use by the same managers who deploy the other property, the capital, entrusted to them by the investors/owners who become shareholders. Why should workers, then, not have analogous legal monitoring/controlling rights vis-à-vis these managers? Indeed, if decision-making rights ought to stem from the taking of risks with one's property, the workers' argument to have such decision-making rights is far stronger than that of the investors/owners of inorganic property. Capitalists, after all, are inveigled into investing in corporations by the amazing privilege of being able to limit their risk. Further, simply by selling their shares they can leave a publicly traded corporation pretty well any time they do not like either its management or the direction of its management. This ability is commonly referred to in the books as the shareholders' right and power of "exit." Workers have neither of these luxuries available to them. Employment is hard to find. Workers cannot exercise the right of "exit" whenever they doubt management's ability. While their incomes and economic welfare—just like that of shareholders—are put at risk by management (as in Westinghouse), in addition their very physical integrity, their lives, are also put at risk by management (as in Westray). No shareholder faces that risk.

If the defenders of capitalism, the market, and the corporation were genuine in their argument that those who risk the most by investing should have the most say, they would be forced to argue that the legally imposed rules of corporate governance should be the very opposite of what they are. Workers should have the greatest amount of decision-making power, not shareholders.

This argument is even more persuasive when it is noted that, for the classic market proponent, the right to retain the yield of one's investment rests on the principle that that yield was earned. Indeed, this is how conventional wisdom justifies the eye-popping material inequalities that characterize capitalist economies such as Canada's.

The reasoning is that, provided that every individual is given the same opportunity to participate in profit-maximizing activities, those who have the most talents and resources, and/or uses those talents and resources better than others, should be entitled to profit more than those who are less well-endowed and/or less adept. But for this market justification of gross inequality to retain the moral support it needs, an individual's investment of talents and resources must be shown to have returned profits to that person because of her or his own efforts. The right of some to become richer than others is to be justified by evidence that they have *earned this by their own endeavours.* This has been the moral defence of a private property-based polity, of capitalism, since the time of the philosopher John Locke. It underlies Adam Smith's loathing of incorporation, where doing and profiteering are separated.

Here another troubling issue—troubling for the corporate ideologues, that is—comes to the fore. People who invest in a corporation do so by giving their individual capital to the corporation, where it will be managed by others so as to yield a profit for each of the investors. That the investors/owners do not exert any personal effort to yield that profit is of no interest to corporate law. That they have a limited risk is sufficient to give them legally enforceable decision-making rights in the governance of the corporation. What would Locke have said about this? And, worse still, the managers to whom the capital is entrusted also do not personally do any of the profit-making work. Rather, it is their task to get others to do this work. These others are the workers, who have a legally enforceable right to a contractual wage, but are given no legal ownership rights in the products or services that result from their efforts. Nor do they have a legally enforceable right to tell the managers how or what to produce, when to produce it, and how to do it. The owners/investors/security holders/shareholders, none of whom do anything, do have some such rights vis-à-vis the managers.

All of this is the obverse of what a private-property or free-enterprise model, one justified by the philosophy of John Locke, is supposed to be. Not to give the actual workers any legal standing to participate in decisions made by non-workers should be indefensible within the tenets of market capitalism. Indeed, in some West European countries, where social democracy has had a longer and deeper history than it has had in North America, workers have been given some legal standing as decision-makers in corporate affairs.

Various jurisdictions provide for workers' committees that participate in decision-making in respect of disciplining and firing of fellow employees; elsewhere there are committees that have a legal right to participate in decision-making about the introduction of new technology and/or the introduction of methods of work that could undermine the health and safety of workers; in some jurisdictions there are legally mandated positions for workers' representatives on boards of directors. While none of these mechanisms give ultimate corporate decision-making power to workers, they do go much further than anything yet developed in the United States, the United Kingdom, Australia, New Zealand, and Canada—that is, in countries in which the common law underpins the ideology of the market in a particularly strong way. Inasmuch as some of our workers have won some rights over corporate decision-making that has an impact on their working conditions, these are still very limited rights, not imposed by law but won by private contract-making.

What Kind of a Canadian Citizen Is the Canadian Corporation?

The publicly traded corporation is an ideal vehicle through which to attain the capitalist goal, namely, the accumulation of capital by the exploitation of the value produced by other people's work. The design of the legal corporation invites investment that is to be managed by professionals who are to extract profits from the work of others. But this reality is to be hidden, because the achievement of capitalism's central goal is not one that is readily acceptable to the general public, constituted mostly by people who are to be its victims. After all, they are expected to earn what they get by working for it. As a consequence, the legal corporation is portrayed as an instrument through which individual owners of property continue to act as autonomous marketeers, each contracting with other people who are equally interested in maximizing their resources and talents.

But the system of governance in the publicly traded corporation seems to negate the sovereignty of the individuals who contribute their property to the corporate endeavour. Corporate protagonists are forced to make a number of problematic arguments. Even if these arguments are given some credibility, the internal logic of the reasoning pushes forward another capitalist truth—that non-property owners, those who contribute their bodies and souls to the corporation, are treated as inferior beings. While this dovetails with the tenets of capitalism, which demand that the working classes remain inferior to, and the antagonists of, the ruling property classes, it does not sit well with the legitimated and legitimating market model that is supposedly served by the corporate vehicle.

These technical rules of corporate governance reveal how dramatically anti-market and, more importantly, anti-democratic the legal corporate vehicle really is.

The tangled web that the defenders of the corporate vehicle are forced to spin causes them to argue that, as the corporation is an umbrella under which individual contractors gather, it should be treated as a private institution, one not to be subjected to public scrutiny and control unless it is efficient to do so from a corporate point of view. They talk about the corporation as a private island, one that is to be left alone to govern itself, just as private, human individuals are left alone. Indeed, one of the drafters of the *Canadian Business Corporations Act*, John Howard, captured this sentiment by arguing that a publicly traded corporation is much like a private state. It has citizens (shareholders) who elect a government (the board of directors), which is to carry out their wishes, and only their wishes. The system puts into place rules of fair play to elect the government (the voting), to govern the supervisory and administrative functions of the government (the enforceable directors' duties of care, to be honest, to act as fiduciaries), and to prevent a majority from unfairly oppressing a minority (the right to seek an oppression remedy), just as the state has created such rules to control the public, electoral, and executive spheres.

But these arguments are, at best, wilfully blind. At worst, they are deliberatively deceptive. They ignore how corporate citizenship—that is, the right to participate as autonomous individuals in a corporation—is granted only to those with property investments, and not to those who work for the corporation. The workers are considered not to have invested any property, and therefore they are not entitled to citizenship. Worse, even the property-contributing investors are not equal citizens within this private state, within the corporation. Those who put in more property get more say.

Indeed, the language of corporate law is Orwellian. When the corporations' propagandists speak of how the corporation is to be run, they speak of corporate governance, invoking the image of liberal-democratic government. Yet when they write and draft policies to implement what they term to be corporate democracy, they reveal that what they are actually pursuing is the antithesis of democracy. It is not people who count, but money. Inside a corporation it is not one person, one vote; it is one dollar, one vote; no dollars, no votes. In Canada, one or two persons own the controlling number of shares in approximately 80 per cent of publicly traded corporations. This means that in most such corporations the group called "majority shareholders" is constituted by a tiny minority of the number of the people who are shareholders, whereas the minority shareholding group includes an overwhelming numerical majority of the shareholders.

Conrad Black has more say in what his invisible friend, Hollinger International Ltd., does than do the hundreds, perhaps thousands, of retired workers whose savings have been invested in Hollinger because they believed that its management would safeguard and grow their capital to help them take care of their retirement. But as shareholders, they have been given a legal right, the oppression remedy, to relieve hardships imposed by other shareholders who have used their greater corporate citizenry power, that is, their greater voting power, to have directors and managers favour them at the expense of the suing shareholders, who have less voting power.

As non-property investors, workers get no votes at all. Those who bear most of the risk of the decisions of the very few (one person in the Westray mine case, or a handful of directors acting under the influence of a few shareholders in the Westinghouse Canada case), have no legally enforceable right to say anything about their jobs, indeed, about the security of their very lives.

The internal structure of the corporation, both legally and functionally, is not just undemocratic. It is positively anti-democratic. This is why democrats and their allies should pay close attention to the rules of governance of publicly traded corporations. An understanding of those rules raises more than technocratic issues; it also draws attention to the essential nature and character of the predominant economic institution in our political economy. The rules themselves reveal why corporations do what they do. The profoundly anti-democratic nature of the publicly traded corporation brings it into conflict with the liberal-democratic polity in which it is supposed to flourish. Inevitably, it seeks to force that liberal-democratic polity to change to suit the corporations' hierarchical, exploitive goals. To this end, the publicly traded corporations set out to adulterate, pollute, and pervert the tenets of liberal democracy.

SEVEN

When Big Corporations Speak, Governments Listen

Wherein we learn how the invisible friends of our flesh and blood captains of industry, finance, retail, and everything else have won the right to speak and how this is used to give those flesh and blood captains of everything added political clout with which to pervert our democratic institutions.

I n 1978, worried about the impact of advertising on children, the Quebec government passed legislation to ban, in the province, all advertising directed at persons under thirteen years of age. Irwin Toy Corporation objected to this legislation, and the reason for its objections were obvious. The toy manufacturer advertised its products heavily on Saturday morning television, and it wanted to continue building the market for its products. It wanted to pursue the only meaningful goal that any red-blooded corporation has: to make money. Of course, when it went to a court to ask it to strike down the advertising-limiting legislation, Irwin Toy did not say anything as crass as that. Rather, it swaddled itself in the clothes of a civil libertarian advocate. It argued that the Quebec government was attacking the freedom of expression as guaranteed to all Canadians by Canada's Charter of Rights and Freedoms—that is, a right guaranteed to us, the people, by *our* Constitution.

In the end, the Supreme Court of Canada (1989) held that the Quebec legislation limiting advertising should stand because, in this particular case, the government had proved that its attempted restraint of a citizen right was a reasonable restriction. But the Court did agree with Irwin Toy that the law violated free speech rights. It held that, in different circumstances, a corporation would be able to have legislative restraints on the citizenry's freedom of speech struck down.

Another corporation, RJR-MacDonald Inc., did find the right circumstances. This company's product, tobacco, is known to cause ill health; it can kill. The federal government, prompted into action by the overwhelming scientific evidence about the noxious attributes of RJR-MacDonald's lawful products and by the mounting body count associated with them, passed legislation that set out to limit advertising by tobacco manufacturers. While the legislation did not make the production and sale of tobacco products unlawful, it did threaten RJR-MacDonald's profitability, which motivated the company to fight back. It asked the courts to rule that the statute violated the free speech rights of the Canadian people. The federal government put forward an argument, supported by scientific evidence—as if it were needed—that tobacco caused harm and that, therefore, it made good public-health sense for the government to act to dim its appeal.

The Supreme Court of Canada (1995) found (i) that RJR-MacDonald Inc., a corporation, had standing to raise the issue of a violation of the constitutional right to free speech granted to human Canadians by the Charter of Rights and Freedoms, (ii) that RJR-MacDonald Inc., a corporation, had proved that this particular piece of government legislation violated these free speech rights by interfering with the publication of advertising slogans, and (iii) that the federal government had not provided sufficient proof that its ban on advertising was a reasonable measure for curbing the ills inflicted by the sale of tobacco products.

The ordinary human being's mind, uncluttered by corporate lore, cannot help but boggle at the workings of the judicial mind that invented and perfected corporate mythology. So, even though we cannot see corporations, we cannot hit or hurt them, we cannot lift them or smell them, according to the highest court in the land we can hear them, and they should be left free to speak so that they can make us listen. It is true, of course, that all around us there is corporate noise-making. The noise that corporations make is not only treated as speech by the courts but, judicially, is also treated as being worthy of the TLC that liberal law reserves for the protection of the integrity of democracy. How did we get to this absurd position?

Free Speech in a Liberal Democracy

However difficult it may be to give a precise definition of "democracy," it cannot be doubted that individual freedom of thought and belief is a corner-stone of any form of democracy. To accord individuals that kind of freedom is really easy: it requires no one to do anything. No one knows what we privately think or believe. Difficulties arise, however, as soon as individuals decide they want to act on their thoughts and beliefs. Usually the first step in giving shape and form to one's ideas is to put these thoughts and beliefs into words, to tell others about them and to persuade those others of the worth of the speaker's ideas. If it is elemental to protect freedom of thought and belief, it becomes logically necessary to safeguard freedom of speech.

Any country that pretends to be a liberal democracy, therefore, proclaims its devotion to freedom of speech. Canada had done so well before the advent of the Charter of Rights and Freedoms in 1982, but in that year the country embedded a guarantee of freedom of expression in its new Constitution. Section 2(b) of the Charter of Rights and Freedom now provides, as a "fundamental freedom": "Freedom of thought, belief, opinion and expression, including freedom of the press and other media of communication."

Freedom of speech is clearly one of our most highly prized rights. Still, it can never be totally unfettered in an interdependent society. It may well be that the freely expressed views of one individual will cast unwarranted slurs on other individuals. These insulted people may be given the right to protect their reputations by suing for defamation, or the right to bring legal actions to be compensated for an undesired invasion of their privacy. The Charter of Rights and Freedoms does not purport to give a guarantee to the kind of speech that inflicts these kinds of harms. Further, if a lawfully elected government legislates to limit our freedom of expression to attain, what it claims to be, legitimate social goals, freedom of speech still may be curtailed by it, even after the introduction of the Charter of Rights and Freedoms as the bulwark against state attacks on our basic rights. But the Charter has imposed a burden on any government that seeks to restrain speech in support of its explicit and legitimate public policy. It must be able to show a court that its limits on our free speech rights are no greater than they need to be to achieve its (otherwise) acceptable goals. An unelected court must find that the elected government's proposed limitations are reasonable in a free and democratic society. As we have seen, the government succeeded in meeting this burden in the case of Irwin Toy, but not in that of RJR-MacDonald's tobacco advertising.

The government must be wary lest it undermine the purposes that the guarantee of freedom of speech serves. The first purpose of the guarantee is that it enables individuals to further their pursuit of individual liberty, autonomy, and self-realization. As well, just as the self-seeking economic acts of Adam Smith's individual butcher, brewer, or baker in a free market are expected to benefit the economic welfare of all, so an individual's freedom to articulate thought and expression is seen as leading to the enrichment of the political welfare of society as a whole. Liberal luminaries such as John Milton, John Stuart Mill, and Oliver Wendell Holmes have argued that giving the greatest possible latitude to freedom of expression will produce a political climate in which everyone can be asked to accept majoritarian-based decisions. This is so because each individual will have had the right to air an opinion on any matter and will thus have had a concrete opportunity to influence the majority's decisions. The people then should accept these decisions, even if some do not like them. In a liberal democracy, they will get new opportunities to change those decisions, and, in the meantime, it is not unjust to force them to accept them if they do not do so willingly. To complement this argument, which is—without any apparent sense of irony— referred to as "the market place of ideas" argument, its advocates often note that, just as competition in the economic market will ensure that the most wanted goods and services will be produced at the lowest possible cost, a political climate in which all ideas may be heard, good as well as bad, will ensure that, eventually, the most worthwhile ideas will triumph.

Freedom of speech, this argumentation holds, makes for a stable, yet flexible, polity. In addition, the proponents of a constitutional guarantee for free speech argue, the capacity to speak and to criticize creates an atmosphere in which public officials can be held accountable and in which abuses by them will be discouraged. The burden of these mutually supportive lines of reasoning is that the individual's freedom of speech is guaranteed because it will enrich the political life of each individual, as well as that of political society as a whole. From this perspective, the kinds of speakers to be protected should be *political* speakers, and the kind of speech to be protected should be *political* speech. How, then, did actors such as the Irwin Toy Corporation and RJR-MacDonald Inc., specifically created to be *economic*, rather than political, actors, get the Supreme Court of Canada to give them standing to protest invasions of freedom of speech? How, then, did Irwin Toy Corporation and RJR-MacDonald Inc. get the Supreme Court of Canada to say that it was ready to protect their kind of speech, which the corporations themselves characterize as economic or commercial speech?

To answer these questions it is pertinent to identify the logic that justifies giving corporations a right to speak at all.

The Need for Commercial Speech

One of the essential ingredients of a market economy is accurate information. For the market to work effectively, individual sellers and buyers must be able to make sovereign choices about what to make, what to sell, for how much, and what to buy, for how much, and so on. The sellers and buyers must have accurate information (i) about each other—so that they can make judgements about creditworthiness and trustworthiness, (ii) about the quality of the product or service on offer, and (iii) about any particular vendor's price for a product or service as compared to other vendors' prices for these things. Market actors, therefore, should purvey and seek accurate, useful information. As André Ouellet said as federal minister of consumer and corporate affairs in 1975:

> False and misleading advertising and unethical promotional practices distort a free economic system which is built on honesty and fair play. They deny the consumer the information required to make wise and effective buying decisions, and they deprive ethical promoters and honest advertisers of the deserved rewards for offering better quality, more competitive prices or, simply, the undoctored facts.

Capitalist law, therefore, must, and does, facilitate the propagation of accurate commercial information. It does so in two ways: negatively, in that the law sets out not to prevent commercial actors, including corporations, from speaking about themselves, their products, and their services; and positively, in that the law actively prohibits commercial actors, including corporations, from misleading other market actors about themselves, their products, and their services.

The Nature of Commercial Speech

Contemporary Canadians are bombarded by information generated by the producers and sellers of goods and services. In the aggregate, producers and sellers want to make people want to buy—anything and everything.

Individually, each one of them sets out to make the public aware of the existence of its products and services and to make them seem more attractive than those of their competitors. The point of the exercise, then, is to persuade, not to prove. Science and truth have little, if anything, to do with advertising. Data concerning the utility, durability, operational problems, actual price, and costs of maintenance have become less and less central to the messages sent to the markets. Indeed, it is fair to say that these kinds of information are paid scant attention. Consumerism for its own sake, brand-name recognition ("Just Do It"), the creation of images of what life would be like if someone uses a particular service or product (retirement on a gorgeous island if you buy London Life Insurance, becoming a sex object if you drive a Nissan), the seduction into beliefs that translate into lifestyles (clothes make you attractive, it is good to be attractive, use the right credit card and you will be treated with respect) which, in turn, help construct new markets— this is what advertising is all about. In his amusing book on words and phrases David Olive defines advertising as "Words and pictures, often set to music, designed to correct the mistaken impression among consumers that their lives possess meaning in the absence of a receipt for a particular product in their sock drawer." He defines marketing, which is what is done through advertising, as "a decision against letting the product speak for itself, recognizing that it may not be the most credible spokesman." Canadian humorist and economist Stephen Leacock was even more direct: "Advertising may be described as the science of arresting the human intelligence long enough to get money from it."

There we have it: the commercial speech protected by our courts is nothing but hucksterism. The titles of some of the books that analyse advertising tell the tale: *The Hidden Persuaders*; *Captains of Consciousness: Advertising and the Social Roots of the Consumer Culture*; *Sultans of Sleaze: Public Relations and the Media*; *Mythologies*. Despite this awareness, though, sadly, the hucksterism works.

It is safe to assume that commercial actors, whose only object is the maximization of profits and who are expected to behave as Rational Economic Men in the pursuance of that goal, would not spend all those advertising dollars on something that does not provide them with tangible returns, and they do spend lots of dollars. Large publicly traded corporations spend vast amounts of money extolling the merits and desirability of particular goods and services, as well as on touting the merits of consumerism. We can get some indication of how effective advertising is thought to be by its purveyors from just one figure emanating from the United States. This figure is relevant to Canada because so much of U.S. advertising pervades the Canadian economy. According to John Bellamy Foster, U.S. business spent 60 per cent more on marketing in 1992 than the United States, as a nation, spent on all private and public education. Worldwide, the figures are mind-boggling. In 1999 Zenith Media reported that, globally, spending on advertising would be $304 billion that year, $323 billion in 2000, and $342 billion in 2001. A fraction of this unproductively used money could do much to alleviate the pain, suffering, and misery of millions of people.

Manifestly, under the guise of the provision of information to make the market work, there is a giant propaganda/educational machine that is intended to, and does, influence our beliefs, values, customs, and social relations. The principal advertising firms that concoct these dreams and images are corporations. Further, most of the propaganda machine's output is done on behalf of, and in the name of, huge corporations, as in "McDonald's does it all for you," "Coke is the real thing," "IBM, solutions for a small planet," "Can a bank change? Bank of Montreal," or "AOL: They just keep making it better and better." Indeed, of the twenty-one thousand television commercials that the average adult in the United States sees each year, 75 per cent are paid for by the one hundred largest corporations in that country. The extent of these big corporations' influence on our thinking is not measured solely by the number of adults reached by their advertisements. Like all religious evangelists, they understand the need to convert the young. Kevin Mattson estimates that the average U.S. child has been subjected to 380,000 television commercials by the time she or he graduates from high school. Most of these commercials will have been paid for by the largest corporations, pushing lifestyle patterns and habits on people when they are most impressionable. The intention is to make these corporations, their products and services, integral, indeed "natural," to our lives. From this perspective, the Quebec government's attempt to limit Irwin Toy's ability to manipulate children was a meek and mild effort. Yet its effort to restrain corporations' freedom to mould and shape the minds of kids was reprimanded by the courts, and its legislation only just avoided the judiciary's final solution, namely, being struck down by the Supreme Court of Canada.

Clearly, corporations, as commercial actors, have been duly accorded a way of expressing themselves and influencing us. The market model makes it logical that they have a right to express themselves. But, having been given the privilege of speech, they now speak about far more than that required by market logic. They have used the tolerance inherent in our political devotion to freedom of speech to massage us not just commercially, but politically. In doing this they have been aided directly by the courts and the Charter of Rights and Freedoms.

The Charter, the Courts, and the Debasement of Freedom of Speech

From time to time governments exercise the right to curtail commercial speech by passing special legislation aimed at a particular problem, such as tobacco sales or advertising that influences children. In addition, general statutes regulate speech rights. For instance, the federal government has passed legislation aimed at misleading advertising, making it a criminal offence to put out false information. With restraints on advertising potentially undesirable because they restrain freedom of speech, it has been relatively easy for economic actors to persuade government to give this misleading advertising legislation a limited scope.

Outright lies about a product or service will be punished. For instance, the company making Listerine, a mouth wash, advertised its product as having beneficial medicinal properties (which the manufacturer knew perfectly well it did not have). The corporation was subsequently charged and punished for its attempt to trick the population into buying a product for the wrong reason. Similarly, Sears Canada repeatedly advertised that its jewellery was discounted when it knew this to be false, and later it advertised a price for air conditioning units as if it included the installation charges when it did not. In both cases Sears Canada was fined. Straightforward lying—which is rarely detected—is not permitted.

But "mere puffery" is a different matter. Now, much of advertising is known, recognized, as puffery—in other words, as exaggerated praise or commendation. Michael Jordan and Mia Hamm ask, "Is it in you?" Michael Jordan says, "Just do it!" The idea is that if we drink Gatorade, or if we buy Nike shoes, gear, and equipment, not only will we be able to jump, kick, and dribble as well as Michael Jordan and Mia Hamm, but perhaps we will also be able to be considered just as good-looking, cool, charming, likeable, or successful as they are. Similarly, we should want to drink a pop drink manufactured by McCain because Elvis Stojko says he likes it, and we are expected to believe that a man who does Canada so proud would not steer us wrong. We should wear jeans with the sign GWG on a hip pocket because we can trust the Great Wayne Gretzky (GWG himself), who wears these jeans and we would like to be as cool as he is. In one surreal case, a famed Australian footballer changed his name by deed poll. Known to his fans, and to his mother, as Gary Hocking, he took the name Whiskas, the name of the pet food product he was paid to advertise. The Dunlop Tires Canada Ltd. has reportedly offered $25,000 to people with the name "Dunlop" if they will change their names to "Dunlop-Tire." Soccer, football, hockey, tennis, and golf players, as well as their various sports venues, are branded with product names. In films, the names of products subtly wink at us from the background (drinks, food, cars, clothes), and actors use products such as cigarettes and whisky as soon as they walk into a room. This is known as "product placement." The hope is that we will remember the names when we go shopping, that we will think they must be good (drinks, foods, cars, clothes), that we will be seduced into imitating the actors' habits, ape their obvious desire for "things," use the kinds of products they manifestly crave.

All of these explicit and implicit messages are treated by law—and only by law—as "mere puffery," which is something of a legal term. In law, "puffery" turns out to be claims and images that may be misleading but do not mislead the public in any material way. What the devil could this possibly mean? All of the ads in question are devoid of information about the products or services being held. All of them are effective. They sell goods and services and promote specific lifestyles. Worse: the legality and the legitimacy of "mere puffery" have been a Trojan Horse in the war waged on our liberal-democratic rights. Corporations have crawled out of the belly of this Trojan Horse and overwhelmed us.

We know that advertisers spend megabucks on messages and images that tell the markets relatively little by way of objective truth. They do so because these content-less messages are effective selling tools: they have a concrete, material impact. Why would the law, then, not treat all such fact-free offerings of opinions, values, and fantasies as being "material"? Somehow, while regulators have convinced themselves that no one is fooled by "mere puffery," commercial actors continue to spend billions on inventing more and more effective "mere puffery." It is all around us.

Increasingly, corporations have made full use of the law's tolerance of puffery to engage in corporate image advertising. Basically, such advertising is non-product oriented—that is, from a market perspective, it contains no useful facts at all. Often, a particular corporation is the product line being pushed by the advertising. It tries to set itself apart from other corporations. Another variant of this use of the freedom to advertise, of the freedom to speak, is the attempt by some major corporations to persuade the consumer markets that they are expecting too much from the corporate sector. Thus, banks may try to offset the perception that their profits are too high by launching a campaign to the effect that the latest numbers on the profitability of banks are just simply wrong or really not all that high given the banks' sterling services. Oil companies use scientific-looking pie charts to prove that the greatest part of each dollar spent at the pump goes to unproductive governments in taxes, not to the hard-working oil companies. Forest companies conduct campaigns that have their employees declaring how delighted they are to be working as environmentalists first and forestry employees second. They tell us that their corporate employer has given them the scope to protect Canada's forests as they had always dreamed of doing when they were young idealists, before they became employees of what (misguided) environmentalists see as an enemy. Or corporations spend buckets of money telling us that the *raison d'être* for their pursuit of profits is really their unselfish devotion to the creation of meaningful employment for thousands of Canadians.

Unlike the empty-headed corporate-product puffery of "We do it all for you," "Coke is the real thing," or "You are in safe hands with Allstate," this kind of corporate promotional advertising sets out to change public expectations and/or to change the symbolism of what the corporation means to society. It is aimed at the creation of a climate in which governments will be more wary of interfering with private corporate behaviour. Governments become conscious that the electorate may believe that corporations would improve social and economic welfare for all if left alone. This project can have a chilling effect on politicians who might otherwise have set out to curb corporate profiteering, at least to some degree.

All of this has been going on for a long time, certainly since well before the constitutionalization of the guarantee of freedom of speech granted by the Charter of Rights and Freedoms in 1982. But the Charter has clearly given the major purveyors of puffery, corporations, an additional weapon in their never-ending drive for the maximization of profits and the marginalization of the public sectors.

The Charter has allowed corporations to argue—as they always have—not only that it is unwise for governments to regulate corporate behaviour, but also that, now, it is *legally* wrong for governments to inhibit commercial speech unless they can justify such a restraint. Prior to 1982 the government had also been reluctant to restrict commercial speech, as manifested by its timidity in drafting its misleading-advertising legislation and by the poor record of enforcement of even these minimal standards. But then the government was not as yet hindered by the notion that it might not be legal for it to restrain speech if it thought it necessary to do so. Thus, when a government was bolstered by what it believed to be popular support, it did forbid on-screen drinking of alcoholic beverages; and governments all over North America could, and did, force advertisers to offer at least a portion of truth about their products. For instance, governments required tobacco manufacturers and vendors to add a rider to the image of freedom and sexiness that was used to sell cigarettes. This rider noted the brute truth that tobacco is dangerous to the users' health. In doing this, governments were acknowledging two social facts apparently rejected by the basic laws regulating advertising. First, such explicit governmental restraints make it clear that governments really do know that image-making, or so-called "mere puffery," does have material impact. Why else prevent impressionable people from seeing the images conveyed by good-looking, fun-loving, and sexually successful actors drinking alcoholic beverages on screen? Second, whenever a government acts in this way it is clearly acknowledging that the market can be misdirected as much by omissions as by positive lies. Why else force tobacco manufacturers and vendors to tell smokers that the puffery (pun intended) about Marlboro Man or Joe Camel doesn't tell the whole story?

While governments only rarely interfered with advertisers in this way—they preferred to pretend that everyone could recognize puffery for what it was—until the advent of the Charter they at least knew that they were fully empowered to regulate commercial actors' speech. What inhibited more stringent regulation of advertising was a lack of political will. When commercial actors, especially large corporations, crossed the acceptable boundaries—that is, when they used their right to speak as market actors in what was clearly a misleading way—governments had no qualms about restricting such practices. It was legally and politically easy for governments to say that such speech did not serve market efficiency. When corporations abused the right to speak as market actors to mouth opinions to influence electoral politics, governments' need to give an appearance of fairness to the electoral processes led them to pass various political financing laws that limited the participation of corporations in politics. They did so because it was all too clear that the unfettered right to participate in the electoral political sphere would give the corporate sectors, with their unmatchable economic resources, a disproportionate amount of political say.

Then came the Charter, with its protection of freedom of expression as a fundamental right, as a necessary condition in our individual and public political lives. Some commentators had always argued that any form of speech was political (and, therefore, worthy of legal protection) if it helped the self-realization of human beings in any way whatsoever. From this perspective, protection was not to be granted solely to thoughts, ideas, and speech related to political issues as popularly defined, but also to any thoughts, ideas, and speech concerned with "philosophical, social, artistic, economic, literary or ethical matters." The U.S. Supreme Court listed these categories of protected speech in a case called *Abood v. Detroit Board of Education*, decided in 1973. This wide concept of speech that could be protected turns out to have had overwhelming appeal for our courts, especially for the members of the Supreme Court of Canada.

Our judges assumed that the introduction of the Charter of Rights and Freedoms into our Constitution cemented their role as the bulwark against any assault on the rights of the individual by the potentially oppressive majority acting through the state, that is, through government. From the day of the Charter's proclamation onwards, our courts ruled that governmental attempts to restrain freedom of speech should be viewed with disfavour, no matter what legitimate goal the government claimed to be pursuing. This reading of the Charter of Rights and Freedoms imposed a heavy burden of proof on government.

The extent of the zeal of the courts when asked to protect freedom of speech can be measured by comparing it to their approach when trade unions complain about restrictions by government on their activities. For example, in 1974 the Trudeau government imposed wage restraints on trade unions, effectively denying trade unions the right to bargain collectively; in other words, denying them the use of the right to strike to improve their conditions of work. The trade unions took this issue to the Supreme Court of Canada. They complained that the *federal* legislature had abrogated their *provincially* guaranteed right to bargain collectively. The federal government argued that it had a right to interfere with provincial rights whenever a national emergency existed. In this case the national emergency was that effective collective bargaining might raise the rate of inflation. The trade unions responded with masses of empirical data and expert evidence to make the case that the government's fear that excess inflation would be fuelled by collective bargaining was scientific and economic nonsense. The trade unions argued, therefore, that the government had not established the existence of a national emergency that warranted restriction of their provincially guaranteed freedoms. Nonetheless, the Supreme Court of Canada (1976) upheld the federal government's legislation. The judges held that the government had met its burden simply by stating that there was an emergency. No serious proof to counter the union's evidence was required.

This cavalier approach to union rights contrasts sharply with the Supreme Court's stand in the RJR-MacDonald case. There the government produced evidence—albeit not all the scientific evidence available—showing that smoking is bad for health. That is, it did much more than the government had done in the anti-inflation law case—even though most people might have thought that little-to-no proof was needed to support an argument that tobacco is harmful to people's health. Yet the Supreme Court of Canada held that the government had not met the criteria necessary to justify its restraints on tobacco advertising. The freedom of speech of corporations proved to be much better protected from state interference than was the trade unions' right to look after its members' needs.

Another example concerns several pieces of legislation that suspended collective bargaining rights in Alberta, Saskatchewan, and the federal sphere. In contrast to the Trudeau anti-inflation legislation, these statutes were enacted after the Charter of Rights and Freedoms had become part of the law of the land and had given everyone a constitutional guarantee of freedom of association. Unsurprisingly, trade unions attacked these statutes as violations of their right to strike or bargain collectively in an effective manner. The legislation, they contended, had abrogated their Charter-protected freedom to associate. In 1987, contemptuously, the Supreme Court of Canada dismissed their argument. It held that the freedom to associate meant just that: people could join any group they liked, even a union; but this gave them no right to act in any way that they would not have been able to do as individuals. As an individual cannot strike—it takes at least two people to withhold labour in concert—the right to strike was not a fundamental right protected by the Charter of Rights and Freedoms.

To state it baldly: in freedom-loving, Charter-governed Canada, individuals start off with all the rights, and governments, if they want to modify those rights, must justify their proposed modification to a court. In freedom-loving, Charter-governed Canada, individuals are allowed to join a trade union of their choice; but the rights of that union, as opposed to those of the individuals who comprise it, are the rights given to it by the government, and no more. Governments need not satisfy a court that they have an acceptable legal justification to regulate unions in any way they like. There is no burden of proof to be discharged by government.

Corporations, however, have been able to force governments to justify proposed restraints on corporate speech, just as governments would be forced to offer an acceptable rationale if they were seeking to restrain the right of speech of the actual individuals who create corporations. Governments find it tough going to prove to courts that they have discharged their burden when justifying the abrogation of corporate speech.

The advent of the Charter reinforced the decision-making approach that the courts had favoured from the dawn of liberal capitalism; namely, the protection of the individual and that individual's property from the majority exercising power through the state. With this ideological starting point reinvigorated, the judicial attitude has been that, if the marketplace of ideas (writ large) is protected, the sacred sovereignty of the individual will be protected automatically. This is why the courts have chosen to read the constitutional protection of the individual's freedom of speech as including any kind of speech whatsoever. This has led to such a wide reading of "political speech" that the expression is now virtually devoid of meaning. As Michael Mandel notes, the logic has spawned the unappetizing conclusion by Madam Justice Beverley McLachlin of the Supreme Court of Canada, in 1992, that even lies—in this case disseminated by Ernst Zundel, an unreconstructed Nazi holocaust denier—attract the protection of the Charter from state inhibitions. Once speech rather than the speaker becomes the issue, and speech is so elastically defined, the courts find it easy to strike down any attempted governmental restraint, regardless of the purpose of that restraint, regardless of the content of the speech, regardless of its source.

Thus it is that advertising of all kinds has had little trouble getting the judiciary to act as its guardian angel. Indeed, it has been easy for courts to hold that advertising should be protected speech given that advertising is mainly concerned with the propagation of values, images, and symbols rather than with hard "nuts-and-bolts" information. Commercial speech tends to be seen as belonging to that category of speech that has the potential to advance the self-realization of individuals precisely because it appeals to values and opinions, rather than to commercial reason. Consequently, the courts treat with deep suspicion governmental restraints of advertisers, of puffery, of image-makers, of values' spin doctors.

The character and nature of the actor who wants the restraint on speech set aside are of little interest to the court. As long as the attempted restraint *could* inhibit the free speech of some flesh and blood individuals, it does not matter that the actual complainants are not flesh and blood human beings with a human need to realize their full potential. It does not matter that they are abstract, bloodless corporations whose only need is to satisfy their drive to maximize profits. Protection of speech, as such, is the thing; the nature of the targets of the governmental restraints are of marginal interest to judiciary.

The ironies are striking. In the name of protecting the *social and political* rights of individual human beings, the state protects the *collective economic* rights of corporations. When flesh and blood workers seek to protect their *collective economic and political* rights through their unions, they do not have the same protections. Even more paradoxically, the right to speak, which was accorded to corporations so that we could have informed markets, has won enhanced constitutional guarantees largely because corporate speech provides hardly any useful market information.

Commercialism, Free Speech, and the Political Agenda

Corporations, then, have once again won the ability to undermine our aspirations, both social and political. The social and political fallout of the Charter and its judicial interpretations provides, for the first time, positive, active legal support for the political rights of those whose only interest in speaking was once thought to be their need to facilitate their participation in market activities. Now they can participate in political life more directly than ever before. As well, the judiciary's willingness to give corporations standing to defend free speech rights has given those with the greatest capacity to speak an awesome new legal weapon. With it, corporations can legally attack attempts by governments to regulate economic markets in which these corporations have an immediate material interest.

The Charter and the courts' reading of it have yet another major impact. Corporations can also legally attack a government's attempt to limit the ability of wealthy persons—whose wealth often is embedded in corporations—from wielding disproportionate influence in the political setting. The judiciary's enthusiasm to bring all sorts of commercial speech within the constitutionally protected freedom of expression guarantee was based, in large part, on the combined effect of the commodification of culture and the corporate perspective on the world peddled by huge corporate actors and their ever-more sophisticated advertising partners. By the time that Canadian courts had to hand down the decisions in the Irwin Toy and RJR-MacDonald cases, commercialism was already colouring everything. The impact of the corporate sectors' propaganda was immense. It has changed our legal and political consciousness.

The trajectory of this change can be tracked through the documented changes in judicial approach to the value of economic talk in the United States. In 1942, in a case called *Valentine v. Chrestensen*, the Supreme Court of the United States was asked whether commercial speech was constitutionally protected speech. The Court rejected the argument out of hand. The vote was nine to zero against granting constitutional protection to commercial speech. From the 1970s onwards, however, the U.S. Supreme Court began to change direction. Clearly, the impact of the commodification of everything was getting to the judges in the United States. Until then extremely strong proponents of free speech, such as the Supreme Court's Mr. Justice Hugo Black, and political and legal commentators, such as Alexander Meiklejohn and Thomas Emerson, who would have protected any and all political speech, contended that the defence of political speech did not warrant the protection of commercial chatter. Commercial speech, these liberal democrats argued with vehemence, was part of economic activity and sufficiently safeguarded by the Constitution's guarantee of freedom of contract.

By the time that the Canadian courts had to tangle with the question, the game in the United States was over. Commercial speech had won constitutional protection. As a consequence, the embrace by Canadian courts of commercial speech as protected speech was largely reflective of what was commonly believed to be the natural state of things. Still, natural though it seemed, the Canadian courts' willingness to protect commercial speech as if it were political speech led to a serious deterioration of political values and, as a result, of political behaviour. It gave corporate actors additional means of setting the agenda for governments.

A good exemplification of the problem is the way in which the Supreme Court of Canada dealt with Quebec's business signs law in the *Ford* case in 1988. This formally passed piece of legislation contained this provision under its section 58: "Public signs and posters and commercial advertising shall be solely in the official language." The official language referred to here was French. Some business proprietors—many of them corporations— argued that this provision violated the guarantee of freedom of expression found in Canada's Charter of Rights and Freedoms. The Supreme Court of Canada agreed with this business position and struck down this very popular Quebec law. It did so even though the Quebec government had been as clear as it could possibly be that it fully respected the rights of Québécois to think and speak freely. The signs law had specifically stated: "Section 58 does not apply to advertising carried out in news media that publish in languages other than French, or to *messages of a religious, political, ideological or humanitarian nature, if not for a profit motive.*"

Now, the justices of the Supreme Court of Canada—all appointed because of their federalist sympathies—were undoubtedly motivated to reach the decision they did by their view of Quebec's political aspirations, but they could not openly admit this. Rather, they justified their striking down of Quebec's signs law, despite its clear disavowal of any intent to restrain true political speech, on the basis that signs were speech and that, therefore, the choice of language for the signs, regardless of the message conveyed by the signs, was political. The Supreme Court of Canada explicitly protected speech, regardless of its nature, regardless of whether a restraint of it advanced or retarded the political rights of a democratically elected government or the people it represented, even if that government was sensitive to the political sovereignty of those people. The decision had an immediate impact on the political battle between Canada and Quebec and a more insidious one on politics writ large.

The struck-down law had gained the support of all major Quebec parties and factions. Both federalists and separatists saw the business signs law as a minimal and necessary guarantee of French language rights. Inevitably—as the Supreme Court of Canada should have anticipated—the federalist-minded Quebec government of Premier Robert Bourassa had to act to set aside the Supreme Court of Canada's decision. It did so by enacting a new business signs law that law permitted English-language signs to be displayed inside the premises of businesses (provided they were smaller than French signs) and permitted only French signs to be displayed on the outside of business premises. To avoid any further interference by the Supreme Court of Canada at the behest of Anglo business persons and/or their corporations, the new Quebec law went on to say that this law was valid "notwithstanding" the freedom of expression guaranteed in the Charter of Rights and Freedoms. The federalist-minded Quebec government had been forced into employing the escape clause that had been inserted in the Charter to safeguard provincial rights. This in effect was the only way a federalist provincial Quebec government had left to say that it could not accept an interpretation of freedom of speech that was acceptable to the rest of Canada but not to Quebec.

The backlash in English Canada was palpable and may have been the straw that broke the camel's back. Around that same time the top-down, orchestrated Meech Lake Accord—which was acceptable to the Bourassa government and seen as a reasonable starting point by some Quebec separatists—was already in critical ill health in English Canada. Many people in the rest of Canada saw the forced invocation of the notwithstanding clause by the trapped Quebec government as a sign that no Québécois government, not even a so-called federalist one, could be trusted. The Meech Lake Accord died right there and then.

The role of the courts in liberal-capital democracies has always been to maintain a distinction between the political and economic spheres. The pretence is that the economic regime is the preserve of private actors and private market activities and that these private activities do not present a danger to the political sovereignty of individuals—that these private activities do not challenge the political ideal that lies at the core of liberalism. The real danger to individual freedoms is perceived to be the potential for coercion by tyrannical majorities acting through state institutions. From this perspective, any advantage an owner of private wealth might have over wealth-less individuals is not objectionable to the regime of liberal law administered by the judiciary. It does not amount to political oppression. Political oppression comes from the state. What the Charter of Rights and Freedoms did was to cement this belief system. Too many Canadians are not aware that the constitutional guarantees of freedoms found in the Charter—and of which they are so proud—are only guarantees against actions taken by democratically elected governments. Thus, the government of Quebec had to justify its attempts to regulate advertising aimed at children and the language of business signs. But Irwin Toy or any business that objected to the legislation that told them how and when to advertise or in what language to print their signs was free to regulate its own employees' speech. Workers are told when they can speak on the job, how to speak to their supervisors, and to whom they might speak about the products and services of their employers. No justification is needed by employers who impose such restraints, because the restraints are said to be imposed as implementations of the terms of privately, freely negotiated contracts. But what really happens is that the owners or managers dictate what is in those employment contracts. This brings home the point: to advance their economic goals the rich can take advantage of the whole gamut of political rights, even if that makes them richer and gives them greater leverage to oppress the non-property owners by their exercise of private economic power. A paradox has now come into view.

By characterizing profit-seeking commercial speech as if it cannot be differentiated from protected political speech, the courts have helped to set in place an instrumental and ideological basis for attacks on government regulation, a regulation that, in part, will always be aimed at protecting the more vulnerable from private wealth-owners' exploitations. At the same time, by treating profit-seeking commercial speech as worthy of constitutional protection, the courts have laid the basis for the idea that anyone who can speak commercially has a stake in political freedom of speech. The way is thus open for direct participation in political life by corporations, which are, after all, legal "persons" created for the express purpose of acting commercially.

The Supreme Court of Canada has indeed been spinning a curious web. The 1988 free-trade election provides an example of what this means to the rest of us. Leading up to that time, the Brian Mulroney-led Progressive Conservative Party government had made it its mission to enter into a Free Trade Agreement (FTA) with the United States. In doing this it had earned the plaudits of the larger corporations—often U.S. subsidiaries—in the land. But when the other main business party, the Liberals, announced that it, like the NDP, would oppose the FTA, the Mulroney/big business agenda was in trouble. Consequently, the Conservatives and their corporate allies consciously combined their efforts and made the 1988 election into as much of a one-issue election as it is possible for any election to become. Though cap-

turing less than half of the vote, the pro-FTA forces won the day. For good or
bad, the birth of the FTA, as it was intended to do, heralded the advent of a
new political milieu. The FTA (like its successor, the NAFTA) is a deal that
binds the signing governments not to interfere with the private economic
decision-making of corporate actors. Governments representing the majority
of the people agree to give up their right to regulate on behalf of those people in respect of certain economic and social matters. It is an agreement that
has changed the very nature of our politics and has granted corporations
more power at the expense of the majoritarian principles underpinning our
democratic institutions. That is why major corporations wanted the deal.
Their attempts to put their stamp on the election were overt, blatant, often
shamelessly coercive, and, in the end, the single largest reason for the
Mulroney campaign's success. The corporations were aided tremendously by
the expanded free-speech rights for money crafted by the judiciary's interpretation of the Charter of Rights and Freedoms.

In 1984 the National Citizens' Coalition (NCC), an umbrella group for
corporations, their representatives and ideological allies, challenged a federal
political financing law. In enacting the legislation, the government had been
very clear about the purpose: to ensure that those with large amounts of
money to spend on campaign funding would not drown out the voices of
those with no spare wealth to expend. The NCC said it was a defender of free
speech and that the limitations put on spending by third parties—non-candi-
dates and associations other than registered political parties—denied these
third parties their right of free speech. The NCC was thus equating the right
to spend money with the right to free expression, an approach advancing the
free-speech right of those otherwise mute "things," corporations. A trial judge
in Alberta, reading the Charter of Rights and Freedoms as if it were a funda-
mentalists' text and, therefore, to be interpreted literally, upheld the NCC
challenge. His view was that speech of any kind was to be protected from
government excesses, regardless of the nature of the speech or the speakers.
Effectively he ignored the democratic impulses that underpinned the restrictions on third-party expenditures. This was a highly controversial reading. In
the absence of an appeal by the ruling federal Liberal government, the decision negated the law of the land. Corporations and the rich would be free to
spend like drunken sailors to persuade the electorate of anything they would
like to promote.

The Liberals did not appeal the ruling. As later events showed, they
might have been successful if they had done so. In the wake of the 1988 election, a Royal Commission of Inquiry (Lortie) recommended restrictions on
third-party spending. While the initial implementation of this recommenda-

tion was defeated by yet another Charter-based challenge, eventually Supreme Court decisions in 1997 and 2000 did uphold such legislative restrictions (well and truly after the free-trade horses had bolted). Anyhow, in 1984, the Charter had opened the door, and in 1988 the corporations burst through the gap, chequebooks swinging. In the end big business spent some $19 million on the 1988 campaign. Corporations paid $1.5 million for a four-page insert in thirty-five English-language newspapers and a mere $75,000 for an advertisement in *Maclean's* magazine. Needless to say, it is difficult if not impossible for non-monied interests to combat this kind of political muscle. These amounts of money are simply not available to the unincorporated, to the majority of the citizenry. If this kind of politicking is effective—and the evidence is that it is, even though it does not always work, as the failure of the Charlottetown Accord, an agreement supported by the same big business interests, shows—it distorts electoral politics. Certainly, the Royal Commission of Inquiry, established in 1990 to examine the impact of third-party spending, came to the conclusion that the Charter decisions that had permitted the pocket-book elections "had destroyed the overall effectiveness of the legislative framework . . . for promoting fairness" and had diminished "the 'democratic' character of our society."

The perversion of logic that led to the legitimation and direct facilitation of corporate participation in politics could be described as delicious irony were it not for the harm done to the democratic institutions of our nation. To recapitulate: free speech is necessary for political freedom in a liberal democracy, and commercial speech is necessary to a smoothly functioning market economy. Political speech has come to include commercial speech, in large part because commercial speech rarely meets the market's requirements for accurate and essential information. It is more often opinion than fact. Commercial speakers are, therefore, political speakers, even if they are corporations. As corporations engage in speech through the expenditure of money, limitations on expenditure inhibit political free-speech rights guaranteed by the Charter of Rights and Freedoms to all Canadians. As a consequence, inasmuch as money can be used to speak, those with more money can speak more often and more loudly.

A circle has been completed. The logic of private economic market activities is that you get to enjoy the goods and services you can afford. It is the quintessential one dollar/one vote sphere. The logic of political liberal democracy, however, posits the legal equality of all human beings who are members of the polity. It is the quintessential one person/one vote sphere. In practice, this ideal has been destroyed. The right of corporations (themselves sites of the one dollar/one vote logic) to participate directly in issue and party politics with the disproportionate clout provided by their money turns electoral politics into the same one dollar/one vote terrain as that constituted by the market for commodities.

In daily parlance, our media are full of the marketing of this or that politician; our U.S. neighbours are candid about the amount of money required to be elected to the Congress or to the presidency, a candour about which we tend to be righteous, pretending that it is an American phenomenon, not a Canadian one. As the case of the free-trade elections shows all too clearly, our democratic forms have been distorted by the corporations' judicially enhanced right to speak, and thereby to act, politically.

Large Corporations, Power, and the Media

The argument is not that, before the Charter-induced judicial tenderness for corporate free speech, wealthy people did not exercise disproportionate power over the political processes. They did. The menace of a capital strike, of a refusal to invest or of a threat to deinvest, always had an impact on governmental decision-making. And, equally, the ability to grease the world of politicians with money always played a role in their behaviour. Thus, in 1977, Khayyam Z. Patiel reported in his *Party, Candidate and Election Finance* that the provision of funds to parties and candidates had never been based on purely altruistic purposes: "At the lowest level the price has been concessions, dispensations, and specific acts of patronage; at a higher level the aim has been to stabilize the field for corporate activity."

The developments in corporate law, complemented by constitutional protectionism, permit these same wealthy people to hide behind their invisible friends, particularly as their invisible friends hide themselves behind other smokescreens, such as outfits like the NCC and Business Council on National Issues (BCNI). More: by legitimating the participation of corporations in politics as if they were just another organized interest group like any other, the very few, the only true discrete minority in our society, the wealthy, are able to trump the wishes of the majority more effectively than if they had to confront them directly on the political battlegrounds. Both capital strikes and participation in political affairs by the rich are more easily portrayed as benign because, on the face of it, they are engaged in by entities with no personal axes to grind. Corporations present themselves as apolitical organizations that act as their apolitical market needs dictate, not as individuals pursuing their own interests in enlarging their political clout at the expense of the political liberty of fellow citizens. This helps the truly rich to normalize the drive for greater freedom for the private economic sector, for the diminution of government. As a result, many people come to see the marginalization of government as an inevitable, natural, and appropriate goal, not as something simply being pushed forward by an identifiable minority of individuals who stand to gain from its attainment.

The "commodification of everything" project—lubricated by the sophisticated corporate advertising industry—also advances this agenda. Similarly, the Charter-augmented rights of corporations to speak commercially about products, services, and the beneficial nature of a corporation-dominated world and accompanying lifestyles add more bite to the never-ending efforts of wealth owners to establish a favourable climate for their exploits and exploitations.

The industry that is compendiously referred to as the media also has a part to play in this push for power. The guarantee of freedom of expression contained in the Charter's Section 2 includes a specific protection for "freedom of the press and other media of communication." The liberal justification for this safeguard is that an independent, fearless media sector will hold public officials—elected and appointed—and private sectors to strict account. So armed, the public will be better able to look after its social, political, and economic interests. A major flaw, among many, in the argument is that the major media outlets are owned and operated as private corporations. Their owners and management are principally interested in the private accumulation of socially produced wealth. Even though most journalists and their editors think of themselves as having a duty to truth and, on a personal level, do their very best to live by these ideals, day-to-day and larger decisions around how news is to be reported, what is newsworthy, and, more directly, what is worthy of public attention are not allowed to interfere with the attainment of the corporate goal.

The media make the greatest portion of their money by selling advertising. For instance, close to 80 per cent of all newspaper revenues come from the sale of advertising space. About 50 per cent of a newspaper's content is advertising material, rather than news or "independent " opinion. Mass media publications, television programs, and radio broadcasts—and now on-line news services—have become conduit pipes between advertisers of products and services and their potential customers. News and opinions, as well as entertainment, are packaged to attract the kind of readers, listeners, and viewers who are the focus of the advertisers. There is competition amongst the media, but it is not about being the most able to present the truth of social and political events and circumstances. It is about the delivery of consumers to sellers, about market share and dominance. For instance, the newspapers rely on the Newspaper Audience Data Bank, a respected outfit that conducts surveys to determine who and what demographic groups read what newspapers so that papers can position and price themselves accordingly in the market. The wooing of corporations that advertise does not make a particularly good fit with serious investigative reporting, idiosyncratic opinion-writing, the raising of unpopular issues, attacking capitalism, or anything else that lives up to the media's self-characterization of being the safeguard of a free and open society. Rather, the media set out to provide the advertisers with a comfortable, and comforting, milieu. They do not attack the sacred cows of corporate Canada. Indeed, their reporting and editorializing place them on side whenever the large advertisers are pursuing a major social, political, and/or economic goal. For instance, *The Toronto Star* was the only major media outlet to oppose the Free Trade Agreement—a remarkable fact given that two mainstream parties and over 50 per cent of the voters opposed the proposals. In a similar way, the media have provided slavish support for the opposition to such anti-corporate governmental measures as the National Energy Policy and the Foreign Investment Review Agency. More generally, the overall major media tone and tenor are fully supportive of consumerism and commodification.

Sometimes even the proponents of a free press as a guardian of the public interest must be embarrassed by the primacy of consumerism. *USA TODAY*, a major tabloid, promises large advertisers that their ads will be surrounded by dovetailing "news" items. Less blatant, but more significantly, newspapers offer commercial happenings—the arrival of a new product, a description of a good place to spend a holiday, the clever way in which certain houses are built, the lifestyle of a visiting entertainer—as if they were news. The disguise is often very thin; the material appears in sections of newspapers or television shows that are nothing but advertisements for consumerism as a good thing in its own right, as well as for particular consumer products or services.

Given this bombardment of commercial messages, the media provide little intimation that another vision beyond that of the large corporations—the market as liberator and the creator of abundance—can be imagined, let alone pursued. It is not as if there is a malignant co-ordinating censor at work. It is simply that, in a setting in which the media are themselves profit-maximizers, operating as corporations whose mission it is to further this agenda, they cannot be expected to serve any other goal—even if their employees want to do so—that clashes with this agenda. Daryl Duke, an eminent director and producer who has worked for CBC-TV and major U.S. networks and who founded a private television station in Vancouver, has reflected on his experiences:

> In Canada censorship is not a single horrific act of state power. . . .
> Censorship is for the most part invisible. . . . It is censorship by private
> power. . . . It affects everything we watch. There is not a writer, performer or
> commentator who does not feel the impact of private power in the elec-
> tronic media. There is no theatre company, no ballet ensemble, no film-
> maker or video artist who is not beholden to private corporate power. No
> matter how large its membership nor how worthy its goals there is no public
> interest organization, no guild or union free of the restrictions private power
> places upon such a group's ability to reach our citizens with its message.

While the media have won judicial protection from state interference with
their right to express any or all thought, then, they are still tied into a system
of private control—which they warmly embrace.

The media provide more than a positive framework for the large corporations' overall project (and, therefore, a negative framework for anti-
consumerism, anti-market perspectives). The actual operation of media
business makes it virtually impossible for alternative political views to be
aired—or, more accurately, aired effectively. As business operations, media
members take a buck from wherever they can get it, even from those who
want to communicate oppositional views. This open-for-business approach
bolsters the media's self-portrayal as being open-minded outlets, promoting
free speech and thought, the virtues that entitle them to Charter protection.
But to use these outlets the non-corporate groups, just like corporate advertisers, must pay, and pay heavily. In the late 1990s, when the Centre for Social
Justice—a small think-tank of leftish activists in Toronto—investigated taking
out advertisements in major newspapers in Ontario, it found that the cost of
a full-page ad was $15,000 in *The Toronto Star* and $33,345 in *The Globe
and Mail* and *The National Post*. If they wanted to place an advertisement in
all of the Southam group's papers, the cost would have been $250,000. All of
these were reduced rates. Obviously, this kind of participation in politics—
that is, on the dollars equals votes basis—is simply a losing proposition for
oppositional groups. When the exercise of free speech is regulated by the
ability to afford that exercise, large publicly traded corporations gain an enormous advantage, as they did in the FTA election.

The major media are not totally closed to opinions and news that put
forward the case of the non-corporate sectors and the plight of the vulnerable.
Most people who become journalists do so because they want to contribute
to democratic debates. Many journalists see themselves as politically astute
when it comes to complicated causes. Further, most newspapers have regular

opinion pieces and columns by columnists who criticize conventional wisdom. But, inasmuch as such critiques do appear, they are surrounded by pro-consumerism, pro-big business agenda reporting and presentation. It is the systemic for-profit agenda endemic to the media that matters. Some time ago, when Hollinger International, Conrad Black's invisible friend, seemed to be purchasing every newspaper in Canada, the Council of Canadians brought an action in the courts. The burden of its claim was that the emerging monopoly was endangering freedom of speech. In particular the Council was concerned that the Hollinger papers would become an unchallengeable platform for the views of their real proprietor, the anti-nationalist, pro-free-trade, anti-social welfare, anti-communitarian, ultra conservative Conrad Black. The case was lost. This may not seem so important now that Hollinger International has divested itself of most of its Canadian media holdings. The hated "Black" factor has disappeared. But the real nature of the problem remains in place. The proprietorship of Conrad Black was not, in and of itself, a cause for what was—and is—justifiable alarm. His disappearance from the scene does not make things better from a free-speech, democratic politics point of view. The media, whether directly controlled by a conservative ideologue or not, are there to defend the large corporations' interests, interests that are congruent with their own. What the highly publicized growth in Conrad Black ownership did was to make this plainer than usual. His sale of Hollinger assets will not improve the situation: the media are there to pursue profiteering, not democracy. They will continue to undermine democratic institutions effectively as long as there are a few controlling enterprises that run them.

The recent integration of the media with a variety of other enterprises has intensified matters. When CanWest, a major television and radio broadcast player, took over Hollinger International's once commanding newspaper position, at a price of $3.5 billion, it gained control of Global TV as well as 50 per cent of *The National Post*—there had to be some divestment to satisfy the feeble competition policy—and 50 per cent of the RoBTv, the latter being a major news web-site provider. The ownership of RoBTv came to CanWest through a broadcasting corporation called WIK, which, in turn, it had acquired after a vicious takeover battle. Vancouver ended up with two major newspapers and two major television stations all owned by CanWest. Now, is there any argument that the real controllers of what were previously Hollinger media interests, Izzy Asper and his son, are less menacing to free speech than was Conrad Black? Such believers might be shaken somewhat by recent developments. By the fall of 2001 it appeared that CanWest Global was sandwiching in informational advertisements during breaks in its televi-

sion service—an appealing approach to advertisers, who gain by having viewers give more credibility to their message, which looks rather like objectively
gathered news in this happy milieu. Around the same time news began to
come out about how Southam newspapers in thirteen cities—papers now
owned by the Asper forces—would be required to carry editorials written at
corporate headquarters rather than locally. John Honderich, a rival publisher,
called this *dirigisme* unprecedented in a society that claims to cherish a free
press. Aislin (Terry Mosher), a cartoonist for the Montreal *Gazette*, a former
Black paper, gave a CBC interview after one of his cartoons critical of his new
bosses was pulled. The cartoon made the point that it was more forthright to
have Black as an opponent than the gentler-seeming Asper forces.

Other movements towards consolidation include the giant, non-media,
BCE Inc. corporation's purchase of the CTV interests and *The Globe and Mail*.
Are we to believe that a significant non-media corporation, as BCE is, has purchased large media businesses because it developed a sudden desire to dis-
seminate truth and to hold the feet of miscreants to the fire of public
opinion? Or is it probable that BCE saw the acquisition as an efficient way of
improving its conglomerate profitability? In the United States the three
major television networks also have become the property of giant non-media
corporations. General Electric is the owner of NBC and Walt Disney and
Viacom are the owners of ABC and CBS, respectively. News, while still
delivered in sober, balanced tones, is really just a way to get more viewers, listeners and readers of the "right" demographic and economic groups to
attract advertisers.

A Distorted Form of Democracy

The emergence of the corporation as a political entity writ large seriously
constrains our democratic aspirations and room to manoeuvre. To summarize
our findings so far:

1.   Corporations are permitted to speak to participate in market transactions.

2.   Corporations, as the principal vehicle of the capitalist project, use their
     right to speak to advance that project. This includes convincing all of us
     that the production of goods and services for the exchange value they
     have should be at the centre of our social relations. Whether or not a
     product or service is needed in what John McMurtry has called a life-
     enhancing, life-serving way is of no concern. The use-value of a product

or service is of little account. The consequence is a remarkably sophisticated and profitable industry, the marketing/advertising business. Its
focus is the creation of demands for goods or services, regardless of use
or need. It is to create an illusion of well-being by relating it to possessions
and certain lifestyles that, in turn, are associated with consumerism, with
selfishness. As part of this image-making, the producers of goods and services, the employers of the advertising industry, have to be given an
acceptable garb. Corporations, the ultimate in artifices, are portrayed as
normal, natural, and benign phenomena.

3. Precisely because the emphasis on exchange value, rather than use/need
    value, requires the creation of wants and desires, advertising by corpora-
    tions is short on facts and long on sentiment, idealized images of life,
    and the privileging of certain values over others. They are exercises that
    resemble political ones. The judiciary, especially since it became armed
    with the constitutionally entrenched Charter of Rights and Freedoms,
    has protected this kind of commercial speech as if it were political
    speech. This has added immensely to:
    (i)   the corporations' standing as political individuals, as citizens, and to
    the legitimation of all of their activities, including the social construc-
    tion of a consumer-oriented economy;
    (ii) the corporations' capacity to participate directly in the political life
    of the nation and to their ability to embed the ideology that corporations
    should be the central economic actors and governments should be
    restricted to the facilitation of these goals; and, thereby, added to
    (iii) the impacts of the complementary role played by large-for-profit
    media corporations whose very existence is intertwined with the advertis-
    ing industry, which does so much to foster this anti-governmental, one-
    dollar/one-vote polity.

In these circumstances there is persistent—albeit not always irresistible—
pressure for elected governments to pursue the large, publicly traded
corporate agenda. That agenda is not the same for all corporations in respect
of particular issues, but it is relatively uncontroversial when it comes to the
fundamental needs of a consumer, commodified economy. In this cause
large corporations have developed a byzantine and effective network of think-
tanks and umbrella groups, as well as closer personal links with government
bureaucracies. Dominant corporations have also established close ties with
dominant for-profit media corporate interests. As a result, government has
become well aware of the interests of large capital, acting through corporations.

The corporation itself comes to be seen as the major actor in these affairs, and the wealth-owners themselves disappear from the political radar screen. For that reason the identification of the evil of the disproportionate influence of a Conrad Black was highly significant. It was a manifestation that, behind the corporate veil, there are flesh and blood human beings who exercise undemocratic power as "their" corporations absorb political attention and ward off government monitoring and regulation. Most often, as we shall see in the next two chapters, wealth-owners in Canada receive special treatment, allowing our basic laws and beliefs—which ought to be safeguarded by our democratic institutions—to be flouted and ignored by the rich and their invisible friends.

Corporate Deviance and Deviants: The Fancy Footwork of Criminal Law

Wherein we learn that corporate actors regularly and repeatedly violate our standards of moral and legal behaviour, do much more physical and economic harm than any other violators of these standards, and continue to be treated as upright members of our society, giving meaning to Clarence Darrow's aphorism that most people classified as criminals are "persons with predatory instincts without sufficient capital to form a corporation."

One measure of the growing ideological and structural influence of the dominant corporation is that when corporate actors commit crimes they are rarely charged; if charged, they are rarely convicted; and if convicted, they are rarely punished severely. Given the great significance that a liberal democracy such as Canada attaches to criminal law, this privileged treatment has important implications.

The variety of legal tools used to regulate behaviour reflect the needs of our liberal political and economic goals. The tools set out to ensure that each individual has an optimal amount of scope to pursue personal interests without impeding too greatly on the capacity of all others to do likewise. This condition requires the marriage of a mix of policy instruments, each with distinct but complementary objectives. Compensation, retribution, rehabilitation, and specific and general deterrence are the interconnected and over-lapping goals of these many regulatory tools.

For instance, a vendor who misinforms a purchaser may have to compensate the purchaser for any ensuing loss. If certain goods are said to be capable of doing two thousand rotations per minute but, in fact, can only manage six hundred such rotations, the loss incurred by an innocent and misled purchaser will have to be made good by the vendor as a matter of the regulatory system that we call contract law. But if the same wrong piece of information was the result of a deliberate deception, rather than an innocent misstatement, by the vendor, the vendor may also be sued under a rubric of tort law and made to pay punitive damages on top of contractual damages. The vendor may even be charged with the criminal offence of fraud.

Similarly, if a manufacturer puts a shoddy and dangerous product on the market, a person injured as a result of that product may be able to sue the manufacturer. The victim relies on the regulatory tool called tort law. The manufacturer may also be subject to administrative sanctions for its violation of a standard set by a regulator appointed by government to oversee this kind of manufacturing. The manufacturer may have to pay damages or a fine, or it could even lose its licence to do business as a consequence of being held responsible for its breach of an administrative rule or policy. If, in addition, the manufacturer is adjudged to have acted with intent to do harm with its manufacturing or as having been reckless as to whether or not its conduct might cause harm, a criminal prosecution may be launched against it.

The purposes underlying (i) the enforcement of a contract, (ii) the right to sue in tort, (iii) the enforcement of an administrative regulation, or (iv) the enforcement of the criminal law are of the same kind. Each regulatory regime is used to set a standard of acceptable behaviour and to enforce that accepted standard of behaviour. When the standard is violated, the wrong-doer is made to redress the harm done—if possible—and a lesson is sought to be taught. The perpetrator is to be discouraged from acting in a like manner again and all others are to learn from that pronouncement of disapproval. As contract law, administrative law, tort law, and criminal law all serve to main-tain consensually set standards, a decision has to be made as to which of these regulatory tools should be deployed in our quest to achieve compensa-tion, retribution, and specific and general deterrence whenever we are con-fronted by a breach of a standard. In making our choice of regulatory system, we reflexively grade the wrongful behaviour.

We reserve the criminal law for circumstances in which our sensitivities have been deeply offended—that is, for those situations in which, in addition to setting things right and educating the individual—and the rest of us—into better behaviour, we want to condemn the behaviour as strongly as possible. We use criminal law to stigmatize wrongdoers and their conduct. The special processes used are publicly initiated and provide extraordinary safeguards for the rights of the accused person, thereby solemnifying the importance of a finding of criminality. The sanctions imposed are severe and are enforced by the state on society's behalf, rather than at the behest of a wronged person. The offence is seen as an offence to us all.

The state, then, is expected to bring its massive coercive powers to bear to eradicate the kind of conduct that calls the criminal law into play. Because of its might and because of the severity of the sanctions available — anything from slaps on the wrist to lifelong imprisonment (in some jurisdictions, death) — the state is restrained in its options for criminal prosecutions. In the common-law system, the suspected violator of a criminal law standard is presumed innocent until proven guilty after a full trial. The state is inhibited in its investigation by restrictions on the searches and seizures it can conduct. It is prohibited from coercing suspected violators into providing evidence against themselves. In these and other ways, the state distinguishes criminal law from other regulatory laws and rules whose violations will not have such serious consequences for the violator. We are to be careful before we reach for the criminal justice system. As the Law Reform Commission of Canada stated: "There is a general presumption that an act is not a crime. . . . At common law . . . nothing is a crime unless the law specifically says so. Indeed in Canada this has been written into our Criminal Code. . . . No one needs to prove his right to an act. Unless the law forbids it, he is free to do it."

Criminal law must, therefore, be narrowly defined. It must set out to restrict freedom only to protect a people's basic values and aspirations. The capacity to prosecute is carefully constrained and, should a conviction be registered after following all the rules, the sanctions imposed on violators must be appropriate to the offence and offender. Otherwise our use of the state's awesome coercive powers could not be justified; that use would not, in the language of the Law Reform Commission, do justice. And, of course, precisely because it is about the safeguarding of our most precious tenets, the law must be applied without fear or favour. It must be applied equally. As the Law Reform Commission also put it, the doctrine of criminal equality "says that a crime is a crime no matter who commits it." This principle means that "under Canadian criminal law, then, all of us are equal unless the law specifically says otherwise." In other words, as the law Reform Commission and all liberal commentators contend, a political system that prides itself on living by the rule of law should surely avoid anything that smacks of preferential treatment.

Justice "for Them" and for "Just Us"

Sample. In the Westray Mine affair, twenty-six people died horrible deaths. *The Westray Story: A Predictable Path to Disaster*, the telling title of the Report of the Westray Mine Public Inquiry by Justice K. Peter Richard, found that the owner and operators of the mine, a corporation and its executives, had "created a workplace that fostered a disregard for workplace safety. . . .Westray is a stark example of an operation where production demands violated basic and fundamental demands of safe mining practice. . . . Management's drive for production, together with its disdain for safety, played a key role in the devastation of the mine." By the time of the explosion, a staggering record of fifty-two breaches of the health and safety standards had been compiled by the overseeing ministry. They never led to any prosecutions under the occupational health and safety legislation that had been so flagrantly disregarded. Two charges, however, were laid under the Criminal Code by the RCMP to try and hold someone criminally responsible for the deaths. These charges were eventually dropped. Even though twenty-six people died, no one was ever convicted of any wrongdoing.

Sample. In April 2000, a man was sentenced to sixteen years in jail in Texas. Like the Westray firm, he had repeatedly violated the law. Indeed, he had spent seven years in prison for various offences, including the theft of a bag of Oreo cookies. This time the prosecutor asked for the awesome sentence of sixteen years to teach this incorrigible recidivist a lesson. He had gone too far: he had stolen a Snickers bar from a grocery. Not just any Snickers bar, but a king-size one, worth one U.S. dollar.

Sample. Hoffman-La Roche, a giant pharmaceutical corporation, pleaded guilty to conspiring with other corporations (some, such as Hoffman-La Roche, BASF, and Rhone-Poulenc, were giants; others, such as Canada's Chinook Group, were relative minnows) to fix the prices of vitamins in several parts of the world. The conspiracy was hatched in 1990 and lasted until 1999. Annual meetings to ensure the smooth operation of the conspiracy were held in Basel, where the headquarters of Hoffman-La Roche were located. Clearly, the criminal activity was not the brainchild of some rogue executives. Hoffman-La Roche agreed to pay a $500 million fine in the United States. Four of its executives were given jail sentences: one four months, one three-and-a-half months, and the other two three months. In

Canada during the decade of cheating, the conspirators sold products for $668 million. Vitamins were sold for 30 per cent more than a competitive market would have allowed; there was an illegal profit of just something less than $200 million. Hoffman-La Roche Canada paid a fine of $48 million of the total fines of $88 million imposed in Canada on the various conspirators. The former vice-president of Chinook, the major Canadian participant, was given a nine-month conditional sentence. He was to be allowed to serve his time in the community, rather than in a prison; he was to perform fifty hours of community service. Given that he had retired, he presumably had enough time on his hands to meet this requirement without much pain.

Sample. Australia's Northern Territory requires, as do many U.S. jurisdictions, that courts impose mandatory sentences on wrongdoers who are repeat offenders. The need to eradicate rotten apples from the social barrel obviously presses hard on these legislatures. On January 29, 2000, a repeat offender in the Northern Territory—an Aboriginal, like most of the persons caught by this provision in this part of the world—was sentenced to one year in jail for attempting to steal a quarter-full bottle of whisky and a half-bottle of beer. Earlier on in the same jurisdiction a boy hanged himself in jail after being sentenced to a year in prison for stealing a box of crayons and liquid paper.

Sample. Between 1960 and 1972, Reed Paper Company poured nearly ten tons of mercury into a Northern Ontario river and lake system. The company was aware that mercury was a known hazard. Reed Paper continued its deadly dumping even after the federal government issued an order banning the practice. Mercury is known to poison fish and to cause Minamata disease—a serious neurological disorder—as well as deafness, muteness, and blindness. In addition to its damaging effects on health, the mercury poisoning was an economic assault on the lives of the Native communities, which lived off the fishing and tourism supported by the river and lake system. Reed Paper Company eventually abandoned its productive activities and the provincial and federal governments and Reed Paper's successors paid out some compensation. No individual was charged criminally for the continued acts of knowing ruinous pollution of the river and lake systems, which had long been the source of life and well-being of the local communities.

Sample. In 1975 a welfare recipient failed to disclose that she had a common-law spouse. As a consequence she had received $1,700 in welfare payments—money she would not have received if she had been honest. She was sentenced to five months in jail. She had four children. In 1993 a mother of two, who had similarly failed to disclose that a male co-habited with her, received $17,425 in welfare payments. Despite uncontested evidence that she was an excellent mother and active community volunteer, her heinous offence was punished by imprisonment for four months. A study of welfare fraud documented that 80 per cent of all persons convicted of welfare fraud of this type were given jail sentences. In contrast, another study shows that "prison" is imposed in 4 per cent of all tax evasion cases, even though the amounts stolen vastly exceed those stolen by welfare abusers. Unemployment benefit frauds reveal the same pattern: the rate of incarceration is twice that experienced by tax evaders. In June 2001 a medical practitioner convicted of fraud for overbilling the publicly funded health-care system by just under a million dollars—money used to take luxury trips to Germany, Italy, California, and New Zealand and stay in five-star hotels with his partner— was sentenced to a conditional sentence of two years, to be served not in jail, but in the community. The medical disciplinary board added to the sentence by suspending his ability to bill the health-care system for a short length of time. The harshly dealt-with practitioner appealed the medical disciplinary board's decision.

Sample. In the 1980s, Eli Lilly, a major pharmaceutical corporation, brought an arthritis drug on to the U.S. market. To do this the company had to obtain approval from the U.S. Food and Drug Administration. It did not inform the agency that the drug was known to have killed a minimum of twenty-eight persons in Europe—a fact that only came to light when the Food and Drug Administration discovered that the drug had possible links to forty-nine deaths in the United States and hundreds elsewhere, as well as to countless liver and kidney failures. Eli Lilly, a corporation that earned $3.1 billion in 1984—the latest financial year prior to the revelations—was fined $25,000. Its chief medical officer, a Dr. William Shedden, was fined $15,000 after pleading guilty to fifteen criminal charges arising out of the marketing of the drug.

Sample. In 1978 the Canadian Union of Postal Workers was engaged in a legal strike, led by Jean-Claude Parrot. The government passed legislation ordering the workers to discontinue the strike or risk being penalized. In addition the legislation required the union's leaders to renounce the calling of the strike. Parrot refused to do so, arguing that it was a legitimate strike when he and his executive called for it and that it would infringe his freedom of speech and belief rights if he had to make a public statement that would be seen as an acknowledgement of wrongdoing in supporting a democratically agreed-to strike action. He was charged with a violation of the new legislation and jailed for three months.

Sample. In the United States a developer was found guilty of defrauding an Oregon Savings and Loan institution out of $55 million in the 1980s. The jury wanted a stiff jail term, but the presiding judge ignored the jury's wishes and in 1993 sentenced the developer to six months in a halfway house—not exactly a prison—and ordered the felon, who had ripped off all of those millions, to make restitution to the tune of $2 million. The prosecutor was outraged, and the judge explained his reasoning: "This man has unique ability. . . People who are able to accomplish what he has, if it can be done honestly, are also stimulating the economy of the country and helping those of us who are professionals to exist."

Sample. A.H. Robins put an intrauterine device known as the Dalkon Shield on the market, even though, during production, the corporation had documented that the tail end of the device had the potential to fray and disperse harmful bacteria into the user's body. It kept the device on the market even after reports appeared that it was connected to deaths, miscarriages, and injuries. Eventually the corporation was successfully sued, and it went into bankruptcy. In the United States alone, the Dalkon Shield was responsible for seventeen deaths and about two hundred thousand miscarriages and other injuries. The judge who presided over the civil litigation against A.H. Robins, the corporation, was outraged by the conduct of the corporation's chief managers (who appeared before him as witnesses but were not personal defendants). In a rather famous statement—famous because it was so unrepresentative of how judges tend to approach these cases—Judge Miles Lord wrote:

> It is not enough to say, "I did not know," "It was not me," "Look elsewhere." Time and again, each of you has used this kind of argument in refusing to acknowledge your responsibility and in pretending to the world that the chief officers and directors of your gigantic multinational corporation have no responsibility for its acts and omissions. . . .You have taken the bottom line as your guiding beacon and the low road as your route. . . .You, in essence, pay nothing out of your own pockets to settle these cases.

Despite this much-publicized judicial indignation, neither the corporation nor any of its managers were ever charged and, therefore, convicted of a criminal offence. Indeed, the civic leaders of Richmond, Virginia, the headquarters of A.H. Robins, threw at banquet for E. Clairborne Robins Sr., one of the men excoriated by Judge Lord. At the banquet, after much praise from the dignitaries, one of the top people behind the Dalkon Shield evildoing was given the Great American Tradition Award by his civic peers.

Sample. Asbestos manufacturers and processors knew about the lethal impact of their products for many years. Indeed, the potential hazards were commercially acknowledged by the private insurance industry, which, as early as 1918, had refused to sell life insurance policies to anyone who worked with asbestos. By the 1930s the asbestos producers had access to detailed and reliable scientific studies establishing the links between exposure to asbestos and asbestosis and other pulmonary diseases. The asbestos industry went out of its way to prevent this information from getting to the workers it employed. The industry doctored scientific reports and agreed with insurance companies, law firms, and some of its medical advisers to remain silent on the problems. By the time exposure came and mass litigation ensued, millions of people had been exposed to the poison—as many as 11.5 million in the United States alone and millions more throughout the rest of the world. Many of the exposed, perhaps as many as 18 per cent, would die painful deaths as a result. As early as 1976 the estimate in the United States was that three hundred thousand people would face premature deaths. Given that many more people later came forward to indicate their exposure, that figure may well have been an underestimation. In Europe, as well, the extent of the asbestos scourge has been recalculated. A 1999 issue of the *British Journal of Cancer* estimated that 250,000 people would contract mesothelioma, a rare disease associated with asbestos. The incidence of deaths by more common pulmonary diseases and cancers would be much higher. In the United States the corporations responded to the litigation explosion by seeking refuge in bankruptcy, and many afflicted workers and families would never recover compensation, let alone gain satisfaction from seeing some of the malefactors held criminally responsible. No one was ever charged with an offence, despite the telling of many lies and the hatching of many conspiracies over many years, despite the gravity of the consequences.

A Bad Fit: The Corporate Hand and the Criminal Glove

Corporate misconduct is clearly treated differently than is misfeasance by the poor, the marginal, workers, and, in general, ordinary citizens. It is not that the corporate conduct is unplanned; it is not that the consequences of the corporate conduct could not have been foreseen. Indeed, in some cases it was foreseen. It is not that the corporate conduct, in the cases presented here, did not clearly breach established standards of behaviour. The irony is that the liberal-democratic polity prides itself on its adherence to the rule of law and on the care it takes with the application of criminal law—to ensure evenhanded treatment and, thereby, the legitimacy of the system. But still it tolerates this apparent privileging of the corporate sectors.

To justify these seeming contradictions, the defenders of the status quo have to participate in some very fancy manoeuvrings. The whole phenomenon is not unlike those thousands of bad jokes spawned by the O.J. Simpson trial. One story went that when O.J. tried on the incriminating gloves and found that they did not fit him very well, he said, "Gee, maybe I didn't do it."

To attract the wrath of the criminal law, the impugned conduct must be a transgression of a rule that reflects our society's shared morality. Before the state can use its awesome coercive powers legitimately, it must establish that the offending conduct involved an *individual who intended to engage in it.* The emphasis, as we would expect in a liberal polity, is on the responsibility of individuals for their actions. This emphasis also dovetails with the basic premise of idealized market capitalism, which posits that we are all sovereign actors, capable of exercising our free will as we go about doing what nature demands, namely optimize our opportunities. Logically, therefore, we will be held responsible for how we exercise our individual choices.

This basic formulation of the constituent elements of criminal responsibility permits us to excuse those who do not have the mental capacity to make free choices and allows us to provide defences for people who acted in self-defence or under extreme provocation or, in egregious circumstances, out of undeniable necessity. In such circumstances criminal culpability does not attach because the transgressing individual did not have the freely formed intent, known as *mens rea* to lawyers, that demands criminal punishment.

It is easy to manufacture reasons that render corporations immune from the application of a branch of law that requires an individual to have committed an act with a subjectively wrongful intention. Unsurprisingly, defenders of the status quo and of the corporation's legitimacy have employed all of these many easily available arguments at various times. While most of those arguments have been rejected, over time a useful climate, from a corporate point of view, has been created. The application of criminal law to corporations continues to be seen as aberrational, as a matter requiring justification.

Initially the defenders contended that, because a crime required an intentional breach of a legal norm, a corporation could not be a criminal because it was merely an artifice created by the state. We should assume, so the defenders claimed, that the state would never empower its own creatures to act with evil intent. When this argument did not bite, the advocates offered a variant that had a somewhat longer shelf life: as a non-human, as a mere fiction, the corporation could not have a state of mind, nor could it carry out an act. This old—and now discredited—argument demonstrates, once again, that the captains of industry, finance, retail, and everything else, who use invisible friends to produce and protect their profits, are willing to resort to any argument, no matter how threadbare, how transparently insincere, to avoid responsibilities. Today, the same people, still seeking to avoid responsibility for acts committed via their invisible friends, make a diametrically opposed argument. Now they argue that if anyone is to be held responsible, it should be the corporations, rather than the human beings who act through them.

The courts began to make inroads on the "a fiction cannot commit a crime" contentions by holding that, if the offending conduct was the omission by a certain party to do something that the law required to be done by that party—for example, to build a bridge—a corporation could be held responsible for its failure to act because there was no requirement in that case to prove the intentional nature of the act. That courts even resorted to this logically feeble argument shows that they were looking for ways of pinning criminal responsibility on the creatures to which they had given legitimacy, corporations. This pressure resulted in the gradual expansion of the concept of corporate criminal responsibility. Next, courts went on to hold corporations criminally responsible if their conduct constituted a public nuisance in that it inconvenienced the public and/or breached a statutory standard; and if the statute merely stated that an offence was committed if the act was done, regardless of the actor's motive or state of mind—for example, trading on a Sunday when that act was forbidden by legislation.

What motivated the courts to extend the application of the strictures of the criminal law to corporations was their recognition, from the nineteenth century onwards, that corporations' activities had the capacity to impose a great deal of harm and costs on society if left unchecked. This acknowledgement of the need to hold corporations to account permeated the whole of the regulatory field—civil, administrative, or criminal—demonstrating the interconnectedness and complementary nature of the discrete spheres of regulation. Thus, in 1915, the British House of Lords held that a corporation could be held civilly liable for the damages its activities had inflicted on another person. This pronouncement came in an unusual civil case in which civil law, like criminal law, required some evidence of an intention to do an act by the defendant. The defendant corporation had taken the still fashionable point that it was incapable of forming an intention. The House of Lords held that it was sufficient to demonstrate that those who made the corporate decisions had the necessary intent. This intent would then be taken to be the intent of the corporation. The intention of the people who were characterized as the guiding mind and will of the corporation was to be attributed to the corporation. The corporation could now form an intention and do an act. This doctrine of attribution, which became known as the identification doctrine, was to become the way in which courts could determine whether corporations had formed the necessary intent to be held criminally responsible. But it would take a while before this radical civil ruling crystallized as the rule in criminal law.

After the House of Lords decision in the civil law case, corporations continued to make arguments as to why the criminal law proper should not be applied to them. Most of these arguments were technical and procedural and were relatively easy to overcome when the political will was mustered to do so. These arguments included the self-serving one that, as corporations had no body and no soul, punishment meant nothing to them. Flogging and incarceration, or deportation, made no sense; the stigmatization of a non-human was a nonsense. Accordingly, the argument went, other regulatory regimes, those that did not require the infliction of physical and psychic pain, should be deployed to control corporate behaviour. To counter these lines of defences to the application of criminal law to corporations, all the courts needed were amendments that gave them an arsenal of different sanctions, such as the right to fine instead of jailing, the right to make restitution orders, or the power to supervise reformed structures and future behaviour or to order the making of public apologies. Some of these measures were duly established; others are still being urged. In any case the arguments against applying criminal punishment to corporations were not ones based on principle. Their rebuttal required no rethinking of the fundamentals of criminal law.

Another argument maintained that to charge corporations criminally would deny them due process and, therefore, be unfair. The point made was that corporations, unlike human defendants, could not appear physically and could not confront their accusers directly—that is, corporations, because of their nature, could not be extended the safeguards that the criminal processes offered flesh and blood accused persons to help offset the might of the coercive state. This was an argument being put forth by the same group that contended that, because a corporation is not a human being, criminal law should not be applicable to it. Here, showing a certain unmitigated gall, the same sector was now claiming that the corporation should be granted the safeguards bestowed on human beings because of their very, well, human nature. Inevitably, this fanciful argument was trumped. The courts held that a corporation could indeed appear in court through its guiding mind and will and/or lawyers.

These and other similar made-up difficulties disappeared when the courts finally determined that they could no longer justify not applying criminal law to corporations. Evenhandedness in the justice system and the concrete impact of corporate harm mandated this change in approach. By 1941 a Canadian court had used the identification doctrine developed by the House of Lords in the 1915 English civil case to hold a corporation criminally responsible for a fraud committed through its leading director and executive. Since then neither legal principles nor technical difficulties have inhibited the uses of criminal law vis-à-vis the corporate vehicle, although the political will to do so remains a long way from being cemented in place. What is obvious, though, is that there was a pressing need to vanquish the long-standing corporate opposition to the potential employment of the state's most repressive weapon of regulation. The relative immunity of corporations from the criminal process tended to bring into view some delegitimating features of the corporate vehicle.

We have already touched on the spectacular deviances of Hoffman-La Roche, Reed Paper, and A.H. Robins, among others. The neglect and/or wilful disregard of well-known standards of behaviour attributed to countless other large corporations has caused grievous harm: Shell (allegedly associated with brutal repression in Nigeria), Union Carbide (of Bhopal fame), Dow (which had earned a nasty reputation for its production of Agent Orange before it cranked out malfunctioning breast implants), Ford Motor Company (manufacturer of the Pinto, which proved to be explosive rather than reliable), General Electric (leading light in the still notorious heavy electrical equipment conspiracy), and Johns-Manville (a leader amongst the asbestos killers). The shareholders in these and other corporations have little financial incentive to ensure that the managers involved behave legally, ethically, or decently. As investors who do not legally own the property used to do the harm, they have no personal responsibility for its deployment by the corporation's managers. Further, the privilege of limited liability means that they are unlikely to be seriously hurt by the losses incurred by the corporation should it be held responsible for the management's failure to make a profit as a consequence of the harm-doing or for the corporation's losses should it be made to pay damages to third parties or a fine to the government. In law, the shareholders are personally untouchable, which includes their private wealth. In law, then, the shareholders of wrong-doing corporations are irresponsible.

The position is little better when it comes to the managers who make the corporate decisions to carry out acts that we now want to characterize as criminal. Precisely because we identify these senior managers as the guiding minds and will of the corporation—that is, because we identify them as *the* corporation when they are thinking and acting on its behalf—they are not seen by law to be thinking and acting in their own right, as you and I would be, as ordinary, not incorporated human beings. Unless they expressly make the impugned conduct their own, it will be attributed to the corporation, not to them. In law, the senior managers who constitute the guiding mind and will of the invisible friends of the rich are, like the rich themselves, irresponsible.

Now we can see why Judge Miles Lord was so frustrated when confronting the major shareholders and managers of the feckless Dalkon Shield maker. The legal structure of the corporation deprived him of the tools to hold them responsible, as they should have been if the criminal and civil laws of the land could have been evenhandedly applied. He was faced by the fact that corporations are *criminogenic.* Just like some substances or chemicals that, by their very nature, without any malice, induce cancers and are, therefore, labelled carcinogenic, corporations, by their very nature, without any malice towards any particular victim, will engage in criminal behaviour. They will do so because there are no strong internal disincentives for them to do otherwise; while, at the same time, their single-minded goal—profit-maximization—which is also the driving motivation of the irresponsible shareholders, makes it rational for them to do so.

The early failure to hold corporations responsible for criminal activities, then, drew attention to the understanding that no one (not shareholders, not managers) was being held responsible for the evils inflicted on consumers, the environment, workers, and the markets. That is why the identification doctrines evolved and why the laying of criminal charges against corporations was eased. That is why, today, some of the barriers to bringing criminal charges against senior managers, the guiding minds and wills of corporations, are—as we shall see—being removed. Gradually, courts and legislators are distorting the legal construction of the corporation to make it amenable to the criminal process. But, precisely because the judicial and legislative responses have distorted, rather than changed, the legal structure of the corporation, the defenders of the status quo have not solved their problems. Corporations continue both to be anti-social and to evade legal responsibility for many acts. The corporate hand may have been twisted into shape to fit inside the criminal glove, but it still seeks to revert to its original, ill-fitting, shape.

Corporate Ugliness – Corporate Recidivism

Despite our new legal capacities to hold corporations responsible, every day corporations engage in anti-social and illegal behaviour, in the process inflicting an enormous amount of economic and personal harm. The full dimensions of the problem are hard to quantify, in part because our policy-makers, politicians, and most criminal law and criminology scholars concentrate their efforts on the evils of street crime. "Law and order," a favourite slogan of politicians of all stripes, focuses public attention on the need for safe neighbourhoods, on wars on drugs, and on morality plays such as assaults on pornography and prostitution. One of the consequences in a world of limited resources and unidimensional thinking is that there is no systematic collection of data in the realm of what is called "suite crime," or corporate crime. The difficulty of determining just how much corporate crime occurs on an everyday basis arises partly from a continuing sharp dis-agreement around definition: around, indeed, whether corporate criminality should be treated as crime at all.

Nevertheless, in the United States a 1980 study examined the annual law-abiding records of a great number of corporations and found that 40 per cent of the 582 largest industrial corporations had not been held culpable of an illegal act. In other words, a remarkable six out of ten corporations had at one time or another that year been engaged in an illegal activity. Some eighty-three of the guilty corporations had been found responsible in respect of more than five violations of the law in that year. If a flesh and blood human being possessed this kind of record, every law and order proponent in the land would be completely scandalized, and would make no bones about saying so. Yet record-breaking corporate wrongdoers continue to be held in high regard.

Part of the problem is that some of the various harms, and damages, resulting from corporate wrongdoing tend to be vastly different in kind from the results of so-called street or (what we think of as) ordinary crime. Brutal crimes, such as sexual assault, domestic violence, and murder, carry with them great, perhaps incalculable, psychic harms as well as bringing costs to the social fabric. But so too do the destruction of a piece of the environment and the pulverization of a community's way of life—as happened, for instance, to the Grassy Narrows and White Dog reserves because of Reed Paper's merciless dumping of poisonous mercury. These kinds of harms, because of their scale and their long-lasting effects, are arguably far graver and more destructive of the social good than anything produced from the ranks of individual street criminals, especially because much (but, of course, not all) street crime amounts to self-abuse by the perpetrators, such as drug and alcohol abuse and related dysfunctions.

In economic costs, the handiwork of burglars, muggers, and thieves—those mortals we are taught to fear because they act up in the streets—does not appear to be in the same league as the wrongdoing by corporations and the people who act under their umbrellas. A 1987 study of FBI statistics, for instance, found that the economic costs of robbery, burglary, and motor vehicle and other theft were insignificant when compared to the costs imposed by corporate monopolistic and standard-breaching manufacturing. A conservative estimate is that the economic costs of corporate wrongdoing are ten times greater than the costs generated by street criminals. One study cites the U.S. Bureau of National Affairs to make the point that this ten to one ratio does not include the economic costs of anti-trust violations. As the case of Hoffman-La Roche illustrates, these kinds of illegal activities are the biggest ticket items of all. Indeed, just one criminal act, the "Heavy Electrical Conspiracy" involving General Electric, Westinghouse, and other corporations that, at the time, formed the core of the respectable manufacturing sectors, cost the economy more than all the thefts committed in one year by the much-ballyhooed and despised street criminals. The dollar amounts involved in corporate rip-offs are gigantic. The price-fixing by major petroleum corporations in Canada between 1958 and 1978 took an extra $12 billion out of the pockets of consumers. A handful of corporations fraudulently manage to get their hands on some hundreds of millions, sometimes billions, of dollars at a time.

The dollar figures are one thing; the human costs are another. When people die in workplaces the cause is often a matter of corporate wrongdoing: exploding products, the release of deadly chemicals and pharmaceuticals, poisoned environments, reckless or violating conduct. Other less violent but no less costly crimes (both economically and in human suffering) are also rampant: systematic tax evasions; bribery (the Lockheed bribery scam of the mid-1970s not only led to anti-corruption legislation in the United States, but also brought down a Japanese prime minister and embarrassed a member of the Dutch royal family and the Italian government); and outright fraud on investors and depositors. The Savings and Loans scandal of the 1980s cost the U.S. economy a staggering amount of money; an estimate of the General Accounting Agency of the U.S. Congress placed the amount at a minimum of $352 billion and a maximum of $1.4 trillion—more than the total U.S. defence budget in 1989, when the calculations were made; and three and a half times more than the Saudi Arabia Gross National Product at the time. The recent Enron events—a more spectacular version of the Long-Term Credit rip-off of 1998 and the more modest Canadian-grown Bre-X and Royal Trust scams—are guesstimated by the well-respected economist Felix Rohatyn to have bilked investors to the tune of $90 billion, roughly the Gross National Product of Indonesia.

As well as these frequently recurring deviances inflicting economic harms, "our" corporations also use their ability to act across borders to do injury to "foreigners" when we—in the United States and Canada—will no longer tolerate some of their profit-seeking activities at home. They simply export their harm-causing activities and products, as Occidental Petroleum did when, after the production of its pesticide was found to have caused sterility amongst its workers, it produced and sold the product in countries that had not as yet proscribed it.

The other heavy element in this pattern of criminal behaviour is the rate of recidivism: the corporations that do wrong, that inflict harm, tend to do it not just once, but again and again. Corporate crime is not an aberration. The recidivism is of such a high order that if the "three strikes and you're out" rule were applied to the lists of corporations on the Fortune 500 or the Financial Post 1000, those lists would take up half as many pages of precious paper, and the rest of us would have so much less to admire.

When Hoffman-La Roche was caught conspiring to fix vitamin prices, it was certainly not the first time its reputation had been besmirched. In 1980 this corporation's Canadian branch was found guilty of a most unusual crime: it had been too generous. In order to kill off competition in the tranquillizer market, Hoffman-La Roche had given away vast amounts of Valium to hospitals and had provided monetary awards to doctors who prescribed the drug. This offence, called predatory pricing, is deemed anti-competitive in that it leads to monopolies and, then, to overcharging. Hoffman-La Roche's executives coldly calculated that, by giving away the product, not only could the company crowd out competitors, but it would also get medical advisers and hospitals into the habit of prescribing its drug. This is precisely the sort of drug-peddling that, when conducted out in those high-profile mean streets of America (or Canada), has led to those much-publicized wars on drugs. When it happens in corporate corridors, again what we get it mostly silence and a return to business as usual.

Hoffman-La Roche's attempts to create monopolies for its tranquillizing products were not confined to Canada. The Monopolies Commission in the United Kingdom also found evidence of similar tactics there on the part of the company. In addition, the commission found, the corporation had falsified its manufacturing and processing costs to justify vastly overmarked prices. Hoffman-La Roche presented its calculated costs to monitoring government bodies after its subsidiaries had created a paper trail of transfer costs that were grossly out of whack with the actual costs incurred by the company—a practice apparently adopted everywhere. In this way, in Canada it managed to inflate its selling prices by some 140 times the original costs and 20 times the total costs of production. This highly desired ability to over-charge is assisted not just through the falsification of records but also by eliminating competitors. False documentation goes hand-in-hand with anti-competitive practices. In England, after eight years of litigation arising out of its deceptive practices, Hoffman-La Roche had to agree to roll back prices by 50 per cent and to repay some of its excess profits. Germany, the Netherlands, and Denmark also confronted the company over similar shady practices.

Given this atmosphere of "anything goes" created at Hoffman-La Roche's headquarters in Switzerland, we shouldn't be so surprised to find that deviant behaviour also occurs on the company's peripheries. For instance, its officers in Kenya bribed government pharmaceutical buyers to purchase its products. The bribes led to the jailing of the government officials—though not of the Hoffman-La Roche employees. The government, through its bribe-accepting officials, had contracted to buy enough Hoffman-La Roche products to last it for ten years, even though most of the products acquired would become unusable after two years. This lack of interest in the well-being of consumers also showed up in Morocco, where two Hoffman-La Roche executives were jailed. Their offence was to have erased the expiry dates on their products, enabling them to continue to sell the drugs long after they were deemed safe to use. In the meanwhile, in Seveso, Italy, a Hoffman-La Roche subsidiary was involved in one of the most deadly spills of toxic materials ever recorded in Italy. Eventually two executives were jailed, although the corporation itself was acquitted on appeal. Stanley Adams, an ex-senior executive of Hoffman-La Roche, turned whistle-blower to provide information on the incident.

Prior to that, the same Stanley Adams had reported to the European Economic Community (EEC) that his employer had systematically engaged in falsifying transfer-pricing documents, in collusive market-sharing with sup-posed competitors, and in giving illicit rebates to favoured customers, among other shady practices, all in violation of the EEC's trading rules. Amazingly, the EEC gave the identity of the whistle-blower to Hoffman-La Roche. Shortly thereafter, Stanley Adams was charged with treason against the Swiss Confederation, Hoffman-La Roche's host nation, and later by Italian authori-ties for the commission of ill-defined crimes. He was jailed in Italy after losing his business and his family, without ever having been given a satisfactory explanation for his imprisonment. The EEC did pay him some compensation.

The Stanley Adams story, which is not yet over, has become something of a minor *cause célèbre* amongst civil liberty advocates in Europe. It is a story that highlights not only the pervasive deviance of this large pharmaceutical corporation, but also its ability to enlist the power of the state despite its record as a major recidivist. When the Canadian court found Hoffman-La Roche guilty of predatory pricing, it imposed a fine of $50,000 (the company had given away $2 million worth of Valium by then). To the court's way of thinking, to give things away could not be seen as evil, and the company's executives were decent people working for a decent corporation that was promising to clean up its act and thereby avoid a repeat of this odd failure to abide by the law. The court, it would seem, was not aware of Hoffman-La Roche's full history, and the court functionaries may not have read a book written by one of the company's former executives, who recorded that the corporation's connections to illegal drug-peddling between the wars was so well-known that the League of Nations Opium Advisory Committee had been advised that the corporation "was not a firm to which a licence to deal with drugs should be given."

The Exxon corporation provides another ready example of major recidivism. This is the company whose ill-equipped, overloaded, poorly maintained, badly captained container ship, the *Exxon-Valdez*, had despoiled the coast of Alaska in March 1989. Exxon's role in that violation of all the anti-pollution rules of civil, administrative, and criminal law, is notorious; but it is only one in a long list of peccadillos involving this giant corporation. In January 2001, for instance, Exxon agreed to pay U.S.$7 million to settle claims arising out of the underpayment of royalties for oil extracted from federal lands. (Some nine other oil companies were found doing the same thing.) The underpayment had occurred because Exxon had misstated the amount of oil extracted. This was not a one-off, regrettable, happening that came as a surprise to this huge corporation. A month earlier Exxon had been ordered to pay $3.5 billion to the Alabama state government after a court found that ExxonMobil internal documents showed that the company considered Alabama to be inexperienced in the natural gas business and determined that it could get away with underpaying the neophyte government. To this end, it had deliberately misstated its levels of extraction to avoid paying royalties to the state. If this practice had gone undetected, the corporation would have "earned" an extra $1 billion over thirty years.

A different brand of Exxon flim-flammery occurred in the Hudson River scam. In the summer of 1983 Exxon decided that its refinery at Aruba, near the coast of Venezuela, was short of fresh water. The company found a nice way around this problem. Its tankers plying the Hudson River would discharge the sea water they carried as ballast into the river; and, after rinsing, the tanks would be filled with fresh Hudson River water. This cheap way of finding a water supply for the Aruba operations removed a few hundred million gallons of water from the upper reaches of the Hudson River yearly. It polluted the river and imposed large clean-up costs on governments and financial costs on fishing people.

Occidental Chemical was yet another chillingly bloody-minded recidivist, beginning with its involvement in the infamous Love Canal saga. The company's subsidiary Hooker Chemic Company had dumped chemical hazardous waste into a huge trench near Niagara Falls, New York, over a ten-year period. The owner of that same trench sold the land to a school board. Neither the vendor nor the school board told anyone about the land's virulent potential, and the horrible fallout came when a housing estate was built on the land. The incidences of cancers, skin diseases, and other illnesses, as well as catastrophic property losses, were so great that the words "Love Canal" became synonymous with environmental disaster. The corporation that did the dumping did so in full knowledge that it was breaching pollution regulations. A subsequent Congressional Inquiry found that the company's top managers had been aware of the problems presented by the chemicals and even when they came to know that the chemicals were escaping from the ground still did not warn residents of the dangers. The corporation's managers had fudged test results to hide the inculpating data from the environmental authorities.

The same Congressional Inquiry noted that, in California, Occidental Chemical had knowingly and illegally dumped pesticides that endangered children in the area of its operations and had not warned anyone because this might cause it to incur substantial legal liabilities. The same corporation had contaminated water in Lathrop, California, by its deliberate illegal dumping of waste materials. Once again, the corporation's officials had deliberately misled government agents about its practices. On another occasion Occidental Chemical hid a scientific test that showed that one of its products caused testicular atrophy in rats, and the company continued to expose its workers to the substance, which led to internal bleeding and extraordinary rates of sterility amongst the workers. After the product was banned from certain uses in California, Occidental Chemical exported the noxious substance to countries oblivious of its dangers or without the regulatory power to keep it out.

In the year 2000 the City of Toronto was trying to deal with a major problem: the disposal of its ever-growing piles of garbage. One of the proposals, eventually rejected for diverse political reasons, was to transport the garbage to an abandoned Northern mine, the Adams Mine, near Kirkland Lake, Ont., and to have it processed there. The operator of the disposal site would be a subsidiary of the world's largest waste disposal corporation, Waste Management Inc.

The opposition of this plan did some research and found that Waste Management Inc. had some character flaws. The company had been criminally convicted ten times in five U.S. states, paying more than $5 million in fines. It had been convicted of twenty-three price-fixing offences in twenty-three states. It had been convicted of twenty-two environmental regulation offences and another eighty-seven vaguely described administrative offences. In addition, it had been found guilty of defrauding its own investors. As well, it had been forced to arrange a deal with shareholders who had accused the corporation of inflating its stock prices by lying about its earnings. That settlement alone cost the corporation $220 million. Still, the Toronto administration—led by a group with a "law and order" orientation—was fully prepared to enter into a contract with this corporation, whose criminal record makes most Snicker bar thieves look rather respectable.

This is hardly an unusual story: recidivism does not inhibit corporate profit-seekers. Thus, in the year 2000 a great deal of anxiety came to the fore concerning revelations that certain Firestone tires were fitted on certain vehicles that had been rolling over regularly, leading to a number of deaths and serious injuries. Firestone had allegedly known about its tires' defects for some time as reports of accidents had rolled in from all over the world—from North America, Saudi Arabia, and Venezuela, among other places. Rather than initiate a recall, the company had determined to "ride it out." Eventually the parent corporation was forced to issue a public recall. For those with long memories, this recent story, as yet unfinished, has an uncanny resemblance to certain events of the mid-1970s, when Firestone placed a steel-belted radial tire on the market. One year after the tire went on sale, the director of development at Firestone told the board of directors that the tire would have a tendency to belt-edge separation. In turn, Firestone did nothing—or, rather, it did a lot. It continued to sell the tire for another five years, issuing no warnings, neither to government nor to consumers. It sold some twenty-four more million tires. There were a huge number of "accidents," and eventually the federal government would attribute at least forty-one deaths and many more injuries to the proneness of the tires to blowout.

Firestone was also one of the conspirators that set out to wreck the public transport systems in some of the largest cities in the United States—and largely succeeded in this endeavour. The conspirators, who in the end pleaded guilty to charges of criminal conspiracy, cooked up a scheme that inveigled cash-strapped municipalities to have their public transport systems run by a certain bus company, one of the conspirators. As a result of these transactions, the municipalities discarded electric railways and other such non-automobile conveyances, and automobile, oil, and tire sales in those communities were exponentially increased. Pollution, energy waste, the cost of insurance, and the cost of traffic jams and accidents also increased: no small feat. One of Firestone's co-conspirators was Mobil—now merged with Exxon, one of our chosen recidivists—and the other was General Motors. When General Motors pleaded guilty to criminal conspiracy, it was fined the princely sum of $5,000.

General Motors has also, not surprisingly, shown recidivist tendencies. One of its better known acts of mischief—better known because one of its former luminaries, John DeLorean, revealed the facts—was its shoddy production of the Corvair in the early 1960s. The GM engineers involved knew that car had rear-end suspension problems that made it—in the phrase that has become part of idiomatic language—"unsafe at any speed." Even though its own engineers cited its product as a rolling time bomb, General Motors refused to recall the car. Indeed, General Motors kept on telling the world that the allegations and rumours about the Corvair were completely unfounded, when it knew otherwise. As a result, many people were killed and many others suffered serious injuries. The only conclusion to be drawn is that injuring and killing are part of this major corporation's modus operandi.

The Corvair story had a reprise when Ford Motor put the Pinto on the market. The car maker decided not to recall a car it had made to be competitive in the small-car market for the next ten years, even though its tests had revealed that its placement of the gas tank at the very back of the trunk meant that the car would be engulfed in flames if anyone collided with its rear end at very low speeds. The company made a calculated decision not to place an $11 barrier around the tank to substantially diminish the risk, because the added fixture in total would cost more than the expected compensation that would have to be paid to people immolated in burning Pintos over the car's market lifetime. Although the manufacturer was eventually charged criminally, it escaped criminal responsibility because of the way in which the presiding judge framed the legal issue, rather than because Ford was morally blameless. The recidivist General Motors, supposedly Ford's fierce competitor, sent Ford a congratulatory letter when Ford was acquitted.

General Motors, like the rest of mainstream corporations, was appalled that business decisions made to protect profits and that led to death and economic harm could be treated as immoral. After all, Ford had made a routine decision, no more, no less. It had been the kind of decision made regularly by all companies in their business practice, and one that Ford had made in the past without being labelled leprous. In the 1970s Ford Motors had produced a number of models with transmission design flaws, causing the cars to slip into reverse without warning. The company's customers were not warned, even though, in 1971, internal memos warned company officials about the defective design. The company did nothing until 1979, by which time 98 deaths, 1,710 injuries, and thousands of consumer complaints had been recorded.

Ford was also heavily implicated in the more recent Firestone "tire tragedy" of 2000. The auto company used Firestone tires as standard equipment on its Explorer four-wheel-drive SUV, as well as on other passenger cars. Ford management noticed a certain number of recurring accidents with the Explorer, with the vehicles rolling over more than might have been expected. The executives and managers kept any concerns to themselves, not wanting to tell the markets that its vehicles were unstable, at least not until they had irrefutable proof to that effect. By the end of the year more than one hundred people had died as a result of accidents with the Explorer, and by mid-2001 the Firestone tires were being linked to 203 traffic deaths and more than seven hundred injuries in the United States. Many lawsuits were pending against Firestone and its owner, Bridgestone Tire and Rubber Corporation. Ford eventually blamed Firestone for having supplied bad tires, whereas Firestone eagerly pointed to Ford's faulty SUV designs to explain away the "accidents"—in which people die and get injured—that were occurring when cars with Firestone tires inexplicably went into rollovers. If there had been no human costs in this affair, it might have been amusing to watch these recidivists turn on each other.

These and all the similar stories that might be told, backed by the more lifeless aggregate data, indicate the scope of the problem: massive wrongdoing, with a great deal of recidivism. In his pioneering study of what he called the criminal careers of the seventy largest corporations in the United States, Edwin H. Sutherland determined that there had been an average of fourteen registered convictions for offences against each of those corporations. Rather scathingly, he described them as akin to habitual criminals. Many years later, in 1980, Marshall Clinard and Peter Yeager's similar findings recorded that, of the 60 per cent of large corporations that had committed crimes annually, 42 per cent had been charged with more than one violation and 25 per cent had been charged with multiple cases of non-minor violations; 83 of the major corporations studied had been found responsible for more than five violations of the law in the year of study. A few years later, in a study of the commission of crimes by *Fortune 500* companies, the team of Kesner, Victor, and Lamont found that the mean for firms engaged in illegal activities was three acts. Deviant behaviour by large, publicly traded corporations is a common occurrence. Recidivism is far from aberrational; indeed, it is almost the norm.

Theoretical Explanations, Incontrovertible Facts

The most obvious feature of corporate deviance is that it is fundamentally different from the illegal activities engaged in by individuals who commit assaults, murders, robberies, thefts, or abuse, or who deal in drugs. Such people break the law not only to suit themselves, but because they want to hurt others. These individuals will therefore be excused from any finding of wrongdoing if they are shown to have lacked the necessary malicious intent, the *mens rea*. They will be excused if they were coerced or incompetent or had to defend themselves or were provoked. Other than that, society holds them responsible for their acts. They are stigmatized and made to pay very serious penalties if their behaviour breaches our norms. Why, then, do people ever engage in such behaviours? The literature fairly bristles with explanations. Some analysts point to biological factors, such as certain bumps on people's heads that indicate that they are prone to criminal behaviour; or they suffer from chromosome imbalances or have a peculiar psychiatric disposition. These causal explanations are not all that far removed from the more ancient views that deviance and evildoing were committed by bewitched persons. Some explanations for deviance are sociological and psychological. For instance, the strain theory as to why people commit crimes is posited on the idea that we all have a relatively fixed amount of emotional drive that must be released. When there is no outlet, some people may act out, and engage in prohibited, that is, criminal, conduct. Variants include the argument that if individuals are taught to aim for certain goals and feel frustrated because they cannot reach them, their frustration can lead them up the criminal path. Others may suffer from anomie, or be influenced by the people they associate with and become part of criminal subcultures; they may be labelled in particular ways and then try to live up to the label. Or all of these causes may act in mysteriously synergetic ways.

However elaborate these causal theories of criminality may be, the distinct nature of corporations makes such explanations inapposite. As E.H. Sutherland wrote over fifty years ago: "We have no reason to think that General Motors has an inferiority complex or that the Aluminium Company of America has a frustration-aggression complex, or that U.S. Steel has an Oedipus complex, or that Armour Company has a death wish or that the Duponts desire to return to the womb." Corporations engage in deviant, harmful behaviour because it suits their agenda. They set out to maximize profits. They are legally created for that purpose. Indeed, they are legally constructed to facilitate the exercise. As part of that, corporate law, by creating incentives for both shareholder and managerial passivity—limited financial risk and personal immunity for responsibility—has emptied the corporation of moral and ethical constraints that might otherwise inhibit profiteering at any cost.

Still, why do directors, managers, and employees of a corporation engage in wrongful conduct on behalf of the corporation, conduct that they might well eschew as unincorporated individuals? Again, the scholarly literature dealing with this issue is voluminous and refined. A causal explanation might centre on the observable fact that large, publicly traded corporations are extremely complex in structure, with many divisions operating with relative autonomy from one another and often created as legally—if not functionally—discrete corporations acting as subsidiaries of a common parent corporation. This intricate, tangled organizational architecture can lead to a lack of oversight at the various levels of management, especially as you get closer to the top. Each division is under pressure "to perform optimally." The management of each division is given the impression that the corporation as a whole does not much care how that optimal performance is achieved, a condition that creates a structural recipe for a flouting of legally mandated, but profit-inhibiting, behaviour. The arrangement is further complicated because the eventual law-breaching conduct may be the cumulative result of a series of small decisions, each of which is innocent enough if not put in the context of the driven-for result. There is little incentive for overseeing managers of a division to provide a context for all the contributing actors and decision-makers. Often, then, it is difficult to pinpoint who in particular might have actually committed a wrongful act, with the appropriate intention. Diffusion and delegation serve both the goals of efficiency and the not-so-worthy abdication of responsibility.

Then, too, the explanations go, when some individuals do knowingly engage in deviant behaviour, they may believe (whether sincerely or not) that their actions are not reprehensible. The corporate culture may have taught them that the legal restraints are unwarranted. Sometimes, perhaps often, managers become corporate creatures, to some degree alienated from mainstream society and conventions. Through their work they form certain tight bonds, perhaps as a result of frequent movement from one corporate site to another, or from associations with peers and memberships in the same associations and clubs. As a result, they see the world through a corporate glaze; profit-maximization at virtually any cost becomes an incontestably good thing. As well, rational managers who make decisions that lead to violations may calculate that the profits yielded by the illegality will earn them kudos now, while the fallout of discovery of the wrongs done will come long after they have left the organization.

The very search for these many causal explanations for the deviant behaviour exhibited by those who act for the corporation indicates above all else that for these people, for their wrongdoing, the standard explanations relating to individuals as suffering from strain, frustration, anomie, or lack of conventional bonds, or as being victims of labelling theories, and so on, do not work. They have no plausibility. In the end, though, despite all the scholarly explanations, we are left with a few incontrovertible facts:

(i)   the large corporation is *legally* constructed so as to become a site of irresponsibility and, thereby, criminogenic; and

(ii) the large corporation has spawned internal structures that make it logical for the actors within the corporation to take deviant actions if this leads to profits, even if the human, environmental, social, and economic costs are horrific; and

(iii) the large corporations' deviance profits flesh and blood entrepreneurs who, for the most part, are able to proclaim their ignorance of wrongdoing, their lack of blame, while pocketing the ill-gotten proceeds.

The examples furnished in this necessarily abbreviated account support these contentions. In the stories told, the corporations and their decision-makers acted after a degree of planning. Often they knew the harm they would do and understood they would be in breach of existing legal norms, let alone ethical ones. Sometimes their initial conduct may have been careless or reckless, rather than premeditated, but then, having found out that they had committed a wrong, they compounded their culpability by hiding, lying, or falsifying. Wrongful corporate behaviour is, more often than not, systematic. H.C. Barnett documented how corporations tend to commit those crimes that relieve their particular market difficulties. For instance, manufacturers are much more likely to breach environmental laws than are corporations involved in distribution industries; while service industrial corporations are more likely to violate trade regulations than are manufacturers. It is, in other words, the need to capitalize on their opportunities that drives corporations to criminality. They are rational calculators. Thus some market circumstances have been termed criminogenic. For instance, one well-known study documented how the automobile manufacturers' ability to control the profitability and livelihood of their franchised dealers caused those dealers to cheat their customers and, occasionally, their franchisors. They were impelled to take these tremendous risks because the contractual demands made on them by the franchisors negated their potential for profit-making.

Contrary to some arguments, I would contend that the capitalist agenda, as pursued via the large corporation, causes corporate actors to violate supposedly precious laws and norms. The evidence gathered here indicates that corporate skulduggery is aided and abetted by the dominance of this agenda in mature liberal democracies. It is this dominance that causes us to treat deviance benignly. When this comes into plain view, a legitimacy problem arises for the wealthy ensconced in their corporate cocoons. The next chapter considers just how they deal with this problem.

"It's Not a Crime" – Reclassifying Corporate Deviance

Wherein we learn that the captains of industry, finance, retail, and everything else get their invisible friends to take the blame for violations of rules at the same time as these violations have come to be seen as minor infractions of the law of the land, actions that carry no stigma and attract a more friendly police force, regardless of the actual harms done by, or the moral bankruptcy of, the captains of everything who made the corporation "do it."

The puzzle is why the world is not more outraged by the substantial record of harm and damage inflicted by large, publicly traded corporations— conduct that, in lay terms, would be labelled criminal. To the contrary, often these same corporations maintain a place of great respect in our polity; and their major shareholders and managers, who lurk behind the strategically placed veils, are seen as the *crème de la crème* of our society. They, unlike our robbers, thieves, rapists, drug users and peddlers, and vagrants, are bound to be on the "A" list of invitees to all the important political and social gala events. Corporate deviance has been redefined and recast in a way that averts the stigma that would be attached to corporations and corporate bigwigs, and to the capitalism they serve, if those deviant acts were dealt with as

144

if they were what they truly are: unspeakably repugnant behaviour on a par with, or worse, than most street crime.

There are two related sets of reasoning and policy decision-making that deflect social disapproval from the large corporations and their managers that engage in deviant behaviour. The first, law-related, stems from the legal treatment of the corporation as if it were a person and from the associated legal starting point that criminal law is devised to control individual behaviour. Inasmuch as this first reason for the problem is a technical matter, it is correctable. But there are limits to the extent of the correction possible. They arise out of the second reason that renders the corporate sector relatively immune to the strictures of criminal law. This one is a structural matter, founded on the nature of the belief system that underpins our political economy. This belief system does not envisage that the corporation, as capitalism's primary vehicle, or its major movers and shakers, as the drivers of that vehicle, are to be subjected to a regime of law designed to regulate non-capitalists. Because this rationale cannot be acknowledged in a political setting that claims to be devoted to the legal equality of all individuals, a great deal of effort has gone into the development of an ideological support system for a separate regime of legal regulation of capitalists (mainly to favour large corporate capitalism, although the tenets of liberalism demand that it be seen as applicable to small-business firms as well as to individuals).

The contention then becomes that, given the availability of this alternative scheme to control corporate behaviour, the differential application of criminal law proper that seems to favour large corporate actors is no longer a blight on the legal/political scheme. There should hardly be any need to rely on criminal law to attain our social ends when corporations violate established standards; corporations can be more appropriately disciplined by other means. Acceptance of this proffered line of reasoning instantly relieves the corporate sectors of any stigma attached to the harms arising out of their profit-chasing activities. Name-calling, such as the labelling of corporate wrongdoers as "criminals" or "recidivists" becomes inapposite. Certainly, this is not a bad trick if it can be executed. The corporate sectors' champions expend a lot of effort, therefore, on turning the trick that legitimates the reclassification of corporate wrongdoing.

The Nature of Criminal Law vs. the Nature of the Corporation

The corporation is an aggregation of once-separate capitals, assets, investors (equity and credit suppliers), managers, and workers. The law's need to *pretend* that the corporation is an individual, so that it can hold property and to purport to act as a stereotypical market participant, does not make it an individual in fact. But this pretence that the corporation is an individual, which makes run-of-the-mill criminal law notionally applicable to it, raises questions when criminal law is not applied to corporate actors in circumstances that would lead to the use of that law against real individuals. Pretending, however, is for those who want to avoid the objective facts of life. To treat the corporation—especially the large, publicly traded corporation—as an individual is a distortion of reality. The consequence is that when calls are made to employ criminal law sanctions against corporations because they are just individuals, there is an hesitancy, a reluctance. Something unnatural is about to be done.

Still, there has been considerable pressure to make criminal law applicable to corporate deviance. That deviance has been recorded; it occurs frequently, does a huge amount of harm, and the conduct often ignites public anger and resentment. Our social values are perceived as having been assaulted by corporations and their often well-known, but legally invisible, managers and shareholders. There is an expectation that the state should use its most stigmatizing and coercive legal weaponry, the criminal process, to set things right. The courts and legislatures developed the identification doctrine as a means of tackling this problem, but in doing so failed to address the underlying causes, instead creating a myriad of new and very practical difficulties.

In the first place, ere the corporation can be held culpable, "the law" has to find the persons to be described as *the guiding mind and will*, and the justice system must then prove that these people have engaged in criminal conduct. Investigators and prosecutors are then confronted by difficult evidentiary questions. Who did the act? Was it the same person who had the required subjective intention, the *mens rea*? And, if so, was this person (or set of persons) senior enough in the particular structural organization of this corporation to enable any personal action and intention to be attributed to the corporation? These issues are further bedevilled by the lack of jurisprudence firmly establishing which human being will be adjudged to be an actor who may be characterized as the guiding mind and will of the corporation. Courts waffle on the issue. In Canada we are willing to go lower down in the hierarchy of a corporation than are the English or Australians to find the guiding mind and will, but not as far down as some of the U.S. states. The question, our appellate courts keep on telling investigators and prosecutors, is to be decided on a case by case basis. This approach enormously increases the difficulties of the investigators and prosecutors. They are naturally chary of putting scarce resources into complex corporate investigations and charges if it remains likely that the wrongdoing they think they may find will, in the end, not be attributable to the corporation whose conduct they want to have judicially condemned. The quandary this poses is aggravated by the fragmentation of decisions and actions in large, publicly traded corporations, some of which are organized, supposedly for efficiency, as a group of affiliated but separate corporations. Often, distinct legal entities operate under the same general corporate umbrella, so that, in the end, a multitude of people—not always legally linked—play a role in the thinking and doing that, together, make up the corporate conduct that is the object of investigation. The authorities find it difficult to identify any one person, let alone the requisite senior person, as having had the legally required intention and hands-on participation. Incidentally, this also makes it extremely difficult to hold individual executives responsible for criminal conduct engaged in as executives on the basis that their action shows that they intended the conduct that caused the corporation to violate the law to be conduct for which they would be personally responsible. It will be easier, of course, when the corporation is a small, closed organization in which the directors, major managers, and employees are basically the same group of people. This goes some way towards explaining why so few directors and executives are criminally charged when a large corporation's conduct has breached our laws.

This was the reason that Judge Miles Lord was so frustrated in the Dalkon Shield case. He believed that the directors and executives who appeared as witnesses in the civil case against A.H. Robins ought to have been held responsible, but no civil actions or criminal charges had been brought against them. While we do not know why that did not happen, it is plausible that litigants and prosecutors deemed it too difficult to pin, on senior managers in a very large corporation, a participatory role related to the final fatal outcome of a great number of more or less neutral decisions taken, and acts done, in many divisions and departments. The resulting failure of many prosecutors to bring charges against corporate executives often leaves judges, like Judge Lord, presiding over a trial of a humanless corporation with a feeling of uselessness and impotence.

A less emotive, but equally palpable, irritation was shown by Chief Justice Evans of the Ontario Supreme Court when he had to deal with Amway Corporation's fraud on the Government of Canada, a case that went to court in the early 1980s. The brunt of the charge, to which the Amway Corporation pleaded guilty, was that by means of a web of shell companies, dummy invoices, false price lists, and fraudulent oral and written representations (the same sort of tactics used by Hoffman-La Roche to whip up prices in England and Canada), the corporation had avoided $30 million worth of customs and excise levies. The prosecution, in return for a guilty plea by the corporation, had dropped its charges against the senior managers—who were also major shareholders in this huge corporation. This plea bargaining, which enables senior managers to avoid responsibility for corporate conduct that they initiated or controlled, is commonplace. It is clear why managers like it. Its popularity with prosecutors stems, in part, from the prosecutors' difficulty of proving who carried out the act with the appropriate criminal intent and, in part, from the difficulty of proving that the guiding mind and will of the corporation, and therefore the corporation itself, had behaved illegally, without the co-operation of the people who make up the guiding mind and will. While plea bargaining with the individuals who might have been guilty of bad behaviour in their own right may lead to the conviction of a corporation, it leaves a bad taste in the mouth. Precisely because a corporation cannot be shamed, because the need for revenge is not easily satisfied by seeing a corporation pay a fine while its activist managers and shareholders remain unscathed, this partial result is a most unsatisfactory state of affairs, one that revives the spectre of lack of evenhandedness in the criminal justice system. Undoubtedly, this turn of affairs is what fuelled Chief Justice Evans's anger. Those whom he perceived to be the real miscreants were not before him as accused persons. He wrote:

> One can hardly say that these are good corporate citizens. . . . Mr. Humphreys [the corporation's lawyer] has given . . . his usual very excellent presentation in mitigation, that these are men who are very responsible citizens in the United States. Well, they weren't very responsible corporate directors in Canada. The pleas of guilty on behalf of the defendants has undoubtedly saved the cost of the lengthy trial. However, this is a sort of death-bed confession of guilt. It comes of the—as we are getting close to trial, after many months of preparation and much expense on behalf of the Crown and of course there is another side to the coin, the pleas have enabled the accused to avoid the heavy costs to which they would have been exposed, had this matter continued to trial.

Not grammatical, but very clear.

In addition to (i) the problems created by the ill fit between a regime of law that is posited on the sovereign decision-making of a flesh and blood individual and a regime of law that wants to advance collective economic activities while purporting that the collectivity it calls a corporation is engaged in market endeavours, which are just like individuals' efforts, and to (ii) the evidentiary problems that investigators and prosecutors face, an ideological bias exists against the institution of criminal charges against corporate actors. This bias saturates the efforts of the police forces, prosecutorial offices, and policy-making institutions. This ideological bias exacerbates the evidentiary difficulties that the prosecutors need to resolve and goes some way towards explaining why it is that, on the relatively few occasions that corporations and/or their managers are held criminally responsible, the punishments are so slight. This inhibiting mindset stems from some deep structural understandings of our political economy and is, therefore, not an ideological perspective that will be easily shed.

Class-Based Corporate Capitalism vs. Consensus-Based Criminal Law

Criminal law is reserved for intentional violations of those values that constitute our social fabric, those values that reflect our shared morality. While we are clear that it is wrong for individuals to kill others without an appropriate reason, such as self-defence, or without lack of capacity to form the requisite intent, and we know that it is wrong for individuals to assault other persons physically or sexually, not much else is clear. Shared morality is an elusive concept. Indeed, serious scholars offer mushy definitions. In one of the more famous formulations of the dominant approach, Lord Devlin argued that we know that conduct needs to be treated as criminal when the reasonable man or woman thinks the conduct is unacceptable to our moral fabric and threatens to tear that fabric. How we are to know who the reasonable person is, what she or he thinks, or whether or not this thinking is reasonable is left to be determined by luminaries such as Lord Devlin, to politicians and to judges. This kind of formulation leaves everything up in the air and, worse, subject to manipulation.

When it suited the times, those in power treated witchcraft as a heinous criminal offence because of its supposed threat to the social fabric. For a long time gambling, now the lifeblood of many governments, was seen as a similar threat. Our essential value system is a moveable feast. It makes little sense from a historical perspective and little sense at any one time. Today's criminal law bristles with offences that make no sense if the basis for criminalizing conduct is that it offends our supposed shared morality.

It is a crime to sell or to use proscribed substances, that is, drugs. Heroin, cocaine, marijuana, and crack-cocaine are out. Not only are peddling and abuse of these drugs criminal offences, but they are also serious offences, which preoccupy our police forces, courts, legislatures, and politicians.

People who sell and use these drugs are treated as moral lepers and, there-fore, as criminals. But people who sell or use tobacco are not criminals. The harm inflicted by tobacco on social programs such as health care and on individuals who use the product (actively and passively) exceeds the harm inflicted by the sale and use of proscribed drugs. So it cannot be the conse-quences of selling and using these drugs that cause us to wage full-scale policing wars on proscribed drug-users and sellers. This leaves us with the embarrassing proposition that the selling and use of the proscribed drugs are justifiably criminalized because that selling and use offend our shared moral-ity, whereas the selling and use of tobacco products do not. This reasoning is patently absurd, because it cannot possibly be the case that the peddling of some sources of harm that lead to addiction are morally more offensive than the vending of other substances that have the same adverse effects, often to a worse degree. It could be argued that this absurd proposition jibes with the views of most contemporary reasonable persons, and that this condition justi-fies the criminalization of heroin sales, but not of tobacco vending, which would accord with the view that conventional thinkers, such as Devlin, take of how we define our shared morality. But this is argument is at best an unconvincing cop-out. It might well be the case that the reasonable person's view was produced over the long term by the initial decision to criminalize one set of drugs and not the other; that is, that the logic is upside down.

There are many examples of such inverted logic. Indeed, it is safe to say that the contradictions are the norm, rather than the exception. For instance, we could make the same comparison between the immorality of selling and using heroin and the apparent moral legitimacy of selling an addictive and hazard-creating substance like alcohol or, perhaps less obviously, Valium. After all, the Hoffman-La Roche predatory pricing crime in Canada (chapter 8) was not the socially endangering act of making Valium more readily avail-able and more of a habitual drug, but rather the anti-capitalist act of giving away—*free*—something that had a commercial value. To take another exam-ple, today the charging of interest on loaned money to the fullest extent allowed by the market and the law is a very respectable way of making money. Who is more righteously proud of his role as a pillar of society than a banker? Yet only a short time ago, in historical terms that is, usury, the charg-ing of interest, was considered the most despicable of activities, one worthy of bearing the full brunt of criminal law. And even today, based on this not-so-very-old perspective, church activists and other moral leaders are calling into question the propriety of the International Monetary Fund's and World Bank's legally endorsed enforcement of the debts, with their ever-increasing interest burdens, against poor countries. Yet the lending of capital to earn interest remains one of our most prestigious activities. It is in no danger of being criminalized by any modern politician. How did our supposed shared morality change so abruptly, so quickly?

The answer to these apparent conundrums is that the undefined shared morality that justifies the use of the state's coercive criminal law powers turns out to reflect the premises of the dominant ideology at any given time. At the present time, it reflects the needs of a matured capitalism. The term "shared morality" is not a scientific one, but a slogan that hides the highly politicized nature of an exercise that classes certain conduct as criminal and certain actors as criminals. The people who hold the balance of power—whether the power is economic or political (or more likely, both)—are not likely to want to have their everyday activities described as being criminal or to be stigmatized for doing what the current dominant practice requires them to do. It is their needs, and, therefore, their political representatives' efforts, that determine the kind of values that our criminal law is to protect.

Unintended support for this assertion is furnished by a most conventional source. The Law Reform Commission of Canada, in its widely respected and quoted 1976 study of criminal law, argued that criminal law should be defined narrowly, only encompassing that conduct that presents a danger to the truly fundamental values of Canada's liberal-capitalist democracy. Criminal law, it contended, should be used to protect the values of peace, order, and good government and the liberty of the individual. It is manifest that none of these values are definable with exactitude. Values such as liberty of the individual are abstract in nature and require interpretation before they can have any practical meaning. The meaning, then, will depend on who is doing the interpreting. Typically, one person's exercise of liberty infringes another's; or one interpreter's view as to what constitutes order and good government is bound to clash with that of others who hold different but (what they sincerely and not unreasonably believe to be) viable opinions. This approach is a delight to lawyers who grow rich and get to feel important as they play a crucial role in the ensuing fights centred around this (undemocratic) structuring of some of the fundamental elements of social relations. But a criminal code based on undefined, always contestable principles can hardly lay claim to being anchored in the uncontested values of society. Rather, what is presented as a shared morality is that complex of values and beliefs dear to the hearts and minds of those who can exercise control over the political struggles that define the shared morality at any one moment of history. In modern Canada those are the beliefs and values of the dominant capitalist class.

The mainstream Law Reform Commission of Canada clearly identified this state of affairs. After stating that criminal law had to safeguard basic values—such as liberty of the individual and peace rather than violence, and social or political order rather than chaos, the Commission went on to say that in all capitalist countries, including Canada, the protection of private property is the most important function of criminal law. Indeed, the Commission pointed out that theft—legally defined as the taking of another person's property with the intention of permanently depriving the original owner thereof—is the paradigm crime.

There we have it: the protection of those who own property is the main focus of the criminal justice system, regardless of the popular portrayal of murder, assaults, rapes, or drug-related crimes as *the* problems to be addressed by criminal processes. Now, even relatively poor people usually have at least a small amount of private property to protect and, with so little going for them, they are very anxious that what they do have is protected. That is why the dispossessed often strongly support law and order politicians and police officers. The poor are also the most likely victims of street crime, which also means that criminal law is not seen as being primarily concerned with the safeguarding of the truly wealthy. But the apparent evenhanded approach to physical safety and property-protecting goals should not be allowed to deflect attention away from the major focus of criminal law in a capitalist polity. That focus is to safeguard the physical integrity of property and the mainte-nance of the power—of those very few who have it in our most unequal economy—to accumulate ever more of it by engaging in the exploitation of the socialized efforts of those who must work for a living. To make this goal more easily attainable, those wealthy few, along with their army of support-ers, find it necessary to erect barriers that stop their wealth from being subju-gated to the strictures of the criminal law. It would be counterproductive if the true capitalists were inhibited in their capitalist activities.

Other concrete aspects of the criminal justice system bolster the appear-ance of evenhandedness. The criminal justice system does treat wealth-owners similarly to the poor in some cases; when, for instance, the wealthy commit certain offences, such as murder in anger or passion, or sexual assault or drug abuse, that are not primarily calculated to advance private property accumulation by productive market activities. Even then, though, the wealthy are more likely to gain a better end result in the justice system, simply because their money allows them to exploit the vagaries of that system to their advantage. In the eyes of the administrators of the justice system, the wealth-owners also start with a more appealing image than do the poor of the world. Still, the potential of criminal law to treat wealthy people, in some circumstances, in the same way as it does poor people does help to counter the impression that the criminal justice regime does not abide by liberal-democratic principles; but in most cases, thanks to the corporate veil, the wealthy remain largely immunized from criminal prosecutions for what would ordinarily be punishable behaviour.

The key to this largely acceptable departure from evenhanded treatment is the way in which we have been taught to think about corporations' market activities. We take it to be true that when the investing classes engage in market activities through the corporate vehicle, their focus, like that of the corporation's, is single-minded: to make money. Any harm inflicted is an unintended effect of otherwise laudable activity, namely, trying to be productive in order to make a profit. Productive activity for profit is good, even though all productive activity entails risks. It is regrettable when the risks materialize but, as they inhere in useful activities, the risk-takers and creators should not be treated as criminals, not even as deviants. Rather, they should be allowed to do what comes naturally, subject to any rules and standards imposed by the democratically elected government. Their meritorious endeavours should be monitored and controlled and encouraged, all at the same time. Criminal law should be saved to punish conduct that cannot lay claim to being productive, in the market sense, even if it is owners of wealth who are engaged in such illegalities. This special place accorded market-productive activities justifies the establishment of special behaviour-regulatory monitoring schemes that do not condemn market-productive efforts that go wrong. Such wrongful conduct does not, cannot, menace our fundamental values. Such misfiring is to be avoided, but not criminalized.

Special Regulatory Regimes and the Laundering of Corporate Criminality

In liberal-capitalist democracies, such as Canada, governments, wedded to the primacy of creating welfare via the private sector, set out to establish optimal conditions for private entrepreneurship. In recent years this goal has meant a dismantling of much of the existing regulatory apparatus. The very existence of this regulatory apparatus in the first place is, in part, a result of governments' need to be seen to be acting on behalf of the public in general. Governments must be seen to be willing to mediate the worst impacts of an economic system that, if left unfettered, will inflict grave harms on the citizenry by its unrelenting pursuit of profits. Scholars refer to this as "legitimation and accumulation," the dual, tension-filled attempt to legitimate the system while furthering the accumulation of private wealth.

By their very nature, the ensuing administrative and regulatory regimes are particularistic. They address specific problems arising out of discrete forms of productive activities. By definition, unlike the criminal law proper regime, they do not purport to reflect a shared morality that holds our social fabric together. They merely provide a framework in which market activities can be conducted. They draw a balance between the benefits provided by uninhibited market activities and the amount of harm that people, as members of a society, should be willing to tolerate to enjoy those benefits. The justification for this kind of scheme is that it attains a proper balance between costs and benefits. The balance may, indeed is expected to, change as we get to know more about the level of benefits and harms brought about by certain forms of productive endeavours. But what does not change is the underlying premise, namely, that market capitalism is per se beneficial and should be promoted whenever possible. If there is an equivalent to the shared morality that supposedly underpins the criminal justice system proper, it is that private profit-seeking activities are an unalloyed good and need to be protected from anti-market zealots who would save lives and the physical environment at any cost. John Kenneth Galbraith quoted the pithy observation of John D. Rockefeller that captured this sentiment: "The American Beauty Rose can be produced in the splendor and fragrance which bring cheer to its beholder only by sacrificing the early buds which grow up around it . . .This is not an evil tendency in business. It is merely the working-out of a law of Nature and a law of God." Regulatory laws reflect this Darwinian starting point.

This understanding of market regulatory laws, such as misleading advertising legislation, pro-competition laws, occupational health and safety and environmental protection laws, consumer protection, and fair trading regulations, legitimates special treatment for those regulated by these schemes. If fierce competitive and aggressive behaviour is to be welcomed and promoted by a regulatory apparatus, there are bound to be a few people (read: for practical purposes, a few corporations), who use excessive aggression, who breach the regulations. But the logic is that the basic endeavour ought not to be faulted, just the means used this time by this actor (read: for practical purposes, by this corporation). This approach creates an atmosphere in which violations are unlikely to be seen as serious misconduct. Indeed, so difficult is it to tell the difference between acceptable and admired aggression and unacceptable and sanctionable aggression that it will be hard for violators to admit that they have done anything wrong, or at least it will be difficult for them to believe that they have done something morally repugnant, something that ought to lead to their vilification.

A number of studies verify this finding. For instance, a senior Westing-house executive was asked why he had participated in something as plainly wrong as the "Heavy Electrical Equipment" conspiracy, which involved clandestine meetings to fix prices. Rather perplexedly, he responded, "Illegal? Yes, but not criminal." This kind of insensitivity to normal appreciations of what is right and wrong is reinforced by what has been called the "structural immorality of corporations," or, in my own words (chapter 8), the structuring of the corporation as a site of irresponsibility. The managers work in a sub-culture of immorality, a climate endorsed by the regulatory assumption that violations are the unfortunate, but natural, outcome of fundamentally admirable behaviour. It is this approach that explains why it is that, when corporations and their movers and shakers breach the standards set by regula-tors, they are infrequently charged; and when charged, rarely convicted; and when convicted, extremely seldom punished severely. The schemes are not perceived as ones maintaining important values; rather, they are characterized as regimes whose prime purpose is to facilitate hard-nosed, aggressive market participation, in which the dominant motif is winning at (almost) any cost.

Thus, while violations of regulations of this sort are wrongful, they do not lead to a stigmatization of the violators. Indeed, the first reaction of the regulators is to try to get the offenders to comply voluntarily with the rules. The investigators sent out to monitor compliance do not behave like the police. The powers-that-be usually give the investigators certain names that make it clear they are there to help the regulatees meet the standards imposed by the market-administrating regime. They are inspectors or officers and they share the ideology underpinning the regime they patrol: production is good and state intervention should be kept to a minimum. Charges, fol-lowed by punishment, should be a last resort. Eric Tucker established how this approach had been followed ever since the Ontario government had passed the first Factories Acts to try to alleviate some of the slaughter in the up-to-then unfettered workplaces. To get a sense of what this approach means in practice, imagine that a police officer catches a burglar breaking into a house. Instead of taking the would-be thief to the police station and laying criminal charges, the police officer tells him: "Now, now, you know that breaking into people's houses to steal is against the rules. Think about it; I will check your actions over the next few weeks, and if I catch you again I may be forced to throw the criminal law book at you." This is, of course, pre-cisely what, time and time again, occupational health and safety inspectors tell countless corporations that engage in rule-breaking and life-threatening practices. Indeed, the administrative regulatory policy to seek voluntary com-pliance first and to use the stick of prosecutions under the regulatory regime much later (and only if all else fails) is so well-established as a recognized and much-commended strategy that it has been given a name: the pyramid method of regulatory enforcement. The understanding is that the potential of punishment is merely a means to get voluntary compliance with the regulatory schema. If a need to impose the sanction actually arises, it indicates that the regulators have not been getting their message through to the corporate regulatees. Indeed, if the criminal law proper needs to be employed to condemn a failure to abide by the standards set, this eventuality is taken to be damning evidence of a failure of the administrative regime.

Given this regime, then, the charges against corporations and their functionaries are few; convictions are fewer; and penalties, when imposed, are light when corporations are found to have breached the law of the land. As often as not, corporations suffer no more stigma than do we ordinary mortals when we are caught jaywalking. They benefit from being regulated by laws designed to help their main endeavour—the advancement of market capitalism. From the perspective of regulatory law, the results are logical and, therefore, acceptable. To have it become part of conventional wisdom that market capitalism, especially as carried on by the corporate sectors, is to be ruled by the principles of non-criminal law has yielded a highly satisfactory state of affairs for the corporate sectors. It is something of a coup.

But this coup rests on some dubious assumptions and leaves many of the underlying tensions unresolved. The various legal regimes used to attain social, political, and economic goals have overlapping and complementary features. All of the regimes, including regulatory laws, set enforceable standards that help society preserve the integrity of the person, property, and environment. To make their way in this system, people can choose the regulatory regime that suits their overall purposes best. The decision to bring most market activities under the non-criminal administrative schemes is, in large part, justified on the grounds that corporate actors—and other marketeers—are engaged in productive activities that only harm persons, their property, and environments incidentally. The wrongful acts are not committed with the subjective intention necessary to find true criminality, with *mens rea*. The harm-inflicting acts are, in the language of the legal philosopher H.L.A. Hart, morally neutral. In the much older language of the judges, the marketeer's violation of a regulatory law is a *malum prohibitum* (wrong because it is prohibited) as opposed to a *malum in se* (wrong in itself).

As usual, when courts and lawyers use Latin tags to explain their thinking, they are hoping that no one will notice that they have no convincing reasoning for their judgments. Just as we can't possibly characterize anything as morally neutral or morally offensive without making assumptions about our world and our preferences, to say that something is a deep wrong in itself—*malum in se*—and, therefore, to be forbidden by the criminal law proper, does not tell us why this is different from something that is just wrongful enough to be forbidden by another kind of scheme—why it is to be a *malum prohibitum*. There are no criteria provided by this kind of word game. Yet this game is all our conventional scholars and authoritative courts come up with when they need to draw distinctions between acts that are truly criminal and those that are best left to be dealt with by other, less stigmatizing, regulatory schemes.

The Supreme Court of Canada, in a case called *Sault Ste. Marie*, has endorsed the proposition that the administrative regulatory schemes are different in kind to criminal law and that, therefore, different rules and practices are applicable when regulatory law is deployed. The judges refer to this different legal regime of norm enforcement as welfare law, as distinct from criminal law. The Court recognizes that the aims of welfare law and criminal law are much the same: the enforcement of commonly agreed-upon standards by the imposition of fines and prison terms on violators. How then to justify the different rules and practices, such as the abandonment of the requirement of *mens rea* and, therefore, a lesser need for adversarial policing, as well as a justification for lesser punishments and less stigmatization, when welfare laws are to be enforced? How does one know that a law setting a standard whose violation is to be punished by the state is not meant to be treated as a crime? The blindingly, disarmingly, and totally unhelpful reply by the highest court in the land to these questions was that offences that are listed in the Criminal Code and/or are described by Parliament as crimes are crimes; others are not. The distinction is the result of bootstrap argumentation. It is a crime when, over time, the machinations of our political economy have said it is a crime. In a polity dominated by the wealthy who run their profit-pursuing affairs by means of corporate vehicles, it is not at all surprising that those same forces have found ways in which they can have their profit-making activities treated more benignly than other harm-causing conduct. The only justification on offer to back up this state of affairs—and to reject the argument that the capitalist agenda has been permitted to trump the liberal-democratic agenda—is that corporate wrongdoing does not usually involve malicious and legally and morally tainted intentions. But, unsurprisingly, this, too, is an argument depending on a bootstrap kind of argument. It requires the acceptance of a capitalist spin on the meaning of malicious intent.

Consider the following scenario. A building contractor is retained to build an eighty-storey edifice. The builder's intention is to construct a building according to the given specifications for a price that will yield a profit.

The builder knows, from experience and available statistics, that for every ten storeys over fifty, one more worker will have an accident resulting in injury or death. If workers actually die on the eighty-storey project, should the builder be held criminally responsible for those deaths? The conventional response is a resounding "No." The missing ingredient is that the building contractor obviously never bore any of the workers malice, never intended any worker to be hurt. Yet criminal law does not always demand that kind of malevolence or deliberate intent before it will criminalize conduct. If a person gets into a car blind drunk and kills someone on the road because the object in front of the car seemed to be a cardboard box, the law would hold the driver criminally responsible. It would do so even though the driver neither meant to hurt anyone nor had formed any intention of doing so. It would do so because the driver had been utterly reckless about the well-being of others after getting drunk and before getting into the car. The reckless indifference to life is what causes the law to punish the driver, to stigmatize the offender and the particular conduct. Now, did our hypothetical builder not exhibit the same kind of indifference? From one perspective, the driver is less morally culpable than the builder, who ignored the risk being imposed on others simply because of the final goal of making money. The builder made a rational decision. The driver was just plain stupid.

Not every inadvertent act attracts the displeasure of the criminal justice system. But many corporate acts are at least as condemnatory, at least as reckless in their disregard of human life and well-being, as the acts of the drunk driver in the garden-variety reckless driving/manslaughter case. In the Ford Pinto scenario, for example, the manufacturer deliberately put on the road, and then left on the road, a car that certain executives knew would cause extraordinary harm when it was involved in accidents—and all car manufacturers are aware that their products will sometimes be involved in accidents. It took a while before all the evidence came to light, but when it did the manufacturer was prosecuted for the crime of reckless homicide under an Indiana statute, which essentially followed the kind of reasoning used to hold drunken and reckless drivers to account. The prosecution did not succeed, but only because of a rather peculiar reading of the statute by the court and by its consequent exclusion of what was the most damning evidence of wilful disregard for human life. This evidence was the cold-hearted in-house memoranda that revealed that Ford executives had made a calculated decision that, given the number of cars they had on the road, the number of accidents in which they would statistically be involved, the number of passengers and amount of property likely to be burnt and destroyed, it was cheaper to keep the car on the road, unmodified, than to recall all the vehicles out there and refit them so as to make them less explosive. When this evidence was allowed to be adduced in a prior civil case, the jury imposed huge punitive damages ($125 million, reduced to a mere $3.8 million on appeal), something like a criminal fine. This was the evidence that had motivated the Indiana prosecutors to lay criminal charges in the first place. The prosecutor had reasonably believed that this evidence would be admitted in any criminal trial. Despite the acquittal, then, the lesson is clear: such conduct, although it lacked the kind of personal malice towards a particular person and although the overriding intent of the corporation was to make money, lends itself to criminalization. What is required is the will to use this potential. There is nothing in *legal* principle that prevents the use of criminal law in these kinds of cases of corporate wrongdoing arising out of market activities.

The lack of a real distinction between conduct automatically treated as criminal and conduct seen as being, equally automatically, better dealt with by market-promoting welfare regulatory law shows up in a number of well-known harm-causing cases. Although the activities in these cases are still not treated as crimes, most people would feel comfortable with a decision to hold the corporations and their managers criminally culpable. Thus, in recent times, courts and juries have found tobacco corporations to be civilly liable for having caused illnesses and addictions. Damages have been awarded to people who have demonstrated that they have suffered illnesses as a result of smoking, even though the decision to smoke was their own, and even though the tobacco corporations had presented warnings about the danger of their product on every packet sold. In addition, governments have won huge compensatory awards from tobacco sellers. Their successful argument was that their health-care bills were grossly increased because of the heightened incidence of sickness in people who had voluntarily smoked, despite the warnings. In sum, tobacco corporations have been held responsible because they knew in advance of the likelihood that their legally produced and sold goods would create addicts and cause illness. They engaged in this profit-making endeavour heedless of the harms they knew they would cause. If this case is different from that of the drinking driver, it is only so because the tobacco corporations were far more calculating, far more evil in their studied indifference to the health and life of human beings, than any drunk. A policy that these kinds of corporate planned acts should not be subjected to our most significant means of condemnation—the criminal justice proper— is a *political* policy, not one mandated by legal, or any other kind of, logic.

Some recent gun-makers' cases make this clear. From the early 1990s on, people injured in gun shootings in the United States began to bring actions against the makers of the guns used by the shooters. Certainly, the actual shooters were clearly criminally responsible because they had engaged, as individuals, in impermissible conduct with the necessary *mens rea*. The civil actions brought against the gun-makers to the effect that they should be responsible to the victims of the injured and dead had to overcome the obvious argument that the gun-makers had not intended that anyone be shot, that they had not shot anyone, that an independent actor—by definition, another person legally responsible for his or her own actions—had done the forbidden act with a requisite intention, which permitted that person to be convicted as a criminal. Yet, in 1999, a court in Brooklyn found gun-makers liable. The basis for the decision was that, while gun-makers had nothing to do with any one shooting, nor could they have known that their gun would be used by some criminal somewhere, they were responsible because of their planned marketing practices. The gun-makers distributed their guns to states that had weak laws regulating the sale and possession of guns, which made it easy for persons prohibited from having weapons in other states to get guns and to use them in their home states. The gun-makers were held civilly liable because their marketing practices were indifferent to the outcome of their profit-seeking activities. Note that gun-making and gun-selling are perfectly legal and even respected businesses in the United States. This line of argument, namely, that indifference to outcome is sufficient advertence to be held responsible, *even if the injuring act was committed by another totally independent actor*, suggests that, as eventually happened in the Pinto case, this level of inadvertence could be treated as the kind of reckless indifference to which criminal, as well as civil, culpability might be attached. Of course, that it could be so treated does not mean that it will be so treated. A California court took the opposite approach to the Brooklyn position in a subsequent similar gun manufacturers' case. The point is not that legal logic mandates that the production of guns must lead to criminal prosecution, but that there is nothing in legal logic that prohibits this course. There is no binding logic to tell us that this kind of corporate market behaviour must be left either to civil tort law or to the welfare regulatory regime. Would the public, the aggregate of reasonable persons, truly be horrified if either the tobacco corporations or the gun-making companies were charged with criminal negligence? Are these cases clearly cases in which the planned wrongdoing is morally neutral, a *malum prohibitum*, rather than a *malum in se*?

To ask these questions is to answer them. Let us put the nail into this coffin. If a person holds up another person with a gun and says, "Give me your wallet or I will take your life," does this individual offend our shared morality? Obviously. The brigand will be treated as a criminal. When asbestos manufacturers and processors tell their workers, "We want you to work in contaminated conditions or take less pay if we are put to the cost of rendering them contamination-free," are they not saying, "Your money or your life"? This implicit conversation occurs regularly in settings that call for attention to health and safety standards. Sometimes it is more explicit. Some underground cable work, for instance, was being carried on in an area notorious for the potential danger of escaping hydrogen sulphide gas. An inspector of Hydro-Québec had reported that the employer had not taken basic precautions, such as the use of exposure measurement devices, proper scaffolding, and the provision of hats and gloves for workers. Several workers had complained to the employer about feeling ill after the first day of work and had reported that the ventilation was inadequate and requested that gas measurement devices be provided. The employer had ignored all these complaints and requests. Three workers were subsequently overcome by hydrogen sulphide fumes and died. In this case, implicitly, and rather plainly so, the employer had said, "Take these conditions or leave." No criminal charges were laid.

The refusal to see this scenario as criminal behaviour is based on the assumed fact that the workers consent to a certain level of risk and that the ensuing materialization of the risk should not be seen as morally offensive, as criminal. But, as usual, the explanation is convincing only if the basic premises of capitalism are unquestioned. Again, workers enter into contracts of employment because their lack of disposable wealth forces them to sell their only capital, themselves, to people who do have a choice as to whether or not to invest their disposable capital—that is, to employers. Consent implies a relationship between equal, sovereign parties. The employment contract is not such a relationship, even though it is crucial to a liberal-market political economy that it be characterized as such. Thus, the fundamental reason for the argument that robbery holdups and endangering workplace situations are not analogous is based on an implied assertion that is wrong. More, even if for debating purposes people are willing to accept the flawed argument that workers can truly consent to the risks, the argument is still unpersuasive. It assumes that workers, aided by governments that have been forced to mediate the operations of the unfettered market, fully understand the level of safety risks to which they consent. After all, there can be no consent to a level of risk if its existence or extent is unknown to the supposedly consenting party. This is a problem.

A case involving the B.F. Goodrich company illustrates this problem. One of this corporation's plants was found to have a statistically disproportionate incidence of angiosarcoma, a rare liver cancer, among its workers.

The corporation had been aware of a European study that linked vinyl chloride, one of the substances the company used in plastics manufacturing, and liver cancer, but had continued using the chemical in the United States. Many workers at many plants contracted this disease before the problem came to the attention of regulators in North America. After much bargaining with plastics manufacturers, the authorities required different processes to be used. No criminal charges were brought.

The knowledge possessed by entrepreneurs and employers is vastly greater than the knowledge held by the public or governments, as the Eli Lilly and asbestos stories (chapter 8) demonstrate. In the asbestos cases, the industry knew about the dangers long before any one else did. The eventual anger directed at the asbestos industry largely stemmed from the way in which it hid this information from the people likely to be affected. Similarly, the public's complaint against tobacco manufacturers is fuelled by what is now known to be the industry's deliberate constructed web of lies about its knowledge of the dangers of its products.

In a political economy in which the paradigm is that wealth should be generated primarily by private investors seeking private profits, the primary ability to assess and control the risks associated with all production rests with these investors. They decide what to invest, how much to invest, and where to invest. They decide what kinds of processes and substances to use, and what kinds of skills are necessary. They decide on which workers, and on the number of workers, and which technologies to employ. The investors/employers set the agenda and frame the debate for decision-making about the standards that ought to be maintained. Governments use the data of experience to alter the investor/employer blueprint. They do this largely on the basis of the harms wrought over time by the blueprint's implementation. *We need to be harmed to get regulation.* The workers—like consumers and environmentalists—are in a totally reactionary position.

Workers come to workplaces because they must, and they do so after the agenda has been set. They are always trying to alter what already exists, which truly places them in a feeble position. Yet workers also bear most of the risks. The government has liabilities when the risks materialize, in that it needs to provide such items as welfare benefits, pensions, medical care, and rehabilitation. The investors bear the least proportion of the costs of the materialized risks. They hide behind corporations—which often can pass on the costs imposed by having to compensate or retrain—and enjoy limited liability. Everything is upside down: the persons most at risk have the least control over the risks, while those with most control over the risks are least exposed to them. Yet both liberal and democratic principles would maintain that the people most at risk should make most of the decisions. This is a fundamental principle of liberal capitalism. After all, capitalists always make this same argument whenever anyone tries to intervene with their deployment of their wealth. Its appeal is why elected governments have so much political difficulty justifying their interventions in the marketplace.

Yet none of this supposedly shared perspective of our values and polity applies when it comes to the issue of enforcement of democratically agreed-upon occupational health and safety standards for workers. Here the needs of capitalists are privileged. The logic of capitalism, especially as practised by means of large corporations, contradicts that of liberal democracy. This oft-ignored truth could be brought out by applying criminal law to situations where this is rarely considered to be an option.

The use of criminal law against asbestos processors or the B.F. Goodrich's of this world, as if they were holdup artists, would rely on the argument that there is only a pretence of consent to harm by workers, not a real consent. This argument would go to the very foundations of capital-labour relations, to its legitimation as a scheme based on freedom of contract. Unsurprisingly, this approach is fiercely resisted. It is vital to the legitimation of the extraction of surplus value from workers who contract to work for wages that the contract be perceived as voluntary. To allow an argument to the contrary in the health and safety sphere would menace this valuable starting point. It is the importance of the maintenance of the pretence of consent that stands in the way of using the criminal law in the asbestos kind of case, even when ordinary common sense cries out for such treatment. Efforts to lay criminal charges in occupational health and safety cases, then, have little chance of success, but they do provide a basis for bringing out the contradiction, for underlining the privileging of corporate capital in our supposedly liberal-democratic polity. This is underscored by the fact that, when there is not as much at stake from the perspective of the maintenance of the legitimacy of dominant economic interests, the logic of liberal law will be given more room to operate.

The potential for criminalizing corporate deviance is more likely to be realized when there can be no claim of consent by victims of corporate activities to the harms inflicted, and when acknowledgement of this will not challenge the very basis of the system. This will be the case in environmental destruction cases and in many consumer-harming ones. When harms are inflicted on nature or on people who did not contract directly with the wrongdoing corporations, it is far more difficult to argue that there was an implicit consent to the injuries. The use of the criminal law in these kinds of situations cannot be deflected as easily. Indeed, even in cases in which there is some argument for consent to the potential of injury, the law has had to concede that the consent basis for averting the application of enforcement based on moral fault-finding has little weight. Thus, in the case of the tobacco industry's liabilities, the consent by the victims was not allowed to stand in the way of finding of culpability, albeit only civil culpability so far. What the jury decisions reflected was that the corporations' lying and coverups were anathema and that this wrongdoing needed to be publicly condemned, even if the victims may have been foolish in giving their consent to some harm.

The contention, then, that when corporations are engaged in market activities, authorities should deal with them as entities engaged in morally neutral activities that occasionally go wrong—that is, as entities that should not be regulated by the deep morality-protecting criminal law processes—is just a political position advanced by those who benefit from it. It is not defensible as a legally logical position and is not even empirically reflected in law, because some everyday market-productive activities that went wrong have indeed been treated as serious legal and moral wrongs rather than as morally neutral regulatory peccadillos akin to parking violations. The laying bare of this argument has serious implications. It suggests that a great deal of rather ordinary profit-seeking endeavours by corporate actors could be deemed to be morally unacceptable.

In this regard, the Ford Pinto case, for instance, was really not unusual at all. Every producer for the market balances the cost of safe, healthy, non-polluting production against what the market will bear. Cars that are much safer than the ones on the road could be produced, at much greater cost. Drugs could be far more exhaustively tested before marketing, to eliminate all risks. Mining could stop altogether until more efficient ways of reducing fumes or emissions could be found. Products and services could be safer, healthier, and less polluting. Their costs would be increased and delays in satisfying needs and desires would be incurred, but there would be welfare-enhancing benefits to the public that would come at the expense of private profiteers. In short, as it stands, calculations are made as to what people are willing to put up with and pay for each and every time a product or service is produced or rendered for profit, and these calculations are not necessarily people-friendly. Why is this cavalier treatment of the quality of life and of life itself not a *malum in se*, a crime properly so-called?

To reject this line of reasoning, to make sure that daily corporate decision-making is seen as morally neutral and not criminal in nature, some commentators make an argument positing that market calculations are natural, reflexive, and not to be second-guessed. They argue that if people are not willing to pay for safety, health, or a good environment, they must be deemed to have consented to lack of safety, ill-health, and pollution. In other words, it is the economic need and financial starting position of citizens that should determine what is acceptable behaviour, not objective needs or social and political mores. The intellectual and political weakness of this defence of the status quo lies in the fact that, in a liberal democracy, the primacy of market arguments is contestable and is contested. Many of us purport to have other values and goals than the satisfaction of personal greed.

The struggle between a vision of the political economy that sees economic development as a tool for the provision of human needs, concrete and spiritual, and the vision that regards economic growth as an end in itself, which, incidentally, will provide what people want, lies at the heart of mature capitalist democratic politics. It is the struggle between neo-liberals and social democrats, to translate this into modern Canadian political language. Even during those times when the social-democratic side seems to have been vanquished, the push and pull between these two visions of liberal-capitalist democracy continue to mould decision-making and thinking.

In 1995, for instance, the Supreme Court of India had to deal with workers' claims that they had been damaged by their exposure to asbestos and should be compensated. In the case before it, the Indian court stated that the enshrinement of the protection for the right to life, found in both the internationally applicable Universal Declaration of Human Rights and in the Indian Constitution, supported the workers' claims. It is worth quoting the language used by the judges, as the actual words and phrasing are rarely found in our part of the world:

> Compelling economic necessity to work in an industry exposed to health hazards due to indigence to bread-winning to himself and his dependents should not be at the cost of health and vigour of the workman. . . . Right to life includes protection of the health and strength of the worker is a minimum requirement to enable a person to live with human dignity. The State, be it Union or State government or an industry, public or private, is enjoined to take all such action that will promote health, strength and vigour of the workman during the period of employment and leisure and health even after retirement as basic essentials to live the life with health and happiness. . . . The right to human dignity, development of personality, social protection, right to rest and leisure are fundamental human rights. . . . The right to life with human dignity . . . includes the quality of life as understood in its richness and fullness . . . which makes life worth living.

This vision acknowledges the existence of values (such as the right to life itself, dignity, and respect for human beings) other than commodified values, and it recognizes that much of the supposed consensus on which we base our regulation is just that, supposition. The vision is anathema to capitalist relations of production, and it is treated with disdain by the defenders of market capitalism. Their response is that not to treat commercial activities, typically undertaken by and through corporations, as morally neutral, is to dilute the power and demonstrative effect of criminal law as condemnatory and educational. If all our ordinary productive activities undertaken for profit are to be suspect, then there will be no way to differentiate between decent, useful, economic welfare-enhancing, behaviour and wanton, non-market aggression.

Another, contrasting, statement comes from Richard Posner, a senior judge and formerly one of the best-known advocates of the neo-liberal school of academic thinking. Posner argues: "Only the fanatic refuses to trade off lives for property, although the difficulty of valuing lives is a legitimate reason for weighing them heavily in the balance when only property values are in the other pan." This vision sees human life and, no doubt, all other life, as merely a factor to be put into the calculus engaged in by all rational market actors. Such a vision was illustrated dramatically when the *Wall Street Journal* reported in July 2001 that one of the highly paid flacks that corporations use for selling themselves and their harmful products, a public relations firm called Arthur D. Little International, had tried to tell the Czech Republic to leave Philip Morris's products alone because, on balance, by killing off so many people earlier than they would otherwise die, this public-spirited corporation would be saving the government the medical expenses it would have incurred if these people had lived out their normal life spans. Incidentally, the tobacco companies used this same argument when they were sued by U.S. authorities for the extra expenses incurred by them as a consequence of tobacco-related ills. It was unsuccessful then, but hey, why not try again?

The infliction of harms is portrayed, and conventionally perceived, as a norm that, on some occasions, might be unacceptable. Proof will be required before such a harsh judgement on profit-seeking efforts is to be rendered. Market-capitalist activities are normalized in this way. Only excesses and flagrant abuses should be treated as truly deviant. Market activities should be regulated by a regime that respects the capitalist project and that promotes participation in it while containing its abuses and abusers. In the end, this is a vision holding that the ordinary, the normal, is a society that does *not* put a premium on life-enhancing qualities above private gain-seeking. To maintain hegemony for this vision necessitates establishing that an invigorated welfare regulatory law can by itself bring about acceptable corporate behaviour. The advocates for this line of reasoning make great efforts towards providing such a regulatory, but non-criminal, regime and, as we shall see in the next chapter, they and others expend even more efforts in attempts to persuade us that such a regime, when established, works satisfactorily.

New Corporate Responsibilities – or More Window Dressing?

*Wherein we learn that when legislators mediate the impacts of unbridled
market capitalist acts of their invisible friends, the captains of industry,
finance, retail, and everything else bristle effectively at the political
attacks as they hide behind their invisible friends' Charter rights. They
peek out to argue that they, the hidden ones, are too precious to us to be
held responsible for anything they get their invisible friends to do.*

In the *Sault Ste. Marie* case the Supreme Court of Canada, it was claimed,
showed a lamentable lack of logic when it drew its fuzzy line between welfare regulatory offences and criminal law proper. It is time to offset that
dose of vinegar with some sugar. The Supreme Court of Canada had
become involved in its hopeless quest to draw this line because it had set
itself the task of finding a way of supporting the legislatures' efforts to restrain
harmful corporate maximization activities. Ironically, the corporate sectors
and their legal advisers have been using the courts to undermine the very
legislative regimes that, in *Sault Ste. Marie*, the judges intended to defend.

When the state uses its awesome criminal law processes, a part of its
endeavour goes towards stigmatizing the wrongdoer. One of the safeguards
provided to accused persons is that they are to be treated as innocent until

proved guilty beyond a reasonable doubt. This safeguard makes it more difficult for the prosecution to succeed, which is as it should be, given the gravity
of a criminal conviction. But welfare regulatory law is not meant to be so
tightly constrained. The enforcement of such laws does not set out to stigmatize behaviour as much as it attempts to create an inviting climate for economic activities. To be efficient, the governing regulators must be able to
enforce their regimes relatively easily. That is why this kind of legislation provides that prosecutors of violators need only prove that a violation has
occurred; they need not prove that the accused person had a malicious
intent, a criminal *mens rea*. Precisely because a conviction under a regulatory law is not condemnatory in the same way as a Criminal Code conviction
is, the burden of proof is lightened and shifts from the prosecution. The
Supreme Court of Canada's holding that this shifting of the burden of proof
was valid, provided the offence was created as a welfare regulatory offence,
has many implications for our examination of corporate deviance. In particular, it makes the prosecution's task easier.

Once the prosecution has shown that the welfare regulation's standard
has been breached, the onus falls on defendants to prove that they exercised
due diligence and care to try to avert the breach of the standard. This
approach makes it easier to convict and provides an incentive to government
agencies to enforce their statutory mandate vigorously. This condition helps
governments demonstrate to the electorate that its interferences with the
market on the public's behalf are serious. The passing of relatively easily
enforced rules signifies that government can be, and will be, effectively
tough with those whose market conduct imperils the well-being of the public. At the same time, because these interventions with the market also aim to
facilitate accumulation, they help to do so by providing legitimacy to those
market actors who stay within the framework provided by the welfare regulatory standards. Their conduct is thereby explicitly and powerfully characterized as morally neutral. What this does is boost the legitimacy of market
capitalism and provide stability for entrepreneurs. All of this, in turn, helps
make the case of those who argue that there is no need to reach out for criminal law proper—that is, there is no place for that scheme of law that we
reserve for truly shaming and condemning bad actors.

The force of this reasoning, however, has been diluted somewhat by the
selfishness of individual market transgressors and by the facts on the ground.
The first of these factors reminds us, if we need reminding, that corporate
actors have no shame. Even though the predominant purpose of lowering
the burden of proof is to help governments sell market capitalism, some
individual capitalists care more about their own well-being—as good selfish

persons truly should—than about capitalism's well-being. When the Charter of Rights and Freedoms became part of the fundamental law of the land, a number of corporations fastened on the guarantee that everyone should be presumed innocent until proved guilty beyond a reasonable doubt. They argued that the reverse onus of proof when enforcing welfare regulations, specifically endorsed by the Supreme Court of Canada in the *Sault Ste. Marie* case, was a violation of their Charter rights. Eventually, the Supreme Court of Canada (in *Wholesale Travel*, 1991 and *Ellis Don*, 1992), rejected this argument. Even though the Court made hard work of coming to this decision, it really had no option. It would have been contradictory to hold that charges initiated because of a need to punish and condemn behaviour severely because of its malevolence, that is, treating the behaviour as crimes, were not to be treated differently than charges initiated to punish conduct that, the Court itself had held, was not criminal because it did not require a subjective, evil intent. It would have made a mockery of its prior and emphatic endorsement of the distinction between the two spheres of control.

Still, that courts even found the argument to be plausible does show that the law is predisposed to the kind and gentle treatment of economic actors. After all, it was corporations that had made this argument based on the Charter's recognition of the need to safeguard human beings from the power of the state. The judicial schizophrenia revealed is intriguing. What the Supreme Court of Canada did in the *Wholesale Travel* and *Ellis Don* cases was to uphold its own decision that it is justifiable to treat corporate economic activity as non-criminal and, therefore, that corporations in those kinds of cases did not require the normal criminal justice protections. Yet it did give serious consideration to the corporate demand for protections that human individuals can claim when prosecuted for serious criminal offences. This ambivalence reinforces a particular perception: not only is there something special, something peculiarly worthy of protection, about market activities, but also corporations are entitled to solicitous handling. These subtle signals from on high may well have a braking effect on the zeal of regulatory agencies.

The second factor in this argument is that there has been no diminution in the number and gravity of the harmful and undesired outcomes of corporate activities. The media do an increasing number of exposés of high-profile catastrophes, from Bhopal and Exxon-Valdez to the tobacco and asbestos sagas, from the Nestlé infant formula affair to the collapse of banking and investment institutions, from the investment by corporations in countries with recognized evil, anti-human rights regimes, to the kind of securities/law fraud now being labelled "Enronitis." All of this attention is whipped up at the same time as governments fall over themselves to demonstrate that they are willing to create a more friendly investment climate for corporations by diluting the existing regulatory apparatus. There is a tendency for the perception to develop that the flood of unwanted and unacceptable outcomes of corporate capitalism is related to the stepping aside of the state. The perception of corporate mayhem creates policy difficulties for the forces seeking to legitimate economic welfare creation via the corporate vehicle on the basis that corporations are adequately controlled without the aid of criminal law. And the perception of mayhem has a concrete basis; it cannot be ignored easily.

One worker dies on the job every day in Ontario; about one thousand a year in the whole of Canada. In addition, the workers' compensation agencies record over one million debilitating injuries every year; ten thousand workers die every year of occupationally related diseases, and countless others suffer from such diseases but do not die. Pharmaceutical mishaps, the spraying of harmful materials on people and lands, the polluted air, undrinkable water, contaminated lakes, and exploding products are daily news bulletin fare. In this context it has become commonplace in some quarters to lump clear illegality that does physical harm together with physical harm arising out of ordinary market activities. The anxious public mind, troubled as it is by the repetitive impact of intolerable harms, tends to lose sight of the need to establish actual violations of rules or laws. The analyses tend to focus on harm by corporations, rather than the legal nature of corporate conduct. For instance, the numbers of assaults and murders may be compared with the numbers of injured and dead in the workplace by researchers who want to demonstrate that workplace tragedies represent a far more serious social and moral problem than regular, everyday "crime." Such comparisons raise the spectre that unfettered corporate capitalist conduct should be characterized as harmful, in and of itself. "Capitalism is toxic" is the implicit catch cry—to adapt a phrase coined by Frank Pearce and Stephen Toombs to describe their findings after a much more extended argument. This perception is dangerous to the status quo. The state needs to show—again and again—that it can exercise control and is able to balance the costs against the benefits of corporate market activity, even in these deregulatory times. One of the ways in which it does this is by increasing the penalties when corporate actors are convicted under such welfare regulations as do remain on the books. The pressure for this elevation arises both from the increased public focus on undesired outcomes and from the historically derisory nature of sanctions.

In the "Heavy Electrical Equipment" conspiracy, which took about $1 billion 1960 dollars out of consumers' pockets, the fines imposed on General Electric, after a vigorous denunciation by the presiding judge who decided that capitalism was being brought into disrepute at a time when it was fighting a war to the death with Soviet-style communism, was $437,500. This was the total assessed in respect of seven confessed-to conspiracy charges and twelve others to which the corporation pleaded *nolle contendere*, that is, to which it agreed to accept punishment without contestation if no conviction was registered. This much-noted fine was the equivalent of a $3 parking fine for a man with a $175,000 per annum income at that time. Clinard and Yeager, in their major study of giant corporations' wrongdoing, found that 80 per cent of all fines levied in 1976-78 against these huge corporations were $5,000 or less. Clarke made similar findings for the United Kingdom. Ermann and Lundman provided an insight into what these kinds of fines really mean. They calculated that a U.S. corporation with annual sales of $300 million, forced to pay the average fine of $5,000, would be paying the same amount as an individual who earned $15,000 a year and who had been fined 2.4 cents. If the same corporation was fined $100,000, a rare occurrence, the equivalent for the $15,000 per annum person would have been 50 cents. Stanbury made similar calculations for corporations punished for anti-competitive practices in Canada. He showed that fines imposed for blatant conspiracies by large firms amounted to the equivalent of a $131 fine on a person earning $15,000 a year. The fines represented tiny percentages (8 per cent in one case, 0.5 per cent in another) of the cash and short-term investments of the corporate deviants, and the profits earned in the conspiracies were greater than the fines imposed.

This dismal state of affairs is rendered even more depressing when the consequences are death or injury on the job. In these cases, when penalties are imposed they are totally out of whack with the seriousness of the outcome. In the first place, unless the gravity of the consequences attracts considerable attention, charges might not even be laid. When the cases do appear in court, the consequences of the act or practice are not in issue when the court considers the appropriate sanction for the fact of violation. Thus a fine for failure to lock-out electrical equipment may be of the order of a few thousand dollars even when a worker suffered horribly before dying by burning as a direct result of that failure. This apparent indifference drives the family, fellow workers, and the general public to distraction. When an incident occurs on the street, it makes a lot of difference whether a drunken driver killed someone rather than damaged another car. Not so in the corporate welfare regulatory world: here the transgression, not its impact, is the concern. This is so because it is assumed that there is no intention to harm and all harm is incidental.

The Corporate Response to Welfare Regulatory Changes

The welfare regulatory schemes clearly have not frightened the corporations, especially the large, publicly traded ones, to any great degree. The continued manifestations of harms and the loudly proclaimed deregulatory atmosphere have put pressure on the state to reinforce what is left of the apparatus of non-Criminal Code regulation. This has happened. It is common now for statutes, like environmental protection and occupational health and safety laws, to permit the imposition of fines of up to a million dollars. Thus when fines are imposed they are larger than they used to be, with increased room to manoeuvre between the minimum and maximum. In certain spheres of business deviance, fines have increased even more, which explains the historically huge fines incurred by the likes of Hoffman-La Roche for their anti-competitive practices. It has always been the case that when corporations breach the rules most directly related to the capital markets—stock exchange rules, or regulations governing competition practices—the regulators have been more willing to take a serious view of the offences. Rogue capitalists are not to be allowed to bring capitalism into disrepute if, at the same time, this disadvantages law-abiding capitalists.

Still, the legitimating aspect of this demonstrated willingness to heighten the cost of violations cannot be discounted. Nonetheless, it may not be all that successful. The little evidence (largely anecdotal) that exists on this issue suggests that the largest fines are generally imposed on corporations that have no assets. For example, on February 3, 1992, the *Windsor Star* trumpeted the imposition of what was then the largest fine imposed for an occupational health and safety violation penalty in Ontario under its invigorated sanction regime. It was $400,000. But the guilty corporation, Elan Corporation, was bankrupt by the time the fine was to be levied. It has also been documented that the prosecutors tend to go after smaller and more vulnerable firms when enforcing their regulatory rules. Part of this is due to the rather cozy relationships that develop between very large corporations and the regulators who supposedly monitor them; in part, it is due to the difficulty of effectively proceeding against outfits with vast resources and complicated organizational structures. The emphasis of regulatory enforcement in any one area of welfare regulation is biased against the marginal firms, the small entrepreneurs, the small corporations—that is, against firms in which the individual wrongdoers are not as powerful and perhaps more easily visible.

All in all, however, the increase in the penalties available, which also include jail sentences for individuals, has gone some way to re-establish the claim that welfare regulation can take care of corporate deviance, that the Criminal Code is not necessary and remains inapposite. This line of reasoning is given more credibility by a recent upsurge in the bite added to the personal duties imposed on directors and managers by welfare regulatory law. Senior managers are responsible for setting money aside for revenue collection authorities, such as income tax, retail tax, and goods and services tax collectors. They are to ensure that premiums payable to schemes such as the Canada Pension Plan and employment insurance are paid. Failure will make them responsible for the sums outstanding, as well as liable to be charged with an offence. Indeed, governments have had to pass legislation of this kind because corporations, their owners, and their managers can be expected to evade the clear responsibilities that all of us owe to revenue authorities. Under the *Business Corporations Acts*, directors can be liable for unpaid wages owed by an insolvent corporation; and under environmental and occupational health and safety statutes and the *Competition Act*, they can be liable for a variety of obligations; and under employment standards statutes they can be held personally responsible for some liabilities owed to workers.

Most of these responsibilities kick in when a corporation has been found to have violated the pertinent regulatory scheme and the senior manager has authorized, assented to, acquiesced in, or participated in the commission of the offence. The senior manager is held responsible because the corporation has committed a wrong in which that manager has played a part. Under some statutes, the senior manager may even be held responsible when the corporation has not yet committed a wrong but the senior manager has allowed the development of a situation in which the corporation might commit a wrong. The penalties that can be imposed on senior managers under these various provisions include fairly large fines and jail terms for up to one year.

In essence, what has been done is to endorse what has always been the case: those officers of a corporation who have made an illegal corporate act their own have always been civilly and criminally responsible in their own right. But now this potential is more likely to be realized. What had been difficult in the past was to make a factual finding that corporate officers made corporate acts their own, especially in large, complex organizations. Making directors and senior executives directly responsible for wrongful acts if they did not actively seek to prevent them has made the laying of charges against individuals much easier.

These changes to the approach to welfare regulatory regimes make them, on their face, more realistic alternatives to the Criminal Code processes. The hope, therefore, is that the cries that the welfare regulatory system does not regulate effectively will no longer be heard. But, precisely because the underlying agenda is, as it always has been, to give corporate capitalism as much leeway as possible, and because, at the same time, self-seeking individual capitalists will continue to try to detooth state interventions designed to help capitalism as a system, this hope may not be satisfied.

The success of these attempts to make corporations comply with existing regulations depends on the depth of apprehension felt by the guiding minds and wills. It depends on their perception that they will be personally impaled on the welfare regulatory hook should they fail to comply with the rules. This fear will be tempered by the realization that the mere occurrence of a violation does not necessarily co-relate to personal liability. The defendants will not be held responsible if they can prove that they exercised due diligence. "Due diligence" has been interpreted as the setting up of systems of operation that, for instance, make the workers at the coal face aware of their legal regulatory duties, to have them report what system they have put in place to ensure compliance, and to report on whether that system is working; and for the managers to act when it is not. There are potential defences for the managers, then, should there be a violation. Nonetheless, the new personal duties on managers will make some difference.

By imposing personal responsibilities of this kind, the legislatures are, in effect, indirectly but very strongly telling corporations how they should be governed in respect of some aspects of their operations. Companies will need to set in place new directives, following the so-called "due diligence" operational guidelines. The lack of legitimacy arising from not applying stringent enforcement methods against corporations has demanded a restructuring of organizations that were initially constructed as sites of irresponsibility. But, in the end, the impact of these indirect means will depend on the nature and scope of the welfare regulation schemes. If the standards set are low and being lowered, the incidence and seriousness of corporate conduct may not be abated. Similarly, the effort put in by regulators in monitoring compliance with these standards will influence the extent to which managers pay attention to the new dangers they notionally face. So far, the prospects are not promising.

Directors and their allies have furiously attacked the increased range of managerial obligations. The centre of their argument is that their lives have become so fraught with risk, so burdensome as their duties are multiplied dramatically, that society is in danger of throwing out the baby with the bathwater. Directors and managers, knowing that it is now more probable than ever before that they will be held personally responsible if something goes wrong, will be less inclined to take risks. This will set back economic welfare creation. This tendency will be aggravated because corporations are going to find it harder and harder to recruit the best and the brightest to be directors and executives if these risks are imposed. This "anti-responsibility for management" campaign reached a crescendo in the early 1990s as, in the grips of a recession, several corporations left creditors holding empty bags, leading to demands for directors' blood. The evident public appetite for holding corporate directors and managers responsible for corporate failures and wrongs led to vigorous counterattack. Business journalists and academic shills for corporate capital adopted a hysterical tone in expressing their worries about liability chills and directors being driven from boards and becoming the new "fall guys."

From the corporate sectors' perspective, there was also a positive side to all of this action. The fury of the managerial sectors helped the cause of those who wanted to argue that the welfare regulatory regimes clearly could now exercise all the necessary discipline over corporate actors while striking an acceptable balance between social costs and benefits. But the actual outcomes of the new direct responsibilities of directors and managers did not lead to results that afforded lasting credence to this argument. There is as yet no solid evidence that significantly more directors or managers have been held personally responsible for corporate failures and wrongs than was the case before the latest wave of direct duties on directors and officers. There is no systematic record-keeping on this matter, but it appears that it is directors and executives of small, closed corporations who are having the new book thrown at them. It may well be that practices inside large corporations have improved markedly, but this does not mean that the harms inflicted by these corporations have lessened. There is no evidence of that at all, nor is there any evidence that there has been such a chilling effect that the best and brightest do not want to be directors and executives of major corporate actors. Indeed, the reverse is true. Famous and supposedly intelligent people are continuing to fall over themselves to become directors of large publicly traded corporations. The only available study found that, despite the sharp increase in statutory responsibilities, no evidence existed of a paucity of directors or any accelerated loss of directors due to resignations brought on by the increases in risk.

This is not to say that the corporate world has no reason to be concerned by the targeting of flesh and blood directors and executives. What they fear, perhaps intuitively rather than consciously, is that this development is the first step on a slippery, and to them, very dangerous slope. The new, if slight, attention may reflect a growing social and governmental awareness that, behind the corporate veil, real people are doing the acts that cause harm, that real people are profiting from harmful conduct. A certain angst surrounds the state's evident perception of the necessity to isolate some human beings because *someone, some actual person*, ought to be held responsible. The necessity arises from the state's need to claim with credibility that it can tame the corporate beast. The corporate fear is that this direction will lead to a political acknowledgement of an elementary truth: that the corporation is a device that irresponsible profiteers use to their benefit because through it they can avoid being subjugated to the norms and values that the rest of us have to accept.

The unspoken fear is that if directors and executives are being explicitly asked to keep more of a watch on corporate methods and mechanisms in the the pursuit of profits, why should shareholders not be asked to do so? The logic would be that shareholders are happy to receive the ill-gotten profits from corporate deviance and illegality engineered by their chosen managers, but remain unaccountable because they can claim that they were not active decision-makers in all of that dirty business. Their passivity is their excuse. But, of course, shareholders are anything but passive when their directors fail to deliver the profits, or begin to consider selling corporate assets or control. Then they show a firm interest in how corporate decisions are made. They may, then, be passive towards wrongdoing only because there is no duty on them to be active. This licence to be passive was, once upon a time, also granted to directors and senior managers. If managers can be forced to take responsibility by means of positive legislative enactments to that effect, why not shareholders?

Still, the increase of direct responsibility for directors and managers is hardly so awesome that we are anywhere near developments of this kind. But to prevent this possibility from even being considered—a possibility that, if realized, would call into question the very legitimacy and utility of the corporate vehicle—the war against the establishment of responsibility for directors and senior management has been fiercely fought. One of the tacks taken by law and economics scholars such as Ronald Daniels is that it would not be "efficient" business practice to hold directors and senior managers liable. Rather, the argument goes, if anyone is to be held responsible for non-compliance with the criminal law or welfare regulations, it should be the corporation. The reasoning is that this will ensure that the directors and managers will continue to take the necessary business risks and that the pools of managerial talent will remain full of desirable fish. Another element in this argument is that if the directors and managers cause their corporation to be held responsible financially for some kind of law-breaking, shareholders will then, as a result, take steps to discipline their boards and managements. Not only will directors and managers, in turn, lose financially, but also their marketability will decrease. This is the other side of the argument: the market will work its usual magic, if left alone. There is no need for draconian persecution of well-meaning entrepreneurial risk-takers.

The very adoption of this argument indicates once again that the corporate sectors and their allies know no shame. Once the argument was that corporations could not be held responsible because they had no soul to damn and no body to punish. Now the argument is that soul-less and body-less corporations must be held responsible because we should not punish decision-makers who have committed reckless and immoral acts on behalf of the corporation. This, we are told, is the efficient way of doing things.

The argument, again, is brazen. Despite a myriad of proposals for more innovative sanctions when corporations act illegally, such as counter-publicity, special issues of shares, and the designing of restructuring orders to be monitored by courts, the tools used by courts and regulators are limited. For the most part, the innovations remain the preserve of law journal debates. Policy-makers have basically stuck with fines for corporations and fines and jail for executives on the very rare occasions that they are held to account. That is, after all, why there has been an impetus for saddling directors and senior managers with *some* responsibility for the corporate conduct they initiate. The advocates of this approach believe that it might solidify the image of welfare regulatory law sufficiently to ward off the cries for criminalizing corporate capitalism. The counterproposals to turn back to corporate, rather than human, responsibility will most likely not sit well with the general public, which is greatly troubled by the impersonal nature of accountability. Apparently public disaffection does not worry the intellectual gatekeepers of corporate capitalism, or, if it does, they consider it the lesser of the evils. Their agenda should be understood for what it is: they want to shield the investing classes and their managers from the application of our democratically expressed values, the values that we have rendered clear by enshrining them in law. To effect this they are willing to pretend that to hold corporations responsible, rather than the people who own and run them, will work to educate the people who own and run the corporations.

The defenders of the investing classes and their managers understand full well how difficult it is to hold a corporation legally responsible. Yet this holding to account must be carried out if their scheme—punish the corporation, which will lead to the disciplining of management—is to work.

Knowing how difficult it is while pretending that it provides an *efficient* means of regulating corporate behaviour reveals the hypocrisy of their preferred solution. Further, even if a corporation is held responsible, it is most unlikely that its management will ever feel the sting of investors' revenge. For shareholders to react to a holding of corporate liability, the potential losses they face in punishing the corporation must outweigh the corporation's potential profit to be gained by engaging in unacceptable conduct. This need puts a premium on calibrating fines and punishments with a great deal of precision. The problems for a sanction-imposing tribunal are obvious, especially if fines continue to be related to the fact of violation rather than to the harm inflicted or the profit made by the wrongful conduct. This difficulty of calibrating sanctions has been the subject of heated public policy and scholarly debates, all leaving the issue unresolved. While the defenders of the status quo keep arguing that punishing the corporation is the efficient way to go, individual corporations, looking after their own interests, are continuing to erect hurdles that make it difficult to punish them.

For example, in the *Amway* case, after the corporation pleaded guilty to fraud in a criminal court, the case was then pursued in an administrative proceeding. The government wanted to recoup the losses incurred as a result of Amway's fraudulent pricing strategies and had brought an action to levy fines under the quasi-criminal statute that provided for such a compensatory remedy. The government lawyers sought to get evidence by examining the company's senior executives, who also happened to be the major shareholders. These men took the point that, because they were the guiding minds and wills of the corporation against which the fines were to be levied, they were indeed the corporation itself, and to make them give evidence would be to make the corporation give evidence against itself. This was a "no-no" under the Charter of Rights and Freedoms. They, or rather their well-paid lawyers, took the identification theory to its logical conclusion. The judiciary, embarrassed, eventually held that a corporation was not entitled to the privilege against self-incrimination because that constitutional right was meant to protect the dignity and privacy of individuals, and a corporation could not enjoy these qualities of life. But the Supreme Court of Canada has not been consistent on this matter. Thus it also has held that a corporation can hide behind the Charter of Rights and Freedoms guarantee that people should be free from unreasonable searches and seizures. Given that this guarantee exists to protect individuals from the state's prying and invasions of privacy, the declaration of the difference between real human beings and corporations drawn in *Amway* has been blurred. More importantly, with regard to the effectiveness of the new welfare regulatory regimes, the ability to ward off state inspectors from an examination of company records aids corporations enormously in staving off prosecutions, and it has a chilling effect on regulators who are expected to get tougher with corporations. The Supreme Court of Canada ameliorated the situation somewhat by subsequently holding that the corporate right to privacy of documents does not exist where the investigators or would-be prosecutors are trying to get at commercial records in a non-criminal offence circumstance. But, of course, this finding raises the issue of what is criminal and what is non-criminal, which is far from easy to decide. As well, the Supreme Court of Canada's decision that there should be a different treatment for corporate non-criminal illegality and criminal wrongdoing reinforces the argument that ordinary corporate business practices that breach the law are not all that serious.

A bizarre Supreme Court of Canada decision handed down in 1999 neatly illustrates the practical and ideological significance of this point. When a court imposes a fine on a corporation—and, remember, this is the preferred option of the law and economics scholars to get at the movers and shakers in deviant corporations—the corporation will often claim the fine it then pays as a deduction to be offset against its declared taxable income. This practice may be offensive to common sense, but it is not so to law. In a case called 65302 *British Columbia Ltd. v. Minister of National Revenue* (1999), the Supreme Court of Canada determined that, unless Parliament explicitly says otherwise, a fine imposed on a corporation is deductible if the corporation can show that the fine was the result of a violation committed while trying to earn income. The argument is that the corporation has to declare the income from illegally conducted business and pay taxes on that income; and therefore it should be allowed to deduct the expenses it had in earning that taxable (illegal) income. These expenses include fines and levies. Indeed, the Court noted that, until the statute was amended, a company could deduct the cost of paying bribes in order to get profit-making business. The decision only reinforces the great difficulty, in the absence of a clear legislative statement, of distinguishing appropriate and inappropriate means of making profits. Like the Charter decisions, this tax deductibility judgment also points, more directly, to how corporations will fight like hell to make enforcement of conduct difficult and ineffective—at the same time as the resistance to the personal responsibility of directors and managers and, some far-off day, shareholders, has led corporate supporters to make demands that the corporation be made the prime target for enforcement.

The Averting of Condemnation, and a Growing Unease

This is not to say that corporations are never punished, nor that directors, executives, and other managers are never held to account. They are. Sometimes the fines are steep, as in the Hoffman-La Roche case. In the Exxon-Valdez case the penalty was of the order of $3.5 billion on top of a costly clean-up order. Sometimes executives do get sent to jail. Indeed, in the United States, a number of well-publicized corporate manslaughter, assault, and misdemeanour charges have been laid. In one case a corporation was charged with, and convicted of, criminal assault with a deadly weapon. The corporation had operated a clandestine mercury reclamation plant, exposing unprotected workers to hugely excessive doses of mercury. In England, too, there has been a recent spurt of such charges, leading to the conviction and jailing of the executives or owners of small corporations. In Canada, too, there have been occasional, but rarely successful, attempts to use the criminal law proper against corporations and their managers.

All of this activity, though, remains the exception. In general, corporations have been able to avert the social condemnation that comes from being held to account by the criminal law process, our most solemn means of voicing disapproval. They have been able to do so, in part, by relying on the unease intuitively felt when we are asked to take criminal law aimed at individual actors and apply it to a functional collective. In part, the corporations' success derives from the instrumental difficulties created for prosecutors who have to prove the corporation's malicious intent and conduct via the intentions and acts of leading individuals inside the corporation. Recently these problems have been exacerbated by the way in which corporations have been permitted to employ the Charter of Rights and Freedoms. Added to this complex picture have been the very real problems posed by devising effective punishments for corporations. Further, corporations and their owners and managers have been able to take advantage of the ideology of a liberal-capitalist democracy, which holds that participation in market activity is a good that must be promoted by law. From this starting point, the tendency is to treat corporate excesses as unfortunate by-products of worthwhile endeavours. This means that they ought not to be seen as undermining our fundamental values, the values that criminal law is designed to defend. They ought to be governed by more market-friendly regulatory regimes.

All of these arguments are open to critique. For instance, the argument that some harmful outcomes of corporate conduct are not real crimes and should be regulated by non-stigmatizing welfare regulatory regimes depends on upside-down forms of reasoning. Occasionally the faults in this reasoning become all too obvious, threatening the legitimacy of the logic underlying the treatment of corporate wrongdoing as merely incidental to laudable activities. The question as to whether ordinary corporate capitalist activity is distinguishable from behaviour that we regard as criminal is then placed on the agenda. Certainly, the appearance of evenhandedness, vital to liberal democracy, comes under severe stress, especially as the public awareness of the costs of doing corporate business increases and as economic welfare becomes more unequally distributed. This is why the Law Reform Commission of Canada which, in 1976, wrote about the need to decriminalize, to unfetter individuals from control by the state, was, by 1985 and 1986, publishing papers recommending the creation of new crimes: a crime against the environment and a crime of endangerment of workers. The idea was that special crimes, analogous to criminal negligence, should be created because the pollution of the environment and the endangering of workers violated fundamental social values and could not be left to regulatory law. These recommendations came to nought. After the Westray killings and the failure to hold anyone criminally responsible for them—that is, as having done an act that demanded denunciation and condemnation—the New Democratic Party floated the idea of creating a corporate manslaughter offence. What is arresting is that these kinds of recommendations are thought necessary by those offended by the lack of state control over odious corporate acts. After all, the existing Criminal Code provisions, on their face, are already available. This speaks volumes about the success of the corporate sectors in undermining the use of the Criminal Code in the corporate setting.

To anyone concerned with them, these matters have left a considerable feeling of unease. There is evidence that corporate harm-doing is treated differently and more benignly than other sorts of injury-doing. This puts pressure on lawmakers to devise new means to hold corporate actors to account. The pressure in turn leads to sophisticated ripostes by corporate-sector allies. They achieve a lot of success in this, too, in large part because they have the power to discipline governments that make life too hard for them. The result has been approaches that do not rely on anything like repression of uncontrolled, harmful corporate behaviour. There are movements afoot to ask corporations to be more thoughtful of the citizens' needs. They are being asked to be socially responsible. These movements, like any that seek to civilize corporate capitalism, invariably find that they have huge mountains to climb.

(image speech bubble: "YOU REALIZE THAT THE CAPACITORS IN THAT TV WERE MADE IN A SWEATSHOP.")

The Legal Corporate Social Responsibility Movement: A Politics of Impotence

Wherein we learn how reformers try to exploit the apparent gap between the ownership of the corporation by invisible friends and the control of the corporation by the captains of industry, retail, finance, and everything else; and how the reformers fail because their efforts are, in liberal and capitalist terms, illogical, and because the various captains of industry and everything else would rather be damned than permit their invisible friends to be used for the public good.

Nestlé peddles its infant formula in poor countries in which women have to mix the baby food with unclean water. Mothers have been gulled into doing so by Nestlé's pseudo-scientific representations that this manner of feeding is healthier for their babies than their uncontaminated breast milk. The results are horrifying.

Shell sets up oil-drilling and outfits refineries in Nigeria, destroying the environment and way of life, first of the Ogoni and then the Ijaws people. Local resistance brings the use of lethal, repressive force by the Nigerian government; people die, attracting the outrage of the world. The Nigerian poet Nnimo Bassey writes:

183

We see open mouths
But we hear no screams
Standing in a pool of blood
Up to our knees
We thought it was oil
But it was blood.

Nike contracts with heavy-handed employers in Korea, then Indonesia, then Viet Nam, as it moves about in its endless search for women employees who will make shoes at the lowest possible wages. The shoes are then sold at exorbitant prices in far-flung parts of the world. One woman, working ten hours a day, six days a week, takes one month to earn one-half of the retail price of a pair of sneakers in North America. In any one year, Nike pays Michael Jordan to advertise its sneakers more than the combined yearly earnings of thirty thousand Indonesian workers. The swoosh associated with Nike becomes the "v" in the word "slavery" used by Nike's detractors in the First World.

Talisman Energy is a joint venturer in the development of oil interests in Sudan. The royalties it pays, it is said, go a long way towards helping the Sudanese government wage a fierce and brutal war against a part of its population.

Occidental Petroleum provides heavy support for the Colombia Plan, the name of the U.S. Trojan Horse-like war on drugs in that South American country. This backing earns Occidental governmental and military support for its development of the oil fields in Colombia, which requires displacement of the U'Wa peoples of the area. The Colombian government meets their resistance with force.

In the *maquiladoras* and free-trade zones everywhere, major corporations have set up factories and plants that allow the superexploitation of local labour and provide inexpensive access to raw resources. These operations displace labour in the corporations' home countries and produce goods for our consumer markets at lower costs, yielding great profits.

Anglo-American and European corporations are exploiting the conditions in the Third World to accumulate profits for their predominantly Anglo-American and European shareholders. In most of these cases, the corporations are able to maintain that they are acting within the limits of the law in the countries they operate in, even if they are acting in ways that would lead to condemnation in their home countries. In short, these are, once again, extreme, and extremely well-known, examples of corporate capitalist behaviour that may well be technically legal but is socially so reprehensible that, using conventional criteria, it could easily be criminalized. But in these kinds of cases, which take place outside our jurisdictions, we in the First World appear to have even less power over corporate conduct. Still, because the final profiteers are within our jurisdictions and because many of us, as consumers, seem only too glad to benefit from the exploitation of Third World peoples and their environments, an increasing number of people feel a certain amount of concern, and sometimes guilt, about the uglinesses that seemingly arise naturally from how market capitalism is practised by our major corporations. These feelings are exacerbated by knowledge of the many domestic unpunished, or lightly punished, violations. The response in turn leads to protestations, and in this all the angered people are supported by the many victims of insecurity in the First World—that is, by the large segments of the population who feel that the riches created by private corporations have not trickled down to them in any tangible way.

The number of disaffected people in our part of the world is significant, and, even more important, these people tend to be politically and commercially significant. A study by the Conference Board of Canada found that only 7 per cent of Canadians strongly agreed with the statement "Successful business should focus on money and profit rather than on social and community issues." A whopping 78 per cent strongly or moderately disagreed with the statement. In Britain a 1999 poll showed that only 25 per cent of people thought that big business profits made things better for everyone, while 52 per cent flatly disagreed with that notion. A U.S. study focusing on views about the conduct of corporations vis-à-vis customers and workers revealed a strong anti-corporate sentiment. While 78 per cent of respondents rated corporations highly when it came to profit-seeking and profit-making, and 53 per cent believed that corporations did well on producing quality products, 55 per cent thought corporations did poorly when it came to paying decent wages; and 69 per cent indicated that they did very badly when it came to the provision of job security. Many of those polled believed that corporate behaviour was a greater problem than government behaviour, despite the widely disseminated notion that the state provides the real brake on prosperity.

These indications of growing public disenchantment with the corporate sectors imperil the legitimacy of the relentless pursuit of profits via the corporate vehicle. The disillusionment is fed not only by the awareness of the more disagreeable outcomes of market capitalism, but also by a host of pronouncements from opinion leaders in the political, business, academic, and judicial spheres that, in turn, are buttressed by the clear anti-corporate mood revealed by the polls. For instance, in 1994 Courtney Pratt, president of

Noranda Inc., called for corporations to become more socially responsible. "Without losing sight of its basic economic role, or its need to make a profit, the modern corporation has concerns, ideals and responsibilities which go beyond the economic," he said. "It must accept community responsibilities as well as private obligations." The well-known journalist Will Hutton became one of the leaders of a movement in England urging that corporations be made to accept this role. He wrote of the need to create a new financial architecture in which private decisions could lead to the development of a less degenerate capitalism. Charles Handy asserts that, while profits are one of the objectives of the corporation, they are not the only goal. He states that corporations should be reconceptualized as servants of communities with members such as customers, suppliers, financiers, and workers. All these interests should be treated as stakeholders in the corporation. In England, Prime Minister Tony Blair jumped on the stakeholder bandwagon, giving an indication of its import. He made clear his own ambition to create a stakeholder society, a society of inclusion, one that must provide opportunity to all and afford advancement on the basis of merit, and that should exclude no groups from full participation. All of this reflects the latest trend in a movement that has existed for a long time, a movement that calls for corporate managers to act in a socially responsible way even if that means a relaxation of the single-minded pursuit of profits.

If this is the political push generated by the corporate stakeholder/social responsibility movement, a vast change could be at hand if that movement wins the battle for the minds and souls of the people. There is support for such radicalism, occasionally even from within the judiciary, the very institution that validated the self-seeking corporate vehicle. In a widely cited declaration, Justice Thomas Berger of the B.C. Supreme Court wrote:

> The classical theory is that the directors' duty is to the company. The company's shareholders are the company and, therefore no interests outside those of the shareholders can legitimately be considered the directors. . . . A classical theory that once was unchallengeable must yield to the facts of modern life. . . . If today the directors of a company were to consider the interests of the employees no one would argue that in doing so they were not acting *bona fide* in the interests of the company itself. Similarly, if the directors were to consider the consequences to the community of any policy that the company intended to pursue, and were deflected in their commitment to that policy as a result, it could not be said that they had not considered *bona fide* the interests of the shareholders.

While many fellow judges have quoted this statement from *Teck Corporation Ltd. v. Millar* (1973) with apparent approval—they, no doubt, like to feel they are part of a caring institution—it has rarely been given any legal effect. But in the context of the contemporary excitement about the reconceptualization of the corporation as a socially responsible institution devoted to its stakeholders, the *Teck* statement has recently been revivified as a means of legitimating the position of the proponents of the stakeholder theory.

All of this has been sufficiently noteworthy to raise alarm amongst the apostles of the corporate world. For instance, Terence Corcoran, a business journalist who is a not-insignificant intellectual gatekeeper of the status quo, has trumpeted his disgust about the very rumour of the stakeholder idea. In a 1990s piece Corcoran argued that the substitution of stakeholders, in the *Teck* sense, for shareholders as the intended beneficiaries of corporate activity, was a novel idea whose time had not come and should never be mentioned again. Corcoran is not a scholar, but a front man for corporate Canada, and his assertions were ill-informed. At the time the stakeholder concept was far from being novel. He argued further that the idea was an abomination because it was just a way of sneaking a post-Marxism kind of socialism in while no one was looking. He was wrong about that as well. He went on, however, to say that the concept was incoherent. He was right about that; his instincts, which move him to protect capitalism, led him to the right conclusion. By contrast, the instincts of the more sophisticated proponents of greater corporate social responsibility do lead them astray.

As they urge changes in corporate governance and behaviour, the proponents of the stakeholder/social responsibility movement essentially offer two lines of argument. They do not always keep these lines distinct, but they are different in nature. The first line of argument is that, given the actual mode of operation of large corporations, it makes legal and operational sense to have them *legally governed* so as to reflect interests other than those of shareholders. The second line of argument is that we must, *somehow, any-old-how*, force corporations to behave more altruistically or else we are lost.

The first argument's limitations arise out of its avoidance of the irreducible essence of a corporation: it is a vehicle that is legally and ideologically devised to pursue profits to the greatest extent possible. Changes to its fundamental structure, therefore, would reduce it to being a corporation in name only. The second of these arguments is more clearly born out of desperation, and we will leave discussion of its line of thought and limitations to the next chapter. Here we will concentrate on the difficulties facing those who would advocate legal and potentially radical kinds of reform. We begin by asking why advocates for change believe that they could effect such radical changes.

The Lineage and Schizophrenia of the Legal Stakeholder/Social Responsibility Movement

As we have already seen (chapter 6), since the inception of modern corporate law market capitalists have faced a grave problem: the separate legal personality doctrine, complemented by the limited liability of investors, heralded the arrival of a new dawn, one in which the investors of property did not control, or even care all that much, about its deployment. Adam Smith deplored this state of affairs because it meant that the managers of the capital would not act as efficiently as they would if they were single-mindedly pursuing their own interests with their own capital. The situation would minimize the efficiency promised by a market operated by owners. Smith was truly bearish about the potential utility of the corporate vehicle as a tool of market capitalism: hence his scathing view that corporations should only be used for enterprises that required hardly any entrepreneurial imagination. By 1904 Thorstein Veblen was noting that, indeed, the functional separation of ownership and control impelled by the use of the corporation had given management a great deal of discretion, which it exercised rather freely to suit itself. He bemoaned how corporate managers were joining the parasitic bankers and promoters to devise schemes for personal profit while purporting to act on behalf of the corporation and its shareholders. This critique gave substance to Adam Smith's worst fears. When Berle and Means published their famed study in 1932, they added overwhelming evidence of the tendency for owners of capital to lose control over that capital by leaving it in the daily care of the corporate managers appointed by them. They found that the number of publicly traded corporations controlled by identifiable shareholders was a remarkably small minority of their sample, some twenty-two, whereas those controlled by non-owning managers numbered eighty-eight. By 1963 a replication of their study revealed that the problem had deepened, with a hundred and sixty-nine out of a sample of two hundred corporations being management-controlled while only five were clearly privately owned or controlled. If separation of ownership from control makes the corporation a market-defeating institution, Berle and Means provided proof positive that the market was being distorted by the publicly traded corporation.

This clear and present danger to the legitimacy of capitalism's favourite vehicle, the invisible friend of the captains of industry and everything else, soon gave rise to a massive amount of revisionism by legal scholars, led by the law and economics school. This school's claim is that there is no real bifurcation between owners and managers, in that the managers are just contractual agents of the owners and, as such, have a contractual and fiduciary responsibility to carry out the wishes of their principals, the shareholders. That is, managers are there to carry out the specific and known wishes of the true owners. If there is some slippage (and even these corporate optimists concede there is a good deal of slippage), this problem can be rectified by the efficient operation of the market. Discipline over wayward managers will be exercised by the market for managers, which will punish poorly performing managers. The markets for control over the corporation will also exercise control, as investors use those markets to buy control over a badly managed corporation, believing that, with new managers, they will earn a profit on such a purchase. Similarly, discipline will be exercised over managers as a result of the decline of a corporation's share of the market for its goods and services, inasmuch as the decline is attributable to poor management. If any or all of these markets work imperfectly, then governments can always step in with corrective rules that will impose the terms of the contracts that would otherwise have been struck between owners and managers if the markets were perfect. These ingenious, if somewhat overly optimistic, arguments are made by these defenders of the corporate form to counter the proposition first adumbrated by these scholars' hero, Adam Smith, that the separation of ownership from management would naturally lead to inefficiency.

This vigorous revisionism first gained impetus when certain critics saw the gap between ownership and control as a problem for the legitimating claim of efficiency made on behalf of corporations. It gained extra impetus when it was seen as a promising opportunity by those who regarded the unfettered for-profit corporation as a menace to the welfare of the community. Soft-hearted antagonists of the status quo believed that they could use the same observed split of control from management to make the corporation do things that the corporation's defenders hated. They argued that the discretion that inevitably has to be ceded to corporate managers should be exercised by those managers to look after the welfare of those harmed by or simply connected to the corporation's activities, as well as looking after the interests of shareholders; and that there should be a law to that effect. Here it is not irrelevant that the Berle and Means study saw the light of day when corporate capitalism was failing to deliver general welfare. Indeed, it was failing spectacularly on this score. The Great Depression of the 1930s destroyed any belief that the trickle-down impact of the single-minded pursuit of profits by corporations would enure to the benefit of all. Nor was it any longer clear to the world that the market, let alone the corporation, was an efficient means by which to pursue general economic welfare. In this context, the Berle and Means findings prompted calls for more efficiency and for economic actors, especially corporations, to act as if they had a social conscience. For the system, and corporations as key components of that system, to be viewed as legitimate, changes were in order. Indeed, the impact of the failures of the 1930s on corporate lore, rather than law, is of direct interest to the discussion of legal remedies that follows.

In a riposte to Corcoran's 1990 attack on the stakeholder notion, Max Clarkson noted that Corcoran was wrong about the novelty of the concept because, as early as the 1930s, General Electric (later found to be a flagrant violator of the laws of the land) had identified consumers, employees, the general public, and shareholders as stakeholders to which it owed an obligation. Similar statements were offered by major corporations such as Johnson & Johnson and General Motors (also both well-known deviants, despite these pious sentiments). Of course, it was the severe Depression conditions of the 1930s that influenced major corporations to reach out for measures that would add to their social legitimacy.

On the academic front, the drive for more corporate social responsibility received a lift in the postwar period, with its economic prosperity. The strong economic climate gave a boost to a movement that saw the corporation as a potential public engine for social good. Its claim was that, if it ever had been right, it was certainly true *now* that managers of large corporations could easily satisfy the desire for reasonable profits and still have sufficient capital left to look after the stakeholders. Now it was more appropriate than ever that managers should exercise this discretion for the public good. That the new prosperity and the preceding failures might give rise to a new legal entente of this sort was given support by social science arguments that had gained currency. As early as 1926 John Maynard Keynes portrayed this managerial role, namely acting on behalf of the common weal, as making good corporate sense. He pointed out that the obvious rise of real managerial power was evidence of a tendency of enterprise to socialize itself. As it did so, managers perceived the need to avoid criticism from the public that they were not serving society's general interests. This meant that shareholders should be given adequate, rather than maximum, dividends so as to permit management to take costly measures to avert criticism of corporate economic power. The trade-off would be that the stability of the corporation would be safeguarded over the long haul. Somewhat later, a slightly different and more technologically narrow view, purveyed by James Burnham, treated the dominant decision-making power of large corporations' managers as a sign that there had been a managerial revolution that had turned managers of large corporations into a new, somewhat benign, ruling class with noblesse oblige functions.

These acknowledgements—that the dominant way of doing business had created an unbridgeable gap between the owners of invested capital and its managers, which reduced the objective need to treat the shareholders as privileged members of the corporation, and that efficiency in the pure market sense was no longer the objective leitmotif of the corporate vehicle— paved the road for the postwar period reformers. Earlier arguments to the effect that managers had a duty to exercise their discretion on behalf of non-shareholders were revivified and invigorated. As early as 1932, E.M. Dodd had argued that the Berle and Means evidence supported the case that managers were trustees for many people other than shareholders. Berle himself, although originally opposed to Dodd's perspective, came to embrace it in the changed circumstances of the postwar period. At that time there was a felt political need to honour the promises made to the generation let down by corporate capitalism in the 1920s and 1930s and that had been asked to make huge sacrifices during the war. In addition to honouring those promises as a matter of decency, there also was the pressure felt from the emergence of an alternative political economic regime, the ever more visible military and productive might of the U.S.S.R. At the same time the anti-colonial revolts sweeping the world heralded turbulence ahead for the hegemony of corporate capitalism. In this context, the observed fact that managers of large corporations had discretionary powers and that these large corporations were not only the means of creating economic welfare, but were its most significant, virtually only, beneficiaries, led to claims that the managers' discretion should be used consciously to enrich the lives of the formerly ignored and maligned.

The idea that corporations should be managed *directly* for the social good emerged, then, from arguments built on the problems created for market efficiency by the separation of control and ownership in major corporations. By the 1970s, as a result of changing political economic circumstances, the idea had gained concrete support in many quarters, spawning a host of proposals to reconstruct the legal governance of corporations. These proposals envisaged a corporate management team charged with the legal duty of balancing the concerns of employees, consumers, and the environment, among others, against those of the shareholders of the corporation. This movement is alive and lively today, but it does face difficulties. The movement for change is diametrically opposed by another wing of activists on the corporate reform bandwagon, the revisionists, whose vision is that such abuses by the shareholders' managers that do take place should be redressed by perfecting market conditions. Legislative changes to corporate governance could be contemplated only if made absolutely necessary by the failure of the markets. The revisionists' agenda is to use corporate governance legal reform to ensure that the corporation retains its character as an institution legally designed to maximize profits on the shareholders' invested capital. Community and stakeholder values need only be respected to the extent that they are protected by existing legally enforceable rules.

What this means is that there is a continuing struggle over exactly how corporate behaviour is to be reformed by law, because the two goals for reform are, on their face, incompatible. Given what we know about how law sets out to privilege the for-profit corporate agenda, guessing at the outcome of this battle should be a no-brainer. The stakeholder/social responsibility movement, the modification of the legal corporate agenda to look after a slew of stakeholders, will have the much harder row to hoe than will the countermovement to retain the corporation as a single-minded site of profit-maximization.

A Conceptual and Legal Ideology Problem

While a great deal of public support for asking corporations not to behave anti-socially comes from the corporate record of flagrant violations of the law, that issue is not what engages the stakeholder/social responsibility movement. If violations of existing standards were the only issue, the civil, welfare, and regulatory offences and criminal law regimes could be strengthened and refined. But the push is not just for corporations to obey the law, but also to have them behave better, with more regard for the people whose lives are hurt or severely limited through the corporate pursuit of profits. A positive set of obligations being urged would require corporations to be altruistic and compassionate, and this would take place at the expense of their investors. This approach, though, faces a tall conceptual hurdle arising from the very legal and/or political terrain that is to be used to put this kind of change in attitude and behaviour into effect.

Imagine a man who comes across a baby trashing upside down in a small pool of water only about nine inches deep. The man has a horror of getting wet and decides to walk on, leaving the baby to drown. Although we might consider this man to be a moral leper, he will have committed no legal wrong. In law, there is no obligation to rescue. Only if the law has imposed a positive duty on a person or class of persons will it step in to demand a positive rescuing action from anyone. In the imagined case, a parent or legal guardian of the baby, a police officer, or a doctor who had undertaken treatment of the baby would be legally bound to help.

This hands-off approach fits in with the individualistic, egoist model of liberal law and with the capitalist market model: we are not to be fixed with a responsibility to help our neighbours. Underlying this precept is the anxiety that, if individuals were legally bound to be their brothers' and sisters' keepers, there would be arguments to the effect that to rescue them from poverty and privation we should share our personal wealth with them. This argument postulates a political economy of a totally different kind than the one that liberal law is designed to maintain and perpetuate. This omission does not mean that individuals can do as they like without regard for the interest of others. Rather, a sophisticated array of civil, administrative, and criminal laws requires each of us seeking to attain our own goals to do so without intruding unnecessarily on the ability of all others to do the same. But this feature does not mean that we have a *positive* duty to help our neighbours. Rather, the duty is a *negative* one: we are not to engage in conduct that harms our neighbours by breaching existing legal rules and standards. Altruism, as a legal obligation, is a non-starter in the ideological world of liberal market capitalism.

The terrain is tilted, therefore, in favour of retaining the corporation as a vehicle for pursuing profits, rather than as a vehicle for promoting the common good even at the expense of profits. Of the two wings, one starts off with an advantage: the one seeking to reform the legal governance and operation of the corporation to ensure that management does not abuse the discretion granted it by the principals, the shareholders. The prevailing legal ideology does not object to its agenda, which does not require anything by way of new qualitative duties for managers. All that this wing of reformers is promoting are the kinds of duties that will better ensure the ability of managers to carry out the existing legal task—the maximization of profits for the corporation and its shareholders. This wing's opponents, however, want to change the nature of the corporation. They would like a slew of novel and hard-to-define positive legal duties to be imposed on the corporation's governing body. Their need is all the more difficult to satisfy because the contents of these duties are unclear, contradictory to the point of being incoherent. That is where the journalist Corcoran got things right.

Clear Conservatives, Uncertain Progressives

For the status-quo wing, the only reason for legal reform is the possibility that, as things stand, the agents/managers of the corporation are in a position to abuse their power and thereby to cheat their principals. This possibility exists because the existing rules of corporate governance leave managers with a great deal of room to manoeuvre. The board of directors that, as the elected representatives of the shareholders, appoints managers is legally held to a loosely defined standard of care. Directors are charged with exercising a reasonable standard of care in acting in the best interests of the corporation. In large, endocratic corporations, they are entitled to delegate tasks to professional managers. The directors are policy-setters, rather than operatives and executives (although some directors may also be executives). These hands-off supervisors of the corporation's operational managers must rely for their information on the very managers they are supposed to supervise. As the law stands, they will have done their duty if they do their best to ensure that managers report properly and act upon the ensuing directors' instructions when they get them. To stop the remaining potential for abuse by the managers engaged in the everyday running of the corporation, what may be needed is the spelling out of specific duties for named directors and the creation of special committees of directors to vet specific tasks of the management team. In this way, directors will be able to monitor better two aspects of management behaviour: whether managers are acting in the best interests of the corporation when they make choices amongst the various decision open to them; and whether managers' choices lead to the optimal profit performance to which the corporation (read: shareholders) is entitled.

A plethora of such legal reforms have been initiated and suggested. The appointment of independent directors and unrelated directors is one of the favoured suggestions. Here the idea is that at least some of the directors on boards of large, publicly traded corporations, notionally elected by shareholders, should come from slates comprising persons not directly connected to the managers of a corporation. These directors would, therefore, be independent of management. Some enthusiasts recommend that some directors should come from a slate of persons not at all connected with the enterprise(s) of the corporation. They are referred to as unrelated directors. This push for independent and unrelated directors arises from the repeated findings that boards of directors chosen in the traditional manner tend to be thoroughly unprofessional and ineffective.

As a pioneering study by Miles Mace concluded, directors generally do not adequately perform any of the three major functions normally carried out by a board charged with supervising executives. First, directors are to establish basic objectives, strategies, and policies. It turns out that they leave these crucial tasks to the very managers they are supposed to guide. Second, to discharge their legal task satisfactorily directors should be asking discerning questions inside and outside board meetings. Mace found that they do not do this; rather, managements have convinced them that board meetings are not intended to be debating forums. Third, board members should also take the lead in respect of the selection of the president of the corporation to ensure that the right person gives the executive its marching orders. Again, he found this was not happening. As a matter of practice, that task was also being left within the domain of management.

The ability of managers to usurp the directors' functions stems from the practice, at least in the early days of corporate capitalism, of appointing directors based on their reputations for success and/or trustworthiness as "gentlemen," rather than for their business acumen. They were like parsley on a fish: decoration rather than substance. This is why the legal duties of care and the requirement to be diligent in pursuit of the corporation's best interests were traditionally stated in such vague and non-demanding language. The assumption was that directors would often be running small family businesses or be members of the political and social lists' elites, appointed to the boards of large corporations primarily for the prestige they added. Amateurism was the modus operandi. As the modern corporation—huge, complex, with many sub-branches and affiliates, operating in many jurisdictions, employing thousands of people—came to dominate the economic landscape, the rules and ideas based on these quaint old notions made no sense. Indeed, they were counterproductive, rather than simply outdated, because the very complexity of these institutions has now permitted the executives—the professionals in the trenches—to dictate names of board members to the shareholders. With their minimal legal obligations to supervise and monitor, directors have become managerial lapdogs, which is perhaps a step down from their ancient status as ornaments adorning the corporate crown.

It is in this context that the clamour for independent and unrelated directors, preferably professional directors, has arisen. This push is meant to advance the efficiency of the corporation as a vehicle maximizing profits for investors. It is the preferred means of overcoming the inefficiencies produced by the wrongful exercise of discretion by a management that has nothing to fear from its board of directors. But, as it turns out, such empirical evidence as there is suggests that the presence of independent and/or unrelated directors has brought but little observable change. Still, that is neither here nor there. The point is that this kind of legal reform fits in with the status quo advocates' agenda. So too does the proposal for legally mandated internal auditing committees. The law already requires the appointment of external independent auditors to assure the investing public of the accuracy of the reports put out by the corporation when disclosing new circumstances and/or when going to the public to solicit investment. Internal audit committees, overseen by directors, are meant to keep managers honest in matters such as salary demands, adherence to stated policies, and the like. Again, this kind of measure is aimed squarely at advancing the cause of profit-maximization. It has nothing to do with the promotion of the views favoured by the stake-holder/social responsibility movement.

By way of reprise, this argument also applies to the new direct duties imposed on directors (chapter 10). These new duties have been imposed to ensure the meeting of the existing legal obligations of the corporation to the revenue authorities, to environmental and occupational health and safety legislation, and to competition laws. Even though the right wing of the spectrum has resisted this increase in responsibility, in truth it is an alteration that helps to legitimate the corporation as a profit-chasing institution. All that is being done is to make sure that corporations constrain their profit-maximizing activities enough to stay within the boundaries of the law. This requirement is not novel in any way and remains a long distance away from making corporations act altruistically. To make them do so will require serious restructuring of corporate legal governance, and to attain this radically different goal is a much more difficult task.

One way of working towards that goal is to have special directors appointed to the boards of large, publicly traded corporations. These directors will be charged with the duties of seeing that the corporation respects certain rights and interests and of promoting certain kinds of productivity on the basis of their great communal value rather than their profit-making potential. In a mechanical, superficial, sense, there is an overlap here with the status quo adherents' agenda. These progressive reformers, like their conservative counterparts, are also calling for a set of directors independent of, or unrelated to, the managerial executive team. But the tasks to be given to these other directors and how they are to act are much more nebulous. These difficulties stem from the reality that these directors are meant to inhibit profit-maximization on behalf of the corporation and its shareholders so that other groups will benefit. Profit-maximization is to be tempered and made secondary in some circumstances. But the circumstances are hard to identify and, by their very nature, highly contestable. For instance, what special interests ought to be recognized as worthy of protection from profit-maximizing conduct that legally causes harms? Should a director stop the making of a shoddy product because the public should not be exposed to inferior goods? After all, one person's shoddy product may be just what is wanted by someone else, a person who cannot afford the better product that the special interest defenders might demand. In a world of imperfection, how are appropriate standards to be set if not by majoritarian governmentally imposed decisions or by the operation of market forces?

Further, as the special interests are to be protected within a profit-making regime, the people seeking the improved behaviour must make decisions about how much less profit makes sense from the direct investors' perspectives and from the general welfare-creation point of view—which would be a perplexing problem indeed for a director. Stakeholder and corporate social responsibility proponents try to skate over these kinds of questions. Stanley Beck, former dean of Osgoode Hall Law School and chair of the Ontario Securities Commission, is typical of the cadres who pretend that there is nothing too complex about any of this. In 1985, he wrote: "Vague social issues need not be substituted for profit maximization. That is not the issue. The issue is one of responsible profit-maximization rather than maximum profits at all costs." This is a common line of reasoning found in the stakeholder proponents' tracts.

The inherently contradictory nature of reaching for an absurdity such as "responsible profit-maximization" to avoid the implications of the corporation's ceaseless need to accumulate has been dismissed rather sharply by clear-thinking progressive scholars. Lord Wedderburn rightly refers to the Beck-like statements as belonging to the "fudge school" of thinking. Logically, the stakeholder/social responsibility movement starts from behind the political eight ball, and from there it gets worse. Many other factors compound the difficulty of balancing hard-to-identify social goals against something as unquantifiable as "reasonable profits." How many special directors looking after stakeholders' interests should a board have? Should they be in a majority? What mandate should they have? Should each one represent a specific interest, or should they just be directors who represent specific slants or expertise but who still have a responsibility to ensure the profitability and viability of the corporation? Should these directors be elected and, if so, who is to be allowed to vote? If directors are not to be appointed as representatives of specific interests and are asked to guide the corporation towards socially responsible behaviour, even at the expense of profits, does this mean they will choose between competing social goals without ever having been given any kind of legitimating democratic authority for such choice-making? Speaking of competing choices and values, how should the interests of, say, environmentalist and workers be balanced when they conflict?

All of these difficulties are well known, basically because it is self-evident that a corporation, a vehicle specifically designed for profit-maximization in order to advance the private accumulation of socially produced wealth, is ill-fitted to be used as a vehicle for the promotion of public policy. This does not still the controversy. Some scholars argue that the difficulties can be resolved; some of them argue that they cannot. I would argue that the nay-sayers have the better of the argument, simply because the others start off from a very weak political, as well as poor logical, base: after all, they are call-ing for unelected private-sector actors to impose public policies in the corpo-rate realm—public policies that cannot democratically be put on the agenda of the public sphere.

Some commentators have tried to remove this fundamental hurdle by arguing that shareholders may not in fact be single-mindedly interested in profit-maximization and that, therefore, they may not be opposed to the directors pursuing stakeholders', rather than just shareholders', interests. Daniel Greenwood points out that shareholders are a varied bunch of people who have preferences that may include concerns such as local community welfare, the well-being of the environment, or the good of the corporation's employees, and therefore it should not be assumed that they want managers to pursue profits at any cost. Shareholders, in other words, might very well want to look after stakeholders other than shareholders. This different ratio-nale for stakeholder proponents does not require abandonment of the argu-ment that the corporation's best interests are being served when social values other than profit-maximization are treated as corporate objectives.

The difficulty with this alternative rationale is that there is no easy way to support the claim that investors desire a variegated approach to manage-ment. There is also no obvious way for managers to gauge which of the many potential alternative objectives are in fact preferred by the thousands of share-holders of any one corporation, or to decide which ones should be given preference even if they can be identified. While Greenwood's point—that individual investors should be treated as individuals with personal views and moralities, rather than as empty-headed profiteers—is respectful and there-fore ought to be respected, he pays less attention than he should (although he does address the issue) to the nature of many investors: a great number of the important ones are institutional investors. They are corporations and their managers have their own maximization of profit obligations. More, his central point is not supported by evidence. Such evidence as there is goes to show that shareholders get quite shirty when corporate management spends money on not-for-profit endeavours. Indeed, Justice Berger's statement in the *Teck* case was a response to the well-established legal doctrine that share-holders are entitled to object to such not-for-profit activity. The doctrine had become well-established as a result of litigation initiated by shareholders who were disgruntled by the non-maximization approach of their corporation's managers. At the very least, then, there is good evidence that some shareholders do not want their managers to pursue any interest but their own. David Olive records a number of instances in which, even in post-*Teck* /pro-stakeholder times, shareholders continue to bring resolutions aimed at forcing corporate directors to rein in managers who are too free with the shareholders' money—by giving it to charity, perhaps, or to the causes of stakeholders—rather than devoting themselves to the primary cause of shareholders: profits. Some shareholders, then, may well be willing to forego profits to meet other social needs, but many shareholders resist this idea.

Inasmuch as some activist shareholders do want their corporation to pursue stakeholder needs and values, they tend to meet with relatively little success. Some activists, for instance, buy shares so that they will be in a position to bring shareholder motions to corporate meetings and, thereby, draw attention to their cause. Various groups did this to object to corporations supporting the war effort in Viet Nam. Others did it to raise objections within corporations that conducted business with South Africa during the days of Apartheid. Others did it to attack Nestlé's infant formula sales in Third World countries. Until recently Canadian shareholders have found it difficult to get their proposals for change in corporate behaviour heard, even when the changes they were seeking were designed to improve profit-maximization rather than the advancement of stakeholders' interests. In part, at least, this was due to the technical difficulties that they had to surmount. The corporate voting system was stacked against minority shareholders, who had to make use of something called the proxy system to get resolutions placed on the corporate board's agenda. In the immediate past this scheme required the proponents of a resolution to contact all shareholders of the corporation to ask them for the right to vote their shares in favour of that resolution, hence the name "proxy voting." Manifestly, this task involved a time-consuming and costly organizational effort. It was comparatively easy for any managerial team that did not like the proposed resolution to mount an effective counter-campaign. The managers had control over the workings of the proxy machinery and command over the corporation's treasury. The dice were loaded. When the activist shareholders sent their proposal to the other shareholders, they had to limit the required supporting statement to two hundred words; the management team was not so limited in its response. It could send out brochures, even videos, urging shareholders to reject the activist shareholders' blandishments and to give their votes to the management team to vote as it saw fit. Not only were the boards of directors and their managers thus favoured, but they were also given the right to reject a proposal they did not like without it ever being put to a vote if the proposal was adjudged to be aimed at the promotion of "general economic, political, racial, social or similar causes." Those causes, of course, are exactly of the kind being promoted by proponents of changes in the sphere of corporate responsibility.

It should not, therefore, come as much of a surprise that only once has a court upheld a claim of a dissident shareholder whose proposal to put a resolution to a vote was rejected by a board of directors; and that this case was concerned with a shareholder's effort to make the board of directors more profit-oriented rather than more socially responsible. The shareholder, a Mr. Michaud, had proposed a resolution that would have changed the by-laws of the corporation. His proposed amendment was to allow for the appointment of some directors independent of the executive management team, a team that he believed was not being pressured sufficiently by its tame directors to pursue shareholder wealth. The court agreed that the board of directors should permit this kind of resolution to go forward to a corporate meeting and to be put to a vote. This pro-minority shareholder result was so unusual that it led to an outpouring of commentary. For instance, a large segment of a leading journal was devoted to a vigorous discussion of this potential opening of previously tightly secured floodgates. But "potential" is the key word in that phrase. The decision in the *Michaud* case in no way suggested that the court thought it appropriate that a duty should be imposed on management to look after the interests of non-shareholders. Indeed, despite all the excitement in the wake of *Michaud*, thus far no such judicial determination has been made.

Unsurprisingly, the chilling effect of the hard-to-use proxy voting system was giving the notion of shareholder democracy a bad name: minorities, whether wealth-seekers or do-gooders, were not being heard. In the only major survey done, Raymonde Crete found that 90.3 per cent of corporate respondents reported that no non-management shareholder had ever asked them to include a proposal in the proxy mailings that management sent out as part of its routine search for formal shareholder approval of its decisions. The impotence of Canadian minority shareholders was all the more noticeable because their counterparts in the United States, with much more friendly proxy voting rules, had been able to notch up a number of stakeholder victories. The situation thus generated pressures for legislative reform in Canada, and in late 2001 such amending legislation was passed. Amongst other things, it permits persons to solicit proxies from no more than fifteen shareholders without having to send a dissident proxy circular—that is, without having to clear the hurdle of the alerted opposition of a management team about to be challenged. Further, a person may, in some circumstances, commence a solicitation for votes process without sending out a proxy circular if the solicitation is conveyed by public broadcast, speech, or publication, greatly reducing the time and costs incurred by the old requirements. Notably, the new provisions also eliminate the right of the board of directors to reject a proposal to further general economic, political, racial, social, or other such causes. This last amendment had been fought for by such groups as the churches' Taskforce on Corporate Responsibility, the Corporate Responsibility Coalition, and the Social Investment Organization. Even though boards of directors retain the right to reject shareholder proposals that they deem not to be related in a significant way to the business or affairs of the corporation—a potential pitfall for shareholder activists and a motherlode for the legal profession—the amending provisions represent solid advances for those who want to push for increased corporate responsibility towards stakeholders by taking up a position on the inside. But it is too early to say that the corner has been turned, that the imposition of corporate responsibility by reliance on the amended corporate law is a *fait accompli*.

I sound this note of pessimism because it is not necessarily only the technical hurdles presented by the proxy voting system that have inhibited Canadian shareholder activism. The paucity of shareholder activism in Canada, as opposed to in the United States, where the proxy system has presented fewer hurdles and where shareholders have demonstrated a greater desire to use the system to hold their corporations' directors and managers to account, may be attributable to a difference in control. In Canada, unlike in the United States, most large corporations are controlled by one or two major shareholders. It tends to be impractical for anyone but these dominant shareholders to exercise influence over the decision-making in what, functionally, is "their" corporation. It remains to be seen, therefore, whether the hard-fought-for changes in the proxy voting scheme will be allowed to have much impact on the profit-maximization goals of these dominant shareholding groups.

The distinct and well-known nature of shareholding concentration in Canada has an effect on the arguments made by those who want the law to set different goals for corporations. Unlike in the United States, where shareholding in most large corporations is diffuse, there is no real argument in Canada that owners have given up a significant amount of control over the deployment of their invested property. In Canada something like 80 per cent of all publicly traded corporations are controlled by one or two shareholders. In the United States the corresponding figure is about 20 per cent. Canada, then, lacks the factual bases and premises that generate the theoretical arguments by U.S. scholars about the evils and potentials of relatively unfettered managerial discretion. This gives further pause to those who hope that the new Canadian proxy voting regime will have a positive effect on corporate social responsibility. Even in the United States, the inherent logic of corporate capitalism continues to have more bite than does the postulated logic that social responsibility can be built into the system by forcing managers with discretion to take stakeholders' objectives and needs into account.

A number of statutory changes in the United States allow directors to take stakeholder interests into account when making certain types of decisions, in particular when they are considering how they should respond to a bid for control of the corporation by an outsider. Many observers see these provisions as giving directors and managers new justifications for resisting such a bid, which, while it may suit the shareholders, would bode ill for some of the incumbent managers. These reforms that, on their face, could benefit the stakeholder proponents are thus acceptable to the managers because the changes provide them with the capacity to give their crass self-ishness a patina of legitimacy. They are changes, therefore, that are annoying to the law and economics school, because they do much to endorse the assumption that a gap exists between ownership and control and that this gap, this downgrading of the primacy of ownership, is not such a bad thing. The law and economic scholars want to maintain that there is no such gap and that this nexus between ownership and managerial control makes for efficiency. The new statutory rights to consider stakeholders, which gives the managers freedom to ignore the true owners, are anathema to them. They hate the changes. But, despite the anxiety generated in the breasts of true believers in profit-maximization, these changes do not do much—if any-thing—for the stakeholder/social responsibility movement. They have not led to any serious shifting in how corporations are run.

There are, of course, other kinds of corporate governance reforms. They are more successful because they do not try to advance the stakeholder/social responsibility agenda. They set up outside, independent committees and auditors to avert the recurring instances of poor management of major corporations. The Enron debacle of 2001-2 reveals a little about how easy it is for corporate management to bend supposedly independent directors and auditors to its will. Still, the idea is clear: the watchdogs are there to vet such things as managerial plundering of the corporation's funds by the managers' avaricious allocation of bonuses and perquisites. These reforms are impelled by the need to protect the profit-maximization goals of the corporation and its shareholders. The logic of capitalism requires the provision of this kind of curtailment of managerial discretion inasmuch as the explicit and implicit contracts between the shareholders as principals and managers as agents fail to do so. There are plenty of blue-ribbon outfits that urge and obtain legislative interventions to attain this objective, because the excesses of managerial skul-duggery are well documented, especially when it comes to managerial pay.

In North America, the pay of executives in large corporations has reached levels that have attracted the attention of even the most sleepy observers. Often employees who are called greedy for demanding better pay or who are being laid off complain about the enormous, impossible-to-deserve pay packets of their rich bosses. As a simultaneously horrified and titillated *Business Week* article of September 2000 put it, "People feel over-worked and underpaid, especially in contrast to their CEOs, who now make 500 times the average employee's wages." Shareholders also utter their dis-pleasure at this gross imbalance — but they tend to do so when "their" corpo-ration's executives salaries increase at a time when the share performance of the corporation is declining. This displeasure can turn into anger when the managers have caused the corporation to change their remuneration's basis so that the downturn in the equity markets does not affect their perquisites. Executive remuneration is frequently by way of stock options that they can buy at a set price. Notionally this means that their interest and that of the shareholders in strong stock-market performance coincides. This mechanism of payment, a common one, is justified by, and therefore justifies, the advancement of shareholder interest as the primary corporate goal. It is when managers seek to uncouple themselves from this discipline by reformulating the price at which they can exercise their options that we get pressure for cor-porate governance reforms. Plainly, profit-maximization matters more than anything else, and policy-makers and governments have plainly acknowl-edged this by their actions.

All of this does not mean that the public is never served by legal corpo-rate governance reform. Governments have had to step in, for instance, to impose some personal responsibility on directors to ensure that minimum standards of the law are obeyed. The legal reforms in governance, when they do not directly address the needs of shareholders as profiteers, are there to help governments assure the world that they have done their best to keep cor-porate excesses within legal bounds. This is still a long way from the imposi-tion of the kind of responsibility that the stakeholder and social responsibility movement advocates are seeking to entrench. They would demand that the corporation do more than just abide by existing legal requirements.

The problem for ambitious social responsibility advocates is that they want to disregard the essential nature of the corporation. This makes little sense. After all, the large, publicly traded corporation is attractive to investors because in taking up this vehicle these investors will be beholden to no one. They are free to disassociate themselves from the corporation and its other members whenever the management of the corporation displeases them or whenever they want to put their capital to a different use. This is the *raison d'être* of stock markets. The shareholders have the power of exit if they can find purchasers for their shares on the open market. This practice is efficient from the corporation's perspective, because the amount of capital available is not influenced in any way by these market transactions. It does not matter, either to the corporation or to any one investor, who the investors are at any one time. Nothing could be more impersonal.

The relationships between shareholders are money relationships. These investors accept, indeed embrace, the logic of relating to each other on the basis of wealth, rather than on the basis of any personal characteristics. They understand that shareholders with more wealth invested should have more say over the appointment of directors and managers and, therefore, over the conduct of these directors and managers. They also assume, and are backed in this assumption by corporate law, that all investors, while not equal, belong to the same class of wealth-owners and that, therefore, they owe each other various obligations that they owe to no one else. This why corporate law fairly bristles with remedies for minority shareholders, and it is why corporate law scholarship is mainly about the scope and utility of these remedies. Protections for minority shareholders against oppressive actions by directors and majority shareholders; safeguards in respect of their rights when takeovers or mergers occur; protections when majority shareholders are in a legal position to compel minority shareholders to sell their interest in the corporation: these and other matters are the stuff of corporate governance law reform and the launching pads for the litigation that makes so many corporate lawyers rich. In short, when they come together in a corporation shareholders perceive themselves, and are legally and functionally typecast (whatever their personal views on the environment, community values, or workers' welfare), as being interested only in one thing: money.

This understanding of the legal corporation for-profit makes it counterproductive to pretend that its agents, the management of the corporation, should, or could be made to, act as if they had other interests to protect. This would make the corporation into a different institution than it is designed to be. Its managers are intended to maximize profits to the extent the law permits it, and the law sets its face against the notion that the corporation should be used in any other way. Corporate law has created limited liability for shareholders because it provides them with an inducement to invest precisely because they can, for all practical purposes, disregard the way in which others might be harmed by the corporation's activities. The legal assumption is that those who invest in the for-profit corporation do not want their managers to be preoccupied by such constraints as they chase returns on the invested monies.

Those who want to maintain that shareholders would not be upset by their agents considering stakeholders' interests at their expense show little regard for the concrete reality and ideology of corporate law and practice. They are laudable romantics. The brute fact is that to impose a legal duty on managers of a for-profit corporation to look after public interests is a plausible argument, but not a workable one. It is as plausible to say that one's grandmother could be fitted with wheels to make her useful as a trolley car. In this age of technological wonders, this could be done, one supposes, but it would make little sense to try: it would make for a poor trolley car. More importantly, it wouldn't be all that good for the grandmother either. Not surprisingly, then, the stakeholder/social responsibility proponents have been forced to supplement their demands for a different approach on the part of directors and managers with strategies that do not try to alter the nature of the corporation by means of publicly enacted legal reforms to its governance structures. To get what they want, a kinder and gentler capitalist corporation, they have been lured by desperation into treading the private, undemocratic path — a path on which passage can be secured by money, not politics.

The Stakeholder/Social Responsibility Movement Goes Private

Wherein we learn that the captains of industry, finance, retail, and everything else are happy enough to wrap themselves in a cloak of social responsibility (woven especially for their invisible friends), provided that this feature does not seriously impede their capacity to pursue personal profits as irresponsibly as ever.

Galling as it is to have to admit it, then, Milton Friedman was right when, in 1979, he wrote that the discussions aimed at imposing a legal duty on corporations to act in a socially responsible manner "are notable for their analytical looseness and lack of rigor." The key to the problems that confound the stakeholder/social responsibility proponents is that, while they tut-tut, sometimes very loudly, about some of the practices of the large corporations, they do not quarrel directly with the reason for these practices, namely the chasing of profits that the corporation may retain for future profit-enhancing investments and/ or for distribution to the contributors of capital. As long as they continue to accept the value of that principle and believe that the corporation is an efficient means of giving it life, their noble efforts to invent, and then to implant, more restrictive legal governance structures are quixotic. The strength of this logic—whether they explicitly acknowledge it or not—forces the proponents of a kinder and gentler corporate capitalism to try to pressure corporate managers into change by making it more practically difficult for them to make profits by legal market practices that inflict hurts on people or the environment. Among the main "market tools" these proponents use are economic and ethical investment strategies. We will consider in turn the tactics deployed and their developments and prospects.

Economic Boycotts

Economic boycotts have long been a favoured stratagem of actors trying to force others into more acceptable behaviour. Sometimes boycotts are used by governments to achieve their political ends. Recent examples include the U.S. economic boycott of Cuba, the UN's embargo on Iraq, and the withdrawal of some nations of their athletes, suppliers, and news coverage from the Moscow Olympic Games of 1980 in protest over the Soviet Union's involvement in Afghanistan. In these cases, the state makes it illegal for its citizens, including corporations, to engage in commercial and/or social relations with the targeted nation. Such engagement will be a breach of the law.

More importantly for us here, given our concern with attempts to create conditions in which corporate actors will forego legal conduct that yields profits, is the use of the boycott weapon to pressure certain actors to behave better than existing law requires them to do. This tactic, too, has a long tradition. For instance, trade unions frequently ask consumers and suppliers not to deal with an employer who refuses to accept unionization and continues harsh or unfair labour practice. The California grape boycotts of the 1960s are a well-known example. Unions may ask consumers and suppliers not to deal with employers who refuse to improve working conditions that the trade unions and their supporters believe are unacceptable. The Clean Clothes, Labour Behind the Label, United Students Against Sweatshops, and Rugmark campaigns are recent illustrations. Sometimes a campaign is run in favour of unionization in general, such as attempts to persuade consumers to buy only goods that bear a union label. Or, in support of indigenous people's claims, activists may organize a consumer boycott against the goods produced by the indigenous people's corporate antagonist because it is violating one of their claimed rights to a particular way of life or because of their opponent's denial of their entitlement to some of the fruits yielded by the exploitation of their lands and waters. The recent successful boycott of Daishowa on behalf of the Lubicon nation in Alberta is a good illustration.

In all these cases, would-be purchasers are asked to exercise their market power in favour of a social value. They are not required to do anything; indeed, their act is to be one of omission. From a capitalist market perspective it is an ideal tool: it celebrates the sovereignty of the individual as a market actor. It is, by definition, a tactic that fits with liberal economics and law and cannot be rejected as anti-capitalist or illiberal. It is safe to use and promises rewarding results. It is useful to, and used by, advocates concerned with corporate profiteering that harms workers and the environment, even if many of these advocates' preferred agenda would be to get rid of market capitalism altogether. To them it is a Trotsky-like tool, one that allows them to use capital's logic to bore from within. It is then much harder for them to be marginalized than if they use tactics that denounce the market, *tout court*. By using market capital's own logic, they find it easier to get public support for their campaign to alleviate suffering than when they call for legislative attacks on the market. The public to which they appeal is reassured that its consumer autonomy is being respected, at the same time as it being asked to be involved in the "doing of good" in a rather painless way.

The increased awareness of corporate exploitation of the world's vulnerable has impelled a fresh outbreak of enthusiasm for this kind of campaign. The corporations' own image-making and efficiency-maximizing organization of production have enabled consumer-based campaigns against the likes of Nike, Reebok, The Gap, Levi Strauss, Guess, and Disney to get off the ground. Naomi Klein has aptly described the world of commodification as one in which manufactured consumer identification with brands is the modus operandi of marketeers. The brands have become part of the persona of the people who wear and use and, not incidentally, advertise them by wearing and using them. The success of certain brands has made their purveyors easy to single out for bad practices, especially for their poor treatment of the workers who make the goods. These corporate outfits have developed elaborate contracting-out schemes that allow them to employ dirt cheap labour in the Third World, where unionization, health and safety legislation, and minimal safeguards in respect of hours, levels of pay, and the like are virtually unknown. Inevitably, these large First World corporations claim that what is being done in the Third World for the benefit of the corporations and their First World consumers and shareholders is legal there. In any event, they further point out, it is usually a local firm, *legally* separate from the First World corporations, that employs the workers who are (by First World standards, but not necessarily by their own standards) so badly treated. That is, major corporations run to hide behind the separate legal personality argument, in much the same way as their own major shareholders use that shield to hide themselves from responsibility for acts done for their benefit.

Still, in some of the more notorious instances, the campaigners have been able to overcome these lines of defence. The boycott leaders argue that, while legally there may be nothing wrong with how production is organized, the results, nonetheless, should be, and often are, unacceptable to the consumers in the First World. They have been able to educate large segments of the market to understand that their favourite brands are the product of very unappetizing practices. Here the boycott organizers play on both the guilt and greed of the consumer. They make consumers feel, first of all, that unless they speak up they will be concrete contributors to unacceptable exploitation. Second, they make consumers aware that they are paying far too much for products that are so cheaply produced. They appeal to the righteous indignation of consumers, highlighting how, for instance, Michael Jordan makes more per annum for saying "Just Do It" than thirty thousand workers do for actually doing something, or how Phil Knight, Nike's CEO, a white guy who can't jump, makes even more than Michael Jordan. Consumers begin to feel ripped off when they buy shoes they have been taught to covet.

These projects have had a certain educational success. Polls conducted by the campaign organizers show that most consumers would be willing to pay one dollar more for every twenty dollars spent on an item if they could be confident that the item was not produced in sweatshop cum slavery conditions. While there must be some doubt as to whether or not these kinds of survey responses would actually translate into a market practice should an extra dollar per twenty dollars be charged by a corporation that improved its productive practices, the targeted corporations have had to respond. They cannot take the risk of market-share losses in luxury-type competitive markets, that is, in markets where demand is elastic. Initially, when confronted by a consumer boycott campaign, they simply argue that they meet all the legal standards where production takes place and/or that, in any event, they are not the direct employers of the exploited workers. These responses have been stymied by a paradox: the success of these brand-producing corporations in winning their consumers' loyalty and veneration for their products is, in large part, based on the image of the corporation's greatness, decency, cool, humaneness, and the like. When icon-like corporations are exposed as profiting from their foreign contractors' excessive exploitations, these same consumers cannot be convinced that their favoured corporation is impotent, that, wondrously imaginative and ingenious as it is, it cannot do something about the behaviour of its on-the-ground brand producers. Socially conscious consumers are ready to pierce the legal corporate shield in ways that sober courts are not. The very success of branding is the Achilles heel being exploited by these consumer boycott campaigns.

This strategy, though, has a structural limitation. The tactic is only easy to use when the goods and services sold have a certain kind of imagery behind them. How easy is it to activate buyers into agitation over the way in which bicycle pumps, floppy diskettes, microchips, or television components are produced? How many people know that the capacitors found inside their laptops, pagers, and personal digital and cell phones—the very instruments used by consumer boycott campaigners to educate the consuming public— rely on the mining of coltan mud, which, when refined, produces tantalum, a necessary ingredient for the capacitors of the machines produced by Sony, Nokia, Motorola, and Ericsson? How easy would it be to organize a boycott against these products and producers because they rely on mining in Africa, which leads to self-exploitation, prostitution, and diseases, prolongs armed struggles between Rwandans and Ugandans, and leads to environmental degradation? The mining of coltan mud to produce the tantalum process does all of this. Also, is it likely that buyers are as price insensitive when it comes to items that they consider essential—like gasoline for their cars, or laptops, cell phones, or pagers—rather than items that might, especially to the well-heeled consumer, be more self-indulgent, like a T-shirt, a pair of jogging shoes, jeans, or a racket, with a logo? After all, while, on occasions, there have been attempts to boycott Shell to draw attention to its odious behaviour in Nigeria, or against Unocal for its involvement in Myanmar, these efforts have been short-lived as consumers continue to respond well to price competition on automobile fuels. The gas market, like many others, is a market in which price does matter greatly to the consumers. In short, there are limits on the utility of this tactic. Still, it does have some beneficial possibilities.

Those boycott campaigns that have met with some success have done so because the corporation, based in the North and relying on its image for its success, has had to accept that it has the capacity to control and monitor the contractors it hires to do its exploitation in the South. This capacity is expected to be used for social betterment. When, after the initial period of denial and protestations of innocence, the corporation begins to respond positively, it usually tries to recoup its image by crafting a Mission Statement or a Code of Conduct and proclaiming that it and its contractors will thereafter live up to the promises made. Such proclamations are full of positive phrases about human rights, worker protections, and the environment. Manifestly, this is not a satisfactory response to the sophisticated organizers of boycotts. They see this as a transparent effort at damage control and co-option of the protestors, not as a concrete alteration of the conditions of production.

William Greider's acerbic comment, "If corporate declarations of good intent were edible, the world's hungry would be fed," has had empirical support in a study by Christopher Bart of McMaster University, whose research revealed that the "vast majority" of mission statements "are not worth the paper they are written on and should not be taken with any degree of seriousness." As Wayne Spragge, of the Ethical Institute of Canada, pointed out: "We call these codes of ethics 'ethical artwork.' It's like putting a piece of art on the wall and is of no value." The boycotters do not ease up on the pressure after a company waves a Code of Conduct in their faces.

What they want, and increasingly are getting at least in their successful campaigns, is the acknowledgement by corporations of the need to monitor the implementation of codes and reports on how contracting producers meet specific goals. They want to see proof that corporations enforce their non-legally binding self-regulatory rules. Of course, it is important to specify what kinds of conditions have to be met, and equally important that the monitoring and reporting are independent and thorough. Some progress has been made along these lines, as two well-known boycott organizers, Linda Yanz and Bob Jeffcott, point out:

> Five years ago, many of us would have dismissed codes of conduct as nothing more than company attempts to protect their brand image and/or avoid government regulation. . . . In a few years, we have moved from company codes of conduct with no provision for monitoring or verification, toward multi-company, industry-wide and multi-sectoral codes, with elaborate systems of internal monitoring and external verification, factory and company certification, and mechanisms for NGO and labour participation in monitoring and third party complaints procedures.

These results are satisfying—after all, a good deal of general education goes along with the efforts to redress some specific corporation's misdemeanours. Any one campaign, therefore, can result in immediate improvement in some people's condition, and the accompanying educational effect may well make things better for others in the future. Yet these solid gains do not go to the heart of the problem: the corporate sectors' continued capacity to inflict harms with relative impunity. The boycott strategy suffers from overlapping quantitative and qualitative weaknesses.

On the quantitative side is the difficulty of applying a strategy based primarily on brand identification to the vast number of brandless, almost anonymous productive enterprises. The strategy may touch on the activities of only a small number of corporations and practices; its diffusion is far from guaranteed. Here the counterspins that corporations engage in come into play. It is not as if all corporations under these kinds of attacks just fall back into a defensive position, incorporating codes and establishing monitoring and reporting schemata. Some fight back vigorously, taking a severe toll on the activists who assault them.

These counterattacks have many manifestations and take many forms. One popular tactic is known by its acronym SLAPP, which stands for Strategic Lawsuits Against Public Participation. It is just a fancy term to describe what corporations do best: use their resources and elite corps of lawyers to the fullest degree possible. The idea is to tie activists up in costly court fights to distract and—with luck—discourage the adversaries from acting against the corporate world. Any old legal argument to show that the corporation has been injured—from libel, to interference with commercial relations, to improper use of logos—will do. From the corporate perspective, it does not matter all that much whether the case has a sound legal or factual basis. The idea is to run interference—serious interference. The most famous of these kinds of suits is the so-called McLibel action brought by McDonald's in the United Kingdom. In the end that suit may have redounded to the corporation's disadvantage, because the mighty hamburger chain was publicly portrayed as a bully. Still, it would be wrong to think of SLAPPs as an occasional and not very threatening corporate weapon. Thousands of such suits take place every year in the United States, so many indeed that a number of states, under pressure from free-speech advocates, have passed protective legislation that makes the corporations jump through a few hoops before they can initiate these pre-emptive strikes by way of legal actions. This legislative reaction indicates the chilling effect of the corporate resort to legal blackmail: the strategy cuts down greatly on the number of activist challenges.

As for the qualitative side of weaknesses in the consumer boycott campaigns, first and foremost, the strategy only reinforces the ideology of market capitalism. As such, it has the characteristics of that regime. It is anarchic. It has different impacts—sometimes none at all—in very similar circumstances. Further, the opposition cannot possibly prescribe any common denominator of behaviour, at least not in the way that a legislative standard might be able to do, which adds to the variations in effectiveness. Like all market activities, the tactic works haphazardly. Each campaign is a "one-off." The tactic's standard-setting capacity is limited precisely because it is an extra-legal campaign.

Second, and relatedly, whatever corporate-improvement undertakings are promised, there remains no efficacious means of enforcing them, despite attempts at monitoring and reporting on them. For instance, Yanz and

Jeffcott refer to the ILO Conventions as an exemplar of the monitoring and enforcement framework they want to see developed as an outgrowth of their gallant fights to give consumer boycotts bite. But these conventions are virtually unenforced, even though nation-states have committed themselves to monitor, report on, and enforce the standards they have solemnly endorsed. By the year 2000 *The Globe and Mail* was reporting that surveys were still showing that some 75 per cent of corporations with highly touted (but not legally required) codes of conduct were not adhering stringently to the prescriptions of their own codes. As John Braithwaite once remarked, " If voluntary compliance worked, Moses would have come down from the mountain with the ten guidelines." Leaving the fox in charge of the chicken coop has never been a satisfactory means of ensuring the chickens' welfare. Consumer boycott activists are aware of this predicament and expend considerable effort in trying to devise schemes to make corporations publicly accountable for how they administer and implement their codes of behaviour.

Publicity is the tool of enforcement, and in this the question of resources becomes a factor. Corporations have an advantage. At all times the very corporations that are under consumer fire are doing their level best to convince the same consumers through their sophisticated advertising that it is perfectly alright to continue to keep buying their brand of products; and it is the very success of these corporations' advertising that has created a loyal consumer following in the first place. They are good at it. Sometimes corporations also take steps to refurbish their image as good citizens, as entities deeply concerned about the well-being of the public, by acting philanthropically. They donate large amounts (in absolute terms—even if the amounts tend to be trivial when compared to their revenues and assets) to institutions of learning and research, to sports, to cultural events and agencies. They do this on the basis that their generosity and public-mindedness will be acknowledged by their respected recipients and the governments involved, which are thereby relieved of some funding pressures. Corporation X "buys" concerts. Corporations A, B, and C sponsor a sporting event. A hospital wing benefits from the generosity of Corporation K. It is difficult to stay mad at a corporation that shows so much (heavily advertised) support for the public good, even if, in some other part of the world or some other sphere of activity, that company has strayed from the straight and narrow, perhaps polluting a river here, exploiting some children there, or faking a test result somewhere else.

Corporate law only permits this deployment of corporate monies if the board of directors can demonstrate that such charity will benefit the corporation by reaping it the kind of goodwill that is required in achieving a profitable performance. The law acknowledges, then, that profit extraction at all costs can lead to anti-corporate sentiment and/or fettering regulations and that, therefore, it is appropriate for corporate managers to behave charitably. In market capitalism, charity—supposedly the unilateral, unforced act of bestowing a benefit on others, to be rewarded in heaven because it is a testament to altruism, a valued virtue—has *legally* come to be equated with corporate self-advancement. Then too, the law allows these charitable corporations to pass on the costs of this largesse through the taxation scheme, making it easier to swallow the managerial decision to "divert" capital intended to be deployed for the benefit of shareholders.

Corporations, then, fight back against boycott campaigns by using the very market powers and resources that give rise to the perceived problems in the first place. They are able to use such market strategies all the more effectively because the struggles waged against them are posited on the tenets of the market: on the basis that informed consumers should be entitled to spend their money as they see fit. When the combatants meet on the terrain of the market, the battle reinforces the position of the private sector as the protector of general welfare. The corporate sectors seek to bolster this prime position in many ways. One thing they do is fund the establishment of industrial groups or non-profit organizations that act as quasi-independent watchdogs. These bodies declare that the corporations they "watch" are to be guided by certain values, such as the sustainability of the environment in which they are active, and respect for local customs, workers' rights, the safety of their products, and the like. Given these watchdogs, the implicit argument goes, there is now no need for economic boycotts and other such tactics; the corporate sectors are quite capable of setting norms that enure to the public good.

Typical of such self-regulatory bodies—and there is a great number—is the World Business Council for Sustainable Development, representing 150 corporations in 30 countries. Its stated goal is to advance high standards of environmental management, providing leadership and urging corporations to do more than the law demands as they pursue profits. But, while the World Business Council puts out papers and reports and, therefore, may serve a useful educational function, it does nothing concrete. Indeed, a number of observers have seen it and like organizations as surrogates that set out to persuade governments and international bodies that industry can regulate itself adequately, which in effect limits the extent to which the values of the stakeholder/social responsibility movement can set the agenda for positive change. Of course, these "confess and avoid" responses by the corporate sectors can produce welcome outcomes. After all, the setting of industry standards of any kind will provide norms that consumer boycott campaign organizers, policy-makers, and even courts can use as a guide to pushing for improvements. More, when corporations claim that they are already regulated adequately by their self-generated standards (which, by definition, will be practicable and compatible with profit-making), boycott organizers will more easily be able to hold them to living up to such standards. Given that any reduction of the destruction of life, limb, and the environment that may result will be an improvement on the unchecked project of private capital accumulation, these self-regulatory, critique-deflecting corporate strategies have some positive aspects. That said, it remains probable that the main effect of these much ballyhooed efforts of corporate capitalism to set its own limits will be—as the corporate sectors intend it to be—to blunt legislative interventions, consumer-led boycotts, and like strategies.

The International Organization for Standardization provides an example of this blunting effort. Affectionately known as ISO, the organization is a long-standing (1947) association of representatives of 130 nations that sets product and manufacturing standards. Its goal is frankly profit-oriented. It states that it desires to facilitate the international exchange of goods and services, and its influence is pervasive among trade organizations and large industrial actors. It has a certification system prized by some as a competitive advantage. Inasmuch as its standards require an elevation of the standards set by a great variety of domestic laws, the ISO is a private mechanism that fosters more socially responsible behaviour, and in that it is a positive force. But there are limits to the benefits it can bring, not the least because its major financiers are private corporations, which therefore dominate the workings of the association. The standards are not likely to be all that onerous.

As usual, in respect of those corporations that do not meet even the "sensibly" drafted standards, enforcement remains a problem. All of this is illustrated by the short history of Social Accountability International, SA 8000, a variant of ISO established by the Council on Economic Priorities in 1997. It requires participating corporations, which want to be able to say that they abide by the standards set, to hire certified auditors to evaluate the conduct of individual factories through which transnational corporate productivity is carried on. Again, this can't be all bad: if the fear of government regulation or loss of market share consequent upon militant consumer boy-cotters' actions leads to a more effective self-regulatory response, something positive is achieved. But the optics of the thing may be more significant than its actual outcomes. Mark Levinson cynically notes that, of the sixty-one factories that had received the seal of approval for their labour practices and thus been certified by SA 8000 as satisfactory employers, thirty-four were in China. Levinson asserts that if Chinese workers actually sought to enforce the standards promised by SO 8000 adherents, they probably "would find themselves in jail or an insane asylum." One does not have to be as sanguine as Levinson about China's repression of labour to take his point that there is something odd about how the bulk of certification has occurred in a nation whose human rights record is viewed with a great deal of suspicion by the First World countries and their major corporations. Are private firms abiding by SO 8000 really tackling a social/political problem that their dominant home nation-states dare not take on directly, or are they engaging in a confidence trick, assuring potentially militant consumers that they are not in China to exploit repression?

The suspicion that it might be the latter is bolstered by the findings of Corporate Watch, an organization focused on making corporations more socially responsible and accountable for their activities. The Corporate Watch analysis concerns a spin-doctoring endeavour in another setting. Its evaluation of a United Nations effort to encourage participation in something called the Global Compact, a loose body of corporations signed on to a bunch of appealing general principles about human rights, environmental protection, and workers' rights promulgated by the UN, was not optimistic. Corporate Watch felt that giving credibility to the Global Compact would enable corporations to hold out that, because they were participating in a United Nations-sponsored effort, even one without a specific program, norms, or means to make the agreed upon basic principles enforceable, they were beyond criticism. They would be "bluewashed" by the UN flag wrapped around their corporate body. This then is the conundrum: many of the self-regulatory mechanisms may allow the wolf to cloak itself in sheep's clothing.

The Corporate Counterattack

Corporations are not only able to use market powers and resources to repel assaults on their social legitimacy, but also able to mount attacks on the legitimacy of their adversaries. They are in a position to argue that, precisely because no one has electorally or otherwise legitimated the cause of the consumer-led boycotters, the claim of that opposition—to be doing good by calling on corporations to behave differently—lacks inherent validity. The mere contention that the values they want pursued are superior to the profit-maximization focus of the corporate sectors does not make them so.

Here I pause to state my own perspective. I do believe that acts done with the primary intention of protecting individuals or the environment from legalized exploitation by the invisible friends of the captains of industry, finance, retail, and everything else have more intrinsic merit than acts done primarily for self-serving ends by these same invisible friends of the greedy. I do respect, indeed admire, the organizers of consumer boycotts and the church leaders, unionists, and social groups that participate in them, because I believe that the intentions of these people are genuinely altruistic. Their efforts are morally laudable. But such an undocumentable belief in the merit of their beliefs is neither an adequate logical nor, more importantly, effective political response to the corporate sectors' argument.

The corporations' logic is that they, too, believe they are acting for the public good, but that they allow the markets to determine what is in the public interest; they do not presume to know best. People, they say, vote with their money. People buy goods they want; they work for wages and under conditions they choose; they exchange the quality of the environment for other benefits they treasure. The corporations simply do what people want them to do. By contrast, the economic militants are making decisions for other people when they seek to alter natural market outcomes. Here, the corporate status quo defenders say, the militants lose the high ground. When boycott activists denounce market outcomes, they are actually espousing a perverted application of the market voting system, "one dollar, one vote." As people's values are shaped by concrete conditions, it is quite plausible that the choices that better-off militants would have corporations make might not be the choices made by their less-well-off sisters and brothers if left alone. It is the better-off market actors' values that count most. This premise can be self-indulgent, or self-serving, and might lead to paternalism.

The events of the Battle of Seattle in November 1999 nicely illustrate the politically persuasive strength of this argument. President Bill Clinton had pronounced that, maybe, globalizers should be more aware of the need to protect Third World workers and the environment. Spokespersons from the Third World responded that Clinton's statement reflected a sugar-coated effort by the First World to reintroduce protectionism. Sylvia Ostry commented that Third World countries were saying, in effect, that they needed to be "exploited." Harlan Mandel documented the same kind of Third World opposition—coming from India, Brazil, Mexico, Chile, Nicaragua, Malaysia, and the Philippines—to social contract clauses introduced by the First World during the GATT Uruguay round.

A consumer boycott originating in the First World, that is, engineered by wealthier consumers, against a corporation that exploits Third World workers can face the same problems. It may well be that, objectively speaking, there is a case to be made that no workers should be treated in the way that these workers are. But we live in a world of non-absolutes. Thus it is quite plausible that, horrible as they are, the conditions are a trade-off and acceptable to those workers who, otherwise, would have no means of subsistence of any kind. This being a plausible argument, it is not surprising that some very nasty corporations often defend their practices by relying on it. They try to reclaim something of the moral high ground. They contend that they are providing work to people who had nothing before under conditions that match local standards (and that, therefore, are approved and welcomed by local governments). They may also argue that the complaints are made to protect already richer workers in the First World from competition by the less well-off elsewhere. The corporate sectors' not-so-implicit question is: how high-minded are these do-gooders? A similar critique could be—and often is—mounted against those good souls who campaign for the end of the senseless hunting of animals for their furs while providing no redress for those whose living depends on hunting and killing.

These arguments are far from ridiculous in an economic setting in which the state is not seen as the main vehicle for the creation of the general welfare. In the context of the primacy of the private sector as the engine of wealth and welfare, there is resonance to the argument that these kinds of private-sector campaigns against the private sector's legally permissible practices are run by self-righteous flakes or selfish people pretending to be do-gooders. This response makes it all the harder to pierce the social-legitimacy shield of the corporation-for-profit; it makes it more difficult to get the policy-makers, whom the boycott organizers seek to influence, to enact laws to make corporations more socially responsible or to hold them to standards that promote non-monetary values.

What I am acknowledging here is the persuasive value of the corporate counter-argument, not its objective credibility. The corporate arguments about the activists' supposed self-indulgence and egoism are mischievous. The difficulty is that we do not live in anything like a perfect democracy. The alleged lack of democratic legitimacy of the economic boycotters stems from the lamentable absence of any effective democratic institutions through which an opposition can address the private wrongdoing of the corporate profiteers. Still, in the end, a reliance on measures replicating the very tenets of the scheme that causes the harm may not be all that useful; especially when the goal is to curb the undesirable outcomes that spring from the very heart of that system.

Proof in the Eating of the Pudding

Then too, even if an economic boycott were truly successful, some proponents of more radical change might remain dissatisfied. If, for instance, such a campaign led to a corporation adopting the society-friendly operational model of a Ben & Jerry's or a Body Shop, would that make economic activities conducted through a for-profit corporation acceptable? Critics of corporate behaviour choose these two firms as exemplars because the companies have stressed that they are both profitable and socially responsible. Certain evidence suggests, however, that these firms may not entirely be models of good corporate citizenship. While Ben & Jerry's made much of its use of organically pure ingredients to make its ice cream not only delicious but also good for the health of the consumer, and it made much of a family-type approach to its employees, it turns out that Ben & Jerry's also used labour tactics thought to be the province of red-necked, intransigent, and dictatorial employers. When employees in one small locale became less than convinced that they were being treated as loved members of the family and sought to exercise their democratic right to unionize, Ben & Jerry's turned mean and engaged in traditional union-bashing tactics. Similarly, the Body Shop tells the world that for its products it only uses ingredients that are organic. The company says it is against animal testing of ingredients, and that it encourages indigenous people to trade with the Body Shop; the company buys their traditionally harvested products. It says it preserves communities and cultures while helping them engage in trade, and that the conditions of its workforce are as generous as they can be. But all of these claims have been documented as bogus, in whole or in part. The Body Shop has been convicted of false advertising related to its claim that it does not use animal-tested ingredients. It has been found using synthetic ingredients. Apparently it has purchased only the tiniest amounts of the pure, traditionally harvested ingredients, making its claim about respect for, and fairness to, indigenous people, if not untrue, a rather self-serving exaggeration. In England the Body Shop does not allow its workers to unionize and pays them minimum wages that are well below the official European "decency threshold."

But this carping is a side issue. By now it should come as no surprise that the various captains of industry and everything else, hiding behind their invisible friends, are willing to peddle images that present partial, deceptive portrayals of what they offer and do. Let us assume that the Ben & Jerry's and Body Shops of this world are as socially responsible as they would have us believe and that they are also profitable. From this perspective, it makes sense to put pressure on all corporations to show a regard to stakeholders other than shareholders; after all, there is living proof that it is done, can be done, and should be done. Would that lead to a much better world, even if successful? After all, even ice cream or body lotions made with organic materials by contented workers may not be the best outcome of the deployment of the world's resources and human talents. Yet they will still be produced because there will still be consumers who can be persuaded to purchase them; they will not be produced because they meet the objective needs of people. Inasmuch as such market-dictated productivity uses up resources that could be put to more life-enhancing uses, materially or culturally, little will have changed. Commodification will still rule the roost. Debilitating social engineering by market profiteers will not have been confronted. People will still be persuaded to buy creams that make them feel better, but not be better, while millions of people will be denied the necessities of life.

What is coming into view here are two related issues that ought to trouble those who rely on market-based tactics to reform corporations engaged in market practices. First, as long as for-profit corporations stay within the limits of the law, they can produce and sell anything they want to produce and sell. The ecological, cultural, or moral value of the product sold or service rendered simply does not matter. Its utility in human terms does not matter. All that matters is that there are people who are willing to purchase it—and, as we have seen, such desires are engineered by the very people peddling the products and services. As in war, damage inflicted by permissible profit-seeking activities will be registered as regrettable collateral damage by friendly fire. That damage is regrettable but not to be condemned. The overall goal has been thoroughly legitimated, and continues to be so, by the very tactics used by those who would like a little more social responsibility to be displayed. Corporations continue to be praised for making money, whether it be by making guns or baking bread. More, elected governments and their policy-makers encourage this result. Indeed, they rely heavily on the maintenance of consumer confidence, which means consumerism for its own sake. People are to be encouraged to buy, no matter what, to keep the economy buoyant.

This pathway leads to bizarre, if unwitting, acknowledgements of the moral bankruptcy of market capitalism. For example, in a 2001 article, Gregory Frederick notes that the privatization of prisons has increased at a rapid pace. It has become a good business. As an example he cites Corrections Corporation of America, whose stock rose from being priced at $8 a share in 1997 to more than $30 by 1999, and was still climbing. This has led to promoters setting up conferences to convince investors to put their money into the prison business. As the brochure for one of these conferences states, the corporate takeover of prisons "is the newest trend in the area of privatizing government-run programs. . . .While arrests and convictions are steadily on the rise, profits are to be made . . . profits from crime. Get in on the ground floor of this booming industry now!" One wonders whether there would be investors lining up to snatch at this kind of opportunity, if their identities could not remain a secret hidden by the corporate veil. This kind of profiting from crime might not be considered such a good idea if it were corporate actors, rather than the poor and racial minorities, who became the fodder for the profit-making jails. Then too, this kind of money interest in having a continuous and increasing supply of prisoners may well have an unsavoury influence on law and order policy-makers. To say that corporate capitalism, carried to its logical extension, breeds amorality would be a rather mild way of characterizing its nature. To say that frequently it will have little to zero social utility is to say the obvious. To say that it distorts liberal political institutions is to enunciate the manifest. In short, the use of tactics that do not directly question the legitimacy and viability of corporate market capitalist practices should be a problematic approach for those who want to challenge corporate market capitalism.

The second, and related, issue is that not only do corporate market practices, maintained by consumerism, lead to the objectionable commodification of everything and anything, to waste and exploitation and deepening inequality, but they also endorse a value system that encourages corporations to produce only if there is a demand for a particular good or service. Production and sale will only be entertained if there is a buck to be made. This issue is neatly illustrated by the way in which health products are parcelled out by the market. Recently, for instance, the South African government scored a victory. It had defended itself against a suit by big pharmaceutical corporations, affectionately known as the collective "Big Pharma" to those who profit from their endeavours. These corporations had taken legal objection to the South African government's announced intention to ignore the patent rights held by Big Pharma in respect of drugs combatting HIV infections. The issue was of vital importance for South Africa, which has a human tragedy of epic proportions on its hands and needs to be able to supply drugs to a huge number of infected citizens who could not afford Big Pharma's prices ($240 a month). At the time the equivalent drugs were available in a generic form at a cost of $48 per month. The government sought to exploit a rarely used legal clause that enables governments to modify corporate patent holders' exclusive right to market a product. In court Big Pharma was disputing that move, claiming its own right to protect its profit base, regardless of the human cost—which amounted to withholding a product from the millions who might die without it. This time the corporations lost, at least to some degree. The adverse publicity they received was such that Big Pharma dropped its legal action and agreed to supply the needed drugs at less exorbitant—but still profitable—rates.

In a way, the AIDS story reaffirms the point that tangible benefits can indeed be derived from anti-corporate campaigns. But it also illustrates that the starting position for consumer campaigns and the like remains one that favours corporations. The initial assumption is that those who control wealth and, therefore, determine how it shall be deployed are free to do so in their own interests. The depressing tenet that, in a liberal-market capitalist political economy, there is no positive duty to be altruistic, to rescue anyone from harm, is firmly in place. Amongst the many things this signifies is that research and investment are more likely to be aimed at the development of products and services for which paying consumers can be found than to be focused on the creation of products that have life-enhancing purposes, whether or not they lead to profitable sales. It is more useful, from a corporate point of view, to produce creams and beauty products that well-heeled women can be persuaded to buy than use their pharmaceutical know-how and facilities to develop medicines that would address the problems of the poor. This starting point also gives credibility to the Grinch-like stance that denies people access to already developed medicines if it means those medicines have to be sold without making a profit.

Once again, corporations that hide behind the veil of legality to callously put profits before lives do so on behalf of people who, in turn, also hide behind the law. They hide behind the corporate veil. It is quite possible, indeed likely, that investors who, as individuals, are happy to donate money and time to charities that support health and research, allow the corporate veil to be their veil of ignorance. This absolves them from thinking and acting as responsible human beings. It might be much more difficult to pursue profits by denying HIV-infected people medicine if individuals had to publicly declare themselves as favouring such a way of satisfying their greed.

Ethical Investment

The need for large, publicly traded corporations to go to the public in search of capital from time to time presents socially conscious would-be investors with an opportunity. They can use their leverage as potential investors to have the corporation agree to more socially desirable terms of market engagement. The investors, theoretically, can say, "No social conscience, no dough." The assumption is that, in market-capitalist economies, it is politically acceptable to use capital as a tool to achieve political ends. As we've already seen, these kinds of reform projects invariably face ideological and practical difficulties.

But another assumption also comes into play: that there are enough capital contributors out there with social reform on their minds that corporations will have to pay serious attention to them. This is not entirely true. The bulk of capital for these large, publicly traded corporations is obtained by borrowing, which involves institutions such as banks and other lenders. Inasmuch as capital is raised by way of equity—by issuing shares in the corporation to contributors of monies—this is a lesser amount, something of the order of 25 per cent of these corporations' needs. Still, in absolute dollar terms, this lesser amount is a huge amount of money, and it is significant to corporate coffers. The strategy of withholding capital funding from unethical corporations will, then, carry at least some weight. But even then, the largest source of equity capital for corporations is not direct investment by countless small investors. Rather, the greatest amount of equity capital comes via institutional investment houses, such as mutual, insurance, and pension funds. These funds are aggregates of a large number of small-time investors who have neither the know-how nor the time to invest as individuals. Hence, the interposition of intermediaries between the capital-raising corporation and the actual investor creates problems for ethical investment strategies. While it is possible for the institutional investors to exercise their leverage to get the corporations to agree to socially responsible practices, this is a theoretical rather than realistic position. The actual functioning of these capital markets works against the possibility of institutional investors deploying their clout to social responsibility ends.

These funds are aggregates of the little capitals invested by non-professional investors trying to build up savings or nest eggs for their retirements. Each fund competes with the others for the small investors' contributions on the basis that it can provide better returns to these individuals than can the other funds. Each fund sets out to establish a reputation for picking corporations whose shares will yield great profits. This marginalizes any notion that these funds will be, or should be, looking for corporations that concern themselves with stakeholders other than shareholders. More, the funds' managers typically share the worldview of those who manage corporations for profits. In particular, they also view the maximization of profits in freely operated markets to be a moral activity in its own right. Inasmuch as they do have clout, the funds' managers are likely to exercise it to ensure that the managers of corporations in which they invest do not abuse their discretion to line their own pockets at the expense of shareholders. They may interfere, therefore, if the salaries and perquisites of executives get out of line with the performance of the corporation or when the managers try to establish rules that will safeguard their tenure.

Managers sometimes try to make it more difficult for outsiders to take over the corporation. They do so by including rules in the corporate constitution that act as poison pills. This forces the bidder to pay more for shares than it otherwise would, aborting a takeover that could lead to the replacement of the management team. Institutional investors frown on these shareholder rights' agreements—the formal name for poison pills—because they remove the possibility of getting a quick premium on their investment from an anxious bidder. In short, the kinds of actions that institutional investors engage in are the very opposite of what the stakeholder/social responsibility movement wants from ethical investors. They are actions that reinforce the profit-maximization project, rather than actions that temporize profit-seeking. As a matter of practice, large institutional investors engage in computer-trading: they have computers programmed to sell or buy automatically when certain stock-market circumstances prevail. This quick activity makes it difficult to engage in pinpointed investments of the kind needed to further the goals of ethical investment.

What all of this means is that those individuals who have disposable capital and want to deploy it ethically must find ways of becoming significant players and of acting as directors of corporate policies. That is where ethical investment funds come in. Crudely, they are for-profit funds that aggregate the contributions of socially conscious investors. They hold out the possibility of getting enough like-minded capital together to influence corporations that go to the public in search of money. These funds tell potential investors that they can have their cake and eat it. They can get good returns on their investments and sleep the sleep of the innocent. The problems with such schemes arise out of the complicated nature of large, publicly traded corporations, the difficulty of drawing a line between acceptable market-capitalist practices and unacceptable ones, and the need for these ethical funds to be themselves profit centres.

It is relatively easy, first of all, to promise that the fund will not invest in corporations that make and/or sell products and services, such as tobacco, alcohol, or guns, that are, in and of themselves, anathema to some segments of the public. The funds that promise this are engaged in the negative screening of corporations—looking at what the firms make and sell. It is much harder, of course, to promise that corporations will be screened for their practices as they produce and sell—looking at how they treat their employees or at their impact on the environment. It is even more difficult to engage in screening that will be used to tell corporations what to make and to sell things we want them to sell. To engage in this kind of positive screening, ethical investors must employ information-gathering systems, which is time-consuming and costly. The restraints that ethical fund managers think ought to be imposed on corporate activities must always be tempered by the need for a profit to be returned to the ethical investors who entrusted their capital to the ethical investment fund. Sometimes the funds are able to deliver despite the difficulties of their task.

Researcher Anders Hayden reports that the Ethical Growth Fund, set up by VanCity Credit Union, was named fund of the year in 1998 because of its very good returns when compared to those of other, non-ethical mutual funds. Similarly, Investor's Summa and Desjardins Environment have been good performers, as they invested their contributors' monies in what they deemed to be better-behaving companies. These results are not universal. Some critics argue that ethical investment funds do well in their initial years, precisely because they subject the target corporations to more scrutiny than usual, making for better investment decisions than brokers and other dealers might ordinarily come up with. After that, their record becomes indifferent, sometimes even worse than that of other institutional investors. Fosback, the editor of an investors' advisory newsletter, notes that the funds screened for the environment and other social factors performed better than the Standard and Poor's 500 in only two of eight years.

At best, then, the claim that good returns and social conscience are not incompatible is neither proved nor falsified. The case for ethical investment funds as a viable means of holding corporations to better standards is not indefensible, but it is less convincing than its proponents would like it to be. It turns out that the ethical funds, in business to make profits, are under pressure to behave as profiteers. This means cutting corners. Sometimes this leads to outright deception of well-meaning individual investors who want their capital contributions to make a social impact. One report indicates that of twenty-three ethical, socially screened, or green mutual funds or trusts in the United Kingdom, nineteen were scams. Despite their claims to be investing in ethically acceptable and screened corporations, they did not. More typical than outright deception is the slippage from the straight and narrow because of the difficulties faced by ethical investment funds when they try to find and identify the path of virtue in the first place.

Positive screening requires continuing monitoring. David Nitkin found that few ethical investment funds maintained routine files on collective-bargaining practices, environmental cases, military contracts, and other everyday corporate activities that should be of interest to socially conscious investors. Then, as they need to find *some* investment vehicles, ethical investment funds frequently have to make judgements that are rather crude. Hayden found that a much-heralded ethical institutional investor, Vancouver's Ethical Funds Inc. (the parent of the Ethical Growth Fund, which got the accolade of "fund of the year" in 1998) had purchased a Toronto Stock Exchange index fund. Put simply, this meant that the investment fund had bought an interest in thirty-five corporations whose overall performance on the stock market would give the ethical investment fund its return. Of course, this meant that the investment included shares in corporations that socially conscious individuals would normally avoid. They included not only firms that made money from defence contracts and tobacco, but also known environmental polluters.

Even if ethical investment fund managers do their best to screen corporations, they are confronted by an endemic difficulty of market capitalism: drawing a line between socially acceptable conduct and unacceptable behaviour. Ethical investment funds find it difficult to formulate precise operating criteria. Their brochures are full of solemn undertakings. They announce that they will invest contributors' monies in corporations with progressive employment practices, environmentally conscious practices, racially sensitive goals. All of this sounds good, but leaves a lot of discretion with fund managers who are under pressure to find corporations that not only roughly match the vague goals of the ethical fund but will also offer a profitable return on the investment. They have to make difficult decisions with little solid information and only the loosest of guidelines to steer them. Not surprisingly, confusion reigns. Thus, while it is easy to say no to investment in a tobacco corporation, what if that same corporation also engages in activities that might be favoured by socially conscious investors? Imasco not only markets tobacco, but also supports a Montreal job-creation initiative because, its literature says, it is committed to the well-being of the people who inhabit the city where it has lodged its headquarters. This reminds us of the inherent problem confronting economic boycotters. Take McDonald's, a much-despised corporation: it not only uses up beef supplies and destroys forests and is such a bad employer that a "McDonald's job" is the appellation given to dead-end work, but it also runs houses where parents of seriously sick children can stay when they have to leave their homes to be near their ailing infants. As the critical chronicler of McDonald's, Eric Schlosser, notes,

McDonald's also has taken a stand on how poultry farms that want to supply the restaurants—and a great many farms do—should treat their animals, which is a stand much-appreciated by animal right activists.

Even if these positive aspects of McDonald's activities are seen as mere window dressing that cannot offset its overall corporate image of irresponsibility, the complexity of character of many other gargantuan corporations presents ethical investors with serious dilemmas. Typically difficult are those cases in which support for an environment-endangering corporate activity also supports much-needed employment. Thus, David Olive notes that Ethical Growth invested in forest giants, such as MacMillan Bloedel, which are vast polluters in the eyes of some critics but are also key to employment in British Columbia. This decision was the outcome of a balancing act for the ethical investment fund. Not everyone would agree with how it drew the line, but these kinds of balancing exercises are hard to avoid and difficult to fault. Sometimes, when funds do not attempt that kind of balancing, the results can be less than satisfactory. Olive notes, with a suggestion of disapproval, that the same Ethical Growth Fund has a flat rule that it will not invest in corporations that have anything to do with military contracts. That simple rule led it to refuse to invest in Bombardier because, sometimes, that company acts as a defence contractor. But, as Olive points out, Bombardier's major business is the manufacture of environmental friendly means of transport. The ethical fund might be seen as throwing out the baby with the bath water.

If simplistic bright lines don't do the trick, how should enthusiasts of the ethical approach undertake the calibration of corporations? Is it good enough to say that the ethical investment fund will only invest in corporations that abide by the best practices of a particular industrial sector, even if those best practices may still be repugnant? Or how directly involved in unfriendly or unseemly conduct must a corporation be before an ethical investment fund should deem it unworthy of receiving the capital of socially conscious citizens? Hayden suggests that investment in banks—the financial engines of much corporate activity in all spheres, good and bad—might be eschewed by some ethical investors, and not by others.

This litany of difficulties that face ethical investment as a tool for reforming corporate behaviour has much in common with the problems associated with consumer boycotts. At bottom, the conceptual, and attendant practical, problems arise from one point: that all we can usefully say about corporate capitalist activity is that either it is legal or it is not. There is nothing in this political-economic regime that differentiates good from bad. There is no moral lodestar that enables those who would like to use that system's own logic to make it more soulful.

Although some good successes have been, and will continue to be, recorded, the pressure on corporate managers through these means — boycotts and ethical management funds — is unlikely to bring paradigmatic changes. The limits of these various alternative tactics stem from the same fundamental problem: the advocates do not declare that the *raison d'être* of corporate capitalism, the private accumulation of socially produced goods, is just plain wrong. The attacks on corporate excesses by the use of market tools can only have limited success because they do not demand that the corporations give up their capitalist role. The attacks nibble at the flanks of the giant corporate beasts, which only grow larger and larger. Although the brave fights to make corporations act more responsibly, more caringly, towards workers and the community at large, have had their notable successes, for most corporations the ethical investors and boycott organizers, as well as legal reformers trying to alter the framework of corporate governance, are minor irritants at best. Unfortunately for those of us who would like to see a brighter future, no fairy tale ending is yet in sight: the giants remain in firm control.

Government in Their Own Image: Corporations and Political Power

Wherein we learn that giantism as the natural outgrowth of the never-ending private accumulation of socially produced wealth has permitted the captains of industry, finance, retail, and everything else to create governments in their own unappetizing image.

The corporate beast grows ever larger and larger. The size of major publicly traded corporations has become truly mind-boggling. In 1999, ExxonMobil, General Motors, and Ford had greater revenues than the national budgets of all but seven of the one hundred and ninety-one nation-states of the world. The top six corporations together had more annual revenues than the combined budgets of sixty-four nations, which, in turn, boasted over half the world's population.

The size of corporations only continues to increase apace as mergers and acquisitions (M&AS) take on epic proportions. A United Nations report found that the number of cross-border mergers and acquisitions had risen by 42 per cent every year between 1980 and 1999. In 1999 there were six thousand such deals worth U.S.$720 billion (more than a trillion dollars Canadian). If we add domestic M&AS to this deal-making number, the figure for M&AS grows to twenty-four thousand deals, worth a staggering annual total of

U.S.$2.3 trillion. In the United States the latest wave of deals has involved monies beyond everyday understanding. In the 1980s the largest transactions were the U.S.$13 billion Standard Oil acquisition of Gulf Oil and the U.S.$25 billion purchase of RJR Nabisco by its managers and their allies. There has since been an escalation from these giddy heights. In the period 1998-2000, the ten largest M&As averaged U.S.$76 billion. In one massive cross-border transaction, England's Vodaphone shelled out $208 billion for Germany's Mannesmann.

Canadian corporate copulation has more than kept pace. William Stanbury's number crunching in the 1980s led him to conclude that in that decade the largest mergers in Canada were over twice the size of the largest ones in the United States, taking into account the relative size of the two economies. In the result, he found, in line with the earlier Bryce Commission's conclusion that Canada has a greater level of aggregate concentration—that is, non-competitiveness—than the United Kingdom, Japan, or United States. Some recent blockbuster transactions—in Canadian terms—include: Groupe Videotron Ltee's takeover by Quebecor Inc. for a healthy $5.4 billion; Investors Group's payment of $4.15 billion for Mackenzie Financial; the swallowing of Canadian Airlines by Air Canada after the entrepreneur Gerry Schwartz had caused the price to escalate by launching a bid for Air Canada; the capture of Chapters by Indigo, a move underpinned by money from the same entrepreneur Schwartz; and the purchases of Southam by Hollinger, followed by the purchases of Hollinger's media interests by CanWest Global Communications. This intensifying concentration of ownership has great social and political implications, including the heightened prices paid by, and the loss of choice for, consumers. We have already witnessed a continuous stream of complaints about the ability—and the apparent willingness—of banks to treat consumers like dirt, about Air Canada's new-found capacity to gouge all who travel, and, amongst the chattering classes, about the meaning and costs of Indigo-Chapters now getting eighty-three cents out of every dollar spent on the purchase of books. Still, these irritants are not the most sinister outcome of the growth of corporations and the accompanying lack of competition. More serious are the economic inefficiencies and political distortions.

The M&As are of various kinds: horizontal mergers, which are alliances between firms that had previously been competitors; vertical mergers, which are arrangements between firms that were suppliers to each other and did contract work for each other; and conglomerate-creating deals, which bring together firms that operated in different sectors of the economy. Indeed, to characterize fully the utility of this kind of economic restructuring requires a good deal of refined analysis. For our purposes, what is plain is that this continued accretion in size and concentration of capital places serious limits on the abilities of governments and citizens to tame, much less control, corporate behaviour.

Increasingly, these behemoths can dictate terms not just to workers but also to suppliers and buyers, who have no choice but to deal with them. Increasingly, governments, having become dependent on these large-scale enterprises for the provision of society's economic welfare, find it difficult to make major decisions that do not suit the agenda of the megacorporations. These well-known phenomena have led to a series of arguments that corporations should be treated as government-like, quasi-public, political institutions, rather than as mere vehicles for economic convenience. As a study of corporate power and public policy pointed out:

> In a private enterprise market system, such critical matters as the distribution of income, what is produced, the allocation of resources to different lines of production, the allocation of the labour force to different occupations and work places, plant locations , investment levels, the technologies used in production, the quality of goods and services, and the innovation of new products are all matters that are in large part decided by business men. . . . It is largely left to private enterprise to make the critical public policy decisions. . . . Government must, to a significant degree, be acquiescent to the needs and demands of business for to do so is to do no more than to provide good government.

The argument is a variant of a maxim often attributed to Richard Nixon: "If you've got them by their genitals, their hearts and minds will follow." M.V. Nadel has put it in a more scholarly fashion. He argues that, while a government can attach a sanction to its edicts, a sanction that can be enforced via the police and the courts, corporate decisions can be just as effective. He notes that people may not be able to avoid the impact of a corporate decision except at great cost to themselves. Nadel refers to this as "situation bindingness." As an editorial in *Maclean's* pithily put it: "If the CEO's of the big corporations have begun to talk like government leaders, it is not entirely accidental: these days they run the show."

The issue of tobacco production and sales provides a good example of corporate political power. Governments have been shamed into expressing their disapproval of the industry's products, but they cannot bring themselves to outlaw the business. They limit advertising and then run into trouble because they are constraining speech rights about a legal activity. These contradictions are not the result of the collective incapacity of governments to think their way out of a paper bag, as some critics would have it, but rather the consequence of a dependence on the revenues generated by the taxation of tobacco products and of a sensitivity to the efforts, and livelihoods, of a great many farmers who rely on growing tobacco crops. In addition, the tobacco corporations, fighting to retain their profit base, bolster their social legitimacy by sponsoring popular events and causes. Music organizations and artists and sports' spokespersons all lobby governments to permit tobacco companies to continue to put their logos on their events. The headline over a sports column is typical: "Women's Event Should Not Go up in Smoke." The article bemoans how the government's ban on tobacco sponsorship threatens the viability of a golf tournament. The journalist Dave Perkins spontaneously and sincerely says exactly what the tobacco corporations would happily pay him to say: that there is no scientific basis for the ban and that, in any event, the logic that underlies it would allow attacks on all profit-making activities that cause collateral damage: "Doubtless the PC crowd will be strapping on the jackboots any minute now, but I don't buy . . . that sponsoring a golf tournament, or a music or dance festival, causes children to take up smoking . . . the smoking issue is a larger one. . . . What is not a good thing is losing the golf tournaments and jazz festivals and things that help make our lives what they are."

The current, and shameful, asbestos episode provides another example. There can be no doubt that asbestos kills, painfully. In October 2000 the World Trade Organization (WTO) handed down a judgment upholding Europe's ban on the export of asbestos by Canada to European countries. Canada subsequently announced that it would appeal that ruling. Doubtless the Canadian government did not make this response because it wanted to ensure that people in other parts of the world would be poisoned. Rather, our representatives are aware of the existence of a large mountain of asbestos in Quebec on which a great number of livelihoods depend. This is presumably why the Quebec Federation of Labour accepted the support of the Asbestos Institute to make the argument that asbestos work could be done safely and that asbestos could be used safely. The Asbestos Institute is funded by the Canadian and asbestos-producing provincial governments of Quebec and Newfoundland, to the tune of about $50 million since 1984, and also by the asbestos industry. The Asbestos Institute continues, to this day, to wage battles to save the industry. Just as important—perhaps more important—to the Canadian government, Quebec, as a province/nation, has a material interest in the mining and export of asbestos. The political significance of this interest in this always fragile federation cannot be overestimated. The pressures to protect private economic activities stem, then, from many, and sometimes surprising, sources. In the case of asbestos, these pressures have led the Canadian government to take positions that bring Canadians into disrepute in other countries. For instance, Patrick Herman and Annie Thibaud-Mony reported in July 2000 that Canada had persuaded the South Korean government to withdraw labels on boxes of imported Canadian asbestos. The labels, aimed at workers handling the product, directed attention to the hazards of asbestos. The same report also recorded that Canada had given its support to England's disastrous handling of the "mad cow" episode in return for Prime Minister Tony Blair's agreement to delay the ban on Canadian asbestos.

More and more, what is characterized as the natural interdependence between large business corporations, on the one hand, and smaller businesses and workers, on the other, as well as the symbiotic relationship between large, publicly traded corporations and governments, is turning into a dependency relationship in which the dominant parties are large-scale businesses carried on by huge corporations. Ideological constructs and the actual operations of liberal law and the market have naturalized the increasing marginalization of elected governments. Intensified commodification and consumerism in addition to the melding of advertising with the information and opinions offered by the media (which are supposedly there to safeguard the political sovereignty of the citizenry), have led governments and citizens to accept that "there is no alternative" (TINA)—that we have to give the large corporations pretty much what they want. The corporations in turn do let governments know what they want. They have many means of doing so, and they employ them all.

The Orchestration of Public Policy

Amidst the rather feverish activity to promote corporate social responsibility, corporate think-tanks bolster the goal of having government and the law continue to privilege private for-profit corporate activity. As well as creating a generally favourable climate for profiteering, targeted lobbying and influence-peddling carefully work to boost the interests of particular corporations. In his book *The Canadian Corporate Elite*, Wallace Clement recorded the extensive system of interlocking directorships that connected major corporations to one another in Canada's highly concentrated economy of the early 1970s. In 113 dominant corporations, Clement found 1,848 interlocked positions. These spider webs of captains of industry, finance, retail, and everything else remain in place thirty years later, and they continue to make it easier for business leaders (who, on a daily basis, represent distinct interests) to develop congruent views on overall policies they want the state to adopt. To help them with their penetration of the state's policy-making circles, corporate interests have set in place a variety of linkages, all of which, on their face, are natural and even benign. In the mid-1980s John Fox and Michael Ornstein provided evidence of an intense degree of overlap in the memberships of public and private organizations. Public-sector and private-sector functionaries are amicably seated together on the boards of diverse state, quasi-public, and prestigious volunteer agencies. They get to know each other's needs and build relations of trust and reliance. Fox and Ornstein found 3,300 such tie-creating setups, connecting 148 state and 302 private organizations. The same study showed that a great number of politicians and bureaucrats either originally came to public life from the corporate elites or eventually became members. In the 1980s 17.9 per cent of federal cabinet ministers held, or came to hold, corporate organizational appointments. Some 20 per cent of the members of the federal cabinet, the Senate, the senior courts in the land, and university and hospital boards had held at least one senior corporate position either before or after their membership in the public-sector institution.

This interconnectedness is cemented by the opinion-moulding private media outlets. They, and a host of well-funded industrial-sector lobby groups and business think-tanks, combine to propagate a worldview that privileges individual profit-chasing activities over planned decision-making on behalf of the collective good. The Business Council on National Issues, the banks as individual lobbyists and as a group, the Canadian Tax Association, the Canadian Chamber of Commerce, the Canadian Manufacturers' Association, the Fraser Institute, and the C.D. Howe Institute all work to convince elected politicians and their bureaucrats that large corporations should have greater freedom of movement and operation (fewer restrictions, lower taxes), all for the good of the citizenry and, therefore, for the good of government. These organizations have little by way of financial restraint and are not bothered by a burning desire to offer up a complete picture of any particular issue, much less to tell the truth. For instance, the Fraser Institute's "learned" papers, duly reported and given credibility by the "news" media, argue that tobacco smoke is not detrimental to health or that Canada has no real poverty if we define "poverty" as it should be defined: as applying only to people who are totally destitute, devoid of the essentials to survive biologically. According to the Fraser Institute, the lack of the accoutrements necessary to live at a level acceptable to the average member of society, let alone a member of the Fraser Institute, should not be treated as a sign of poverty.

The corporate sectors also contribute heavily to the political coffers of the elected representatives of the people. We've already seen some of the results of that contribution in the discussion of the relationship between corporate speech and the free-trade election (chapter 7). Mainstream political parties and politicians have come to rely on private-sector donations. Robert MacDermid has provided clear snapshots of how corporate financing has become a chief determinant of how electoral politics are conducted and of the decided edge this practice gives to the wealthy, corporate minority, even while the political system continues to hold itself out as reflecting fairly determined majority opinions. A former player, now a disenchanted critic, Mel Hurtig, catches the flavour of the distorted form of democracy:

> I was a member of the Liberal party from 1968 to 1973, and during that time each cabinet minister had an A list, a B list, and a C list, based on financial contributions to the party. Government legal work, as well as work for contractors, engineers, architects, accountants, and so on, was parcelled out largely on the basis of who had put up how much. Many political meetings were devoted to discussions only about patronage. Anyone who thinks the system has changed since 1973 is naive.

Today, some thirty years after Hurtig's experience as a mainstream party member, endless debates still occur about how to diminish the influence of money in the political process. The Manitoba and Quebec governments have enacted legislation prohibiting corporations from funding politicians and their parties. There is a good deal of agitation to have this kind of regulation universalized, indicating at least a general awareness of the problem. Chantal Hebert notes that although the political parties all claim to be in favour of electoral reform, their dependence on corporate funding remains great: "For all their ongoing talk about having the freedom to reinvent themselves, the fact is that rarely have so many parties been so beholden for survival to the generous hands that feed them."

This constant massaging of the political milieu takes place as the result of deliberate decisions by the executives of large, very large, corporations. They decide to register their corporations as members of industrial and commercial organizations. They provide these organizations with money and staff them with luminaries who carry a torch for market capitalism. They fund and run think-tanks designed to establish a "favourable" climate for big business, to finance candidates and parties that are likely to deliver the

specific goods for a particular donor or the general goods for large corporations. But researchers search corporate minutes in vain for resolutions that
empower the executives to deploy corporate funds to these ends. The working assumption is that fiscal and personnel support, both for corporation-
specific lobbying and for general ideology-cementing campaigns, is in the
best interests of the corporations and their shareholders and does not require
detailed discussion with, or accounting to, shareholders. The lack of democratic mandate for corporate boards and executives to act in the public,
political arena draws no discussion in corporate boardrooms—which only
underscores the hypocrisy of the argument that it would be undemocratic to
ask corporate executives to act on behalf of stakeholders other than shareholders. That, after all, was the argument made by Milton Friedman and his
acolytes when proponents of corporate social responsibility, consumer boycott, and ethical investment raised their courageous heads. The other side of
this tendency is that there is never any deviance from the proposition that the
shareholders' interest in profit-maximization is a given. Any other goals that
the shareholders might have as ordinary citizens do not have this same standing, do not command this automatic respect.

All of this manipulation of the political agendas occurs without major
investors ever having to admit that they are using their wealth and the
unequal distribution of wealth perpetuated by corporate capitalism to pervert
the intended workings of democratic institutions. If, to maintain their personal dominance over affairs of state, the various captains of industry and
everything else personally had to threaten to withdraw their personal capital
unless governments gave them what they wanted, or if they personally had to
fund politicians and parties to get personal favours, or if they personally had
to hire flaks—well-qualified flaks though they might be—to gild economic
and social lillies, we might find it easier to see if the liberal-democratic
promises of our political institutions were being kept. But, in large part, these
machinations occur as if they were the "natural" practices of market actors
with no political or ideological axes to grind—as the sensible behaviour of
corporations that are mere technical market instruments. They are thus
effective in a largely hidden sort of way.

Large corporations have been able to persuade governments that corporate concentration is not an unalloyed evil and that, to the contrary, it contributes to the good of the general welfare and helps to ensure governments'
viability. Indeed, we need it, they say, to be "globally competitive." The
result is ever greater degrees of corporate non-competitiveness, which, in
turn, gives the now larger corporations more clout when lobbying governments for yet more favourable treatment. For a time government tried to

preserve at least some competition. Indeed, according to Stanbury the very feebleness of competition policy enforcement led federal governments to begin pressing for changes to its own legislation from 1966 onwards. But the first amendments were not enacted until 1976. Business opposition led to huge delays, and government did not deal with the most significant parts of the policies—mergers and monopolies—because of this resistance. A series of provisions were drafted, some were introduced into parliament, but all foundered because of large business antagonism. Finally, in 1984, a bill received first reading after government made a series of compromises acceptable to the "Gang of Three" (Stanbury's term): the Business Council on National Issues, the Canadian Manufacturers' Association, and the Canadian Chamber of Commerce. The Gang of Three had succeeded in watering down the earlier proposals, themselves pale versions of what governments had originally envisaged in the 1960s. But this bill also did not make it into law. Finally, in 1986, a new version was passed, but only after the government had negotiated it clause by clause with what was now the "Gang of Five" (with the Grocery Products Manufacturers' Association and the Canadian Bar Association added on). This bill was strengthened by a few amendments arising mainly from the demands of small-business organizations.

The corporate sector, then, has been highly effective in its conscious orchestration of public policy-making—"effective," at least, from the lobbyists' point of view. The orchestration is less effective from the point of view of the public interest and maintenance of democracy: the general public has never voted in favour of reducing impediments to mergers and acquisitions, and the increased concentration leads in most cases to undesirable outcomes, including more limited choice for "consumers."

As some observers explain, corporations are supposedly engaged in M&As because of the existence of a gap between the realizable worth of the assets of a corporation and the value attributed to those corporate assets by the market as reflected in current share prices. Purchasing shares (merging the corporation with another or acquiring it for another corporation), even at a premium price, is deemed to be an efficiency-enhancing practice. In theory the changeover will install a new management that will put the corporate assets to better use. That is why incumbent managers must not be allowed to stand in the way of transfers of control, and that is why, inasmuch as legal reform of corporate governance gets off the ground, it leads to the imposition of rules that make it easier for existing shareholders to accept a premium from a purchaser who/which wants to gain control over the corporation's assets. The shareholders are given rights against their managers, who might stand in the way.

But whatever the merits of theoretical contentions about the efficiency-enhancing capacity of unfettered M&As, the empirical record is a sorry affair. In a scholarly summary of the studies of the benefits and disadvantages of the merger movements in the United States, Richard Du Boff and Edward Herman concluded that, at best, mergers had a neutral impact on economic efficiency; at worst, a negative one. There was no evidence of a positive effect. Today many observers defending the relentless merger movement featured in our business pages—often in romantic and sentimental terms about the boldness and vision of the CEOs involved—do so on the basis that the activities advance the cause of shareholders. Rather than measure the merit of the M&As phenomenon by reference to the chestnut of economic efficiency, the contention now is that it should be viewed from the perspective of the gains and losses of the shareholders of the corporations involved in the mergers and acquisitions, particularly the outcomes for the shareholders of the acquiring corporation. The finance capitalist's position, rather than the productive capitalist's one, is what should be evaluated. Given that approach, M&As, in general, will prove to be beneficial. But Du Boff and Herman throw cold water on this theory as well. They note that parasites—that is, people who promote M&As and who have no particular interest in any one corporation's longevity or profitability—do extremely well; but on average the shareholders of the acquiring corporation either lose or derive no benefit from the transaction. This historical analysis is supported by a recent survey by the consultancy firm KPMG, which found that 30 per cent of mergers created shareholder value, while 31 per cent destroyed value; this finding actually reflected an improvement on other periods, when only 17 per cent of mergers created value while 53 per cent destroyed value.

The separation of finance capital from productive capital, which inheres in the argument that what matters is immediate shareholder value—rather than corporate efficiency over the long haul—raises complex questions. For instance, just focusing on whether or not M&As are useful and effective by reference to their impacts on one set of financial capitalists (shareholders) distorts the reading of balance sheets and hides the social and human costs of these humongous transactions. As to the first point, shareholder value improvement is often yielded because the new acquirers sell some of the less productive assets of the acquired corporation, causing share prices to rise. The acquirers often sell assets because they borrowed money to make their acquisition. But the sale of assets can undermine the security that other lenders to the corporation thought they had achieved when they lent money to the corporation before it was sold. The IOUs they held will not be as valuable. Some financial investors, then, lose precisely because others gain.

Sometimes these losses are so great that the lenders' IOUs are transformed from valuable investments into what the market descriptively calls "non-investment grade junk." Rather than an increase of overall wealth as a result of the transaction, there may be, then, a redistribution of wealth amongst fractions of the investing classes. This means that from an efficiency perspective, despite rising share prices, little of utility has happened. But, inasmuch as all of this activity may be a harmless, if wasteful, wash, much of the feverish, unproductive profit-chasing inflicts pain and harm on workers.

Much of the evidence indicates that workers all too often pay the price of M&As. "Merging workers wait and worry," offered the headline of a September 2001 article describing the anxiety of employees of Hewlett-Packard and Compaq as they awaited the fallout of a much-heralded merger between the two companies. The salivating attention paid to that merger stemmed from its size: $25 billion. The corporations announced that, after the change of control, some of the efficiencies promised would be obtained by sacking fifteen thousand workers. In May 2001, Clairol's workers were left on tenterhooks after the purchase of their company's shares by Procter & Gamble for $7.6 billion. Again, "savings," an article announced, would be achieved by getting rid of about four thousand of Clairol's workers. Another would-be blockbuster merger was to be General Electric's purchase of Honeywell International at an announced price of a mammoth U.S.$41 billion. The European Community balked at the possible harm the merger would do to competition within its jurisdictions and convinced the European Commission to put a kibosh on the transaction, despite President George W. Bush's personal intervention on behalf of the U.S.-based megacorporations. But, while the merger was still a real possibility, the merging actors wanted to show the capital markets that it would lead to economic efficiencies and, therefore, should be rewarded by good stock-market prices. To get this favourable treatment, the would-be couplers announced that, after the intended merger, about thirty thousand jobs at Honeywell and around eleven thousand jobs at General Electric, would be "trimmed" from the payrolls. Stock markets find this sort of thing to be very cheering, but it is not very comforting to workers. In a similar vein, JDS Uniphase announced huge losses, of the order of U.S.$7.9 billion in one quarter—losses that came after the firm had written down U.S.$38.7 billion in "goodwill." This last figure was a formal admission that JDS had paid that much too much for its acquisitions of other corporations. This vast miscalculation had led to the shedding of seventeen thousand jobs. The darling of Canadian stock exchanges, Nortel Networks, had to get rid of thirty thousand workers, in part because of equally disastrous errors of judgements when it spent monies on corporate acquisitions in the same way a drunken sailor spends on a short shore leave. But, unlike most sailors, corporate spendthrifts do not end up paying for their self-indulgences. Externalized costs are picked up in part by the state, which has to subsidize job searches, employment replacement incomes, and community shortfalls due to diminished revenues. Mostly, however, workers pay for the mistakes and greed of the captains of industry and everything else, as well as for the hustling practices of well-clad bankers, stock analysts and dealers, and accountants and lawyers, all of whom are disconnected, at least in functional terms, from productive relations.

While some reforms in corporate governance law work to inhibit managers from safeguarding their own security at the expense of shareholders, these affairs as a whole are essentially intra-class disputes. The protagonists belong to the same class and, therefore, law is not to be used too harshly against one set or another of the contestants. Thus, it has become a legally endorsed practice for managers to bargain with their own corporation to get an incentive not to oppose changes of control — that is, to bargain for an extra reward to do what the law already requires them to do. They arrange for golden parachutes, ensuring money-laden, soft landings for managers whom, perhaps, the market has adjudged not to be as effective as they ought to have been. On the understanding that they will not use their governing powers to oppose takeovers or mergers, managers are promised vast sums to go quietly. For instance, when Qwest and U.S. West were merged, U.S. West CEO Sol Trujillo got U.S.$15 million by way of severance pay, $46 million in stock options, plus $11 million to cover the taxes payable on this gift of options. Even this was not quite enough, and Trujillo also received U.S.$24 million worth of shares in Qwest to keep him happy. When the AOL-Time Warner transaction (U.S.$106 billion) was consummated in 2000, efficiencies were to be attained by the usual trimming of employees from the now joint payroll. An initial announcement of two thousand layoffs, to be followed by many more, was news at the same time as it was revealed — to a rather breathless business press — that stock option bonanzas of U.S.$3 billion had been allocated to two AOL and five Time Warner executives to help them get over their loss of control over their corporations.

On occasion, managers do not play by these generous rules, and then the underpinnings of the merger movement threaten to be revealed for what they so often are, a series of manoeuvres inspired by the personal greed of a few powermongers rather than the natural workings of efficient markets. Allegedly this is what happened during Vodaphone's bid for control of Mannesmann AG for $208 billion. German prosecutors alleged that, to convince the German corporation's managers not to put up too much resistance to a bid that the managers of Mannesmann perceived as a hostile one when they received it, Vodaphone sweetened the already saccharine pot by offering more than $72 million to the Mannesmann CEO and his senior executives. Vodaphone denies that it tried to bribe its potential opponents, although it is true that the Mannesmann CEO received $43 million when he left and other executives shared packages worth $20 million.

Nice work if you can get it, and managers involved in M&As get it all the time. Workers simply get no work. Whether or not you see efficiency being enhanced by a M&As depends on who you are and what relation you have to the corporations involved. The various captains and their suited go-betweens—the bankers, brokers, accountants, analysts, lawyers—want these actions portrayed as enuring to the general welfare. As usual, they equate their own interests with those of the public.

Manipulation, Coercion, and Obfuscation

Our adherence to a market economy, both because of its potential efficiency and claimed congruence with political freedom, has established a widely accepted belief system that government is doing its job when it goes out of its way to remove fetters on the private market. This ideological starting point is reinforced in many ways. But when large corporations are the economic actors protected and privileged by these starting positions, a host of distortions arise because these firms behave in ways that undermine the idealized market and liberal-democratic models. This ought to create a public backlash, which rarely occurs. Large corporations have woven a web of associations, political mechanisms, and influence-peddling organizations that supplement their inherent economic and political power, that very power that distorts the liberal-political and market-economic models. In the end this corporate power rests on the right to withdraw the wealth accumulated inside the corporations.

The norm is the creation of a state of mind that has politicians of all stripes believing in the interdependence of democratically elected governments and large owners of private wealth, with those owners screened from view by the legally provided corporate veil. The whole system is posited on manipulation and coercion, and the obfuscation of how the privileging of one minority—the wealthy—is incompatible with liberal-democratic theory. Politicians of all stripes believe that, when they take the needs of big corporate business into account when making laws and policies, they are doing what comes naturally. Politicians and pundits and other onlookers tend to ignore or downplay a basic conundrum: that a somewhat functionally useful interdependence may actually have become a politically and economically distorting dependence. The effects of all this go a long way towards explaining a number of conditions that result in the perpetuation of inequality and misery in this wealthy and supposedly democratic society.

Item. This framework of understanding helps explain why the criminal law proper is rarely thought to be apposite to corporate deviance. Welfare regulatory law is to be preferred for the desirable endeavours of government's main instrument to attain its goals.

Item. Inasmuch as regulatory law is preferred, the move from interdependent relationships to one in which the governments become more obviously dependent on the corporate sectors makes it sensible for government to consult with the regulatees as to whether or not there should be any regulation at all, and, if there should be, what standards ought to be imposed. Stanbury's account of how competition laws were drafted reveals much about how this process works. Among the countless examples of this trend is the way in which the Canadian Chemical Producers' Association has used its influence. In the 1980s chemical producers were faced by the growing environmental movement, sparked by Rachel Carson's now justifiably celebrated *Silent Spring* (1962). In response they set up a program called Responsible Care, a self-regulatory scheme to avert government regulation. Industry thinkers believed that it was necessary to do something drastic to maintain the legitimacy that would leave producers largely unregulated. As one senior chemical corporate executive put it, "[We] just cannot advertise our way out of it." The "it" referred to the growing disenchantment with the increasing revelations about costly pollution and harmful practices (for example, Bhopal) and products (for example, Agent Orange) But awareness of the continuing and increasing degradation of environmental conditions led a 1994 Standing Committee of Canada's federal legislature to begin deliberations, despite the industry's public relations' efforts. The Committee's initial report called for chemical producers to phase out all persistent bioaccumulative and toxic substances. Douglas Macdonald reports how this created panic in industry circles. During the earlier period, to avert the potential regulation the industry had taken on some self-imposed costs through its Responsible Care program. But in the United States, the industry had been forced to spend only 1.4 per cent of its total sales to meet the requirements of the self-regulatory standards: a small cost given that it slowed government regulation to a crawl. The 1994 menace of a total ban on some highly profitable products might not be so easily minimized. The wagons were circled and, evidently, were very heavily armed. Macdonald, much like Stanbury did in respect to the competition bill debate, shows how the Canadian Chemical Producers' Association used its influence with the heavyweights in government (sending letters to members of the ruling Liberal Party and holding meetings between government bureaucrats and their political masters with specially established blue ribbon committees of the chemical producers, for instance) to convince the government to abandon its own committee's recommendations. The Liberal Party members of that committee eventually voted against the Bill enacted by their own government (in 1999) because the government had accepted industry's demand that the policy return to its original position, namely the management of the release of toxic substances rather than the prohibition of their use altogether.

A similar story is unfolding over the controversy whether or not to allow the use of genetically modified foods and, if so, how to regulate that use. The Royal Society of Canada, in response to a government request, set up a panel of experts that was very critical of government's approach on the issue thus far. The government, though, seems to have shelved the report and instead has placed greater faith in the report of Canadian Biotechnology Advisory Committee, a group handpicked by ministers of the Crown. The Advisory Committee turned out to be much more big-business friendly in its treatment of the problem.

Item. Inasmuch as the questions of regulation and standards require an evaluation of the utility and potential hazard of an activity or product, research must be done. Governments do their own research, but their resources are limited and the number of activities and products, if not infinite, very large. They therefore place great reliance on research done by independent institutions and large corporations. But, of course, these so-called independent institutions often rely on private-sector contributions. In capitalism there is no such thing as aimless money—that is, money not deployed to make more money. The logic of corporate law is that funds should not be spent unless the corporation receives a healthy return. While the corporate executives who decide to fund a program may clothe themselves in the vestments of philanthropists or the costumes of organizations eager to further knowledge for its own sake (and to get a tax break for their image-enhancing largesse), the funds are targeted and those who depend on these funds know that.

This is why Eyal Press and Jennifer Washburn, in an article in *The Atlantic Monthly*, concluded: "Corporations not only sponsor a growing amount of research—they frequently dictate the terms under which it is conducted. Professors often own stocks in companies that fund their work. And universities exhibit a markedly more commercial bent." Citing the *Annals of Internal Medicine*, the two authors record that 98 per cent of papers based on industry-sponsored research reflected favourably on the drugs tested, whereas the figure dropped to 79 per cent when the research was not so funded. They cite a *Journal of the American Medical Association* finding that studies of cancer drugs funded by pharmaceutical companies are roughly one-eighth as likely to reach unfavourable conclusions as not-for-profit funded studies. My personal favourite of their many illustrations, in part because it fits so snugly with the example of how the privatization of prisons has become a morally acceptable profit opportunity, is the story of one Charles Thomas, a criminologist frequently published by mainstream media. Thomas reportedly made $3 million from consulting fees from the private prison corporations in which he also held shares. His academic prestige was used to give evidence to a Congressional Committee examining the advisability of privatizing prisons. These kinds of conflicts or, better, circumstances which should be acknowledged to be rife with unacceptable conflict, are commonplace. For instance, the U.S. General Accounting Office reported serious deficiencies in the Environmental Protection Agency's establishment of advisory tribunals: a significant number of the experts on which it relied for advice worked for the very chemical companies whose products were under scrutiny by the government regulatory body. For these very reasons eleven respected medical journals are requiring researchers who submit papers to them to explain their connections, if any, to parties potentially interested in the results and to give an account of sponsoring corporations' role in the research. Things must be at a pretty pass if such obvious conflicts require special rules because they are ignored by many so-called scientists and researchers.

All of this is not surprising, precisely because we already know that large corporations often doctor and/or lie about the known hazards of their products or activities, from tobacco to asbestos to the safety of cars, drugs, contraceptives, and airplanes. Deception for profit, particularly deception of the government with the help of righteous and well-qualified scientific in-house experts, is systemic, not extraordinary. This is why the more egregious examples of large corporations' attempts to get the scientific results that their profit-making agenda needs, regardless of human costs, should not be seen as aberrational. They are merely the clumsier efforts to cook the books.

In 2001, for example, two cases associated with the University of Toronto drew attention to the agendas of the more sophisticated manipulating private financiers of research. Dr. Nancy Olivieri, a medical researcher at the Hospital for Sick Children, affiliated with the University of Toronto, had contractually agreed with Apotex, a producer of drugs, to do a study for the company. She signed a confidentiality agreement with Apotex when accepting the assignment. When she discovered that the drug had harmful side-effects, she wanted Apotex to stop the study; when it refused, Olivieri contacted her hospital, which, in turn, counselled her to change the consent form that her patients signed in agreeing to subject themselves to the drug being studied. Her patients thus would be "better" informed by her findings of hazard. Apotex removed Olivieri from the study. Her hospital not only did not support her but, some time later, allegedly for different reasons, also demoted her. The second case involved Dr. David Healy, who, after a lengthy period of negotiations, was offered an appointment to the Centre for Addiction and Mental Health, an institution affiliated with the University of Toronto. Appointment to the Centre would lead to an appointment at the University of Toronto. It happened that, at a conference held before Dr. Healy was to take up his appointment, he gave a talk in which he questioned the uses made of Prozac. In particular, he argued that there was sufficient evidence of this drug's connection to increases in the incidence of suicide for it to warrant further research. In somewhat disputed circumstances, the Centre for Addiction and Mental Health reneged on its offer of an appointment. It came out that Prozac is a product of Eli Lilly, a company that is a significant financial contributor to the Centre for Addiction and Mental Health; and it was also alleged that the Centre's executives may have had a conversation with a noted expert in the field who acted as a consultant of Eli Lilly and held shares in that corporation. But these factors were all said to have played no part in the decisions of the Centre and university.

These kinds of incidents draw attention to how universities make more and more money by patenting and licensing products and designs that are useful to profit-seeking corporations. At the same time universities are downsizing their humanities and other "non-profit"-related departments as government funding decreases. They place increasing reliance on corporate financing, which flows more easily for types of research and training that suit the world of commerce. This is why universities are increasingly joining forces with dot.com-type operations to deliver education for dollars. None of this does much for the development of independent research undertaken for the public welfare, but it does do a great deal for individual corporations that want an immediate bang for their bucks and even more for the propagation of the belief that what is good for large corporate business is good for all of us and ought to be promoted by government.

Here it is good, as always, to remember who profits from all of this deliberate manipulation. All of this "puffery," "omissions to tell," soft-soaping of specific research, and the like is done in the best interests of flesh and blood human beings who are happy to remain ignorant of, or sometimes to be wilfully indifferent to, the massaging of truth and public policy-making.

Item. Inasmuch as governments and policy-makers agree on the need for more socially responsible action by the corporate sectors, their inability to enforce existing laws, let alone pass new, more rigorous ones, leads them to become cheerleaders for legitimacy-seeking and damage-controlling tactics developed by the more thoughtful corporate leaders and think-tanks. They approve of consultation and mediation, rather than direct enforcement and punishment, to get corporations to abide by existing standards. They openly say this approach makes sense because, otherwise, corporations would stop investing, hinder inspectors, or hide malfeasance. Better, then, to rely on the corporations' sense of decency, to let them self-regulate as much as possible. This reliance on non-enforceable regimes is referred to, rather tellingly, as a preference for soft law—the preferred instrument for governments that have now been gulled into accepting the virtues of trade liberalization, privatization, deregulation, flexibility, and global competitiveness. The preference to permit corporations to call the shots is nicely illustrated by how the Clinton administration inserted itself—because it felt it had to do so—when the public educational campaigns of boycotts against sweated labour in the garment/fashion industry became successful and government had to show it cared. In 1997 it established the Fair Labor Association (FLA), the members of which would commit themselves to decent, monitored working conditions. Signing on would permit a corporation to put a "No Sweat" label on its products. This tangible result of economic boycotts clearly was something of a success, yet it resulted in soft law, not binding law. Even then, by 1999 *Business Week* had reported that a pitiful total of four corporations had signed on to the FLA.

In a slightly different setting, Laura Cram documented how the setting of standards by the European Commission had overwhelmingly concentrated on the enactment of legislation that established general frameworks for behaviour with no direct impact on individuals in member states. Symbolic legal pronouncements predominate. Another very active sphere of Commission intervention has been the enactment of *non-binding* legislation, which is, again, soft law. Similarly, although a Labour Agreement is attached to NAFTA, all that the signatories of NAFTA did was to agree to enforce the domestic standards that already existed in the countries that were party to the agreement. There is also no way for employers or workers to bring labour conditions directly to a NAFTA agency for settlement of a dispute. They must bring their complaint to a secretariat of the member state whose law allegedly has been violated. If this does not lead to settlement, a tri-national ministerial agency may seek to deal with the matter by consultation with the parties. If not settled, the dispute is to go to a tribunal of a committee of experts. Eventually trade sanctions on the breaching party, or even a fine on an individual violator, may be imposed. By contrast, when it comes to violations of the trade agreement that hurt individual entrepreneurs, those individuals can bring direct actions against the member state on the basis that its policy, even if it has democratically been made into a law of that state, offends the corporate entrepreneur of another nation/party to NAFTA.

The so-called "investor/state" provision of NAFTA allows a corporation to sue a country for lost profits or opportunities for profits. Ethyl Corporation used this to force Canada to reverse legislation that banned a gasoline additive (MMT, produced by Ethyl Corporation), which the government considered a danger to the health of Canadians. Once again, here was a major corporation insisting on its right to make profits at the expense of human beings. Similarly, while the large corporations sing the praises of self-regulation and soft law when it comes to the protection of the non-corporate sectors, they warble a very different tune when there is a need to safeguard themselves from other rogue corporate actors that might try to get an advantage in profit-making by cheating and avoiding competition. Thus, recently, the Organization for Economic Co-operation and Development (OECD) managed to get an agreement on bribery. It is meant to be enforceable as if it were hard law, although the likelihood of effective enforcement is far from ensured.

Item. Inasmuch as governments still purport to act on behalf of the public good and inasmuch as they have become increasingly reluctant to direct the captains of industry and everything else as to how to deploy the assets accumulated inside corporations, they have become more and more like the beggars they try to sweep off the streets. The large gobs of wealth that corporations control allow them to force governments to compete for investment. Some cheerleaders for corporate capitalism call this well-known phenomenon good government. In Nova Scotia, for instance, the provincial government is willing to more than double the subsidy that neighbouring New Brunswick pays to U.S.-owned call centre companies for every job created. With New Brunswick paying $10,000 per badly needed job created, Nova Scotia was reportedly ready to spend up to $24,000 of its citizens' money per job created. From the governments' perspective, these initiatives earn them kudos with both the electorate and big business. They justify these corporate handouts by arguing that the newly employed citizens will repay the costs through taxes and consumer spending that would not have been possible but for the subsidies. For their part, the corporations, which have no sense of place or loyalty, happily move about to "earn" this kind of bonus. It is good money. EDS Corporation, a Texas outfit, established a nine-hundred-person call centre in Sydney, Nova Scotia. In return for this largesse, EDS Corporation got $21 million by way of subsidy from the taxpayers. *Private enterprise* is a wondrous thing. Having received the incentive money, our private leaders of everything do not feel any moral obligations about staying when the going gets tough or going back to the public trough when they sense that a mendicant government is likely to cave in to yet more demands and threats.

Between 1982 and 1997 Pratt & Whitney Canada, whose major product is gas turbine engines, received more than $950 million by way of these kinds of subsidies, more than any other private Canadian corporation. In 1998 alone it laid off nine hundred workers. In 1999 Pratt & Whitney was back, begging bowl in hand. This time the federal government ladled $154 million into the business: money given for research and development. While this subsidy, perhaps, might seem to be justifiable as a matter of good government, it is significant that before receiving the grant Pratt & Whitney had threatened to pull up stakes unless it received financial aid. By then, too, the government surely must have known that after receiving subsidies the company had less than a stellar record as a serious contributor to the welfare of Canadians. No matter; the government gave this known wastrel the money. IBM, too, obtained $33 million for research and development in 1999 after it threatened to move its Internet project and fifteen hundred research and development jobs out of Canada. Even Nortel Networks Corp., the huge and for a while marvellously successful corporation, was dipping deeply into the public purse. By 1995 Nortel's vaunted research and development had been subsidized by taxpayers to the tune of $800 million, followed by another $300 million in 1999. In addition, because Nortel is (or, better, was) a "global" Canadian corporation, it received $400 million from the Export Development Corporation, a government agency, between 1988 and 1993 — all this for the company that laid off some thirty thousand workers within a few months in 2001. On average in the 1990s, $13 billion a year was doled out to "help" corporations. Precisely because this aid is the result of direct or hidden power plays, the largest bulk of these handouts go to the largest corporations, those with the most power and greatest access to the government.

According to that most conservative of think-tanks, the Canadian Taxpayers Federation (CTF), 49 per cent of all federal grants and loans went to seventy-five of Canada's largest corporations. When the aid is given by way of loans, it might seem unfair to refer to it as subsidies, but according to the CTF, only 15 per cent of the loans are ever repaid. Similarly, the tax deferments that corporations get under certain circumstances are rarely, if ever, paid off. At any one time the corporate sectors owe the Canadian revenue authorities some $40 billion. This figure appears as a receivable asset on the books, but it is unlikely to become a real asset any time soon.

Taxpayers and workers pay for the subsidy system when it fails to deliver the goods. The captains of industry, finance, retail, and everything else never have to pay the price for the failures of these policies, which, in the first place, are the consequence of their naked power over, and sophisticated manipulation of, the political regime. In the early 1970s NDP leader David Lewis ran a successful federal election campaign around the slogan "Corporate welfare bums." This slogan, though still apt today, may now have less resonance because of the wild success that the large corporations have experienced in convincing our policy-makers and many of the rest of us that "there is no alternative."

The Distortion of Democracy

When we speak of the corporate sector, the corporate view, corporate culture, and the like, we signify our understanding that the economic size of large multinational corporations gives them a special set of characteristics. We implicitly concede that their size and centrality to our political economy are making it increasingly difficult for the nation-state to impose its will, even though this will, in principle, is the will of the majority of human beings in the nation. What we are acknowledging is that government is acting on behalf of these corporations in the hope that this will somehow benefit the majority. What we tend not to openly acknowledge is that these corporations do not exist for their own good, but rather for the good of a small number of dominant investors. But, while we rarely say this, it gnaws away at our political consciousness. Our current system of governing—which is to favour corporations immediately so that, in the future, somehow or other, this favour will turn to the advantage of the non-investors, the huge number of people with no wealth to invest—enures to the benefit of a handful of wealth-owners whose identities and faces are hidden from view.

Given the capitalist system, government has become increasingly dependent on corporate goodwill for the necessary generation of wealth. The corporate sectors in turn have become ever more clever in telling governments what is needed to keep them (and, therefore, their major shareholders) happy. An array of think-tanks, schemes for interchanging functionaries between the public and private sectors, the corporate slant of the media, the systematic funding of politics: all of these conditions boost the structural power of accumulated wealth. Approaches based on the corporate perspective become the only viable policy alternative. The privatization of government functions is made to look natural and beneficial in a setting in which it is assumed that the pursuit of overall welfare should be left to private market activity. The deregulation of private economic enterprises has become a *sine qua non* of a modern liberal-capitalist economy. More trust must be placed in market discipline to safeguard us from environmental and occupational health and safety harms, from shoddy products and inferior services. Less trust must be accorded to Big Brother, the state, which, with its bureaucratic and coercive approaches, is more likely to do harm than good. While governments continue to be pressed to demonstrate that, notionally, at least, they can control even the largest corporations, they soften and deregulate behavioural standards for private economic actors. They urge large corporations to comply voluntarily with the standards that are still in place. Occasionally they do prosecute violating corporations; sometimes they pursue directors and senior managers. But these are not the preferred regulatory routes.

Strategies such as boycotts and targeted investments are, in a way, acknowledgements of the radical change in the political entente, one in which the reliance on the private sector for all major decisions and policies has become a dominant motif. Whereas corporations were once created by the state to facilitate very specific goals—such as the construction and operation of a canal or a railway, or an exploration of a foreign source of resources that required large accumulations of capital—today corporations can be formed simply as a means of facilitating the goals of any individual. Inasmuch as the state benefits, it does so indirectly as a result of the economic activity generated by the enterprise. At one time corporations—which had special privileges, such as separate personality and, eventually, limited liability for investors and a market for the shares of the corporation—could only be used for the precise purposes granted by this privileged certification. If the incorporators sought to use the vehicle for different purposes, its contracts and decisions became unenforceable. They were beyond the legal boundaries of the corporation's legal personality. These actions were, in legal jargon, *ultra vires*. Today, in Canada, the *ultra vires* doctrine has been all but abandoned.

A corporation is free to maximize profits by engaging in any lawful business activity it chooses, that is, anything that its senior managers and dominant shareholders choose for it. While it remains true that, in a liberal democracy such as Canada, governments have unlimited power to act, as long as their citizens give them this leeway, in practice our governments are restrained by the structural right that large economic actors have to withhold capital and by the ideological hegemony that corporations have established to make governmental self-restraint the norm. It is now more appropriate to speak of the need of government *not* to act *ultra vires*—that is, outside the functional boundaries created by large corporate power. Corporations pay the piper and the rest of us are left to dance to their discordant tune.

The flesh and blood captains of industry and everything else are the real governing party of nation-states such as Canada that have hitched their wagon to the star of corporate capitalism. They are not likely to be dislodged by strategies that tacitly—if unwillingly—accept the very premises of corporate capitalism as their starting point.

Outing the Captains of Industry, Finance, Retail, and Everything Else

Wherein an attempt is made to devise strategies arising out of the findings of this book to make the captains of industry, finance, retail, and everything else the target of political action, thereby opening the way for a new, participatory project.

In this critical evaluation of the role played by corporations and corporate law in our political economy, one of my central themes has been that wealthy property owners are able to hide behind the legally created corporate veil as they distort the very economic and political model by which they ask the majority of the population to live. They profit hugely from these perversions, to the disadvantage of the majority of people in our society. Lewis Lapham, editor of *Harper's* magazine, wrote, in 1996, that there now are two governments in the United States, the permanent and the provisional. The permanent government is constituted by the corporations on the Fortune 500 list, plus the attendant lobbyists, media and entertaining syndicates, research institutions and universities, law firms, and the like. What characterizes the permanent government is that it is "obedient to the rule of men, not laws" as it controls production and the way in which people are to live. The rule of men (and the gendered nature of this ancient expression remains the

252

right one) is, of course, the rule of rich men, rendered virtually invisible by the artifice and miracle of corporate law. The provisional government is based on the notion that it is subject to a rule of law and not of men. Consequently, Lapham writes, "It must live within the cage of high-minded principle" while controlling very little of real substance.

What is true in the United States is equally true in Canada. But I can hear the question, "So what?" After all, do the United States and Canada not enjoy a greater abundance of wealth than do most other nation-states, despite these distortions? Don't they enjoy more democratic trappings than most other nation-states, despite the corporate-led erosion of democratic institutions? Well, perhaps they do, but even then something still needs to be done. After all, study after study shows that the economic wealth generated is not shared equitably; indeed, it is hardly shared at all. The bottom 40 per cent of Canadians enjoy 1 per cent of all the country's wealth between them. Millions of people in the United States and Canada struggle miserably to live decent lives or even just to survive. Whether it's called malnutrition, hunger, or "food insecurity," or a housing crisis or homelessness, or unemployment or joblessness, the problems are deeply felt; countless human lives are diminished, and a great many more are damaged severely, sometimes irreparably.

Further, much of the wealth generated for the United States and Canada comes at the expense of the peoples of other nations. UNICEF's 2001 *State of the World's Children* recorded that every year ten million children under the age of five are dying because of hunger and disease: 27,000 children every single day of every year. The gross maldistribution of the wealth concentrated in countries like Canada and the United States and of which we boast ("Canada's the greatest country in the world" may be Jean Chrétien's most often-used phrase) comes at an enormous cost to the helpless and hapless of the world. More, even the casual liberal observer cannot but help note the emptiness of the democratic institutions that the elites hold up as proof of our superior political achievements. Richard Gwyn has written, with echoes of Lapham, that "the expansion of the power of corporations" means that "there is less and less to vote for." As a consequence, he writes, "The political parties and Parliament are becoming shells, like those downtown churches whose parishioners have all moved to the suburbs." The continued pretence that our citizens are able to participate in the vital decisions related to their own welfare and values asks us all to live a lie. This is politically, socially, and morally intolerable.

Yes, something needs to be done. What can be done? I tackle this question, which I feel I cannot avoid, with some trepidation. My apprehension stems from a fear that my readers will concentrate on any recommendations for change—which are necessarily speculative and at best partial and, there-fore, perhaps easily dismissed—to the detriment of the observations and find-ings that preceded them. I hesitate in presenting such recommendations because I believe that the findings presented in the chapters so far have a value in their own right, apart from any use I would ask people to make of them. In other words, whatever readers think about the suggestions for change offered, I hope they will not jettison the earlier observations and analysis. I would hope that there is material there that could help to fortify activists who want a different world.

I stated early on that knowledge is not power. But knowledge and under-standing are necessary precursors to intelligent action. As a United Church on Keele Street in Toronto once proclaimed on its billboard: "Think like a man of action. Act like a man of thought." Pierre Bourdieu pointed out that, at any one time, a social regime has a series of principles and tenets that it wants to be taken for granted. These are what he terms *doxa*, and doxa are not debatable because their premises are deemed to be good. People can raise questions about the implementation of these undebatable foundation principles, but not question their fundamental verity. The dominant voices silence heterodoxical questioning or co-opts it so that it becomes part of the orthodox debates, of the doxa. To this end the powers-that-be employ the major means of communication and a host of intellectual gatekeepers for the status quo. It is not as if there were conscious sets of manipulators out there, although there are some. The process is more insidious. As E.P. Thompson noted: "The truth is that our liberal intellectual often does not notice the real forces which determine our political life, because he does not feel himself to be unfree. In his island of mild dissent he is able to speak, to argue, and to communicate with others like himself to his heart's content. . . . He may say what he wants because he wants to say so little."

All of us who share a desire to create a different kind of world need to find ways of transcending the tactics permitted by the doxa. My hope is that, whatever the utility of my suggestions, the actual findings will support a gen-eration of questions that challenge the basic premises of the system of liberal-democratic capitalism. As Sue Hickey, a speaker at a conference on citizenship in New Zealand, said, "If you always do what you have always done, you will always get what you always got." Certainly, for far too long, what the majority of us have been getting is not good enough.

A Framework for Meta-Level Strategies

When it comes to the functioning, legal architecture, and nature of corporations, most of the ills that need to be addressed actually arise out of the logic of capitalist relations of production rather than because capitalists use corporations. As the bishops and superiors of religious orders in Brazil proclaimed in 1973—at a time when conditions appeared to be more hopeful than they are now—"Capitalism must be defeated: it is the greatest evil, the accumulated sin, the rotten root, the tree that produces all these fruits which we know so well: poverty, hunger, disease, death. . . . We must pass beyond private ownership of the means of production (factories, land, commerce, banks)."

That starting point, though, raises a fundamental question: how useful is it to address these grave problems via political actions whose logic rests on an analysis of the corporate vehicle? After all, it is just that: a vehicle. It is not the thing itself. It is logically true that capitalism would still be able to exist even if there were no corporations at all through which it furthered its agenda. Certainly, much existing evidence indicates that capitalism would persist if it used different kinds of corporate vehicles. The kinds of corporations that the advanced Anglo-American legal systems have thrown up are not those developed in European and Asian settings where capitalist relations of production are also firmly established.

In the Anglo-American settings, the corporations and their conduct are characterized by their emphasis on the provision of short-term returns for a diffuse investor population. In Europe the commanding heights of the economy are often occupied by family-controlled firms whose primary interest does not rest in the fate of their corporations' valuation by large, impersonal equity markets. These capitalists' interests, as protected by their laws, are very different to the interests pursued and safeguarded in our parts of the capitalist woods. In some European countries corporate law has spawned a series of mandates that are unknown to our corporate world. In Germany, an understanding that some corporate directors have to represent workers' interests has given life to the well-known "industrial democracy" model of corporate governance. The Netherlands, while it has no such legally required direct worker representation, does have a commitment to the maintenance of the corporation as a viable site of production—as opposed to just treating it as if it were a disposable vehicle for short-term investor profit-seeking, as we do and as evidenced by our prevailing non-productivity-oriented takeover/merger mania. The Dutch and like approaches place a great deal of emphasis on the duty to maintain employment opportunities for a corporation's work-force, even at the expense of shareholders' returns. Shareholders often do not have the right to vote, a factor that creates a distinct set of goals and correlative duties for boards of directors and a totally different environment for mergers and takeovers. Profiteering, which still is prized, occurs in distinct and different ways. Researcher Douglas Branson, after reviewing the literature, concludes that in many parts of the capitalist world corporations are designed and envisaged as firms based on family and close-knit personal relations as well as being embedded and imbricated in the host nation's political agenda around capitalist relations of production. For instance, forty million Chinese in various diasporas dominate economies through their family corporations. According to Gordon Redding these firms have remained culturally distinct—some say Confucian—wherever they are situated, and they behave very differently than the operations of Western as well as many Asian-run businesses. The South Korean miracle economy—as it was for a while—was based on the chaebol: large, indeed huge, conglomerates run by tight family networks and strongly patrimonial in character. In Indonesia major corporations are also family-based organizations, although they are intimately intertwined with military officialdom, which gives them yet another, perhaps a more feudal, slant. The Indonesian version of the corporation, like that of many European and Asian capitalist countries, then, is a long way removed from the purer market model with its impersonal relations favoured in North America.

Even this bare-boned digression into the varieties of corporate architecture and behaviour indicates that cultural and state-based characteristics have much to do with how capitalism is practised. Localized politics, state-based politics, remain important and relevant, despite the oft-heard claims of the death of the nation-state. But what this also indicates, for me, is that any tactics generated by our understanding as to how corporations work in our parts of the world are necessarily a meta-level response to the much larger problem of the persistence of capitalist relations of production throughout the world. They do not address the ills that arise directly from the logic of that regime. They are not immediately revolutionary, in the technical sense of that term.

Still, although my offerings here do not lend themselves to the positing of strategies that challenge capitalism full bore, the data and the observations based on the data point to the possible political strategies that, in turn, may lead to a more revolutionary set of attacks on the regime. They have that potential because, unlike "capitalism" as a thing, corporations do provide a target.

Capitalism is a set of relations. The symbioses and conflicts generated by these relations create a comprehensive regime. What people react to are the impacts of this regime on their lives. Because differently situated people experience the outcomes of capitalism differently, a sense of connectedness between the opponents of the system is extremely hard to find, or develop. It is very hard to build a common consciousness about the regime and its drawbacks. Capitalism, as a system, instinctively understands this and does its best to exaggerate the distinctions and differences between its victims and exploited. Its proponents love to type opponents as special-interest groups whose narrow goals can only be satisfied by rolling back the entitlements of other non-capitalists. Workers are said to be in conflict with environmentalists, workers in the First World are pitched in battles against workers in the Third World, residents are pitted against migrants and refugees, and so forth.

All of these divide and conquer strategies have been on display during the anti-globalization demonstrations and uprisings that began in the second half of the 1990s: the large number of very impressive gatherings of people from all over the world to protest the meetings of organizational acronyms that do large capital's planning work. In Vancouver in 1997 it was the Asian Pacific Economic Cooperation (APEC) and in Seattle in 1999 it was the World Trade Organization (WTO) whose workings were interrupted by a massive display of people's power. Others followed: the meetings of the World Bank and the International Monetary Fund (IMF) in Washington, the Asian Development Bank in Thailand, the Organization of American States in Windsor, the World Economic Forum in Melbourne, the IMF and World Bank again in Prague, the Summit of the Free Trade Area of the Americas in Quebec City, and the dramatic and violent meeting in Genoa. The intensity and effectiveness of these protests can be measured, in part, by the increasingly vicious police repression and the new search for out-of-the-way spots to hold meetings (like the isolated resort of Kananaskis, Alta., where the G8 summit was held in late June 2002). In part, the impact is also reflected by the evident attempts to cast the protestors as the flotsam and jetsam of political life.

Famed and respected intellectual gatekeepers, such as Thomas L. Friedman of *The New York Times*, remark that the stand of the people in the streets "against globalization" lacks any kind of merit: "To be against globalization is to be against so many things—from cell phones to trade to Big Macs—that it connotes nothing." However, the claim, by some protestors, that globalization is a good thing but that there should be a debate about its implementation is characterized by Friedman and his allies as a useful kind of intervention provided it is not co-opted by the unwashed nihilists. Friedman's warning to such decent protestors is that they should be aware that "anar-chists and leftover marxists," who just hate capitalism, and protectionist trade unionists, who are intent on looking after their own narrow interests, will inhibit the globalization processes, which, "if properly managed, can be the poor's best ladder out of misery." The much more scholarly Professor Paul Krugman—who once empirically proved that free trade had more to do with ideology than economic efficiency—has also seen the dangers of vigorous protests for the hegemony of capitalism. After the Quebec confrontations Krugman wrote that the "people outside the fence, whatever their intentions, are doing their best to make the poor even poorer."

These elite responses are echoed within the walls of the acronyms as the various private and public delegates of the corporate giants fight to retain control over the propaganda war. They tell the world that they always have been aware of the need to look after the hungry and the environment and that they will continue to take these issues into account as they go about the vital business of creating a level playing field for entrepreneurs by establish-ing full access to resources and labour markets on a global basis. They argue that it is for the good of the vulnerable that these Herculean labours are undertaken. The goal is not, as the protestors would have it (with much objective evidence on their side), to provide special advantages for the already advantaged. The WTO, World Bank, and IMF are not setting out— they say—to support the dominant transnationals from the dominant nation-states. Rather, their objective is to lift the less well-developed economies out of the mire by permitting them to compete with their giant counterparts. This always has been—they say—the *raison d'être* of globalizers and their agencies. From their point of view, what is regrettable—and has become crystal clear from the surprising support for the anti-globalization protes-tors—is that their goals have been misunderstood, which means they should be more fully involving environmentalists, workers, and marginalized inter-ests in the process. Those who will be so involved will be those who do not oppose the process. Those who try to convince them to jettison globalization and/or capitalism can do nothing but harm, especially to the vulnerable of the world.

As E.P. Thompson noted, there always are willing experts and opinion leaders, such as Friedman and Krugman, to give a patina of legitimacy to the claims of the powerful. Their ill-concealed cheerleading for globalization gains effectiveness because the very diverse interests of the anti-globalization protestors may well clash. At Seattle, William Tabb found groups ranging from the United Church of Christ Network for Environmental and Economic Responsibility to Pax Romana in Thailand, from Green Action in Tel Aviv to

Green Library in Latvia, from human rights representatives from Cameroon to the Indigenous People's Biodiversity Network in Peru, from Pax Christi in Florence to the United Students against Sweatshops. They all marched together, a kaleidoscopic assembly that must have represented a wide variety of agendas, many of them undoubtedly contradicting the aspirations of their momentary allies. But to allow the elites and their opinion-makers to emphasize those differences would permit them to succeed in their manifest efforts to save their bacon through their tactics of divide and conquer by co-optation. As Tabb observes, it would be to cede the high ground.

The anti-globalization protests are more than momentary enthusiastic and undisciplined collections of the marginal and disaffected. There is an overarching, important politics. Whatever their differences, the many groups and individuals do share fundamental ideas. At the core is an anger about how decisions touching the lives of everyone on the globe are being made behind firmly closed doors in ritzy settings. The decision-makers are small in number, and they are handpicked. They are in no significant way accountable to the people whose conditions of life itself they are determining. The protestors can also plainly see that the governments of nation-states, which might be held responsible for their participation in these crucial policy-making bodies, are less and less democratically accountable at home. Indeed, the protestors see the government representatives, who argue for less and less government regulation over domestic economies, as being complicit in furthering the agenda of major transnational corporations. The protestors share the view that there is a serious democratic deficit that must be remedied. But just having this view does not make the protestors radicals. After all, the democratic deficit is obvious to all. Even as conservative a personage as the Chair of the London Stock Exchange noted in a speech, in May 2000, that it is the manifest lack of democracy that gives impetus to the environmental, economic, and social protests.

What makes the protestors a reflection of a new mood goes beyond dissatisfaction with the lacunae in participatory rights. Barbara Epstein has observed that the protestors are not as much about stopping globalization in its tracks as they are about opposing the more obvious forms it takes: neoliberal policies at home and abroad and damage done to the environment, job security, and welfare programs. They also militate against imperialism, which, more often than not, means being against U.S. dominance and corporate power. These features give resonance to the pro-globalists' argument to the effect that some, perhaps even many, of the protestors really want to make changes in how globalizing trends become established or to ensure that large corporations become more socially responsible and accountable.

Epstein rightly contends, however, that this grain of truth hides a more important one. The protestors also espouse sensibilities that fly in the face of conventional beliefs. The protestors, diverse as they are, share the conviction not only that outcomes of the dominant regime are unacceptable, but also that substantial equality is a worthy objective. They believe that authoritarianism reigns and should be abrogated and replaced by democracy, and that social relations with very different moral dictates should be pursued. Epstein argues that anarchist sensibilities, rather than old-fashioned anarchism, best characterizes these highly visible and significant uprisings. The activists stress decision-making by consensus, which pushes them in the direction of favouring small communitarian political terrains rather than nation-states with their centralized, potentially authoritarian institutions. These values may inhibit their effectiveness as political agents, but they do signify that the protest movements are creating a basis for the development of a new politics by infusing moral values into the resistance to capitalism.

Those hurt by the regime may be able to coalesce around shared values such as altruism, economic and political egalitarianism, concern for the vulnerable, and respect for distinct lifestyles—with these preferences not treated as just some commodities to be weighed in the scales of economic cost-benefit analysis. The political philosopher Gerald Cohen has made a powerful case that, given the new concrete conditions of capitalism, no overthrow of the system may be possible unless there is a recognition of the sharp increase—rather than decrease—in the numbers of people who are extremely needy but cannot be classified, in the traditional sense, as members of the working class, as people directly exploited by wealth-owners. Cohen contends that now we need to argue for change on a different basis than that the real producers of wealth, the workers, should determine how wealth is created and distributed. That Marxism-inspired argument, he points out, was based on the belief that, as producers, exploited workers were entitled to the product of their labour. It turns out, Cohen says, that, at this time, many impoverished and marginalized people would not be entitled to the fruits of their productive labour, or at most entitled to very little, because either they do not do any of that traditional work or because they are connected only in the most attenuated way to such a process. He stresses, therefore, the logical and strategic necessity of basing arguments and struggles for changes in distribution and democratic control on a moral foundation, emphasizing the righteousness of providing for the needs of people, whether or not they are entitled to a reward for their measurable productive contributions.

The protestors' aspirations for greater substantive equality, regardless of the degree of connection to for-profit production, plus their desire for self-government and respect for distinctions, are helping to build a foundation for a politics of change. The values at the base of this movement should be appealing to the alienated majority, even if the immediate cause of their varied alienations makes them cast their demands in distinct ways. Their evident lack of a unified set of strategies and their shifting alliances, as well as their different demands of their immediate antagonists, should not be allowed to hide the incredibly positive contribution of the morally charged aspirations of the anti-globalization activists. As Tabb put it, "Change does not come about from the mere fact of oppression." There must also be "a belief that a better alternative is not only desirable but possible; not necessarily tomorrow, but when the momentum can be turned about." The egalitarian, anti-authoritarian, participatory values of the anti-globalization movement should be built on and fostered by actions that give them a concrete shape, leading to the necessary change of momentum. At least a small part of this struggle for the development of an alternative politics (to borrow a phrase from Sam Gindin) will take place on the terrain of the corporation—or at least by posing questions about the legitimacy of the corporation.

In this part of the world, the corporation is the preferred instrument for capitalists as they pursue the private accumulation of socially produced wealth. Corporate law and the architecture of the corporation provide much of the necessary camouflage for that dubious agenda. Because they are the creatures of a liberal legal system, corporations are subject to the rule of law and the democratic practices that law upholds. Corporations—and, therefore, the capitalists who use them—can, it is said, be constrained and made to serve societal wishes. Capitalism appears to be benign when it is shielded from direct gaze by the corporate veil.

As we've seen, though, corporations are not what they are presented to be: that is, just another individual participating in neutral and normal market activities. Rather, they are collectives; the market is not neutral, or normal; and the rule of law and democratic institutions are perversely applied—if applied at all—when corporate welfare is at issue. To make these elements clear is the first step of a politics that aims at exposing the illegitimacy of capitalist relations of production. But the task is not finished by simply showing that capitalists, protected by corporate shields, are not living up to the ideological constructs that they trumpet. The friends of the corporations could argue, as they often do, that the only problem is that things have got out of hand as a result of carelessness or neglect. This recognition might lead to corporate reforms, even useful ones, but they would still leave the basic market capitalism system intact. An opposition has to make additional political capital out of the exposé of corporate abuses of the economic and political tenets that corporate actors claim as their own. The purpose must be to retain what is of value to democracy and to build on that by pointing out what and who stands in the way of economic and political emancipation.

We can make no advance by simply improving "the market," by bringing it closer to some idealized model. It is the model itself, with its anti-social privileging of competition, that we need to challenge. In its idealized form the market model is a Trojan Horse that allows the true minority, property owners, to elude our defences and protect their individual private privileges from the public and the collective realms, marginalizing any attempts at participatory politics. If a competitive market has any utility at all, it is as a tool to determine people's needs and desires. The market's role as a facilitating tool to these ends, however, must not be allowed to expand—a blockage that will be difficult to ensure. One of the underlying contentions of this book is that the market is a usurper. It always threatens to become what it is now: a supposedly neutral piece of machinery that has structural, value-laden, anti-democratic impacts on our politics and material well-being. This ever-present danger to our political goals—the perfection of our democracy—must be minimized. Strategies for change must therefore stress the need to democratize the private economic sphere as much as possible and, then and thereby, to enlarge and relegitimate the public sphere.

Given also that, as we've seen, the corporation has perverted the meaning of human beings' hard-won civil liberty rights—a distortion of the body politic that needs to be recognized and then reversed—the goal of reform must also be not just to make corporations more decent citizens, and keep everything else the same. Corporations are not, and cannot be, citizens. The point of civil liberty preservation actions is (i) to make sure that those whose lives must be spent inside the corporate umbrella are able to exercise these freedom-enhancing rights right there, and (ii) to endorse the values of freedom of speech, religion, belief, assembly, association, and the like, as values that people must be able to enjoy in all their activities. These are significant rights, and while there are a host of theoretical arguments to the effect that, in a non-capitalist political economy, they will no longer be necessary, history has taught us that change from one regime to another does not take place overnight. Even the most optimistic should expect a long period of transition during which the old holders of power will seek to hang on to their privileges and new formations and pressures might lead to unacceptable restraints and constraints. Strategies for an alternative politics based on the malfunctioning of the corporations, therefore, must emphasize that the abused values do have merit but that those who hide behind corporate veils will always pervert them.

These fights will be easier to win if citizens have been provided with greater material security. Recent decades have seen a concerted attack on what used to be called the welfare state. For twenty-five years or so after World War II, the Canadian government, like many others, adopted "a loose set of social policies and programs" that provided Canadians with at least a limited level of economic and social support. The premise of this approach is that government and its institutions have a basic responsibility for the well-being of citizens—and that the guarantee of well-being cannot be left to individuals or private corporations, or even to local communities. Besides recognizing the need of the state to protect the more vulnerable with minimal material comforts and security, the development also included a qualitative and quantitative rise in respect for civil liberties and racial and gender differences. Most analysts would agree that in the past two decades, while we continue to pay lip service to the need to protect individuals from invidious discriminations—indeed, to purport that we have augmented safeguards against such discriminations by instruments such as the Charter of Rights and Freedoms—the minimal material protections of "the welfare state" have been under attack, to the point of being dismantled.

As these material, social welfare rights disappear, so too do the possibilities for citizens to act as fully fledged participants in their polity. Thus, in his State of the Union address in 1944, U.S. President Franklin Roosevelt offered to enact a new Bill of Rights when the war, then in progress, was successfully concluded. The bill would contain constitutional guarantees for jobs that paid well enough to provide adequate food, clothing, and recreation for all; it promised the right of every family to a good and decent home, the right to a good education and adequate medical care and protection from the economic fears spawned by old age, sickness, accident, and unemployment. This constitutional amendment was never implemented, and the idea that these promises once made sense in the United States now appears to be bizarre. But they were made during years when the citizenry was being asked to make huge sacrifices for a political economic regime that had failed them abysmally in the immediate past, and there was a realization that the regime would not command legitimacy unless it were immeasurably improved. That improvement required a recognition of what was wrong with the capitalist system embedded in a self-proclaimed liberal democracy.

President Roosevelt's radical proposals characterized the ills he was seeking to cure. He noted that the abstract rights embedded in the Bill of Rights (the sort of rights found in our Charter of Rights and Freedoms), while worthwhile in themselves, "had proved inadequate to assure us equality in the pursuit of happiness. We have come to a clear realization of the fact that

true individual freedom cannot exist without economic security and independence. 'Necessitous men are not free men.' . . . In our days these economic
truths have become accepted as self-evident." What he and others like him
envisaged was that the state would intervene to the extent necessary to enable
citizens to become complete citizens, people with "true individual freedom."

This is a vision that continues to make sense in today's Canada, where a
whole host of social commentators have recognized the need for such intervention, especially in the light of the attacks on the welfare state. Contemporary Canadian studies, as summarized by Jane Jenson in an evaluative
essay, emphasize the lack of social cohesion and all that means: the increasing incidence of polarization and exclusion caused by widening gaps in
wealth and income, the cleavages between urban and rural populations, the
loss of social capital such as the networks that enable communities to work
together, and the huge divide between the rich and their supporters, who are
primarily concerned with economic growth and "global competitiveness,"
and the mass of the population, people still primarily interested in the moral
values of community and security in all aspects of life. Jenson concludes that,
to attain inclusion, less polarization, greater participation, and recognition
and legitimacy for all peoples, issues of social justice need to be addressed
and material goods need to be redistributed, which requires governmental
intervention. Neil Brooks, too, has marshalled evidence that, to achieve an
enriched political citizenship, Canadians need direct state intervention and
economic support for those inevitably excluded by the for-profit scheme.
The case to reinstate the state as a provider and distributor of goods and
services is overwhelming.

But that case goes against the grain of received wisdom in many quarters. In part, many oppositional activists see the state as an oppressor rolling
back the welfare and labour rights won in the immediate postwar period.
They see the state as the front line of the assault waged on the vulnerable and
the working classes. They are, of course, right. Governments are taking away
hard-fought-for material protections and liberties, and they do so largely at
the behest of the wealth-owners hiding behind corporations. The spokespersons for the corporate sectors convince politicians that this is the proper
thing to do because of the internationalization of competition, because of the
logic of the new, supposedly unavoidable phase of capitalism called globalization. Thus, these conservative forces—for very different reasons—echo the
opposition's claim that the state, when it intervenes, is the enemy. This powerful mix lends weight to the authority of the slogan TINA: there is no alternative to a shrinking of the state and to a corresponding aggrandisement of
private decision-making.

To urge strategies that rely on refurbishing state power may, therefore, appear to be somewhat impractical and misplaced. Historically, however, it is through the state that the majority of people have gained democratic rights, such as they are. It is the state's interventions, willingly made or not, that have built citizenship rights, such as they are. It is through the state that there is, at least, a theoretical possibility for democratic control over the decisions that have an impact on our lives. Some critics say that it is sentimental revisionism to think that this state intervention will happen again. This argument requires an acceptance of the claim that there is something truly novel about globalization. Indeed, there are many such claims, both in the popular press and in scholarly literature. Kenneth Ohmae summed up this mainstream literature. According to him, the state "has become an unnatural, even dysfunctional unit for organizing human activities and managing economic endeavor in a borderless world."

Still, the vigour of these claims does not make them incontrovertible. Many serious analysts and activists have gathered their own brand of empirical evidence and present arguments that what is called globalization is just another of the more gaudy phases of the international character of capitalism. Many critics argue, of course, that "globalization" has been with us for a long time. Indeed, some commentators say, this particular phase may not even be much more pronounced than previous such phases. The exports' share of advanced economies is not very different than it was in earlier periods; most trade continues to be between countries in the advanced capitalist parts of the world; in major economies, such as in the United States and the European Community, imports and exports constitute but a small proportion of the Gross Domestic Product; most multinationals do not operate by means of worldwide and integrated production processes, and so on. If the present circumstance is somewhat different, then, these commentators say, it is so because of the new financial flows, although impressive studies show that even this is not empirically true. More, inasmuch as the free-trade agreements, regional pacts, creation of free-trade zones, private arbitration of disputes between entrepreneurs, the establishment and creation of new property rights, and the like appear to undermine the nation-states' capacities to do anything about social cohesion within their borders, still the governments of nation-states themselves have had to do much of the engineering necessary to bring about this apparent dilution of their role. Stephen Clarkson has shown how Canadian governments deliberately changed policies to lay, first, the material groundwork and, then, the new political and legislative framework to make free trade with the United States appear normal and natural.

As governments did have, and did exercise, power to direct the so-called inevitable globalization processes, presumably they could reverse some of their decisions. This is particularly true for the governments of the dominant economies, where the nation-states, as political entities, retain a good deal of autonomy despite assertions that globalization has hollowed them out. According to Frances Fox Piven, while there truly are cross-nation trading and co-operation blocs, it is still the case that some nations remain far more economically and politically powerful than others, and the so-called globalization processes have not truly homogenized political processes anywhere as much as they may have universalized consumer habits. This observation jibes, of course, with the point made earlier to the effect that the culture and the originating nation-state within which corporations operate, and to which their chief owners and managers owe conscious or unconscious allegiance, lead to distinct ways of practising capitalism. Homogenization in governance, structure, and behaviour is not easily attained. The point here is not that there is nothing new—and William Carroll provides an incisive analysis of what is significantly distinct about the present circumstance—but that much that is old is still relevant—in particular, the centrality of the nation-state.

Roaming capital needs political support from nation-states, a great deal of it. Aijaz Ahmad puts this clearly:

> There is a pretence in most kinds of economies that prices are determined—perhaps brutally but "freely"—in the market. This simply is not so. Prices, especially the prices of labor, are determined *historically*, and the nationally constituted disciplines and regimes of labor are a fundamental component of that history. . . . How does U.S. capital arrive in Bangalore today, in the context of a sovereign Indian state, to exploit the cheaper labor and industrial plant there? . . . Is there just an open global market for capital to travel on its own volition? Not at all. That capital must pass through the Indian nation-state, must rely on certain disciplines of labor, wage contract, conditions of industrial peace, chances of repatriation of profits that only the Indian state can guarantee. The nation-state in this case is the articulating principle between global capital and national labor.

But, this said, it is also true that nation-states have become more porous with regard to corporate capitalist flows. Accepting the inevitability—and many accept the desirability—of a world without borders, governments fight to have their nation-states be the one to be exploited by capitalism's roving corporations. It is the state that privatizes government-run endeavours, enlarging the profit-making opportunities for private corporations and their hidden investors. Frank Pearce and Laureen Snider record that as a result of accepting the very dubious logic of TINA, by 1991 more than eighty-eight countries had privatized public assets. This snowball rolling down from the state mountains has increased its size and speed, to the point where it is now an avalanche. Governments have less and less direct democratic input into the economic and social decision-making of the nation, and the vacuum has been filled by the domain of the one dollar/one vote regime, the corporate regime. The nation-state has rolled back collective bargaining and social safety-net provisions, leaving working people open to increased exploitation by the corporations, which profit from the intensified competition for jobs. The nation-state, as it takes away citizenship rights—both material welfare and civil libertarian rights—in order to satisfy the needs of the captains of industry, finance, retail, and everything else, has to impose invigorated controls over the flow of immigrants and refugees and has to incarcerate more and more poor people and in general intimidate people into accepting the worsening conditions of life. Michael Mandel calculated that, by 1987, more people were under state surveillance than ever before, which is a condition that serves to keep us all in line. Unquestionably, that same tendency has become more pronounced in the intervening years.

The centrality of the state to any politics of change should, then, be clear. Given that a major obstacle to a democratic state and a politically participatory citizenship is the architecture of corporate law and its creature, the corporation-for-profit, an alternative politics requires, in the first place, a validation of the public sphere. To achieve this validation the democratic features and institutions of that sphere must be given more sway than now permitted by the corporate agenda. A necessary first step is the democratization, and then diminution, of the political reach and power of the corporations.

My contribution here will be to make a few suggestions aimed at enabling people to take that first step. Some of the strategies are likely to give the various captains of industry and everything else only a nagging toothache requiring little more than an alleviating painkiller. Others are aimed at serious hurt and, perhaps, a defanging of the corporate beasts behind which the captains have taken refuge. All start off from the position that people's everyday problems arising out of the exercise of corporate power should be the basis for calls to action. Given that corporate capitalism is exploitive by nature and design, and that it is a system artificially and politically created, we need to remember above all else that it is a *replaceable* system—and that it should and can be replaced by a system reflecting more humanistic values.

A Sampling of Corporate-Based Meta-Level Strategies

One of my recurring themes has been how the twin legal gifts of separate legal personality for the corporation and limited liability for the investors have created a legitimacy problem for the intellectual defenders of capitalism as practised by means of incorporated enterprises. But these features are more than an issue for scholars playing in academic sandboxes. They not only allow some wealthy people to profiteer while incurring little risk, but also leave a trail of victims. The intellectual debating points should be turned into political slings and arrows.

When workers are left holding the bag after small, closely held corporations bite the dust, the state has fashioned legislative remedies that seek to alleviate the most egregious impacts of the doctrines of legal personality and limited liability. Corporations or individuals who controlled the failed, supposedly separate, firm may be held liable, in some very narrowly defined circumstances, to pay the wages owed to workers. They must be classified as related employers or as directors who were in control of the operations at the relevant time. The idea is to have some persons—people who reaped the benefits of the firm's activities and who might be able to pay—make good some of the debt owed to workers who had no real control over their fate. This makes corporate law *seem* more fair, while upholding the sacrosanct nature of private contractual arrangements, a capitalist ideal. At the same time, though, the features of corporate law that undermine liberal tenets and sound market principles are to be left intact; they remain legitimate tools that the wealthy amongst us can use to continue the pursuit of private accumulation of socially produced wealth with little risk. Precisely because these remedies do not aim to change what needs to be changed to protect workers and the public purse—which usually has to look after the abandoned victims— they rarely provide workers with the relief that, in pure contract terms, is due to them. In any event, even if some directors or associated corporations are stuck with some of the costs, shareholders, as such, are not. Directors may be major shareholders or not. That is, the very people in whose name the business was conducted are not made legally, and thereby not publicly, accountable as such. This condition perpetuates the idea that there is nothing terribly wrong with not holding the quintessential capitalists who hide behind the corporation personally responsible for the fallout of their greed.

There is a pressing political and moral need, then, to personalize responsibility. It would be useful if activists used these constantly recurring cases in which workers have been left high and dry and that force them to engage in, what to them must seem to be, arcane, costly and morale-sapping legal fights, as a fulcrum for a larger political campaign. In each and every case of this kind, the individuals behind the corporate veil—the executives, directors, and major shareholders—should be identified and characterized as *the* persons responsible for the corporation's conduct, whether or not they were hands-on operators. If they made the decisions personally, there can be no doubt that such an argument will make sense to the workers who were expected to obey their decisions and who, by the tenets of employment law and the preachings of the managers, executives, and owners—the employing classes—are conditioned to internalize the need to accept personal responsibility for their working habits and for the need to carry out their employment duties in good faith and with fidelity. Not only do executives and directors resist having anything like the same rules applied to them, but so too do the hidden-from-view investors who accept the results of the corporation's products with glee and who have the legal and functional power to monitor and control the hands-on executives and directors.

A campaign to put this sort of argument at the centre of every case in which an insolvent, closely held, corporation is not meeting its obligations to the workers should be orchestrated with a set of demands for corporate law reforms. One demand should be that no enterprise that seeks the privilege to incorporate should be allowed to do so without proof that it has put aside a reserve of capital that will be available to pay workers their arrears in the event of corporate failure. The logic of this line of argument is simple. It is posited on the notion that, if an unincorporated business fails, its owners are personally on the hook. Evenhanded law should not permit incorporation to give those same investors a different result if they behave in the same way. When a small, closed business uses the corporate form, we know that certain parties—that is, those who rule in the one dollar/one vote sphere, organizations such as banks and other institutional lenders—are able to insist that the investors make themselves personally responsible, whether or not they are going to be hands-on operators. Bankers insist on identifying the real persons intended to be benefited by the corporate veil. They "out" the investors; they do not care whether or not they are passive entrepreneurs. Workers do not have that kind of bargaining clout, and so we should demand that the government step in on their behalf. Until such corporate law reform is won, the oppositional campaign should demand, each and every time a case of unpaid arrears provides the opportunity, a legislative requirement that a small, closely held corporation include a provision in its employment contracts that only it, and not the shareholders who want to profit from the workers' efforts, will be responsible for their wages and conditions. It must be made clear to workers that, behind the veil, there are identifiable flesh and blood human beings who are explicitly too willing to profit from their flesh and blood without being prepared to pay for it or without acknowledging their personal debt for the riches they enjoy. Workers must be told where and how these deadbeat capitalists live. We must blow away these runaway investors' privacy: it is a privacy that hides ugliness and deceit rather than the intimacy that the legally protected respect for privacy is designed to promote.

Similar arguments can be made in respect of other obligations regularly incurred by corporations, such as the costs of environmental cleanup, and for which it is extremely difficult to make the eventual profiteering investors responsible if they left the corporation's daily operations to others. Here again, some legislative regimes already require capital guarantees before, say, a mining venture is undertaken, but this is the exception—certainly in those situations in which small, closely held corporations are involved—rather than the rule.

Of course, one of the counter-arguments will be that this kind of requirement will chill innovative entrepreneurs: the cost of doing business will become too high if firms have to set aside capital to offset the costs of potential harms. More, there will be no point to incorporation and, as the corporate form is a good thing, we will be throwing out the baby with the bathwater.

There are ready answers to these lines of argument. First, it is not true that the cost will be increased. Placing the cost of doing business on those who would profit from it is only placing it on different people, on more deserving people. If there is no such displacement, as the present corporate law envisages, the unpaid debts and unmet obligations are being paid for by unpaid workers and the public purse. The costs do not disappear. They are borne by those who did not profit directly from, or controlled, the corporate activities that led to the costs. To force the corporate sectors into a public debate on this issue would be very useful. It would raise consciousness about the duplicitous nature of market economics when practised by means of the corporation.

Second, the claim that corporations would become useless vehicles would help draw public attention to how, in the small-business settings, the corporate vehicle is not about economic efficiency but is, rather, nothing but a mechanism for avoiding responsibility. What will become more evident is that the corporation represents a negation of the liberal-market tenets supposedly embodied in the activities of small, independent business persons. This revelation would help a great deal in the ideological fight that needs to be waged against the belief system underpinning our economy—that our economy truly aspires to be, and almost is, a political economy wedded to competitive, individualistic principles.

When workers and environmentalists are confronting immediate problems, then, significant issues can be raised. Certainly, it may be more directly responsive to a particular problem to look for less confrontational legislative reforms, such as an insurance fund to look after workers' unpaid wages or compulsory insurances to cover environmental spills. Those kinds of reforms have an instant appeal and do have merit, but an orchestration of demands around corporate law and associated behaviour may well have a more long-lasting and radical potential. Most important, I believe, is the concentration on making visible the actors who use invisible friends to make themselves virtually invisible. Outing these shy profiteers gives an edge to a politics for change. It provides a target; it makes it plain that there are real flesh and blood human beings who manipulate the system and us to satisfy their apparently insatiable greed; it makes it more transparent than it otherwise is that there are people out there who do not care what kind of world the non-wealth-owners inhabit. They don't care what their plight is, provided they, the hard-to-see rich, can enjoy the good life.

In large, publicly traded corporations, undercapitalization is not as serious a problem, although it can be, as the Westray story illustrates. Moreover, large corporations often use a business structure of closely and not so closely integrated corporations and then count on the doctrine of separate legal personality to ward off creditors, revenue collectors, and regulators—a point also neatly exemplified by the Westray case. In various jurisdictions there are reform proposals to deal with these kinds of dodges, but they are technical and preliminary in nature and start off from the assumption that hiding behind the corporate veil is acceptable unless it is strictly forbidden. They are not radicalizing measures, merely alleviating ones. They do not do away with the central obfuscation: that corporate law promotes the everyday avoidance of personal responsibility. Above all, anyone working to devise tactics to help develop an alternative politics must always keep in mind this important point: the obscuring ink sprayed all over us by the octopus-like features of corporate law produces flesh and blood victors, winners who profit from the unrewarded work and toil of others, who do not care whether their welfare is based on injuries and harms inflicted on others. The wheelers and dealers behind large corporations should be seen for what they are.

Corporations often, very often, break the law. Sometimes this is characterized as criminal behaviour; more frequently it is treated as a violation of welfare regulatory law, a legally less stigmatizing offence. This kind of line-drawing is specious at best, heavily biased towards corporate actors' welfare at worst. Those who want to work for concrete change should make it clear that they do not buy into that kind of sterilizing analysis. They should also vigorously thrust their reforming swords through the corporate shields. Following are a few possible steps to these ends.

⚖ Each and every time a corporate violation of law occurs, a concerted campaign should be mounted to prosecute the human actors responsible, as well as the corporation.

⚖ Inasmuch as these actors are senior executives who exercised control over the operations of the violating corporation, or who might have been able to exercise such control, they are also people who have been willing to claim both the intangible—such as praise and prestige—and tangible rewards—such as increased bonuses and options—whenever the corporation does well, regardless of the effectiveness of their personal efforts. To hold them responsible, therefore, is a tactic justified by the paradigm they favour. More, inasmuch as they are presumed to be rational actors and inasmuch as they are presumed to be risk-averse—two presumptions posited by corporate law cheerleaders—their recognition of the possibility that they could be held personally responsible and go to jail could lead to better behaviour. Another result could be an increased unwillingness on the part of many people to become corporate executives. Profiteers usually do not want to take risks, but only desire to impose them on others, and it is politically useful to have this point recognized.

⚖ Controlling shareholders of violating corporations should be prosecuted whenever their corporation has violated a regulatory or criminal law rule. The argument is simple enough. While shareholders will maintain that they have no interest in micromanaging the huge corporations in which they invest and that they are passive, even innocent, bystanders, this is so much nonsense. The *Securities Acts* provide criteria to determine who is to be treated as a controlling shareholder, and they do so because these people have inherent power that must be regulated to protect other corporate investors. These controlling shareholders must not take advantage of their positions as insiders to get a jump in the equity markets; if they buy and sell shares they must disclose this to the capital markets because it is understood that, because of the size of their holdings, they have the power to influence the value of the shares of particular corporations. The same is true when takeovers and mergers are in the wing: as soon as a shareholder gets to a certain holding position, the market is to be informed so that "the investor community"—a misnomer, if ever there was one—can reconsider its investment strategy. It is an assumption of corporate law that, once they hold a certain amount of equity, shareholders have the power to determine the fate of the corporation and, therefore, the behaviour of its managers. This residual, and often exercised, power requires them to be saddled with the duty to act appropriately vis-à-vis other shareholders and would-be shareholders. They are not allowed to assert to the capital markets that they are mere passive investors, innocent bystanders, who have no say over what goes on inside the corporation. They should not be allowed to say this to anyone else either. The reason that controlling shareholders are allowed to hide behind the corporate veil when it comes to the affording of protection for non-capitalists' interests is that the protection of such non-capitalists' interests is not a legal priority. Challenging this point by making controlling shareholders accused persons in a prosecution will have the obvious benefit of drawing attention to how the separate legal personality doctrine favours treating these controlling shareholders as innocent receivers of criminally obtained goods, namely the proceeds of corporate conduct that violated legal standards. To bring this out could inform militant opposition to the corporate way of doing business.

Outing the beneficiaries of corporate violations of laws enacted to protect the majority of the population has the virtue of making it plain not only that there are people out there who enjoy the fruits of wrongful activities, but also that the belief in law and order preached by the corporate elites is only skin deep. This clarity will help make it easier for activists to develop extra-electoral and extra-legal tactics, something that may be called for from time to time.

A few other "outing" strategies could also be of assistance. For instance, Robert Waldrop, the director of the Archbishop Romero Catholic Worker House in Oklahoma City, an organization that feeds the poor and looks after the evicted, has published a list of "Eleven Necessary Measures for Curbing the Corporate Crime Wave." These include the requirement that a corporation convicted of a crime should be registered as a violator with the police offices in the locales in which it operates. The register so compiled should be used by governments at all levels to disqualify the corporation from bidding on contracts put out for tender by these governments. Democracy Watch has made similar recommendations, adding that public pension funds should use such a register to withhold investment in corporations listed on it and that "Ten Most Wanted" lists should be posted wherever possible.

Waldrop's suggestions include the attractive recommendation that convicted corporations should be required to place the phrase "a criminal corporation" on all their advertising copy, images, signs, and vehicles. For instance: Wal-Mart is running advertisements that display its multi-ethnic staff as being delighted about working at the store because it is so easy to make people happy at Wal-Mart. The ad's message is that not only is Wal-Mart a good store, but it is also an employer that treats its workers—called "associates"—with respect and dignity. Someone adapting Waldrop's idea could initiate a campaign to force Wal-Mart to run parallel messages acknowledging that its contractors in Haiti make "Mickey Mouse" and "Pocahontas" pyjamas while paying their workers as little as twelve cents an hour, a full eighteen cents below Haiti's minimum wage rate.

An increased public identification of the significant actors in deviant corporations and of those who profit from the illegalities will lead to a greater awareness of the remarkable incidence of deviance. The convictions of ephemeral corporations that are members of large, complicated corporate groups do not especially catch the public's attention. A set of higher-profile human convicts would reveal that these significant corporate actors and shareholders are really what we would normally call social lepers—people, that is, engaged in activities that offend the fundamental values embedded in our laws and cultural practices. This kind of understanding, in due course, may well move people from a simple outrage at the particular outcomes of corporate deviance to a more serious questioning of the corporation-for-profit competitive model. A part of this, too, involves identifying guilty business leaders as recidivist wrongdoers, which would take more than a bit of the lustre off their freely offered nostrums about the beauties of the market and the utility of corporations. These captains of industry and everything else, after all, have been able to make themselves far less publicly accountable than are the elected politicians and bureaucrats they like to malign and characterize as being cavalier and irresponsible. What we need to demonstrate is that the rules binding our governments and the rest of us together have not been applied to corporate actors, for dubious reasons, which points, in turn, to how democratic principles are excluded from the private corporate sphere.

This demonstration of the skewing of democratic practices lies at the core of the meta-level strategies. The goal is to reduce the sway of the private, one dollar/one vote sphere and thereby enlarge the public, one person/one vote sphere. To aid this endeavour, as people confront specific problems caused by corporations' behaviour, we need to expose the lack of internal democracy that characterizes the for-profit corporation.

Again, while shareholders are given corporate governance rights because of the risks they notionally take, workers are given no such rights. It would be good politics to infuse the fights around workers' compensation and occupational health and safety issues with the argument that this denial of workers' right to participate in decision-making is internally contradictory and morally unacceptable. After all, workers put their emotional sensibilities and physical well-being at risk when they contract to work for the corporation, which is intent on retaining the surplus value generated by this work. This is far more than any shareholders with their limited liability privilege ever put at risk. Every time an issue of safety creates a dispute between workers and their corporation, activists could mount a conscious campaign to remind everyone of those salient facts—wrapping the message in envelopes containing concrete demands for reform to the occupational health and safety regulatory regime.

The concrete demands could include a proposal that workers should have a veto over all decisions that have an impact on health and safety. Under existing practice, joint employer-employee committees have the role of monitoring conditions. These committees have an even number of employer and employee representatives, and they have powers only of recommendation. This system leaves all final decision-making with the employer. As the real risk-takers, workers should be in a majority on all such committees, and the committees should have final decision-making power. This system could be adopted in unincorporated firms as well, although the argument that workers should have as much say as passive, virtually risk-free investors, will not carry as much resonance in that circumstance.

Similarly, no employer should be allowed to introduce new technology or work processes without input from the workers. Workers should also have the right of veto over the decision. While this proposal, in the present anti-worker context, might seem a little romantic, if not utopian, such legal protections already exist in Scandinavian capitalist economies. These proposals are not all that radical. The hope is that they are potentially radicalizing. The argument underlying the proposals will point out, too, that corporations are hierarchical and feudal in nature, that supposed liberal law denies them, in the corporate setting, the sovereignty they enjoy in the non-work setting. The powers-that-be justify this state of affairs on the basis that the economic efficiency attained by a feudal corporation means that the granting of basic values, such as the right to determine for oneself how much of one's life to put at risk, should be left to others who only have their own welfare at heart. For workers to force this crass, anti-human, justification out into the open could help the cause of democracy by showing how woefully short of its tenets we now fall.

To this end we could deploy other such tactics, which require little by way of militancy, but a great deal by way of thinking things through in a different way. In all employment contracts, for instance, the employer retains the right to manage the enterprise as it sees fit, subject to any specific rights to the contrary won by the workers when negotiating their contract. Workers are more successful in gaining some of these contrary rights when they are unionized. Non-unionized workers are left to the relatively unfettered whims of their employers. The retained employers' right to do as they want—subject to a contractual term to the contrary—is referred to as the residual managerial rights, or the prerogative of management, clause. Workers, at least unionized workers, should demand that their representatives negotiate to have such clauses entitled "Limitations on Workers' Rights," because this is what they are.

More poignantly, perhaps, each collective agreement has a clause dealing with the handling of health and safety issues. It is usually called the "Health and Safety" clause. Because employers never undertake to provide risk-free environments and always retain the right to make final decisions about how work is to be done, and what substances, equipment, and technologies are to be used, unions should demand that the clause be entitled "Limitations on the Employer's Right to Maim and Kill." When negotiating managers (as anticipated) reject these demands, the impasse becomes an example of how employers want to be able to exercise power without openly admitting to their felt need to strictly control the life and fate of workers. In corporate settings, managers who are doing the bidding of nameless, wannabe-invisible, owners of wealth exercise fundamental powers.

These kinds of tactics can help raise political awareness and militancy if the total context of bargaining becomes one in which workers are encouraged to question the legitimacy of managers making decisions on behalf of passive, virtually riskless, and hard-to-spot investors at the expense of active, very visible, flesh and blood risk-takers. There are many such possible tactics available to workers employed by corporations. They should be employed to help workers see the need to democratize the workplace, especially the corporate workplace. Workers are to be assisted, as they fight their daily struggles, to see that their aspirations to be autonomous, sovereign, individuals are blocked at every turn by the architecture of the corporation and by the legal privileging of the investing classes. The internal governance of the corporation defies democracy, and the tactics must aim at exposing that brute fact.

At the same time connections can be made between anti-corporation strategies and a larger politics. For instance, it might be useful to conduct a political campaign that demands that every citizen is born a full-fledged trade unionist, that the right to fight collectively against private power is an integral part of everyone's birthright, the indicia of citizenship. Unionization has always been treated as if it were a rare privilege to be accorded in unusual circumstances. In recent times, concerted governmental assaults have been made on those trade union rights that had been won over decades of struggle. Public media join in the refrain that trade unionism has become yesterday's idea. In view of all this, the suggestion may seem to be a vainglorious attempt to hang on to outdated notions. To the contrary, I would suggest that the demand could help to fan the flames of the aspirations of those looking for an alternative politics.

Certainly, we could argue that, in a society that makes claims about the legal equality of all people as a basic democratic right:

⚖️ it is not right that citizens who are wealthy property owners should be able to exercise power over citizens who are much less wealthy and/or non-property owners;

⚖️ it is not right that the wealthy property owners should, as if it were a virtual birthright of wealthy citizens, be allowed to continue to combine their wealth by incorporation and, thereby, to increase their ability to exercise power over the citizens who are much less wealthy and/or non-property owners; and

⚖️ it is not right that the less wealthy and the non-property owners should be forced to compete with each other, thereby increasing the power of the wealthy owners over them, unless they can jump through legally complicated hoops and over major economic hurdles and form a trade union, which will give them a restricted amount of countervailing bargaining power.

For tactical reasons, the argument might have to be made on these liberal political bases, but the purpose is to make it more clear than it is that, despite the great amount of diversity that exists and is justly celebrated in our country, the working class shares fundamental problems. For non-property owners to see some of the great commonalities that should bind them politically is a step towards the development of a belief in the possibilities of establishing that social cohesion that the bulk of our contemporary social science researchers tell us is sadly lacking in Canada. Once a good many people see the potential of having a social regime posited on cohesion, the desire for putting the structures into place to attain it may gain a new urgency. As Jenson argues, this project would require measures aimed at improving the level of social justice. In a context of a deepening appreciation of the corporate sectors' inimical impact on social justice, these efforts could lead to a repositioning and relegitimation of state intervention as the only effective means of obtaining the social justice needed to underpin social cohesion

The pursuit of this argument could also yield more immediate outcomes. While the prime purpose is not to improve the collective bargaining situation of workers, automatic unionization could have that effect. Amongst other things, it would save an enormous amount of scarce monetary and human resources that go into basic organization. More important, however, would be the ideological gains. Automatic union standing would underline the current expenditure of an enormous mount of political capital on obtaining limited rights to combine for the narrowest of economic purposes: to offset the economic power of specific employers. This scheme of unionization has created unions that are—in the literal and not the pejorative sense of the word—reactionary in nature. They are reactions to the logic of the unequal division of private property and are legally and politically structured to mirror the structure of the immediate opponents, who own a disproportionate amount of the economy's private property. Of course, corporate employers represent the paradigm of employers who impose their model of organization on unions. Workers, as members of such unions, learn to take the self-serving characterization of the corporation, as a private economic enclave that facilitates the pursuit of profits, as natural and unquestionable. The corporation's political aspects remain unseen by the workers as their union is legally restricted to economic bargaining. Workers are implicitly, but powerfully, being taught that their economic work lives are separated from their political life as citizens. A different basis for union membership could undermine the foundations of this perspective, which hands enormous economic and political bargaining leverage to the wealthy classes.

A demand for the right to be a unionist as a birthright also has the potential of revealing that this private/public, economic/political divide, which is deeply embedded and perpetuated by the creation of the for-profit corporation, is neither natural nor acceptable. When workers start off from the position that they are not just allied on an employer-by-employer basis, they recognize their commonalities and see that political and social life is not separate from economic life. In recognizing, however tentatively, the seamlessness of their existence, they may become more conscious of how much of what is portrayed as normal is not normal at all. What we need to understand, for instance, is that there is something weird about having a category called occupational health and safety that needs to be treated as if it were a discrete problem. Why is that set of issues regulated on the basis that a certain amount of injury is to be suffered by workers as acceptable collateral damage so that some others can earn private profits? After all, when we are not working, our entitlement to a certain standard of health and safety is quite differently approached. Similarly, as workers we are more likely to become aware of how we have been taught to think of our work lives as incidental to our "real" lives—that our "real" lives are to act as, and enjoy being, consumers and that we work to satisfy this supposedly inherent human need. A debate may open up around how sensible it is to further a system that is so politically impoverished that it equates citizenship with consumerism. In short, making everyone a unionist could well be a positive intervention towards the removal of some of the obstacles that inhibit people from seeing the connectedness of work, their social relationships, and their physical environment. The push is to make it plausible for workers to begin to think about "doing-other" and, in so doing, "becoming-other," to use the language of Sam Gindin and Leo Panitch.

To attain this goal, this proposal would have to be fortified by others with the same thrust. One of these could be the co-ordination of a workers' demand for paid time off from work so that they can pursue an education in how to become better political citizens. This goal has proud antecedents, from the classical Greek writings to the battles around the nature of the U.S. federation. The U.S. judicial decision that first established the modern version of the nature of corporate personality, the *Dartmouth University* case, involved the 1816 attempt by the New Hampshire legislature to turn this private corporate school into a public entity. The legislature stated that it wanted to do this because "knowledge and learning generally diffused through a Community are essential to the preservation of free Governments. . . . Education is a matter . . . too intimately connected with the public welfare and prosperity . . . to be . . . entrusted in the hands of a few." The U.S. Supreme Court rejected this effort to turn the private teaching for the rich corporation into a public institution to serve the public good. It held that a corporation's private contract and property rights should be treated as sacrosanct and could not be attacked by legislation, regardless of the motivation of the government. But what is relevant here is that the litigation neatly illustrated that many people, not so long ago, saw the exploitation of private property for the accumulation of wealth as being antagonistic to democratic ideals and, more pertinently, that they saw the corporation as the embodiment of this menace to the development of free governments.

The suggestion of fighting for political education time off during regular work hours also relates to the notion that becoming a fully participating member of a cohesive society requires time to reflect on what that means. What should be the nature of the campaign to fight for educational time off? The demand for political education time should include the requirement that the time off be paid for by employers and/or the state. It should be wedded to arguments for reduced work time for all to combat unemployment. As well, it could be harmonized with campaigns of support for teachers who are engaged in struggles over their conditions of employment. Teachers, engaged as they should be in the development of political participatory citizens, should, after all, be treated generously and shown a deep respect by governments. Teachers should be urged to consider whether they are preparing students for the kinds of jobs provided by market-driven production (and which perpetuate inequalities) or whether they are expanding the democratic horizons of their students. Educating students to understand the world in order to change it is a necessary step in building the process we call democracy. In this sense democracy is understood, as C. Douglas Lummis puts, as a historic project, rather than a static condition.

Alongside these kinds of meta-level strategies are the already vigorous campaigns to improve electoral politics—which is a necessary element in the unfettering of government from corporate bondage. There has been a growing consciousness of the alarming drop in voter participation. Between 1945 and 1988 about 75 per cent of eligible voters participated in federal elections; by 2000 the figure had fallen to 62 per cent. The number of people making themselves available as candidates has diminished dramatically. The 2000 federal elections had 30.5 per cent fewer candidates than the 1993 elections, a fact attributed to the dissatisfaction with the results yielded by our single-member plurality electoral system, commonly known as the first-past-the-post voting system. For instance, in 2000 the federal Liberals won 172 of the 301 available seats—a huge majority, with 57 per cent of the seats—while they only garnered 41 per cent of the popular vote. In 1997 they won an absolute majority of the seats with a paltry 38.5 per cent of the popular vote. Indeed, in 2000 in Ontario 49 per cent of the population voted against the Liberals. This sizeable anti-Liberal vote translated into but two non-Liberal Ontario representatives in Parliament.

This skewing of the wishes of the supposed sovereign voters has led to calls for changes to the first-past-the-post scheme. Advocates for change propose variants of a proportional representation voting scheme, such as a party list, a single transferable vote, or a mixed-member proportional regime. Others push for reforms to political party financing, which the corporate sectors exploit to the detriment of democracy.

All of these proposals have merit. Still, even if substantial reforms of this kind are attained, Canadians will still only occasionally cast a vote to express their opinions and hopes regarding a huge number of issues. Casting a ballot every four years or so does not constitute a direct attack on the control and power of the corporate sphere. The corporate economic and ideological foothold will only be seriously threatened by a much deeper and wider democratic political movement.

In any case, any political assaults on corporate capital will face a barrage of ideological counterattacks, as well as threats of capital strikes. One way of responding to capital strikes may be to urge workers to take control of the many aggregates of capital created for the maintenance of income during periods of disability, sickness, and old age. These massive funds are the culminations of invested contributions by employers and employees held in trust by workers' compensation and public and private pension schemes. The funds are not controlled by the workers whose income security they insure. They are invested in the competitive capitalist markets, where the ruling classes can deploy them for their profit-seeking endeavours. Now, because the Supreme Court of Canada has acknowledged that, in real economic terms, the contributions to those funds come from foregone wages that otherwise would have been used by the workers to look after their income security, there is an argument that resonates with the conceptualization of private property rights in a liberal political economy to the effect that workers should be allowed to determine how to deploy these capital funds. Hence, many critics argue that it would make sense to put these funds under workers' control and use them as a counterweight to corporate power. This is a noble idea, but a very difficult one to implement unless the political milieu has changed or is being *purposively* radicalized. The strategy is difficult and somewhat dangerous as a free-standing tactic.

Part of the problem is that the various plans are so diverse, ranging from the public pension/insurance kinds, through private collectively bargained-for regimes, to private, individually created schemes. This diversity means that, technically, it is always going to be extremely hard to reassure people not only that their income security will not be imperilled but also that there will be truly democratic control and accountability when the funds are brought under some kind of unified workers' control. The political difficulties are horrendous. Then too, there are as many ways of directing worker-controlled funds as there are advocates. A huge number of such schemes have been proposed, and many have been tried. They include giving workers a way of becoming equity owners in their corporate employer, setting up development funds, creating training funds, developing greater industrial democracy within the employing firms, and establishing new large capital funds. But, in the end, they always are more and less moulded by the existing balance of economic and political power.

In our setting the real danger would be that, even if the enormous technical problems could be solved, as things stand the worker funds could (and probably would) be used to support competitive market conditions, always under the guise that they were being used to protect workers' interests. In 1983 Boris Frankel made a powerful case that this is what must happen to such experiments in a relatively unmediated corporate capitalist polity. The worker-controlled funds, following Frankel's persuasive logic, might be deployed to smooth out the unsettling volatility of stock markets, or to offset the recurring imperfections and busts of our capitalist economy, all of which would safeguard workers' interests in the immediate sense. In short they would be corporate-supporting tools, rather than the opposite, unless they were engineered as part of a movement manoeuvring to create an alternative politics altogether. Only then could it become plausible to talk about using the technically difficult-to-harness funds to provide security for the needy, regardless of their connection to the monetized productive sphere; to think about the provision of financial support for community-based enterprises and co-operatives that would not have to swim in the shark-infested seas of the market; and to give serious assistance to municipally-centred job creation funds, and the like.

⚖

It is vital to have a co-ordinated strategy to delegitimate the private enclaves of power created for the captains of industry, finance, retail, and everything else. Demands for profound change must be made at all levels at the same time. As Frederick Douglass reportedly said, "Power concedes nothing without a demand. It never did and it never will."

In Anglo-American jurisdictions, capitalists have been blessed by a form of corporate law that promotes irresponsibility, criminality, and the perversion of democracy to advance their goal, the maximization of their wealth and political power. The corporation makes it all seem normal: selfishness, avarice, disregard for others, impersonal, commodified relations, the subjugation of the majority to the whims and caprices of the few. The very normality of it all makes the mediation of the impacts of unequally divided wealth, so characteristic of capitalist economies, all the more difficult to achieve. All of this is to be tolerated because it generates wealth. Greed is elevated to a moral value, supported by massive education campaigns and commercial advertising techniques perfected to wrought changes in expectations and wants. To be a consumer is what citizens are taught. As Stanley Deetz noted when describing the effect of the increasingly large corporations on civil society: "Employee obedience to those in power supercedes any private romantic loyalty to church, family, community, or nation-state. The employee is first a resource, never a citizen." Not surprisingly, there is a palpable tendency for elected governments and their bureaucracies to refer to the citizens they are to serve as clients and consumers. Only a few weeks after the devastating events of September 11, 2001, the U.S. leaders, fearful of a recession setting in, were urging their shaken American fellow-citizens to do their patriotic duty by getting back out there and consuming. President George W. Bush told the White House news corps, "We cannot let the terrorists achieve the objective of frightening our nation to the point where we don't conduct business or people don't shop." What could be more revealing of the sorry pass to which corporate capitalism has brought us?

If those engaged in the political struggle for change see capitalism and capitalists as the beast they must defeat, they cannot ignore that beast's major weapon, the corporation. The outline of proposed strategies presented here for facing down and overcoming this beast and its weapon is not exhaustive; indeed, it is somewhat eclectic. It is meant to provide a set of tactics that spring from a central theme of this book, which is that corporations block democracy, at home and abroad. My belief is that only if we recover, and enrich, our political lives as democratic citizens will we be able to become useful and effective participants in local and worldwide movements to tackle the enormous human problems we face. As C. Douglas Lummis argued in *Radical Democracy*, to be a democrat is not an abstraction. It is a state of being: "Democracy is a world that joins *Demos*—the people with *Krakia*—power. . . . It describes an ideal, not a method for achieving it. . . . It is a historical project . . . as people take it up as such and struggle for it."

These proposals take up what we have learned in the previous pages about the enemy of this historical project, and they are intended to help fuel the spirit of would-be democrats as they engage in their struggles to bring together *people* and *power*, break down the corporate shield, and lay the groundwork for a humanizing transformation of our polity.

Notes and Sources

NOTE: Each chapter section begins with references/sources to specific pages (if any), followed by general notes and comments (including sources) on general chapter content.

Introduction

p.5, My stand . . . demands that I avoid: Amin, *Re-Reading the Postwar Period*, p.9.

It may seem strange to talk about the failure of an economic system to give people what they want when it is the conventional wisdom that the economy is booming, with perhaps a slight downturn here and there. But the point is that the measure of welfare created by the economy is about aggregates, not about the distribution of that wealth. Income and wealth inequalities are increasing markedly as the economy is generating more wealth; see Yalnizyan, *Growing Gap: A Report on Growing Inequality between the Rich and Poor in Canada*. This disparity leads to feelings of insecurity and unsatisfied aspirations.

More, while governments have become preoccupied with the generation of aggregate wealth increases rather than its equitable distribution, they have set themselves narrow economic policy agendas that are out of whack with what people really want in terms of quality of life. Despite governments' pretence that they are responding to popular demand when they slash public programs and taxes in order to generate more private wealth creation, large bodies of evidence indicate that the citizenry would prefer a different set of priorities. Evidence on what people really want— security in employment, in old age, public health and education facilities available to all, more environmental protection, etc.— and on what they are not persuaded they need, such as the elimination of all debts and deficits, is readily available; see Graves, Gauthier, and Jansen, *Rethinking Government 94*; *British Social Attitudes Survey* 1984–88.

There is, then, a politicians' failure to act on the well-known wishes of the population. The deficiencies of electoral democracy are not addressed here; it suffices to say that they are exemplified—albeit not proved—by the gap between the rather clear wishes of citizens and their supposedly representative governments' responses to them. For a recent poll showing that people do not support even heavily propagandized governmental views of what is desirable, see a Business Week-Harris poll taken after the November 2000 demonstrations in Seattle. This poll found that 52 per cent of people were sympathetic to the demonstrators and that business had too much power. Similarly, a Pew Research Center survey done in April 1999 found that, during a period when Americans were being bombarded with the message that globalization was "good" and the street protestors uninformed and extremist, 52 per cent of people felt that globalization would hurt them (Tabb, *Amoral Elephant: Globalization and the Struggle for Social Justice in the Twenty-First Century*). People, without the benefit of all the official data and despite the barrage of elite-inspired propaganda, are able to form their own views of what is lacking in public policy as a result of their own observations and experiences. This explains the apparent paradox that, in seemingly good economic times, societal discontent is palpable. Popular writers reflect this gap between the advertised and the real; see Galbraith, *Culture of Contentment* and Sennett, *Corrosion of Character*. This explains why flat pronouncements on behalf of the powerful that all is well and there is no basis for future conflict, such as Fukuyama's *The End of History and the Last Man*, only convinces those who are trying to do the convincing, just as in another era the announcement of the end of the necessity for struggle proved vainglorious; see Bell's *End of Ideology*.

There are plenty of easily observable conditions to keep citizens aware that they are not living in the world of their choice. On the spread and institutionalization of food banks, see Riches, *Food Banks and the Welfare Crisis*; there is now a Canadian Association of Food Banks, comprising 615 food banks in 2000. The number of people using food banks doubled in the decade up to 2000, according to the Canadian Association of Food Banks' annual survey published in October 2000. In 2000 some 130,000 people used food banks in Toronto—the city in which the increases in overall wealth are glossily displayed in new buildings, sporting facilities, hotels, and shiny condominiums by the waterfront. Amongst the 130,000 were 65,000 children, 6,000 seniors, 24,000 disabled, and 16,000 single mothers (*Toronto Star*, Dec. 7, 2000). The journal of the Canadian Medical Association documented child hunger in Canada, finding it affects 1.2 per cent of families with children under eleven. Some 78 per cent of people polled thought hunger to be a serious concern, and 60 per cent believed the federal government had a responsibility to act immediately to relieve hunger (*Toronto Star*, Oct. 17, 2000). Increased homelessness caused the Federation of Canadian Municipalities to call on the federal government to provide affordable housing at the rate of 20,000 per annum to make a slight dent in the problem. The Federation noted that Canada was the only major industrialized country without a housing policy (Shapcott, "Government Fails the Homeless Again"). The tragedy of homelessness, as well as the accompanying street kids' phenomenon, is so well-known that mayors of major cities have been forced to term it a national crisis; see also the Golden Report (Golden, *Taking Responsibility for*

Homelessness, 1999). In 1989, at the urging of Ed Broadbent, the federal legislature unanimously passed a resolution to end child poverty by the year 2000. In 2000, Campaign 2000, a body set up to monitor Parliament's progress, found that the child poverty problem had worsened, by about 50 per cent, with 400,000 more children being adjudged destitute, largely due to the cuts in governmental spending.

In June 2000, Statistics Canada released its report on 1998 incomes. It divided Canada's families into five equal groups. The top fifth of the 8.3 million families were the only ones who had increased their share of the national income since 1989. The increase was 3.3 per cent; the next group had stayed where it was in 1989, while the next two groups had slight drops during this period. The bottom fifth of families, however, lost 20 per cent of its already small share. Statistics Canada noted that, despite strong economic growth, income disparities continued to grow apace; see also the Canadian Labour Congress report, *Falling Behind: The State of Working Canada, 2000*.

Working people feel the impact of inequality every day they go to work. On the increase in working time and precarious job proliferation, see Osberg, Wien, and Grude, *Vanishing Jobs*; Yalnizyian, Ide, and Cordell, *Shifting Time*; Adams, Betcherman, and Bilson, *Good Jobs, Bad Jobs, No Jobs*; Yates, *Longer Hours, Fewer Jobs*; Schor, *Overworked American*; Clarke, *Silent Coup*; Dobbin, *Myth of the Good Corporate Citizen*; Stanford, *Paper Boom*.

On the issue of imperialism/colonialism, there is too much writing to select sensibly. Easy reading is provided by Bartolome de las Casas, *Short Account of the Destruction of the Indies*; Koning, *Conquest of America*; Churchill, *Little Matter of Genocide*; and Frank, *World Accumulation 1492–1789*.

1   The Corporation as an Invisible Friend

The theory of the corporation on which I base the account in this chapter is an amalgam of two theories: the concession and fiction theories. This is only one of many theoretical explanations available to describe the nature of the legal corporation. Wolff, "On the Nature of Legal Persons" (1938), p.494, identifies as many as sixteen discrete theories propounded by scholars; see also Friedmann, *Legal Theory* (1944). While the many nuances are interesting to people in the field, readers need only be aware of the four main strands of theorizing.

The first is the concession/fiction theory perspective. Essentially, the same idea underpins these two approaches. It is that the state has the power to bestow legal personhood on anything it desires; and, when this is done, the creation — which is an artifice — in law is as real as a live person. For a stout defence of the proposition that the statutorily created corporation is as much a person as you and I are, see Welling, *Corporate Law in Canada*. The theory entails the premise that the kind of legal person created by the state is subject to the state's decree. It may be a limited form of person, one that has many of the attributes of a natural person — as is the case under Canada's corporation laws — and its existence is subject to state fiat. This theoretical approach fits most closely with the statutory regimes that govern corporate law in Canada — more closely, at least, than do other competing theories.

One of those theories is the bracket theory. It posits that a corporation is but a legal envelope, or a set of brackets, for the live human beings who have decided to conduct profit-seeking activities in a collaborative manner. This means that, when it is sought to allocate responsibility for the outcomes of this collaborative activity, law can just remove the brackets and identify the responsible people directly. While this approach appeals to common sense and probably jibes with the way that actors in small, tightly knit corporations think of their business arrangements, it negates the very purpose of the creation of a separate, property-holding entity and flies directly in the face of how corporate law works.

The third group is the contract-based understanding of corporations. It first arose during the nineteenth century, when general incorporation began to be permitted, replacing the grant of a charter that gave corporate standing for limited purposes. The idea that began to be propagated was that the aggregation of individual investors via a scheme of contracts was something requiring no state involvement and, therefore, neither the internal rules of the corporation nor its goals were the business of the state. The formalities of incorporation were there to facilitate such contracting; see Bratton Jr., "Nexus of Contracts Corporation," p.74, and his "New Economic Theory of the Firm," p.1471. This theory has been experiencing a renewed popularity amongst the adherents of the school of law and economics; it provides them with ammunition for their argument that limited liability for shareholders and governance rights for shareholders can be justified by reference to contract principles. The theory has been renamed to become known as the contract-nexus theory.

The last group of theories comprises the realist theory and the natural entity theory. The point of departure is that the corporation is an organic whole, one that transcends the mere aggregation of its component parts and people. It is a thing in its own right, to which responsibilities should be attached directly. It is not a fiction in any sense. It has a life and culture that are its very own and not a reflection of those who—necessarily—must act on its behalf. This approach has a great deal of appeal to those who want to hold corporations responsible for their conduct and helps obviate the need for finding a will or act that can be attributed to the corporation. This persuasive way of looking at the nature of the corporation does not dovetail with the manner in which our statutes and interpreting courts have treated corporations, although occasionally, especially when they deal with Charter of Rights and Freedoms' issues, judges seem to rely on natural entity or contract theories; see the notes to chapter 6 and also Tollefson, "Corporate Constitutional Rights and the Supreme Court of Canada"; for an assertion and supporting evidence that corporate statutes treat the fiction theory as the primary theory, see Ziegel et al., *Cases and Materials on Partnerships and Canadian Corporations*, pp.132–34; for a discussion of the origins and attractions of the realist theory precept, see Gierke, *Political Theories of the Middle Age*, p.1900, and note the "Introduction" by F.W. Maitland.

The concession/fiction theorization allows for the possibility that the capacity of corporations may be restricted and taken away altogether. Once this was thought appropriate. Goodrich, ed., *Government and the Economy*, notes that the Pennsylvania statute stated that "A corporation in law is just what the incorporating act makes it. It is the creature of the law and may be moulded to any shape or for any purpose that the Legislature may deem most conducive for the general good." The reality of modern capitalist law is that this is no longer the envisaged starting point. It is the contemporary attribute of an unfettered corporate personality, added to the privilege of limited liability, which imperils the legitimacy of the corporate vehicle, necessitating the legal pyrotechnics discussed in this chapter. The idea that a body separate from the actual capitalists would be considered the entrepreneurial entity for the purposes of attaching legal responsibility worried liberal political philosophers from the inception of modern corporate law doctrine. Adam Smith pronounced the separation of owners from management of their property as a sure cause for inefficiency as managers would not pursue profits at any cost; see *Wealth of Nations*, Bk. III, ch.1 (see discussion in chapter 6). Later, Berle and Means, *Modern Corporation and Private Property* (1932), would argue that the corporation permitted ownership without control over property and control over property without ownership of that property, a distortion of the capitalist ideal. The legal historian Paddy Ireland has recorded how hard the struggle was to permit individuals to combine to form businesses in which they could avoid putting all of their personal wealth at risk. The fear was that innocent victims of profit-seeking activities would have to bear the costs of enterprises which they did not engineer, or desire. For the state to encourage such a possibility by granting charters to limited liability companies was tantamount for it to issue "Rogues Charters," as the ultra conservative London *Times* newspaper called them on May 25, 1824. Ireland demonstrated that, while the economic advantages of large firms led the policy-makers of those times to the belief that they warranted facilitation of the corporate form, safeguards were demanded to ensure that this facilitation did not undermine the dominant mores of personal responsibility. Accordingly, the facility was to be made available to what were truly large enterprises; smaller firms were to operate as sole entrepreneurships or partnerships, legal forms which made real, live people participants answerable for the conduct of the firm; Ireland, "Triumph of the Company Legal Form 1856–1914"; and "Capitalism without the Capitalist." The question of legitimacy that arose out of the separation of the investors from the productive activities of the business in which they invested and out of the grant of limited liability to those investors plagued the legally created corporation from the start; see Hurst, *Legitimacy of the Business Corporation*; Hadden, *Company Law and Capitalism*. Indeed, in the early days, many jurisdictions flatly refused to grant these privileges to incorporators; for instance, A.A. Berle reported that, in 1822, Massachusetts law stated that any member of any manufacturing company was to remain liable in his individual capacity for all debts contracted during his membership of the corporation; Berle, "Modern Functions of the Corporate System," p.433. For similar approaches in California, New Jersey, Pennsylvania, and Maryland, see Cadman, *Corporation in New Jersey*; Dodd, *American Business Corporations until 1860*; Friedman, *History of American Law*; Hartz, *Economic Policy and Democratic Thought*. The potential for roguery and ruinous speculation embedded in the principle of limited liability continues to worry commentators; see Orhnial, ed., *Limited Liability and the Corporation*; Ziegel, "Is Incorporation (with Limited Liability) Too Easily Available?" p.1075.

To counter the assault on corporate legitimacy, supporters of corporate rights often point to the very real advantages that the privilege of limited liability brings. These include its contributions to the massing of capitals and assets that, when used in a co-ordinated manner, will yield more economic welfare than they would if used discretely. More, as the personal wealth of investors is not put at risk, they will be free to parcel out the capital available for investment to a variety of ventures offering limited liability. Losses in one corporation may be offset by wins in another. Limited liability provides incentives for more investment and for more variety in investment. As a device it enures to the general good. There are other supporting arguments, but these should suffice because they are powerful ones. They led Charles W. Eliot, president, Harvard University, to exclaim, "Limited liability is by far the most effective legal invention . . . made in the 19th century" (Cataldo, "Limited Liability with One-Man Companies," p.473). For more staid and thoughtful argumentation, see Easterbrook and Fischel, "Limited Liability and the Corporation"; and Gabaldon, "Lemonade Stand: Feminist and Other Reflections on the Limited Liability of Corporate Shareholders." Today the strand of scholarship known as law and economics advances another justification for the privilege of limited liability. These people contend that, even if the law did not bestow it, limited liability would exist because the investing class would be able to exact the benefit as a contractual term when bargaining with the corporation about whether to invest or not; Easterbrook and Fischel, "Limited Liability and the Corporation," p.89; Galbaldon, "Lemonade Stand," p.1387. In sum, the argument is that there is nothing untoward about limited liability and, inasmuch as it is a distortion of market capitalism ideals, it is worth paying the price.

The many unredressed harms inflicted by corporate actors for which notable individuals are not held responsible, as well as the fact that very often these harms are inflicted by corporations that do not offer any of the economic welfare benefits that supposedly warrant the grant of limited liability—see chapters 3 and 4—continue to draw attention to the question of the legitimacy of the corporation. Consequently, fierce defenders of market capitalism have been forced to suggest alternatives. Halpern, Trebilcock, and Turnbull, "Economic Analysis of Limited Liability in Corporation Law," p.117, argue that limited liability should not be available to small, undercapitalized corporations and in circumstances in which the victims of corporate harm-doing were not in a realistic position to bargain with the corporation about the impact of its activities. In a similar vein, Hansmann and Kraakman, "Toward Unlimited Shareholder Liability for Corporate Torts," p.1878, suggest that, where the impact of corporate conduct amounts to a tort—that is, a wrongfully inflicted harm on someone who was not contractually connected to the corporation—the principle of limited liability should not hold sway. These are acknowledgements of the anachronistic nature of limited liability in a market capitalist economy; they are also vainglorious attempts to repair the damage done by the principle. The suggestions have not been acted upon, mainly because to implement them would be to question the logic of modern corporate law and, thereby, threaten to bring the edifice down.

It is in this context that the movement to impose more responsibility on directors and management must be understood. It is a way of imposing obligations on people without directly attacking the grant of full, human-like, personality to corporations or the doctrine of limited liability to investing property owners. The success and utility of this movement will be considered in detail in chapter 10. For an assessment and literature review, see Glasbeek, "More Direct Director Responsibility."

2   An Ill-Assorted Trio: Capitalism, the Market, and the Corporation

p.19, "There is one underlying motive in business . . .: Olive, *Just Rewards*, p.23.

p.20, This is captured in a truly famous dictum: Smith, *Wealth of Nations*.

p.20, Milton Friedman, one of the gurus: Friedman, *Capitalism and Freedom*.

p.22, University of Guelph philosopher John McMurtry has noted: McMurtry, *Unequal Freedoms*.

p.23, One of the most telling: Macpherson, "Elegant Tombstones."

p.23, There are many other persuasive critiques: see, for example, Lux, *Adam Smith's Mistake*; Heilbroner, *The Nature and Logic of Capitalism*.

The arguments adduced about the economic advantages that the corporate form brings are restricted to large publicly traded corporations, where the bringing together of lots of little capitals, the synergetic impacts of collaboration, and the reduction of transaction costs all make sense. None of these justifications for the employment of the corporate form apply when a small number of investors—a couple of friends, a nuclear family, or even a single individual—form a corporation as a vehicle for the pursuit of profits. This is why the following two chapters treat small business corporations discretely. The point is that the use of the corporate form is an abuse in these circumstances, one that threatens the legitimacy of the corporate tool and, hence, of market capitalism.

There are many blatant efforts by ideologues who purport to be serious political philosophers to characterize human beings as innately greedy animals, making the pursuit of profits as natural as breathing. Among the most prominent are Ayn Rand and her followers, the Objectivists. Not only is it central to their view that selfishness is a laudable moral imperative, but they also hold that substantive equality has no moral value; Rand, *Virtue of Selfishness*. While there are many ardent disciples— including the all-powerful head of the U.S. Federal Reserve Bank, Mr. Greenspan— and unknowing captives of this market-capitalism-favouring philosophy, it is always contested. Capitalism did not arise without antecedents. In pre-capitalist societies, in which people produced for need and law created a system of mutual obligations, greed was considered the worst of sins. "In the numerous treatises on the passions that appeared in the 17th century, no change whatever can be found in the assessment of avarice as 'the foulest of them all' or in its position as the deadliest Deadly Sin that it had come to occupy towards the end of the Middle Ages": Hirschman, *Passions and the Interests*, p.41. See also Heilbroner, *Making of Economic Society*; Monroe, ed., *Early Economic Thought*; Gilchrist, *Church and Economic Activity in the Middle Ages*; and Glasbeek, "Commercial Morality through Capitalist Law—Limited Possibilities." Hence, even Adam Smith, writing in 1759 as the philosopher he was before he wrote his exegesis on political economy in 1776, rejected selfishness as a worthy human impulse: "To feel much for others, and little for ourselves, that to restrain our selfish, and to indulge our benevolent affections, constitutes the perfection of human nature; and can produce among mankind that harmony of sentiments and passions in which constitutes their whole grace and propriety": *Theory of Moral Sentiments*, p. 71. Unselfishness, as a praiseworthy way of life, is a virtue that continues to be inculcated by churches, families, schools, and public pundits. To make "greed," the opposite of this much-endorsed virtue, acceptable as an adjunct to a useful institution such as the market, the greed proponents must also argue that the market itself is acceptable. They do this by arguing that engaging in market activities is a natural concomitant of living in a society; that the market transcends political-economic regimes. It does not matter whether or not feudalism, capitalism, or socialism reigns: people will participate in market activities. From this perspective, capitalism really came on the scene when market activities were liberated from unnaturally impeding rules and social norms. In addition, technological innovations made market activities more sophisticated, created a greater number of things that could be the subject of market transactions, and permitted geographically more dispersed exchanges and production, all helping the advance of capitalist relations of production. Although somewhat dated, the best exposition remains that of Pirenne,

Medieval Cities. If people have, forever and a day, been rational self-interested actors, then market promotion is not offensive to basic precepts and, in as much as greed is a component of this normal activity, it cannot be a harmful characteristic and capitalism's emphasis on greed is not so unappetizing.

This view of the development of capitalism as a natural outgrowth of doing what comes naturally—market participation—is much disputed; see Brenner, "Bourgeois Revolution and Transition to Capitalism"; Ashton and Philpin, eds., *Brenner Debate*; Polanyi, *Great Transformation*; and Wood, *Democracy against Capitalism.* The argument made is that the bartering and trading that preceded capitalism were of a different order. It was about trading between different markets, rather than about competition within any one market. Merchants were really middle persons putting different markets in touch with one another; there was no emphasis on producing competitively to serve one market better than other producers could. Polanyi argued that such limited market activities were subjugated to other social imperatives, such as reciprocity, redistribution, kinship, and community. It is only when the modern market as articulated by Adam Smith takes hold, says Polanyi, that social relations become embedded in the economic project, rather than the other way round. From this vantage point it is not possible to contend that the market—with its technical assistant, selfishness—is the natural state of things. Indeed, Polanyi goes on to argue, as does Wood, what distinguishes the emergence of capitalism is the *compelled* participation in market activities. How this came about remains a vexed issue, but that is not to be discussed here. What is important, though, is that, if the market is an imposed system of economic and social activity, it loses much of its legitimating power. Capitalism is no longer able to rid itself of the damning association with greed that leads to inequality in wealth and power—and which relies on an institutional argument that makes this outcome seem to be inevitable. One way around the undermining notion that the market is not a voluntaristic institution is to depict it as merely an economic instrument that is free-standing. For the flourishing of more humanistic characteristics, the social and moral spheres are to be looked-to—these spheres being, in turn, also free-standing. The peculiarity of this pigeonhole approach is a good indication of the power of the Macpherson-based critique. For an elaboration of the claim that capitalism contributes to freedom as long as our social and moral impulses can be satisfied independently of our economic plight, see Novak, *Toward a Theology of the Corporation.*

The depth of the portrayal of the market as an ahistorical, apolitical institution that naturalizes capitalism is reflected in the relatively recent outpouring of literature that followed the failures of the self-styled socialist regimes. The argument is that one of central planning's deficiencies is that planners make poor choices about what people want and need, leading to an impoverished and impoverishing allocation of resources and talents. The market, in which individuals can express their sovereign opinions, does a better job. Hence some scholars argue for something they call "market socialism"—indicating a belief that the market can be adapted to any political economic regime whatsoever. The more progressive of these writings reason that, while the market may allocate resources and talents better, thereby adding to overall wealth, the market does not lead to equitable distribution and there will still be a need for some central planning, hence, market socialism. See Nove, *Economics of Feasible Socialism*; and Roosevelt and Balkin, eds., *Why Market Socialism?* In a similar vein, the association of the market with political freedom, also posited on the view that there is nothing compulsory about market participation, is popularly equated with freedom and progress. Hence, the media refer to pro-market proponents in the former Eastern Bloc or in China as reformers or pro-democracy politicians. This line of thought sees the emancipatory effect of the market as self-evident, even as material inequality and deprivation increase in these new market economies.

3   The "Small Is Beautiful" Campaign

p.28, Industry Canada tells us: Industry Canada, "Small Business in Canada: A Statistical Overview," March 1, 1996.

p.29, The press release announcing these centres: Government of Ontario, Press Release, Toronto, Oct. 22, 1997.

p.29, Governments everywhere repeatedly pump out: Statistics Canada, Small Business and Special Surveys Division, "Employment Dynamics, Business Size and Life Status," 1993.

p.29, It might be the Toronto Dominion Bank: *Toronto Star*, Aug. 5, 1998, p.C.6.

p.29, There has been an impressive growth: Industry Canada, *Small Business in Canada: A Statistical Overview*, March 1, 1996; Industry Canada, *Small Business Quarterly*, Fall 1997.

p.31, In 1989, two researchers, relying on data: Krause and Lothian, "Measurement of Canada's Level of Corporate Concentration," *Canadian Economic Observer*, January 1989.

p.31, Similarly, in 1990, Statistics Canada reported that: Hurtig, *Betrayal of Canada*, pp.181–83.

p.31, As the Bryce Commission noted: Canada, *Royal Commission on Corporate Concentration*.

p.33, Studies are trotted out to show: Canadian Federation of Independent Business, "Result of a National Survey on Canadians' Attitude towards Employment," Angus Reid Group, March 1991; Analysis of Statistics Canada Survey of Labour and Income Dynamics Database.

p.33, To take just one example: Industry Canada, Entrepreneurship and Small Business Office, March 1, 1996.

p.34, At the same public relations event, Barbara Hall: News release at the launching of the Canada-Ontario Business Service Centre, Toronto, Oct. 16, 1997.

For a fine account of how marginalized most small-business people are and how marginal most small business is to the working of the economy, see Stanford, *Paper Boom*, particularly chapter 6.

The figures presented about the intense concentration of corporate power in Canada are somewhat dated but still pertinent. Control of economic activity continues to fall into fewer and fewer hands, further eroding competition. There are many sources—conservative, formal, and progressive—all to the same effect. For instance, Diane Francis, a conservative commentator, expressed her anxiety about the level of concentration in *Controlling Interest: Who Owns Canada?* Statistics Canada's reports consistently provide evidence of concentration. For left critiques—which like to demonstrate that Canada is run by a few for the few—see Veltmeyer, *Canadian Corporate Power*. Francis noted that there might be something in this critique when she reported that, behind these dominant corporations, there were real live human beings who exercised power and enjoyed unbelievable wealth. She calculated that thirty-two families controlled assets whose combined annual revenues were greater than the federal government's yearly income. For a useful short list of recent literature on wealth and power concentration, see Barlow and Campbell, *Straight through the Heart*, ch. 2 and notes.

Understandably, those who defend existing market capitalism in Canada do have to justify this obvious disparity between the Adam Smith small-business ideal and reality. As the Bryce Commission did, these proponents of the status quo argue that, while these large Canadian corporations loom large within the Canadian economy, they are not able to exercise undue market power — thereby destroying the small business model — because they have to compete on the world stage, where they are mere pygmies, unable to set prices. The market model is well and alive, all appearances to the contrary. For recent examples of this disingenuous argument, note that it was Air Canada's — and the supporting government's — line of reasoning when the Canadian two-airline policy was abandoned to create an effective Canadian monopoly by permitting Air Canada to swallow its only true rival, Canadian Airlines. The government had to promise that new competition would be fostered and helped to thrive. A similar tack was taken by the banks in 1999 when alliances between four of the major banks were proposed; if this reduction of competition had succeeded, there would have been only three banks left. The public anxiety about the fate of borrowers should this occur — largely fuelled by the rather self-interested Bank of Nova Scotia, which had been left out of the dealing and wheeling between the other four major players — forced an electorally sensitive government to put the kibosh on the proposed deals. At the time there was a good deal of indignation because service charges were deemed to be too high while profits were huge and increasing. All this, and the banks were continuously lambasted because they were thought to be unkind to small business. In this context, the government apparently decided that it could not be seen to be bestowing more market power on the banks. While the banks did not succeed this time round — they assuredly will in the near future — they did repeatedly point out that, globally, they need to amalgamate to reach competitive size. This argument has real weight with the elites in the land, including the judges sitting on the Supreme Court of Canada, which, in a hallmark decision, once held that, just because one family group, the New Brunswick Irving dynasty, owned all the English newspapers in the province, it was not exercising undue monopoly power because its newspapers did not openly collude to set the prices of the advertising space they sold.

The Hollinger hoopla of the 1990s illustrates the wide understanding that corporate concentration might lead to the possession of disproportionate economic and political power by certain people and their invisible friends. As Conrad Black's vehicle bought itself more and more control over major newspapers in Canada, largely by using holdings in Southam Press and ousting the Power Corporation/Desmarais interests in Southam via their holdings in Torstar, nationalist Canadians became concerned about the loss of control over their country. In particular, they feared that Black, not-too-hiddenly, would be able to use his potential monopoly over news outlets to dictate a conservative agenda to politicians. Consequently, the Council of Canadians, led by Maude Barlow, brought a legal action that argued that freedom of speech rights guaranteed by the Charter of Rights and Freedoms were in peril as a result of the emerging monopoly. Given the earlier Irving decision, the action never had much chance and did fail. But its mere launching speaks volumes about some of the issues raised: there is a widespread understanding that corporations are vehicles for the private advancement of ordinary human beings who—*legally speaking*—can act unseen to get what they otherwise would find difficult to justify seeking as individuals in a liberal democracy; more, it is understood that there are corporations that dominate our political economy despite the daily cant about the economy being composed of a multitude of atomized, insignificant businesses.

But the liberation rhetoric of market capitalism and the actuality of monopoly capitalism—the phrase coined by Baran and Sweezy in *Monopoly Capital* (1966), their famous analysis of contemporary conditions—have another outcome: the progressive, possibly anti-capitalist forces are deceived into making arguments about the need to adhere to the idealized notions of the market, that is to say, many, small actors, competing vigorously with each other. This ideological approach perfectly suits capitalism and capitalists.

4   The Small and the Ugly

p.39, As one judge of the British Columbia Court of Appeal: Per Galliher, J.A., *Associated Growers of B.C. Ltd. v. Edmunds*, [1926] 1 D.L.R. 1093, at p.1095.

p.42, the "law permits the incorporation of a business *for the very purpose* . . .": *Walkovsky v. Carlton* (1966), 223 N.E. 2d, 6 (N.Y. Ct. App.), (the taxicab case); emphasis added.

p.60, Again, the difficulty of specifying what kind of capital funding: Halpern, Trebilcock and Turnbull, "Economic Analysis of Limited Liability in Corporation Law"; Hansmann and Kraakman, "Toward Unlimited Shareholder Liability for Corporate Torts."

The judicial cases used in this chapter are: *Brown (Henry) and Sons Ltd. v. Smith* (the automatic helmsman case); *Rockwell Developments Ltd. v. Newtonbrook Plaza Ltd.* (the lawyer/real estate and his corporations); *B.G. Preeco I (Pacific Coast) v. Bon Street Holdings Ltd.* (the changing of name of corporation case); *Covert et al. v. Nova Scotia* (the cunning grandfather case); *Einhorn v. Westmount Investments Ltd.* (the Belzbergs case); *Kosmopoulos v. Constitution Insurance Co. of Canada* (the poor uninsured man case); *550551 Ontario Limited v. Framingham* (the clever Silvers and Bilt-Rite case); and *C.R.F. Holdings Ltd. v. Fundy Chemical International Ltd.* (radioactive waste material case). For full details of these and other judicial cases, see the section "Judicial Decisions" in the Bibliography. These cases were among those I presented when offering a basic corporate law course. I used a standard teaching book, Ziegel et al., *Cases and Materials on Partnerships and Business Organizations*, and a traditional text, Welling, *Corporate Law in Canada*. The cases discussed are mainstream examples used to teach would-be lawyers the proper way of manipulating separate legal personalities and limited liability to protect their future clients.

In the foundation case of modern corporate law, *Salomon v. Salomon & Co.*, that famed House of Lords decision held that a person who incorporated his business was a distinct person from that business even if all the world had believed otherwise. G.R. Rubin, in his essay, "Aron Salomon and his Circles," on the circumstances surrounding the case, has demonstrated that all of Salomon's contemporaries thought it incredible that he would seek to rely on the separate legal personality doctrine. They were particularly concerned that Salomon had also made himself a preferred creditor of the company, ranking ahead of other creditors who had lent money to his firm in the belief that he would be personally accountable for the monies borrowed. They had done business with him personally for many years and had found him trustworthy, a man who met his responsibilities. The result in the case must have left these Victorian laissez-faire entrepreneurs bewildered. Indeed, it resounded like a thunderclap in legal circles and contributed to the growth of the use of the corporate form by small businesses, often just as the surprising Salomon had done. Note that the Silvers, like Salomon, were controlling shareholders and preferred creditors, edging out the very creditors, Bilt-Rite's employees, who had depended on their probity.

Lawyers ever since have insisted on the purity of the principles laid down in *Salomon*. The inviolability of the decision, they argue, gives them the assistance they need when advising commercial clients about how to conduct their businesses. Any departure will lead to uncertainty. As a result the *Salomon* decision has gained a reified standing. When legislators believe they must protect their policies from the evasive stratagems used by employers of the corporate form, they are at pains to limit their interventions so as to indicate their continuing respect for the Salomon doctrines. And when courts do pierce the veil by characterizing it as a sham or a cloak or the corporation as an alter ego, they are quickly and trenchantly rebuked; see Pickering, "Company as a Separate Legal Entity," p.481, for a long and sarcastic listing of phrases and words used by courts that try to weasel out of the strictures of the *Salomon* dictates. Courts also seek to finesse their way out of trouble when they are deeply offended by the result mandated by the proper application of the pure corporate law principles. This can irritate practitioners, who feel they cannot advise their clienteles if judges are going to follow their instincts. Knowing that this will happen, they try to formulate rules for courts as to when they should pierce the veil, thus allowing for greater certainty; see Friedman, "Limits of Limited Liability." But the difficulty of formulas was summed up accurately by Madame Justice Wilson in *Kosmopoulos*. Thus far, attempts at fairness have led to arbitrariness. In *Kosmopoulos* itself, Wilson's desire to do justice for the hapless Kosmopoulos led her to radically changing the rules of insurance law. By contrast, her fellow jurist, McIntyre, thought that this would cause chaos in the insurance industry. He, therefore, determined to pierce the veil in this "exceptional" case because he did not think this would threaten the integrity of corporate law and *Salomon* very much. That is, the problems are seen but are not resolved.

The same difficulties, which arise from maintaining the structure of corporate law and trying to meet community expectations in the particular case before the court, prevent proposals, such as denying limited liability to some corporations and not others, in some circumstances and not in others, or to require some, but not too much, capitalization of a corporation, from getting off the ground. There is no principled way in which piercing, some limited liability, or a quantum of capital can be determined. There being no principled way, to adopt these kinds of measures would be tantamount to an admission that there is no principled defence of separate legal personality or limited liability.

As a postscript to this chapter, note that in very conservative Ontario the extraordinary judicial reasoning in *Bilt-Rite* was given legislative imprimatur by the government led by Mike Harris. Note that it required a redrafting of the statute to ensure this result, indicating how extraordinary the court's decision in *Bilt-Rite* was. If we are not to assume anti-worker bias in the court, its peculiar holding is explicable only by its fierce desire to limit any legislative incursions on the *Salomon* doctrines.

5   The Westray Story

For the sources of the corporate machinations and interlocking schemes of avoiding responsibilities and maximizing profit potential, see Curragh Resources Inc., *Annual Report 1990* and the statement the corporation put on the public file when it registered with the U.S. Security and Exchange Commission on Nov. 6, 1989, when it applied to be listed as a corporation entitled to go to the U.S. investment public for capital funding. Whatever steps corporations take to hide their doings from public view, they must tell members of the investing classes what they are doing and how they are doing it. Capitalists are not allowed to mislead capitalists.

The argument that the so-called accident was a highly predictable one is supported by the shocking historical record of mishaps, deaths, and tragedies at the same site. Between 1838 and 1952, 246 miners were killed by explosions; another 330 died because of rock falls, by being crushed to death by coal cars, or mangled by other machinery; see Cameron, *Pictonian Colliers*. This history was also known to the workers, and their support for the start-up of the mine and willingness, even eagerness, to work in it speak volumes about how workers do not voluntarily choose to be employed, but must look for employment, whether they like it or not, whether they risk their lives or not.

For an elaboration of the claim that the disaster was really designed to happen rather than an unforeseen and regrettable accident, see Glasbeek and Tucker, "Death by Consensus." For evidence that coal mining "accidents" can be reduced in number and harmful consequences diminished by increased vigilance, that is, by counter-planning, see Braithwaite, *To Punish or Persuade*. For an account of the Westray episode from a worker's point of view, see Comish, *Westray Tragedy*; for a journalistic report detailing the events and the political machinations, see Jobb, *Calculated Risk*. For the most detailed study of what happened, see Nova Scotia. *Report of the Commission of Public Inquiry: Westray Story*; see also McCormack, *Westray Chronicles*.

Much of the public attention was diverted away from the private economic actors involved in the events because of the media's preoccupation with the wrongdoings and ineptness of politicians and public officials. After all, the story involved political heavyweights such as Donald Cameron (Nova Scotia's premier, 1991–93), the prime minister of Canada, Brian Mulroney, whose involvement was procured by his cabinet colleague, Jake Epp, a Nova Scotia patronage king to whom Mulroney owed his seat in Parliament when first elected leader of the Progressive Conservatives and it was not safe for him to run in his native Quebec. This list also included Robert Coates, a former minister of defence (he was forced to resign because of some tawdry behaviour), who was now acting as a professional lobbyist and had so acted to intercede with his former cabinet colleagues on behalf of Frame. In this context the failure to do decent environmental impact assessments, or to enforce health and safety laws, takes on a much more sinister meaning. As if this was not enough distraction, attempts were made to charge two of the mine-site managers, Phillips and Parry, with the serious criminal charge of manslaughter. Lawyers and Crown prosecutors reduced this attempt to the status of a keystone cops' farce. There were motions by the accused to get more of the information held by the Crown, as fair criminal processes demand.

The Crown, in the end, failed to comply, making the presiding judge mad as hell. He contacted the prosecutors' office and thereby lost the appearance of being unbiased. This caused the Supreme Court of Canada (five years after the explosion) to order that everything had to start from scratch again. In the meantime the Crown, to avoid having to reveal too much information to the accused, had the charges for the fifty-two violations of health and safety regulations—which had been belatedly laid to appease public anger—withdrawn. The legal representatives of Phillips and Parry had gone to the Supreme Court of Canada to ask for a stay on the quite separate ground that the accused could not be tried while the Commission of Public Inquiry was conducting its investigations. They had lost, but this, too, took attention away from the more elemental issues of what had happened at whose behest. In addition, it took time and money and upset the survivors and friends of the dead miners. When, finally, after the Commission's report, the Crown was in a position to start proceedings against Phillips and Parry, it decided to drop the charges. It argued that, while the Report of the Commission had found neglect, recklessness, and flagrant abuses, no single cause or act had been identified as the cause of the tragedy. Hence there was little chance of attributing the necessary intentional act to the two accused. This result foreshadows a problem for the use of the criminal law to discipline corporate deviant actors (see chapters 8, 9, 10). Certainly, it invariably proves difficult to keep the focus on the generators of harm: the corporate structure, the hiding of the master mind, the unavailability of assets and/or humans to settle the score, while not forgotten, were reduced to problems of a lesser order.

6   The Undemocratic Innards of the Large Corporation

p.72, The only trades which it seems possible: Smith, *Wealth of Nations*, Book III, ch. 1.
p.77, But, empirically, there is no conclusive evidence: Coffee, "Liquidity versus Control," p.1277; Gartner, "Institutional Investors and the New Financial Order," p.585.
p.80, Milton Friedman made this clear: Friedman, *Capitalism and Freedom*, chs. 1,2.
p.84, These more "in-the-world" apologists argue: Howse and Trebilcock, "Protecting the Employment Bargain," p.751.

The Westinghouse litigation was based on the union's claim that under the collective bargaining regulating statute employers must bargain in good faith and may not engage in unfair labour practices. Here the failure to inform the union that bargaining might be futile because the plant might be shut and, thereby, the union's certification as the bargaining agent for the employees at that particular site be undermined were claimed to be both breaches of the good faith and unfair labour practices provisions. The actual decision of the Ontario Labour Relations Board need not detain us here; suffice it to note that it was far from clear, leaving it open for employers to engage in Westinghouse-type stratagems in the future. For an elaboration, see Drache and Glasbeek, *Changing Workplace*. What is important here about this case is that the Westinghouse decision underscores the right of a property owner to do with its property as it likes, including removing it. This is what is entailed in the prerogative of management. This elemental right permits employers to stop workers organizing on their premises during working hours; this legally preserved right permits employers to continue to use their properties during strikes; the residual right allows employers to stop workers who seek to protect their jobs from picketing on the employers' premises. In short, this right explains why workers and their unions start from behind the eight ball when they lock horns with their employers in economic struggles.

The corporate form gives this power a particular twist. The essence of this right to deploy one's property as one wishes is the fundamental belief that this is a basic right of every individual in a liberal market capitalist political economy. But when, as in the Westinghouse case, the employer is a corporation, the individual deploying or redeploying or disemploying the property is an economic collective. Collectives are not permitted to combine their economic muscle in a liberal market economy. Thus, workers who seek to do so will be restrained. This is the legal history of trade unions. The right to strike that they have won over time is nothing of the kind. It is only a privilege they are entitled to exercise in very restricted circumstances. This is why the Supreme Court of Canada has stated explicitly that there is no such thing as a right to strike in Canadian law, not even under the Charter-protected guarantee of freedom of association; see *Re Public Service Employee Relations Act; Public Service Alliance of Canada v. Attorney General Canada; Retail, Wholesale and Department Store Union, Locals 544,496, 635 and 955 v. Government of Saskatchewan*. By the legal artifice of treating a corporation, such as Westinghouse, as an individual, in a situation where it plainly is a collective of assets and individuals, individual wealth owners are given a tremendous advantage vis-à-vis the workers they employ; see Glasbeek, "Labour Relations Law as a Mechanism of Adjustment," p.179.

A takeover or merger is an attempted combination of aggregates of assets and people, and is acknowledged to be so. When the combination involves major corporations, one of the considerations is whether it should be permitted to go forward as a matter of competition policy. It might well be the case that the new combination of assets and people would stifle competition in the market. At this point, all pretence that what is going on is a decision by two individuals to buy each other or to set up a new partnership/venture is dropped. The cat is out of the bag: combinations between organizations, each of which already is a large combination, may unmask the pretence that the existence of large publicly traded corporations is easily compatible with market capitalism based on competition between countless actors, none of whom can set prices. Note here that the name of what is now the *Competition Act* used to be the *Combines Investigation Act*.

The discretion enjoyed by boards of directors and management presents a danger to the market principles that are supposedly followed by the corporate structure because they allow people without ownership to exercise control over other people's property. Note the stark contrast between this acknowledgement of directors' and managers' powers and the vigorous claims that directors and managers should not be personally responsible for the wrongdoings of the corporation because they are not acting as independent individuals when they cause the corporation to engage in a particular piece of conduct.

Corporate defenders eschew any notion that directors and managers should exercise their discretion for the public good, rather than just for shareholders. They assert that shareholders are truly the owners of the corporate assets and that senior managers are really just agents with trustee-like obligations. Hence, those managers have no right to act as if they are not beholden to the shareholders/owners/principals. There is no room, therefore, for the corporation to become socially responsible in the sense of being altruistic. The political and logical problems for the corporate defenders arise from their continued insistence on the premise that shareholders are the real owners of the corporation. They are the capitalists who own and operate the venture that has taken on the corporate form. Their logical difficulties would evaporate if they acknowledged, as Paddy Ireland, in "Capitalism without the Capitalist" and "Corporations and Citizenship" suggests, that the shareholder became a person with a financial interest *only* in the corporation very early on and that the productive, industrial tasks of the enterprise were of little daily interest to these financial capitalists. The long-term viability and productivity had become the concern of the corporation as such. This explains the struggles between shareholders and managers in structural terms, but it does not permit an argument to be made that the gap allows managers to engage in altruistic activities while their responsibilities to the viability of the corporation as a profit-maximization centre remain intact. It also does away with the corporate defenders' claim that any misfits between shareholder and managerial interests can be left to perfecting the market and/or appropriate legislative reforms. In practical terms, management has become the effective industrial capitalists. This structural explanation also has very grave implications for the workings of capitalism as the industrial and financial spheres compete for supremacy.

While many people pin their hopes on industrial democracy schemes to give workers participatory governance rights in corporations, even in the most sophisticated regimes—Sweden, Germany—the rights of workers are never elevated to the height of those enjoyed by the people who are deemed to be owners. What occurs is that workers get more power to do things within the enterprise, rather than power over the enterprise. As C.B. Macpherson observed in *Democratic Theory: Essays in Retrieval*, p.47, political power is power over others. Thus, while the advances wrought by industrial democracy schemes may be considerable, qualitatively they fall far short of ownership rights of the kind that are accorded shareholders in some circumstances. For a review of the literature and an elaboration of this argument, see Glasbeek, "Voluntarism, Liberalism and Fairness—Dream, Romance and Real Life."

As to the legitimacy conundrum created when shareholders are treated as governors of the corporation even though they do not work for the rewards: law recognizes that they do not earn their entitlements in the good old-fashioned way, by the sweat of their brows. In legal terms, their protection comes from legislation that goes by the name of the *Securities Act*. To attract the fulsome protections of this statute—and they are bountiful—a claimant must be a security holder. A security is defined as having been established when individuals have invested money in a common enterprise with the expectation that they will earn profits solely through the efforts of managers who will ensure that others will do the necessary work. See s.1 (1) 40 of the Ontario *Securities Act* and the interpretation of this kind of provision by the Supreme Court of Canada in *Pacific Coast Coin Exchange of Canada Ltd. v. Ontario Securities Commission*. This is more evidence of how, functionally, because "dividend payments are made to a group that does not actively participate in corporate affairs, the assumed equivalence between income and productive efforts is broken" (G.W. Wilson, quoted in Campbell, *Control of Corporate Management*, pp.46–47). This facet, too, is easily explained by the Ireland approach, while it remains a knife in the gullet for those who need to pretend that shareholders are real owners directly engaged in precisely the kinds of profit-seeking productive activities envisaged by the ideal market model.

7   When Big Corporations Speak, Governments Listen

p.94, "False and misleading advertising and unethical promotional practices . . .": Ouellet, *Misleading Advertising Bulletin*.

p.95, In his amusing book on words and phrases: Olive, *White Knights and Poison Pills*. The Stephen Leacock quote is also from Olive.

p.95, According to John Bellamy Foster: Foster, "Global Ecology and the Common Good."

p.96, In 1999 Zenith Media reported: *Toronto Star*, June 6, 1999.

p.96, Indeed, of the twenty-one thousand television commercials: Foster, "Global Ecology and the Common Good."

p.96, Kevin Mattson estimates: Mattson, "Talking about My Generation (and the Left)."

p.97, Similarly, Sears Canada repeatedly advertised: *R v. Sears Canada Inc.*

p.101, Nonetheless, the Supreme Court of Canada (1976): *Anti-inflation Reference*.

p.101, This cavalier approach to union rights: *Attorney-General of Canada v. RJR-MacDonald*.

p.102, In 1987, contemptuously, the Supreme Court of Canada dismissed: see *Public Service Alliance of Canada v. Attorney-General Canada*; *Re Public Service Employee Relations Act*.

p.103, As Michael Mandel notes: Mandel, *Charter of Rights and the Legalization of Politics*, p.372; *R. v. Zundel* (1992), and 5 C.C.C. (3d) 449 (Sup. Ct. Canada).

p.104, From the 1970s onwards: see the *Virginia State Board of Pharmacy* case (1976).

p.105, A good exemplification of the problem: *Ford v. Quebec (Attorney-General)*.

p.105, The signs law had specifically stated: *Ford v. Quebec (Attorney-General)* (emphasis added).

p.106, The backlash in English Canada was palpable: Mandel, *Charter of Rights and the Legalization of Politics*; Monahan, *Meech Lake*.

p.109, In the end big business spent some $19 million: Fillmore, "Big Oink"; Dobbin, *Myth of the Good Corporate Citizen*.

p.109, Certainly, the Royal Commission of Inquiry: Canada, Royal Commission on Electoral Reform and Party Financing, *Reforming Electoral Democracy* (Lortie Report, 1992).

p.110, Thus, in 1977, Khayyam Z. Patiel reported: Patiel, *Party, Candidate and Election Finance*, p.107.

p.111, Even though most journalists and their editors think of themselves: These assertions require more elaboration than space and the limited nature of this chapter permit. I will content myself by noting that a highly respected and vast volume of scholarly literature substantiates this claim. The titles tell the story: *The Commercialization of the News* (Baldasty, 1993); *The Media Monopoly* (Bagdikian, 1992); *Deciding What's News: A Study of CBS Evening News, NBC Nightly News, Newsweek and Time* (Gans, 1979); *Manufacturing Consent: The Political Economy of the Mass Media* (Herman and Chomsky, 1988); *Market-Driven Journalism: Let the Citizen Beware!* (McManus, 1994); *Networks of Power: Corporate TV's Threat to Democracy* (Mazzocco, 1994); *Read All About It! The Corporate Takeover of America's Newspapers* (Squires, 1993); *Corporate Media and the Threat to Democracy* (McChesney, 1997); *Democracy's Oxygen: How Corporations Control the Press*

(Winter, 1997); *The Missing News* (Hackett and Gruneau, 2000); *Make Believe Media: The Politics of Entertainment* (Parenti, 1992); and *Inventing Reality: the Politics of News Media* (Parenti, 1993).

p.111, About 50 per cent of a newspaper's content: Glasbeek, "Entrenchment of Freedom of Speech."

p.111, For instance, the newspapers rely on the Newspaper Audience Data Bank: *The Toronto Star* gleefully reported in its columns that it still boasted more readers than its major rivals, *The Globe and Mail* and the *National Post*, amongst the preferred demographic groups: the twenty-five to thirty-four age groups with incomes between $50,000 and $100,000. John Honderich, its publisher, noted that this finding was critical because it means that advertisers "cannot buy around the *Star*." In other words, he believes that advertisers cannot simply cherry-pick a paper that would permit them to reach a narrowly defined group of consumers. If they want the biggest bang for their advertising dollars, he thinks that they must use the *Star*. *Toronto Star*, Nov. 11, 2000, p.E1. Whether or not this is an accurate statement of the state of play in the newspaper advertising industry is neither here nor there. What is important is that it is a game.

p.112, In Canada censorship if not a single horrific act: Duke, "Exiles in Our Own Country," p.10.

p.113, But, inasmuch as such critiques do appear: The context makes these seeming naysayers more like lovable grouches than serious critics. Such columnists seem to be daring only because of the narrowness of the overall context in which they work. This is why the Keynesianism and nationalism of a Dalton Camp—a self-styled conservative—is perceived as being refreshingly progressive. This is why the qualifier "seeming" was used to accompany the description "naysayers" above.

p.114, Such believers might be shaken somewhat by recent developments: see *Toronto Star*, Oct. 9, Dec. 7, 2001.

p.116, Dominant corporations have also established close ties: Glasbeek, "Entrenchment of Freedom of Speech"; and Glasbeek, "Corporate Social Responsibility Movement."

The notion that free speech requires protection and promotion to enhance the sovereignty and self-respect of individuals and the political welfare of all has much in common with the notion that economic market activities are to be facilitated because they advance the causes of economic efficiency, the autonomy of individuals, and political freedom of all. For either of these notions to make sense, it is necessary to posit the existence of a multitude of individuals, eager to act as such and who do not have the ability to exercise any coercive power over any other individual engaged in similar political and economic activities. As we've seen, corporate capitalism, with its tendency to aggregate individuals and concentrate capital, has made a mockery of the market's potential to achieve its ideals. The emergence of for-profit media has had a similar impact on the efficacy of communicating ideas and opinions by speechifying in town halls and on street corners and by pamphleteering—that is, on the very means perceived to be the embodiment of free speech exercises by political philosophers such as John Milton, John Stuart Mill, and Tom Paine.

While corporations generally tend towards the elimination of competition, this is a tendency that is particularly marked in the media industries. This is so because of the high fixed costs of entry into these businesses, and the attraction of concentrated media outlets with huge distribution networks to advertisers; and also because of the media's owners peculiarly enhanced ability to retain the very high cash-flow earnings associated with this kind of business. Those earnings create the foundation for merger and acquisition initiatives as cash-rich media owners look for investment opportunities. See Schmidt, Jr., *Freedom of the Press vs. Public Access*; Canada, Senate Special Committee on Mass Media, *Report of the Senate Special Committee on Mass Media* (Davey Report, 1970), *The Uncertain Mirror*. One major consequence of media concentration and the marginalization of the utility of speechifying and pamphleteering has been that the protection of free speech is to be left—for practical purposes—to the large-scale media that have colonized public space. In this setting it becomes natural to characterize a free press, that is, a press free from state interference, as the bulwark of democracy. Certainly, the major media do everything they can to further this characterization. Presumably this is why, in part, the guarantee for individuals to be able to speak freely in the Charter of Rights and Freedoms includes "freedom of the press and other media of communication." In part, this stems from the influence that U.S. politics and jurisprudence have had on our policy-makers and law-makers. This adaptation of the U.S. approach does not make analytical sense. In the United States there is a more natural tendency to give the press as much leeway as possible because it provides one of the few means of ensuring that government is held publicly accountable on a daily basis. The United States has no equivalent to the Canadian institution of a formal parliamentary opposition whose constitutional role it is to focus public attention on the ongoing operations of government. The fetish-like assumption that a free press is the end-all and be-all of democracy—an assumption that dominates U.S. public debate and influences judicial interpretations there—does not require the same ideological devotion in Canada. Still, the dominance of all debate by for-profit media does militate towards the acceptance of such an approach; but as we look for the antidote to elite propaganda, it would be facile to turn to the media that the Americans trust so much.

The so-called free press hardly reflects anything like the plurality of views and opinions that should be vying for attention in a polity in which free speech is the catalyst for democratic practices. Geoffrey Stevens, an opinion writer (later a publisher at *The Globe and Mail*) observed that, while there were differences between the opinion writers at major newspapers that appear to be veritable chasms in the context, the differences were more apparent than real. "The spectrum spans the distance between 'l' and 'n', rather than 'a' and 'z'." Similarly, Tom Wicker, a columnist with an established progressive pedigree at *The New York Times*, explained that while he and William Safire, his bed-rock conservative counterpoint, had complete freedom, they both knew that there were limits. "I could not argue that we should become socialists," he wrote, even though he acknowledged that there was no one who was telling him not to do so. See Glasbeek, "Entrenchment of Freedom of Speech." Or, as H.L. Mencken declared: "It is difficult to get a man to understand something when his income depends on his not understanding it." (As cited in Krugman, "Right-Wing Wrongs,"in Krugman, *Accidental Tourist*, p.61.)

The public does have the right to write letters to the editor, to offer guest articles, to appear on town-hall shows on television, to participate in talk-back radio, to be interviewed on television, and so on. But, all of this partial participation lies within the discretion of the media. If freedom of speech is to be limited in scope by for-profit peddlers of information and opinion, the freedom becomes illusory. A newspaper publisher appearing before the Senate Committee on the Mass Media (Canada,

Senate Special Committee on Mass Media, *Report*, p.8) pithily stated that freedom of the press amounted to no more than "the right of the public to buy a newspaper each day if they wish, to write letters to the editor, or to start a paper of their own if they don't like it."

In some jurisdictions, notably Sweden and Norway, taxes are levied on advertising revenues gathered by mainstream media and these funds are earmarked to subsidize alternative presses. The purpose is to ensure the diversity of news and opinion. Such measures have been advocated, but not implemented, elsewhere (Matthews, "Promotion of Press Diversity," and *Age of Democracy*; Curran and Seaton, *Power without Responsibility*; Baistow, *Fourth-Rate Estate*). That is, the very state, seen as the enemy of free speech in the American/Anglo world, is actually called upon to protect free speech and thought elsewhere. This is the obverse of our thought processes.

This is not to say that the media here set themselves against all of their domestic governments' platforms. Herman and Chomsky, *Manufacturing Consent*, have demonstrated, convincingly, that when it comes to foreign policy issues, something called the propaganda model works to make the position of large capital, embedded in state foreign policy, the only framework for media discussion and debate. The coverage of the so-called war on terrorism, after the events of Sept. 11, 2001, provides yet another example of the credibility of the propaganda model analysis. For instance, the mainstream media have not released much information about the relationship between Unocal Corporation, a would-be builder of a pipeline across Afghanistan, and the new, acceptable government in Kabul—information readily available in Europe. Alex Carey, in *7 Days* (1986), wrote that historians are likely to record the twentieth century "as distinguished by three developments. . . . The growth of democracy; the growth of corporate power; and the growth of propaganda as a means of protecting corporate power against democracy."

While the corporate media fiercely resist government control over their profit-making activities, they are more willing to be regulated by private-sector actors, by monied people. Sometimes this regulation is quite direct. Coca-Cola pulled its advertising from the World Wrestling Federation television programs because it did not want to be associated with profanity, obscene gestures, and images of pimps fighting over scantily clad women who pull each other's hair as they vie for the attention of the gladiators. The company, in other words, was objecting to all the things that make the program a success but that do not fit with Coca-Cola's carefully crafted image of cool and family-friendly values (*Toronto Star*, Nov. 30, Dec. 1, Dec. 7, 1999). The producers of *That's My Bush* were leaned upon by Comedy Central, their employer, which, in turn, is partly owned by media heavyweights Viacom and AOL/Warner. They were asked to curb their lampooning of the presidential family. The producers bemusedly agreed, although they countered that the purpose of the show was to make President Bush more lovable (*Toronto Star*, Jan. 26, 2001). David Letterman was forced to apologize profusely and frequently for having cracked a joke that maligned the product of an advertiser, Dr. Pepper. The advertiser was also given a free advertising spot during the network's highly rated Super Bowl program, a spot worth about $2.3 million to the sponsor (*Toronto Star*, Feb. 9, 2001). Private censorship is effective. But, when the private monied interests are happy to offend and flim-flam the public, then the most outrageous messages will be published, shown, or aired, and the media will defend these communications as uncensorable freedom of speech exercises, as political freedom acts. The controversial Benetton advertisements are a good example, as is the vigorous defence mounted on behalf of an advertising campaign by an Internet loan company. It had produced a photograph of a socialite in a Chanel suit with her hand up a cow's bottom with the message that one should put one's trust into experts in the field. The ad was described as being a little offensive, but still a clever exercise of free speech rights (*Australian Financial Review*, March 18–19, 2000).

The media corporations and the advertising corporations—trading on their freedom of speech rights—combine to produce ever more non-factual want-creating images and messages. Indeed, the media corporations are forced to compete with other outlets for this socially wasteful and harmful, but extremely profitable, advertising material. On Bastille Day, 2000, *The Globe and Mail* reported that Russia had bedecked—for a cool $1.25 million—its booster rocket for a space mission with a ten-metre high Pizza Hut logo. Not to be outdone, Global TV—a media corporation in the business of selling advertising space to others and requiring a high profile to attract that business—has contracted to cover twenty million apples with its logo (*Toronto Star*, Nov. 11, 1999). Private automobiles are being wrapped in vinyl—for a fee, of course—and turned into mobile billboards (*Toronto Star*, Aug. 8, 2000). Nothing is sacred. The Pope has been paid to agree to let his image appear on a telephone calling card, which will also carry his signature and a blessing for those who buy the card (*Toronto Star*, Nov. 12, 1999).

Corporations blend their messages and images with news, opinions, and everyday activities, so that they become inseparable from conventional information, political perspectives, and cultural norms. As Naomi Klein notes in *No Logo*, human beings become brands and the corporations become cultural artefacts. Nike is not known so much as a shoe company as a sporting body; McDonald's is more a story, a narrative, than it is a producer of hamburgers. The brands, images, and inherent messages are so much part of us that the major players have large businesses that trade on their success in identifying themselves as major institutions. Various corporations, such as Ford Motor Co., Binney & Smith, Ocean Spray and Kellog Co., M&M and Nike, run retail outlets cum museums detailing the histories of their products and founders. Coca-Cola has a three-storey pavilion known as the World of Coca-Cola in Atlanta. Its goal is to meet what it has said to be the insatiable demand of the consuming public to "touch and feel" things associated with its products. Hershey's Chocolate World in Hershey, Pennsylvania, attracts more visitors every year than does the White House (*Toronto Star*, Oct. 4, 1999). The marketing is intent on creating fantasies. Those fantasies increasingly become a sort of surreal reality, marketable items in their own right, which is the inevitable outcome of the drive to commodify everything.

As each corporation, pursuing profits for itself, helps establish a milieu in which everything is for purchase and sale—products, services, our human feelings, everything—a totalizing culture emerges. Gerbner (in Gerbner and Gross, "Living with Television," p.173) has, as have others (Deetz, *Democracy in an Age of Corporate Colonization*), likened this enculturation—his word—to the impact of religion on societies. It is not that a particular opinion or view is being moulded, but, rather, that a common consciousness is being created by the bombardment of marketing messages. Curran, in "Communications, Power and Social Order," makes a similar observation, linking the idea to the integration of the media with the corporations-for-profit sphere. He writes, "The communality of the Christian faith celebrated by Christian rites is now replaced by the communalities of consumerism and nationalism celebrated in the media." The dominance of television as a media outlet and a marketing and opinion-forming device has exacerbated this tendency. The picture portrays what is true and false, rather than the word. If it is not pictured it does not exist. The written press is increasingly adopting tabloid formats to compete with television, mirroring the emphasis of a visual representation of reality (Postman, *Amusing Ourselves to Death*). Mathieson, *Viewer Society*, describes our ensuing transformation into a viewer society, one in which the majority view and see, survey and admire, the few, the celebrities and elites. The content of information programming, turned into entertainment, causes us, in Postman's neat phrase, "to amuse ourselves to death." A piece in the *Financial Post*, June 26, 2000, chronicled how investment bankers crowd into a Wall Street neighbourhood establishment to watch re-runs of Seinfeld episodes while munching lunch. One person interviewed there said that he likes all the characters on the show, but especially George because he's "a liar and a cheat and he doesn't care about anybody else." The shaping of minds is integral to the puffery that the law treats so benignly.

Politicians, seeing the effectiveness of marketing techniques designed for profiteers in moulding and lowering public expectations, use them to run elections and craft government policies. The shortfall in democratic practices is serious. Social theorists who in recent times have pondered the utility of the search for holistic approaches—typical of Marxist-informed researchers—might find the picture presented here to be of some interest: the picture, that is, of how the apparent anarchic practices of private corporations and media outlets, dictated as they are by the overarching need to pursue the maximization of profits, lead to a totalizing view of the world.

8   Corporate Deviance and Deviants: The Fancy Footwork of Criminal Law

p.120, "There is a general presumption that an act is not a crime . . .": Law Reform Commission of Canada, *Our Criminal Law*.

p.121, In the Westray Mine affair: Nova Scotia. *Report of the Commission of Public Inquiry*.

p.121, Not just any Snickers bar: Weissman, "Sixteen Years for a Snickers Bar."

p.123, A study of welfare fraud documented: Martin, "Passing the Buck," p.52.

p.123, In contrast, another study shows: Reynolds, "Observations on Sentencing in 'White Collar' and 'Blue Collar' Fraud Cases."

p.123, In June 2001 a medical practitioner convicted of fraud: *Toronto Star*, June 14–15, 2001.

p.123, Eli Lilly, a corporation that earned $3.1 billion: McMullan, *Beyond the Limits of the Law*; Sherrill, "Murder Inc."

p.123, He was charged with a violation: Glasbeek and Mandel, "Crime and Punishment of Jean-Claude Parrot."

p.124, "This man has unique ability . . .": *New York Times Magazine*, May 9, 1993.

p.124, In a rather famous statement: Lord, "Dalkon Shield Litigation," p.7.

p.125, At the banquet, after much praise from the dignitaries: Mintz, *At Any Cost*; Sherrill, "Murder Inc."

p.125, By the time exposure came and mass litigation ensued: Cullen, Maakestad, and Cavender, *Corporate Crime under Attack*.

p.125, No one was ever charged with an offence: Brodeur, *Outrageous Misconduct*.

p.127, What motivated the courts to extend the application: R. v. *The Great North of England Railway Company* (1846).

p.131, The full dimensions of the problem: see Bequai, *White Collar Crime*; Ellis, *Wrong Stuff*; Michalowski, *Order, Law and Crime*; Snider, *Bad Business*; McMullan, *Beyond the Limits of the Law*; Clinard and Yeager, *Corporate Crime*.

p.131, . . . in the realm of what is called "suite crime": Snider, *Bad Business*.

p.131, Nevertheless, in the United States a 1980 study: Clinard and Yeager, *Corporate Crime*. Most of the existing data on corporate crime come from U.S. studies; but given the dominance of U.S. multinational corporations in Canada, this information provides a strong insight into deviant corporate conduct, and the harm inflicted, in Canada.

p.132, A conservative estimate is that the economic costs: Conklin, *Illegal but Not Criminal*.

p.132, Indeed, just one criminal act, the "Heavy Electrical Conspiracy": Clinard and Yeager, *Corporate Crime*.

p.132, The price-fixing by major petroleum corporations: Canada, *State of Competition in the Canadian Petroleum Industry* (1981); Anderson, "Curse of the Corporate Vampires."

p.132, Other less violent but no less costly crimes: Varette, Meredith, Robinson, and Huffman, *White Collar Crime*.

p.132, The Savings and Loans scandal of the 1980s: Snider, *Bad Business*; Calavita and Pontell, "'Heads I Win, Tails You Lose,'" p.309, "'Other People's Money' Revisited," p.94, and "Saving the Savings and Loans?"

p.133, The recent Enron events: Rohatyn, "Betrayal of Capitalism." For an earlier Canadian exemplar of financial skulduggery, see the $1 billion mugging of the public by the Commercial Bank and Northland Bank in Alberta (Canada, *Report of the Inquiry into the Collapse of the CCB and Northland Bank*, 1986); for money laundering and other deceptions of the world of finance, see Levi, *Regulating Fraud*, and his *Customer Confidentiality, Money Laundering and Police-Bank Relationships*.

p.133, . . . "our" corporations also use their ability to act across borders: see the film *Song of the Canary*; also Braithwaite, *Corporate Crime in the Pharmaceutical Industry*.

p.134, In this way, in Canada it managed to inflate: Pekkanen, *American Connection*, p.81. Germany, the Netherlands, and Denmark also confronted the company: Braithwaite, *Corporate Crime in the Pharmaceutical Industry*.

p.134, The government, through its bribe-accepting officials: Heller, *Poor Health, Rich Profits*; Yudkin, "Wider-World Provision of Medicines in a Developing Country," p.810.

p.134, Their offence was to have erased the expiry dates: Muller, *Health of Nations*.

p.xxx, It is a story that highlights not only the pervasive deviance: Adams, *Roche versus Adams*.

p.135, The court, it would seem, was not aware: Bobst, *Bobst*; see also Bruun, "International Drug Control and the Pharmaceutical Industry."

p.135, In January 2001, for instance, Exxon agreed to pay: *Australian Financial Review*, Jan.10, 2001, p.16.

p.135, A month earlier Exxon had been ordered: Associated Press, Dec. 19, 2000.

p.136, It polluted the river and imposed large clean-up costs: *Globe and Mail*, March 5, 1984.

p.136, A subsequent Congressional Inquiry found: 125 *Cong. Rec.* E 5658, daily ed., Nov. 15, 1978; Albanese, "Love Canal Six Years Later"; Brown, *Laying Waste*.

p.136, Once again, the corporation's officials had deliberately misled: *Los Angeles Times*, June 19, 1979.

p.136, On another occasion Occidental Chemical hid: information provided in the film *Song of the Canary*.

p.137, That settlement alone cost the corporation: *Toronto Star*, Aug. 16, Aug. 25, 2000.

p.137, There were a huge number of "accidents": *Newsweek*, Oct. 30, 1978; *Time*, June 25, 1979.

p.138, Pollution, energy waste, the cost of insurance, and the cost of traffic jams: Mokhiber, *Corporate Crime and Violence*.

p.138, As a result, many people were killed and many others suffered: Wright, *On a Clear Day You Can See General Motors*.

p.138, Although the manufacturer was eventually charged criminally: Dowie, "Pinto Madness"; Maakestad, "State v. Ford Motor Co."

p.139, It had been the kind of decision made regularly by all companies: *The Congressional Record* (Cong. Rec. E 3123–24, June 1979) tells the story.

p.139, In his pioneering study: Sutherland, "White Collar Crime," first published in 1940.

p.139, Many years later, in 1980: Clinard and Yeager, *Corporate Crime*.

p.139, A few years later, in a study of the commission of crimes: Kesner, Victor, and Lamont, "Board Composition and the Commission of Illegal Acts," p.29.

p.140, The literature fairly bristles with explanations: Merton, *Social Theory and Social Structure*; McMullan, *Beyond the Limits of the Law*; Snider, *Bad Business*; Glaser, "A Review of Crime-Causation Theory and Its Application"; Hirschi, *Causes of Delinquency*.

p.140, As E.H. Sutherland wrote over fifty years ago: Sutherland, "White Collar Crime."

p.141, Then, too, the explanations go: for points covered in this paragraph, see McMullan, *Beyond the Limits of the Law*; Snider, *Bad Business*; Gross, "Organizations as Criminal Actors"; Wells, *Corporations and Criminal Responsibility*; Sargent, "Law, Ideology and Social Change"; and Veblen, "Theory of the Leisure Class."

p.142, H.C. Barnett documented how corporations: Barnett "Corporate Capitalism, Corporate Crime."

p.142, For instance, one well-known study documented: Leonard and Weber, "Automakers and Dealers," p.407.

p.143, They were impelled to take these tremendous risks: see also Faberman, "Criminogenic Market Structure," p.438.

p.143, Contrary to some arguments: even though that is a line of argument presented by some scholars; see Gross, "Organizations as Criminal Actors"; Kreisberg, "Decision Making Models and Control of Corporate Crime," p.1091.

The rather dramatic lack of evenhandedness revealed by the text is only important if the legitimation of liberal criminal law is taken at face value, something that the defenders of the status quo ask the citizenry to do. The standard argument is that criminal law is there to protect our fundamental values, values on which we are supposed to have agreed. The shared consensual model claims to defend values and morals that are inherent to human nature and that, in pluralistic societies such as ours, have been mediated to reflect the way in which we have democratically resolved our competing interests. It follows that, with the state acting neutrally to enforce these beliefs, any one who violates the resulting criminal law will be prosecuted and convicted, regardless of their class position in society. This theorization of criminal law has been most sophisticatedly elaborated by Durkheim, *Division of Labor in Society*. It has a hard time explaining away the fact that it is mainly the poor and the propertyless who are the subject of prosecution and punishment. It is here that the causal theorists become active. Most of the causes that they offer to explain the commission of crimes are more likely to be found amongst the poor and the dispossessed than elsewhere. Presto, there is then little surprising about the fact that the jails are full of poor people. The work done by Reiman, *Rich Get Richer and the Poor Get Prison*, which, after studying and analysing the studies, recorded that serious crime is widespread amongst middle- and upper-class persons, that some forms of serious crimes show up as often among the well-to-do (who are largely left alone by the criminal justice system) as amongst the poor (who go to prison in enormous numbers), is discomfiting. It throws a trickle of cold water on the conventional criminal law paradigm. This should really become a torrent when we take into account the impunity of deviant corporations. The sample cases of corporate wrongdoing offered here are but the tip of an awesome iceberg. There is a rich documentation of wrongdoing by means of corporations and of the unpunished nature of these harmful malfeasances. An eclectic sampling follows.

For additional reading on the Dalkon Shield, see Sobol, *Bending the Law*. For a popular accounting of old Firestone malpractices, see Louis, "Lessons from the Firestone Fracas," p.45. For more details on the conspiracy to rip up America's public transit systems, see Kwitny, "Great Transportation Conspiracy," p.18. For more on the waste corporations' deviance, see Crooks, *Dirty Business*, and *Giants of Garbage*; and Block and Scarpatti, *Poisoning for Profit*. For the Love Canal saga, see Gibbs, *Love Canal: My Story*. For more on the mercury poisoning, see Shkilnyk, *Poison Stronger Than Love*. For a famed tale of disregard for workers, see Upton Sinclair's *The Jungle: The Lost First Edition*; for more contemporary analogous stories for very different workers, see W.G. Carson, *The Other Price of Britain's Oil*, on U.K. oil workers, Cassels, *Uncertain Promise of Law*, on the horrendous Bhopal saga (1993), as well as the Appen Report, *Bhopal Tragedy*. And for further proof that recidivism is common, see the tragic account of the role of Union Carbide—the corporation responsible for Bhopal—in the death of coal miners in the 1930s by Cherniack, *Hawk's Nest Incident*. For financial scams, see the bribery scandal surrounding Lockheed (Sampson, *Arms Bazaar*; Boulton, *Grease Machine*). For the cheating of the government by defence contractors, see Tyler, *Running Critical*; Weiner, *Blank Check*. For the frequency of banking offences, stock frauds, and money laundering, see Francis, *Controlling Interest*; Walter Stewart, *Towers of Gold*; Bailey, *Fall from Grace*; Cruise and Griffiths, *Fleecing the Lamb*; Ripley, *Roos of Bay Street*; James B. Stewart, *Den of Thieves*; and Soble and Dallos, *Impossible Dream*. For additional stories about environmental destruction linked to corporations, see Epstein, *Politics of Cancer*; Weir and Shapiro, *Circle of Poison*; Jackson, Weller, and WPIRG, *Chemical Nightmare*; Rachel Carson, *Silent Spring*; Ashworth, *Late Great Lakes*. For the pushing of drugs for profits by legal corporations, see Lexchin, *The Real Pushers*; Silverman and Lee, *Pills, Profits and Politics*.

In addition to this incomplete, ad hoc list of specific tales, there are many more general overviews of corporate deviance. See, for instance, a very early work by Ross, *Sin and Society* (1907); as well as Pearce, *Crimes of the Powerful*; Geis and Meier, *White Collar Crime*; Braithwaite, *Inequality, Crime and Public Policy*; Geis and Stotland, *White-Collar Crime*; Ermann and Lundman, *Corporate and Governmental Deviance*; Box, *Power, Crime, and Mystification*; Hills, *Corporate Violence*; Clinard, *Corporate Corruption*; Pearce and Woodiwiss, *Global Crime Connections*; Parkinson, *Corporate Power and Responsibility*; Wells, *Corporations and Criminal Responsibility*; Pearce and Snider, *Corporate Crime*; Mokhiber and Weissman, *Corporate Predators*; and Winslow, *Capital Crimes*.

In short, a great deal of popular and scientific evidence exists that documents massive, largely unpunished deviance, by actors devoid of any of the human character flaws and deficits that the defenders of the status quo would like us to believe cause individuals to commit crimes. It raises the spectre that there is strength in the other major theoretical explanatory framework for the existence and functioning of criminal law: this is that the law sets out to reflect the actual conflictual nature of our polity, rather than the assumed consensual one. From this perspective, conduct is defined as criminal when it is in the interests of those in power to so define it. The members of the ruling class will, largely, escape the strictures of these rules, precisely because the rules were not designed to apply to them. In a capitalist, class-based polity, the capitalists' influence over the state will protect them from stigmatization. There are many theorists who view the world in this way; see Chambliss and Mankoff, *Whose Law? What Order? A Conflict Approach to Criminology*, for the literature. This understanding does not get perplexed by the manifest lack of evenhandedness in the administration of the criminal justice system. The rich are meant not to be held responsible. This is doubly true when they hide behind the corporate veil designed to afford them irresponsibility.

A final note is that the development of a rather awkward legal doctrine to enable us to hold corporations criminally responsible, even though they lack a mind to form a criminal intent and a body by which to carry out as criminal intent, may be seen as a response to the resonance that the conflict-based theories gain from the impunity to do harm by deviant means, a condition that corporations have enjoyed for so long. At the same time, however, the knowledge that it is real flesh and blood people who cause the corporation to commit a crime tends to be hidden from view once the pressure to hold someone responsible has been somewhat relieved. The holding of a corporation as having the capacity to commit a crime leads to the very reification that serves the wealth-owning classes so well. They are helped in this by some finely crafted theories suggesting that, when enveloped inside a complex organization, individuals act as organizational "men" rather than as individuals. The more progressive of these analysts call for a special set of criminal rules that would pursue corporate deviance, arguing that those involved are not behaving as criminals as commonly understood, even if their behaviour is more unacceptable than most individual criminal conduct; see Sargent, "Law, Ideology and Social Change," p.97; Wells, *Corporations and Criminal Responsibility*; French, *Collective and Corporate Responsibility*; and Parkinson, *Corporate Power and Responsibility*. While some slight legislative movements have proceeded in these directions, they are far from mainstream. In the meanwhile, liberal law allows every step taken towards unmasking corporate mystification to be countered by the captains of industry, retail, finance, and everything else (see chapter 10).

9 "It's Not a Crime" – Reclassifying Corporate Deviance

p.146, The question, our appellate courts keep on telling investigators: *Canadian Dredge and Dock Co. Ltd. v. The Queen.*

p.148, He wrote: *R. v Amway*, unreported, 1983.

p.149, In one of the more famous formulations: Lord Devlin, *Enforcement of Morals.*

p.151, The Law Reform Commission of Canada: *Our Criminal Law* (1976).

p.153, Scholars refer to this as "legitimation and accumulation": O'Connor, *Fiscal Crisis of the State.*

p.154, John Kenneth Galbraith quoted the pithy observation: Galbraith, *Age of Uncertainty*, p.48.

p.155, For instance, a senior Westinghouse executive was asked: Geis and Meier, *White Collar Crime.*

p.155, . . . the "structural immorality of corporations": Box, *Power, Crime, and Mystification*; and Jackall, *Moral Mazes.*

p.155, The managers work in a subculture of immorality: Lane, "Why Businessmen Violate the Law"; Geis, 1967; Clinard, *Illegal Corporate Behaviour.*

p.155, Eric Tucker established how this approach: Tucker, *Administering Danger in the Workplace.*

p.155, . . . given a name: the pyramid method of regulatory enforcement: Ayers and Braithwaite, *Responsive Regulation.*

p.156, Indeed, if the criminal law proper needs to be employed: Shapiro, *Wayward Capitalists.*

p.156, The harm-inflicting acts are: Hart, "Immorality and Treason."

p.157, The blindingly, disarmingly, and totally unhelpful reply: *R. v. City of Sault Ste. Marie*, (1978); *R. v. Vasil* (1981).

p.158, The prosecution did not succeed: Maakestad, "State v. Ford Motor Co.," p.857.

p.158, This evidence was the cold-hearted in-house memoranda: Dowie, "Pinto Madness."

p.158, When this evidence was allowed: *Grimshaw v. Ford Motor Co.*

p.159, From the early 1990s on, people injured: *Toronto Star*, May 20, 1994.

p.160, A California court took the opposite approach: see Sterngold, "California Justices Ban Suit against Gun Manufacturers."

p.161, No criminal charges were laid: Coroner's Inquest into the Death of Daniel Tardif, Francois Lamarra, Robert Paquet, Nov. 13, 1978, case no. 1660–78.

p.162, No criminal charges were brought: *New York Times*, May 11, 1974.

p.165, The judges reasoned: *Consumer Education and Research Centre v. Union of India*, pp.940, 938.

p.166, Another, contrasting, statement: Posner, *Economics of Justice*, pp.83–84.

The *Canadian Dredge* case was concerned with a lucrative criminal scam. In essence, the government put out tenders to ask private actors to bid for the contracts to dredge the government-regulated lakes and rivers. The main competitors in the field got together to avoid the rigours of market competition. They engaged in pre-bid discussions as to which of them should submit the lowest bid this time round. The winning bidder would disburse some of the too-highly priced contract proceeds to the fellow conspirators. The means deployed to hide the fake transactions were sophisticated. For the conspirators every tender was a win situation for all of them; for the taxpayers and the government every contract registered a loss. The acknowledged losses were more than $4 million in respect of the seven counts of the final indictment, a number much smaller than the prosecutors' original wish list. Initially there had been twenty accused corporations and individuals. Eventually, after bargaining, the number was reduced to thirteen accused parties; forty allegations of other conspiratorial incidents were dropped altogether. The caper came to be known as Harbourgate. In fact, it was run by a handful of human beings who turned on each other. Thus it was not all that hard to uncover the guiding minds and wills behind all the corporate wrongdoing. Even so, the practical difficulties that attend the application of criminal law to corporate deviance were on display. The miscreants had created a huge web of corporations through which to practise their skulduggery. The court record shows the difficulties encountered (even though the main human offenders were well-known) in trying to identify who was with what corporation, who controlled which one, and who had switched capital investment where and to which other legal person in the web of intrigue. All of this was complicated by the frequent changes in the corporations, creating apparently new, distinct legal persons. That is, even when it comes to tightly held and controlled corporate empires, the task facing prosecutors is daunting and costly, which inhibits the laying of charges. The corporate world and the legal profession that serves it slavishly know this and trade on the difficulty. Ringleb and Wiggins, "Liability and Large Scale, Long-Term Hazards," p.574, document a widespread and conscious use of the separate legal personality trait by captains of industry, retail, finance, and everything else. Roe, "Corporate Strategic Reaction to Mass Tort," has argued how this is an inevitable by-product of efforts to attribute responsibility to profit-maximizers entitled to employ the corporate business form.

The *Amway* cases—the first case concerned the criminal responsibility of the corporation for its fraudulent transfer pricing; the second focused on the quasi-criminal process to exact an administrative penalty from the guilty corporation—featured another trait that inhibits the effective use of criminal law in corporate deviance cases. While, as in *Canadian Dredge*, the actual human wrongdoers were clearly visible and, therefore, it was easy enough to identify the persons who constituted the guiding mind and will of the deviant corporation, it was not easy for the Crown to gather the evidence of intentional wrongdoing. This put the captains of Amway in the driver's seat. They did a deal that is all too common in this field. They agreed to have the corporation plead guilty, helping the prosecution no end. But the price was that they were to be given immunity from criminal prosecution, even though, as the court bitterly noted, the leaders of Amway had behaved scandalously. This did not worry these now legally immune wrongdoers, as it rarely does any of the many executives and shareholders who use this kind of bargaining leverage. Indeed, having been excoriated as moral lepers in Canada, the chief executives and major shareholders of Amway had the gall to get the corporation to take out advertisements in major U.S. newspapers. These advertisements explained that the corporation had pleaded guilty to the violation of some rather technical Canadian laws and had admitted its guilt, not out of shame or because it had actually done something seriously wrong, but rather so that it could get on with making money for its beloved shareholders without the distraction of having to deal with Canadian regulators. The Republican Party and Ronald Reagan must have been reassured, because they continued to accept political and financial support offered by Amway's leaders. This is truly a world in which the actors have little or no shame.

Inasmuch as these aspects of corporate personality shed some light on why it is that, because of technical hurdles and devices, corporate deviance is treated more favourably than are street crimes, the Law Reform Commission's frank statement that the principal goal of criminal law is the protection of the sanctity of private property goes a long way towards explaining a phenomenon noted in the previous chapter, namely that welfare abuses are treated as being far more serious than tax-law violations are. Welfare recipients, people who have no property to protect, are seen as taking money from the state, that is, from other people's pockets. They need to be monitored and disciplined. By contrast, tax evaders are seen as trying to protect *their* property from the state and, therefore, they are justified in taking steps to do so, even if the particular steps taken turn out to be unacceptable. Welfare abusers are portrayed as never-do-wells, while tax evaders are perceived as good guys who might have gone too far. This is all due to the internalization of a capitalist starting point, one that views existing inequalities as neutral, not problematic. For elaborations, see Sossin, "Welfare State Crime in Canada"; and Glasbeek, "Looking Back towards a Bleak Future for Lawyers." Acknowledgement of the deep-rooted nature of this starting point also helps us to understand better the findings by scholars such as Reiman, *Rich Get Richer and the Poor Get Prison*, to the effect that many well-to-do individuals commit serious violations and are far more favourably handled by the criminal justice system than are the poor and the working classes. This is what an unequal polity, one based on class differences and conflict between the classes, would lead us to expect. Liberal theorists and conventional pundits have a problem because they pretend that formal equality and equality of opportunity are enough to guarantee evenhanded treatment. This creates an endemic problem for liberal law in a capitalist economy, as the working classes and the poor are made the butt of coercive law and find it hard to offset the hurts caused by the economic activities of the economically and politically powerful. It is this problematic that, in part, is sought to be resolved by the introduction of welfare regulatory law.

Welfare regulations, intended as constraints on corporate behaviour vis-à-vis workers, consumers, and the environment, have not come easily. They have required herculean efforts by those who want to mediate the harsher impacts of corporate capitalism. Snider, *Bad Business*, p.97, notes, "It took a series of deaths, injuries, accidents, and investigations before meaningful laws governing the manufacture of food were secured." She records similar hardships and struggles in all major fields of modern welfare law. And, as these regulations came, the corporations worked at making the inevitable mediations less restrictive to them. They used, and use, their economic clout to make welfare regulation work in their favour. There is much evidence about both their strenuous efforts and the degree of their success; see Kolko, *Wealth and Power in America* and *Roots of American Foreign Policy*; Domhoff, *Who Rules America?* and *The Higher Circles*; and Snider, *Bad Business*. All of this leads some observers to be sceptical of the utility of the regulatory welfare schemes. Morris, "Help! I've Been Colonized and I Can't Get Up . . ." argues that these regimes, especially environmental ones, really regulate citizen input rather than corporate behaviour. While many see this strong view as, perhaps, a little too slighting to the legions of well-meaning people who have fought—and are fighting—valiant battles to get better governmental responses to corporate capitalism's inherent brutishness, Snider, a scholar who does take great care to pay respect to those struggles, has had to record (in "Relocating Law: Making Corporate Crime Disappear") that many of the protections that had been won in recent decades were being rolled back at an alarming pace by the 1990s. Corporate capital, using the umbrella and mantra of intensified competition in an era of globalization, is now flexing its muscles ever more effectively.

10   New Corporate Responsibilities – or More Window Dressing?

p.171, For instance, the numbers of assaults and murders: Reasons, Ross, and Paterson, *Assault on the Worker.*

p.171, "Capitalism is toxic": Pearce and Toombs, *Toxic Capitalism.*

p.172, This much-noted fine was the equivalent: Geis, "Criminal Penalties for Corporate Crimes," p.377.

p.172, Clinard and Yeager, in their major study of giant corporations' wrongdoing: Clinard and Yeager, *Corporate Crime.*

p.172, Clarke made similar findings: Clarke, *Business Crime.*

p.172, Ermann and Lundman provided an insight: Ermann and Lundman, *Corporate and Governmental Deviance*; see also Snider, *Bad Business*, p.163.

p.172, Stanbury made similar calculations: Stanbury, "Penalties and Remedies under the Combines Investigation Act 1899–1974," p.571.

p.172, The fines represented tiny percentages: See also Goff and Reasons, *Corporate Crime in Canada.*

p.173, Rogue capitalists are not to be allowed: Shapiro, *Wayward Capitalists.*

p.175, "Due diligence" has been interpreted: *R. v. Bata Industries*, (1992).

p.176, The evident public appetite for holding corporate directors and managers responsible: The business papers' headlines of the day tell the story: "New Challenges for Directors" (*Financial Post*, July 23, 1992); "Don't Drive Directors from Boards" (*Financial Post*, Aug. 10, 1992); "Liability Chills Heads for Liability Freeze" (*Globe and Mail*, July 31, 1992); "Why Would Anyone Be a Director?" (*Financial Post*, July 3, 1992); "The Fall Guys" (*Toronto Star*, March 14, 1993).

p.176, Business journalists and academic shills for corporate capital: For instance, note the title of a piece by the now dean of the University of Toronto Law School, R.J. Daniels: "Must Boards Go Overboard? An Economic Analysis of the Effects of Burgeoning Statutory Liability on the Role of Directors." See also Daniels and Hutton, "Capricious Cushion," p.182.

p.176, Famous and supposedly intelligent people are continuing to fall over themselves: Glasbeek, "More Direct Director Responsibility."

p.176, The only available study found: Cited by the Toronto Stock Exchange's report, "Where Were the Directors?" (1994).

p.177, If managers can be forced to take responsibility: Glasbeek, "Why Corporate Deviance Is Not Treated as Crime," p.393.

p.178, Despite a myriad of proposals for more innovative sanctions: On counterpublicity, see Fisse, "Use of Publicity as a Criminal Sanction against Business Corporations," p.107; and Fisse and Braithwaite, *Impact of Publicity on Corporate Offenders*; on special issues of share, see Coffee, "'No Soul to Damn: No Body to

Kick'"; and on the designing of restructuring orders, see Glasbeek, "Corporate Social Responsibility Movement."

p.179, This difficulty of calibrating sanctions has been the subject: Glasbeek, "More Direct Director Responsibility"; Parker, "Criminal Sentencing Policy for Organizations," p.513; Macey, "Agency Theory and the Criminal Liability of Organizations," p.421; Saltzburg, "Control of Criminal Conduct in Organizations," p.421; U.S. Sentencing Committee, "Sentencing Guidelines for Organizational Defendants": Becker, "Crime and Punishment"; Block, "Optimal Penalties, Criminal Law and the Control of Corporate Behaviour."

p.179, Thus it also has held that a corporation can hide behind the Charter of Rights and Freedoms guarantee: *Hunter v. Southam* (1984).

p.180, The Supreme Court of Canada ameliorated the situation somewhat: *R. v. McKinley Transport Limited* (1990); *Thomson Newspapers v. Director of Investigations and Research* (1990).

p.181, The corporation had operated a clandestine mercury reclamation plant: *People v. Pymm* (1990); see also Cimino."Workplace Safety Violations," p.1007.

p.181, In England, too, there has been a recent spurt of such charges: *R. v. Kite, Stoddard and OLL* (1994); see also Slapper, "Corporate Killing," p.1735.

p.181, In Canada, too, there have been occasional, but rarely successful, attempts: Tucker, "Westray Mine Disaster and Its Aftermath," p.91; and Glasbeek and Tucker, "Death by Consensus."

p.182, This speaks volumes about the success of the corporate sectors: Glasbeek and Rowland, "Are Injuring and Killing at Work Crimes?" p.507.

One of the intriguing features of the attempts by legislators to assert their relative autonomy, while undergirding the legitimacy of the accumulation process, is how different factions of the state work in conflict with each other, sometimes in contradictory ways with themselves. This incoherence springs from the limited sovereignty that the state enjoys within capitalism, the strength of market ideology—particularly amongst judges— and the strenuous efforts of individual corporate capitalists to undo constraining regulation even if this regulation serves capitalism well as a system.

A good example is furnished by the recent Ontario Court of Appeal decision in *R. v. Inco.* As noted, there have been invigorated efforts to make welfare regulations more efficient by, amongst other things, reversing the burden of proof, in part at least, and by holding individual directors and senior managers personally responsible for their failure to set up and implement due diligence systems. These efforts were buttressed by the *Bata* decision, another decision of the Ontario Court of Appeal. But, that same court, in *Inco,* held that inspectors who suspect a violation of regulations need to obtain a warrant before they can investigate. This limitation on unannounced inspections and investigations could become inhibiting to those charged with the duty of monitoring the activities of the regulatees. This is all the more true as the Court of Appeal did not provide much by way of guidelines as to how inspectors are supposed to determine when they should obtain warrants. Most likely this decision will be appealed by the government, or perhaps additional legislation will be passed to offset its chilling effect. But in itself the case illustrates the fierceness of the corporate legal world as it seeks to ward off any and all restraints on profit-maximization. The strength of that corporate desire is nicely caught by the title of an article welcoming the *Inco* decision: "Righting an Old Wrong," by Edwards and Parris.

Inco made its case by relying on s.8 of the Charter of Rights and Freedoms, namely the section that provides individuals such as you and me with protection against unreasonable searches and seizures by the state. The issue of whether a corporation could use this kind of political protection designed for citizens was not a problem, as it already had been decided in favour of corporations by the Supreme Court of Canada in the *Southam* case in 1984, a scant three years after the drafting of the Charter. That corporations would be able to exploit the Charter to attack democratically enacted regulatory schemes was not something that was made entirely clear to the public when they were being offered the guarantee of rights. Some critics had issued warnings (see Hasson, "How to Hand Weapons to Your Enemies"), but the powers-that-be categorically denied that fat non-human cats would benefit. Jean Chrétien, as Minister of Justice, and his officials were reported as stressing that the wording of the proposed Charter was designed to benefit individuals, not entities. It was only after the infamous kitchen meeting in late November 1981, at which Quebec's fate was sealed, that Roy McMurtry, the Attorney General of Ontario, let the (fat) cat out of the bag. He spoke at a meeting of the corporate elite and their worried lawyers in Toronto. As a man reaping much kudos in Central Canada for the constitutional deal-making that had brought us the Charter, he went out of his way to tell his audience not to be anxious about the Charter because the newly declared freedoms would not give consumers and workers an edge in their battles against the corporate world. While the Charter spoke of protections for individuals, McMurtry averred, "Our courts would not engage in such narrow and mean-spirited interpretations as to deny the protection of the Charter to corporate entities." A panel of expert lawyers at this same meeting supported McMurtry and argued that "with some liberal interpretations . . . the rights' code might give corporations greater legal protection from a number of restrictive laws." See *Globe and Mail*, Feb. 6, 1982, p.A12.

The corporations have got their liberal interpretations. While the Supreme Court of Canada (in *Amway*) gagged on granting the privilege against self-incrimination—so clearly aimed at safeguarding human beings from torture and other direct coercion—to a corporation, acknowledging that, in the corporation, courts were giving legal personality to a fictitious being, they have found ways and means of allowing corporations to speak and spend as if they were speaking, to claim privacy rights, to assert their religious right to conduct retail business on Sundays, to be relieved from undue delay in being brought to justice, and so on. They made those successful claims in order to ward off the application of regulatory laws, not because they wanted to defend fundamental political principles. The reasoning used by the courts in acceding to these claims, falsely clothed in civil liberty garb, varies from permitting corporations to make Charter claims if human beings could bring them, even if they have no interest in doing so, to reading the Charter provision as if its content, rather than the person engaged in it, is what needs to be protected, to characterizing the corporation not as a fiction but as a real person. For a good analysis of this tendency, see Tollefson, "Corporate Constitutional Rights and the Supreme Court of Canada," p.309. Whatever the merit of the reasoning, the superior courts have not engaged in narrow and mean-spirited interpretations when it comes to corporate rights. This approach speaks clearly to the judicial desire to reify the fictitious person it has done so much to establish, to have this entity perceived as the equal of the sovereign individual whose welfare is said to be the ultimate goal of the Rule of Law. This legalization of corporate capitalism's legitimacy has gone a long way and invites corporations to challenge democratically enacted laws. Significantly, the bench of judges that decided the corporation-favouring Charter decision in *Inco* was presided over by this same McMurtry, now Chief Justice of the province. For elaborations offered at different time periods, indicating the constancy of the trend to protect corporations from interventionist governments, see Glasbeek, "A No-Frills Look at the Charter of Rights and Freedoms or How Politicians and Lawyers Hide Reality," p.293.

Corporations counterattack on all fronts. In addition to clever and plausible-sounding legal arguments, they are willing to engage in emotional blackmail, ignoring such evidence as does exist and relying on specious arguments offered by intellectual gatekeepers. Thus, at the very time that corporate and financial experts were raising the spectre that the legislators' well-meant but ill-thought-out imposition of new responsibilities on senior management would lead to a dearth of qualified managers to govern our wealth-producing corporations, an impressive list of well-known personages were queuing up to get the prestige, money, and inside information bestowed by directorships. At about the time that the Molson Company's brief to the Toronto Stock Exchange argued that "this imposition of directors' liability will inevitably lead to the diminution of qualified business advice and counsel," a former Progressive Conservative finance minister was accepting a position on the board of Amoco. He was to be paid $44,000 in cash and stock for attending meetings held monthly. Former Prime Minister Mulroney became a director of American Barrick Resources, at $12,000 per year, plus $600 per meeting attended, all this in addition to generous stock options. His wife, Mila Mulroney, was appointed to the board of Astral Communications, and a former cabinet member, Don Mazankowski, went to the board of Gulf Canada Resources. This list of Progressive Conservatives success in corporate ranks is mirrored whenever Liberals leave government, which goes to demonstrate a number of points. First, these people are not frightened by the new sets of responsibilities; second, the work is not too arduous; and, three, the rewards are high. It also shows the integration of large corporate capital and elected government, a matter that must duly influence the stringency (or not) of regulation and enforcement. The directorship is a cheap, persuasive tool utilized by corporations to dilute interventionism. For elaboration of the lack of empirical and intellectual foundation for the arguments to the effect that no decent leadership for corporations will be available in the future, see Glasbeek, "More Direct Director Responsibility."

These impediments to holding corporations to account for the harms they do and the violations they commit undergird the efforts of critical scholars and activists to find other ways of holding corporations responsible for their actions. This is why the notion of using publicity of corporate wrongdoing as a deterrent and educational tool gains some momentum. The difficulty of making this tactic work is obvious. After all, the leaders in the making of opinion and of public manipulation are to be found in the very corporate sectors sought to be controlled. They are likely to outwit and outspend any state bureaucracy charged with the daunting task of making them look unattractive. Indeed, two of the more enthusiastic and scholarly supporters of this tactic have found that the results of adverse publicity on discovered wrongdoers have been mixed. In their seventeen case studies, Fisse and Braithwaite (1983), found that only in four cases were the results positive, in the sense that the corporation felt it necessary to give itself a new image by setting up tighter monitoring and governance systems. In some, there were no discernible outcomes, and in four there were negative consequences, in that the violating corporations had been able to exploit the attendant notoriety to their benefit. Perhaps this is one of the reasons that these two serious analysts have come to favour the creation of a category of special crimes that would be easier to prove because they would be tailored to the behaviour of the corporation as an aggregate that is more than the sum of its parts. This organizational approach has been supported by a number of scholars; see Fisse and Braithwaite, (1985–88); Wells, *Corporations and Criminal Responsibility*; and Sargent, "Law, Ideology and Social Change."

While this approach has not yet gained favour in the courts or in most Anglo-American legislatures, in Australia the federal government has enacted legislation that will hold a corporation criminally responsible if it has a cultural predisposition towards deviance. The mountains to climb to establish such a predisposition are very high; Glasbeek, "Occupational Health and Safety: Criminal Law as a Political Tool," p.95. Other clever, but as yet unused, proposals include the equity fine suggested by Coffee, "'No Soul to Damn: No Body to Kick,'" p.806, who notes that the fine needed to deter a rationally deviant corporation was an amount that equalled the sum expected to be made from the violating conduct multiplied by the calculated chance of being caught and convicted. Thus, if the anticipated ill-gotten loot would be $1 million and the chance of getting found out 10 per cent, the fine would have to be a minimum of $10 million. The rational sums are too large and would not be imposed by courts concerned with the maintenance of the corporation, which has creditors and workers, among others, who depend on its continued existence. Coffee argues that what could be done was to force the corporation to issue shares. This would punish all the existing shareholders, including the negligent or criminal managers, by diluting the value of their holdings, without threatening the immediate viability of the corporation. The very need for such cleverness points to the deficiencies of the ordinary legal processes by which we regulate wrongdoing. Interestingly, what is rarely suggested, even by the more progressive forces, is that the major shareholders— that is, the real captains of industry, retail, finance, and everything else—should be held personally responsible for the conduct of the vehicles that carry on business and commit the wrongs on their behalf. Yet once this approach was considered sensible. For instance, in New York state, corporate law made shareholders responsible for the debts of the corporation to the workers, on the assumption that these debts were incurred on their behalf; see *Mesheau v. Campbell* (and also chapter 14 here).

11   The Legal Corporate Social Responsibility Movement: A Politics of Impotence

p.183, For accounts of the plight of the Ijaws of Nigeria, see the Kaiama Declaration, at www.moles.org/ProjectUnderground/oil/index.shtml. See also "100 Reasons Why the Ijaw Nation Wants to Control Its Resources," *Niger Delta Today*, July 4, 2001 groups.yahoo.com/group.Ijaw_National_ Congress.

p.184, In any one year, Nike pays Michael Jordan to advertise its sneakers: Fudge, "Consumers to the Rescue?"

p.184, Talisman Energy is a joint venturer: For the Talisman story, there are many sources. Easily accessible are reports by business reporters: Drohan, "Into Africa," p.82; and Wells, "Ethics and Oil Brew up a Toxic Mixture in Sudan," p.E1.

p.184, Occidental Petroleum, implicated in the Colombia Plan, is the same corporation involved in Love Canal and the *Song of the Canary* saga.

p.185, A study by the Conference Board of Canada found: Conference Board of Canada, *Market Explorers Survey of Canadians*.

p.185, In Britain a 1999 poll showed: Canadian Democracy and Corporate Accountability Commission, *An Overview of Issues*.

p.185, Many of those polled believed: EDK Associates, INC, "Corporate Irresponsibility: There Ought to be Some Laws."

p.186, "Without losing sight of its basic economic role . . ." Quoted in Broadbent, "Democracy and Corporations."

p.186, He wrote of the need to create a new financial architecture: Hutton, *State We're In*.

p.186, Charles Handy asserts that: Handy, *Hungry Spirit beyond Capitalism*.

p.186, In a widely cited declaration, Justice Thomas Berger of the B.C. Supreme Court wrote: *Teck Corporation Ltd. v. Millar* (1973), p.385.

p.187, Corcoran, "Disclosing the Great Stakeholder Hoax," p.B4.

p.190, Similar statements were offered by major corporations: Clarkson, "In Praise of the Stakeholder Concept"; for a more scholarly account, see Clarkson, *Corporation and Its Stakeholders*.

p.190, Somewhat later, a slightly different and more technologically narrow view: Burnham, *Managerial Revolution*; Ireland, "Corporate Governance, Stakeholding and the Company," p.287.

p.191, As early as 1932, E.M. Dodd had argued that the Berle and Means evidence: Dodd, "For Whom Are Corporate Managers Trustees?"; Berle, "Modern Functions of the Corporate System," and *Power without Property*.

p.195, As a matter of practice, that task was also being left: Mace, *Directors*, and "Directors: Myth and Reality—Ten Years Later," p.293.

p.195, It is the preferred means of overcoming the inefficiencies: Gilson and Kraakman, "Reinventing the Outside Director," p.863.

p.195, But, as it turns out, such empirical evidence as there is: Brudney "Independent Director," p.597; Stapledon and Lawrence, "Board Composition and Independence in Australia's Largest Companies," p.150; Hill, "Deconstructing Sunbeam," p.1099.

p.196, In 1985, he wrote: Beck, "Corporate Power and Public Policy."

p.196, Lord Wedderburn rightly refers to the Beck-like statements: Wedderburn, "Trust, Corporation and the Worker," p.203.

p.197, This does not still the controversy: The literature on the debates between social responsibility proponents and their opponents is too voluminous to be canvassed here. For a discussion of this literature, see Glasbeek, "Corporate Social Responsibility Movement."

p.198, Daniel Greenwood points out: Greenwood, "Fictional Shareholders," p.1021.

p.199, David Olive records a number of instances: Olive, *Just Rewards*.

p.199, Not only were the boards of directors and their managers thus favoured: Section 137, Canada Business Corporations Act.

p.200, For instance, a large segment of a leading journal: *Canadian Business Law Journal*, vol. 30 (1998), pp.20–84.

p.200, In the only major survey done: Crete, *Proxy System in Canadian Corporations*.

p.200, The situation thus generated pressures for legislative reform: *An Act to Amend the Canada Business Corporations Act and the Canada Cooperatives Act and to Amend Other Acts in Consequence*, Statutes of Canada, 2001, c.14.

p.201, Unlike in the United States, where shareholding in most large corporations is diffuse: Beck, "Corporate Power and Public Policy"; Francis, *Controlling Interest.*

p.202, But, despite the anxiety generated in the breasts of true believers: Glasbeek, "More Direct Director Responsibility," p.416.

p.202, There are plenty of blue-ribbon outfits: Toronto Stock Exchange, "Where Were the Directors?"

p.203, As a simultaneously horrified and titillated: *Business Week*, Sept. 11, 2000, p.182.

p.203, This mechanism of payment, a common one: Crystal, *In Search of Excess.*

Instances such as the Talisman case and another issue that has recently captured public imagination, the Sierra Leone diamonds, illustrate the difficulty of drawing a line between aggressive and legitimate profit-chasing and unacceptable profit-maximization. The conventional view is that it is easy to draw the line: Talisman should get out of Sudan, where its profiteering helps a nasty government against good rebels; and diamond corporations are to make sure that the diamonds they peddle do not have an ugly provenance. The allegation in the case of Sierra Leone is that vicious militants use illegally obtained diamonds to finance their unacceptable wars against decent governments and people. Yet what is easy about these cases except that our governments have determined which side they are on in the disputations? Imagine if it were the governments that we favour that used diamonds to finance their wars on rebels: would we want to inhibit the ordinary diamond corporations in the same way, even if the favoured governments kill rebels? Would we feel better about Talisman's ventures in the Sudan if they suited the more appealing opponents of the incumbent government? Dow Chemical made a lot of money out of producing Agent Orange on behalf of the Pentagon when it was thought right to devastate a country. The Talisman, Sierra Leone, and Dow Chemical instances are, similarly, stories of normal capitalist calculations whose impacts we, with hindsight, turn out not to like. Compare them to the production of asbestos and tobacco, endeavours we once did like, although we now seem to regret them, a little at least.

Corporate actors have no guidance, except that they should pursue profits within the limits of the law. Until the law is changed, it is irrational to ask corporations to carry out our foreign policies for us. Until the law is changed, the corporations can claim to be occupying the high moral ground. They can, and often do, argue that, because they are part and parcel of the civilized world, which features liberal market practices, their involvement in the economies of more backwards polities is likely to have a civilizing influence. This is, of course, the argument that was accepted by the governments of the United Kingdom and United States when they refused to impose legal economic boycotts on South Africa. It is, of course, the argument accepted by the advanced industrialized nations as their corporations scramble for markets in China, despite the oft-declared distaste for China's human rights record. Precisely because capital requires production for profit, not need, its chief vehicle, the corporation, has no moral lodestar.

This starting point makes it difficult to count on a strategy that would lead to reforms that would transform directors and senior executives of these amoral organizations into stewards of the public weal, as if they were more like public servants than the representatives of the wealth-accumulating class. The notion that they might be something like public servants arises, in part, from their self-image, and public portrayal, as highly professional people. "Professional" here means not just that they are good at their jobs, but also that they possess responsible citizenship qualities. But, on both these counts, some scepticism is warranted. While a great number of the outside and independent directors of large publicly traded corporations are themselves senior executives of other large, publicly traded corporations and, therefore, deemed to have plenty of business savvy, this does not mean that they want to be held to professional standards when the time comes to measure their legal accountability. They trade on their integrity, their know-how, their professionalism, in social and political settings. This gives them their influence and their big pay packets. When it is a question of legal liability, these captains of industry, retail, finance, and everything else have made their feelings clear: they want to be treated as if they should be expected to have no more ability than the ordinary Canadian, non-business-minded person on the street. Thus, in 1967, when *The Report of the Select Committee on Company Law* (Ontario, the Lawrence Report), recommended that a director's duty should be that appropriate to that of a "reasonably prudent *director*," the corporate bar sprang into action on behalf of its clienteles and got language, which is today's language, that imposes a standard of care reflecting that of a "reasonably prudent *person*." The emphasis is that there is no requirement to have special, professional-like qualifications.

This approach allows corporations to appoint directors whose sad lack of ability makes them decorative, but useless. It allows the appointment of eminent politicians to the boards of significant corporations, to pay them off for past generosities or to hold out to the public that this corporation deserves to be treated with respect and largesse. David Olive, in *Toronto Star*, Oct. 19, 2001, p.A1, provides some nice examples of how some of these politicians must be delighted that they cannot be held to a professional duty of care. Former Ontario Premier Bill Davis was a director of a number of corporations that went belly-up when he was one of their legal stewards. Bramalea, Dylex, and Algoma Steel were some of the corporations with which he was associated. Of course, he may have been just unlucky. Still, he was also with Corel Corporation, whose lack of fiscal discipline while he was there went unchecked by him. The chief executive officer of Corel, over whom Davis and the other directors exercised oversight, allegedly engaged in dubious trading practices. If they were engaged in, they were undetected by Davis and his fellow directors. Equally unlucky might also have been John Turner, a former prime minister, a director of Harvard International Technologies and of Curragh Resources Inc., the Westray mine owner.

Despite these evident lack of legal standards—which makes the idea that all would be well if only the executives were given the legal green light to look after stakeholders look pretty far-fetched—executives and directors keep on arguing that their arduous tasks and the responsibility of their position earn them the right to big bucks—very big bucks. They fear, of course, that the outside world does not understand the weight of the personal and legal burdens they bear and would, therefore, like to keep their earnings as secret as possible. When the Canadian regulators sought to bring our executives into line with those in the United States (where executive remunerations and their bases for calculation had to be disclosed), there was a howl of protest from our various captains of industry and everything else. Eventually they had to bow to the inevitable, but not before they had pulled out all stops. One of their arguments resisting public disclosure was that they would be put at risk: once envious people "out there" knew what specific executives earned, they might become kidnap targets.

The lack of any formal, measurable professional qualifications reflects an ideological starting point: that to engage in profit-seeking activities is natural and is every person's birthright. This starting point also encourages self-serving behaviour by all those with access to profit-making opportunities. As seen, managers often use their clout to reduce the price at which they can buy shares when the market price of the shares is falling. Gretchen Morgenson of *The New York Times* (reprinted *Toronto Star*, June 28, 2001, p.B8) refers to a number of studies that establish the frequency of this kind of shameless, or better, unprofessional, behaviour.

When the recession of the early 1990s made a bunch of corporate failures a public issue, this very lack of professionalism led the Toronto Stock Exchange to entitle its inquiry "Where Were the Directors?" No doubt another downturn in the economy will show up an equal lack of diligence, greed, and fecklessness. The Nortel and Enron stories already are being told, as if they were unexpected, totally unprecedented occurrences. But these sagas are exhibiting all the usual ingredients: unprofessionalism, greed, and smugness. There will be more such revelations.

The corporation is architecturally designed to let self-seeking individuals conduct themselves in heedless ways. This does not augur well for the proponents of legally mandated corporate social responsibility.

12 The Stakeholder/Social Responsibility Movement Goes Private

p.207, The recent successful boycott of Daishowa: *Daishowa Inc. v. Friends of the Lubicon* (1998).

p.208, Naomi Klein has aptly described the world of commodification: Klein, *No Logo*.

p.209, Polls conducted by the campaign organizers show: Marymount University Centre for Ethical Concerns, 1999.

p.210, The mining of coltan mud to produce the tantalum process: Harden, "Pagers, Video Games and the Congo," p.M1.

p.211, William Greider's acerbic comment: Greider, "Waking up the Global Elite." Bart's research was reported in *Globe and Mail*, Aug. 21, 1999.

p.211, Five years ago, many of us would have dismissed: Yanz and Jeffcott quoted in Fudge, "Consumers to the Rescue?"

p.212, Thousands of such suits take place every year in the United States: Pring and Canan, *SLAPPS*.

p.213, But these conventions are virtually unenforced: Fudge and Glasbeek, "Challenge to the Inevitability of Globalization."

p.213, By the year 2000 *The Globe and Mail* was reporting: *Globe and Mail*, Jan. 15, 2000, p.B9.

p.213, As John Braithwaite once remarked: Braithwaite made this remark when introducing a paper in Kingston, Ont. The paper presented that day is in Pearce and Snider, *Corporate Crime*.

p.213, Corporate law only permits this deployment: *Parke v. Daily News*.

p.214, Indeed, a number of observers have seen it and like organizations: Hawken, *Ecology of Commerce*; Karliner, *Corporate Planet*; McDonald, "Voluntary Action or Elite Lobbying?"

p.215, Mark Levinson cynically notes: Levinson, "Wishful Thinking."

p.217, Sylvia Ostry commented that Third World countries: Ostry, "Will There Be Life after Seattle?"

p.217, Harlan Mandel documented the same kind of Third World opposition: Mandel, "In Pursuit of the Missing Link," p.443.

p.219, When employees in one small locale became less than convinced: "'It's Business, Man!'—Unions and 'Socially Responsible' Corporations," *Dissent*, Fall 1999, p.53.

p.219, In England the Body Shop does not allow its workers to unionize: Entine, "Queen of Bubble Bath"; Klein, *No Logo*; London Greenpeace Mc Spotlight, www.Mcspotlight.org/beyond/ companies/bs_ref.html.

p.220, For example, in a 2001 article: Frederick, Gregory. "Prisoners Are Citizens," p.76.

p.222, The adverse publicity they received: *Toronto Star*, July 26, Aug. 24, 2000.

p.223, The bulk of capital for these large, publicly traded corporations is obtained: Henwood, *Wall Street*; Hedder, et al., *Canadian Business Organizations Law*.

p.225, Researcher Anders Hayden reports: Hayden, "Capitalist Crunch."

p.225, Fosback, the editor of an investors' advisory newsletter, notes: Canadian Press Service, April 20, 1992.

p.225, One report indicates that: Quoting figures from the Ethical Investment Research Information Services, Nitkin, "Socially Responsible Investing," p.75.

p.226, Hayden found that a much-heralded ethical institutional investor: Hayden, "Capitalist Crunch."

p.226, Imasco not only markets tobacco, but also supports: Ellmen, *How to Invest Your Money with a Clear Conscience*.

p.226, As the critical chronicler of McDonald's: Schlosser, *Fast Food Nation*.

p.227, Thus, David Olive notes that Ethical Growth invested in forest giants: Olive, *Just Rewards*.

It is appropriate here to acknowledge a debt. A teacher learns a lot from students over the years, but sometimes the debt is specific. This chapter relies on information that came to me as a result of my ongoing role as a member of Reid Cooper's Ph.D. committee (York University). In his comprehensives, Cooper canvassed a great deal of literature that was new to me. In particular, when reading Cooper's work I first came across some of the ISO and other international umbrella groups. His research also provided me with citations to Body Shop narratives. While Reid Cooper and I part company in our assessments of the utility of much of the newer social responsibility machinery, his work usefully informed what I offer here.

One of the things that stands in the way of efforts such as boycotts and ethical investment strategies aimed at getting corporations to behave more responsibly is that management must be persuaded to have the corporation conduct itself on the basis of the long-term good of the environment, workers, and consumer needs. But on a day-to-day basis managers are judged in terms of their short-term share performance. While the social responsibility movement frequently contends that for a corporation to be socially responsible will, eventually, lead to a better market share for that corporation and, thus, to better share performance, this argument has little resonance with the managers, who have a very different timetable. Many of the problems that their corporate activity creates for others will not even be visible in the short term or, even more significantly, will probably not become a notorious public issue for a long time.

Managers have an incentive not to do much research into the probable harms created through certain productive or marketing practices. There is, then, a structural basis for turning a blind eye. Harms are not necessarily the consequence of deliberate evildoing; they may be the product of built-in tendencies for managers to be non-inquisitive. Managers, who are paid incentives to drive up share price values in the immediate term, are acting as the stereotypical Rational Economic Men they are supposed to be when they ignore long-term harms. By the time the injuries become manifest, they will have earned their bonuses and be gone. Although greed and fraud played their part, this structural feature may well be one of the ingredients of terrible catastrophes such as the asbestos and tobacco poisonings.

The strength of the link between share performance and pay reflects the primacy placed by corporate law on the welfare of the shareholder as profit-maximizer. Unsurprisingly, it is when shareholders feel that managers are in a position to take advantage of them—the shareholders—that the greatest likelihood for corporate governance law reform arises. Shareholders have ideological, as well as material, clout with lawmakers. Social responsibility proponents have been forced to rely on "soft law," statements of principles that do not have the coercive power of the state behind them. Despite some notable success stories, in the end soft law is simply not as effective as real, enforceable, law, even if real law is hardly a success story.

The Sullivan Principles, developed in 1977, provide one success story for soft law. These principles took their name from a Baptist minister and community activist who was on the General Motors board of directors. Sullivan supported a motion presented by minority shareholders—really, people who had bought shares to have their activists' views put on the corporate agenda—that General Motors withdraw from South Africa. The motion failed to carry, of course, but Sullivan persisted and his well-publicized and clever campaigning led to a code of conduct requiring corporations doing business in South Africa to implement integrated workplaces and fair employment practices, and to accept affirmative action: these were the Sullivan principles. Soon many corporations adopted this code of conduct for their South African operations. Indeed, some major institutional investors publicly announced that they would no longer invest in corporations that failed to abide by the requirements of the Sullivan Principles. But, despite this measure of success, Sullivan himself was forced to admit that the tactic had little impact on the practices of Apartheid. He switched tactics and began a campaign to have U.S. corporations simply withdraw from South Africa. A good account of this interesting struggle is given in Weedon, "Evolution of Sullivan Principle Compliance," p.57.

As an example of a positive soft law exercise, the Sullivan campaign is about as good as it gets. Many people have attempted to replicate it in other spheres. For instance, in 1989, after the spectacular *Exxon-Valdez* environmental spill, a broad coalition of environmental groups, consumer groups, labour unions, and church organizations announced the Valdez Principles, which call for an accounting and monitoring system to be adopted by corporations vis-à-vis their environmental practices and standards. These principles are distinct from the Sullivan principles in that they apply to the domestic practices of U.S. corporations and were designed to improve existing and much better standards than the ones being pushed in South Africa. But they are also similar in that they too are legally unenforceable. Their symbolic impact is likely to be greater than their concrete effect; see Pink, "Valdez Principles," p.180. Some twelve years after the spill, Exxon was still in court fighting the $3.5 billion fine imposed on it. It had succeeded in having the matter sent back to trial for a new assessment. At the same time the ship, the actual *Exxon-Valdez*, now bearing a different name and a new coat of paint, was plying the coast off Southern Australia. While it is true that soft law is not very effective, it is also true that hard, notionally enforceable law does not work all that well when it needs to be applied to hard-headed giant corporate actors.

Another difficulty that the users of private, economic tools face in attempts to instil better corporate behaviour is that it is corporations and their business activities, rather than the individuals captains of industry, retail, finance, and everything else, that are the targets of the strategies. What this signifies is that, even if a corporation is made subject to increased social auditing and monitoring, making its cost-saving irresponsibilities harder to hide, and use, nothing prevents the investors and senior managers from leaving this corporation that may no longer be feeding their instant gratification goals. They can take their short-term, irresponsible profit-seeking tactics and attitudes elsewhere. Capital is mobile. Indeed, it is this capacity and the credibility of the threat to use it that crimps lawmakers and the proponents of social responsibility. The trick is not to ask for too much from this class of self-seeking wealth-owners.

This very problem explains such lame ideas as urging that only reasonable profits be pursued. There was alarm, for instance, in social responsibility circles in 2001 when one of the movement's most celebrated symbols, the Body Shop, apparently went on the auction block. The rumoured purchaser was a Mexican corporation, Grupo Omnilife, a direct seller of dietary supplements, vitamins, weight-loss preparations, and other products made with little regard for the environment or conditions of production. Grupo Omnilife is frequently compared to an Amway-style marketer. The problem is, then, that a simple change of dominant shareholders can make socially friendly human and inorganic assets into something potentially anti-social. This is the genius of capitalism. Indeed, while socially responsible folk gave out a big sigh of relief when the takeover was not consummated, capitalists were very unhappy. They liked the idea of a less socially responsible use of that company's assets, or at least the possibilities of making money on the takeover. The shares of the Body Shop dropped 16 per cent in the immediate aftermath of the failed takeover. (*Toronto Star*, June 8, June 27, 2001.) So much for the argument that shareholders are just like the rest of us and really would like corporations to behave better, even if this costs them money.

These kinds of questions, going to the fundamentals of market capitalism, are rarely raised in the debate surrounding social responsibility and stakeholder rights. But they do get asked by thinking capitalists in a different setting. Many dyed-in-the-wool proponents of the corporation as a single-minded site for shareholder profit maximization are alarmed by the corruption of the capitalist financial markets inherent in episodes such as the recent collapse of the Enron corporation. In the United States today's crises follow a string of other scandals—the Savings and Loans (through the late 1980s), Long Term Credit (1998), Prudential Securities (1994)—all featuring large-scale misrepresentations, elaborate deceptive schemes designed to take the investing public to the cleaners. Managers of prestigious outfits have been found wanting again and again. They cash in their options while the share prices are still up, even though they know what the markets do not: the shares are no longer backed by a profit-making venture. In the Enron case they did that while they coerced the workers to hang on to those devaluing shares, imperiling their pensions. Auditors, the investors' watchdogs, turn out to be more like the deceiving managers' lapdogs. They do not reveal practices of dubious propriety and, as in the Enron case, endorse book-keeping systems that hide the true state of the corporate venture from public gaze. As Felix Rohatyn wrote in a tellingly entitled piece, "The Betrayal of Capitalism," this confidence-eroding conduct is exacerbated by the complicity of financial analysts, brokers, and underwriters, all of whom are supposed to serve the maintenance of the integrity of capital markets as they facilitate their workings. Rohatyn notes that, as the markets soared with the popularity of dot-com stocks, independent analysts and brokers "made fantastic claims about their favorite stocks in the hope of generating investment-banking business for their firms. . . . These claims were often supported by creative accounting concepts. . . . A large part of the market was becoming part of show business, and it was driving the economy instead of the other way around."

David Olive (*Toronto Star*, Feb. 28, 2002) cites a study by the Center for Economic and Business Research Ltd., that the stated profits of U.S. corporations in 2001 was overstated by 27 per cent, or about $130 billion. This should mean that the Dow Jones index of share values, which hovers around the 10,000 mark on the basis of the stated profit statements, the ones used to induce the public to invest, should really be in the range of 5,000 to 7,500. Another study cited by Olive—by Alan Newman of CrossCurrents—supports the credibility of this assessment, revealing that eighty-seven managers of bedrock technology corporations (the likes of Microsoft, IBM, and Intel Corp.) had sold the stock they held in their firms, while only three managers had bought any. Olive contends that the vending managers know how over-valued the shares are because they know how misleading their reports to the market are. Olive goes on to quote Gordon Nixon, the chief executive of the Royal Bank of Canada: "We find ourselves burdened by concerns about the integrity of business, the vigilance of management and boards of directors and the credibility of public infor-mation and financial statements."

The Enron debacle, its predecessors, and its inevitable successors draw attention to how market capitalism today is not so much about the production of tangible wealth for the whole of society as it is about making a few speculators wealthy. What these high-profile failures bring into view is that the industrial and financial capitals have parted company as a consequence of the developments of equity markets supposedly designed to foster the aggregation of productive capital. In the process, dominant market actors corrupt the very scheme they are meant to promote. The main game in town is the maximization of shareholder value, of putting shareholders into position to make profits on their shares, regardless of whether profits are being made by the corporation warranting these gains. When the corporation's daily focus is so distorted, it becomes a poor vehicle for the creation of general welfare. Corporate capitalism's legitimacy is endangered because the market, in whose name the corpo-ration acts and which is acclaimed as the preferred means of maximizing the efficient uses of our resources and talents, may come to be perceived as a cloak for a much more problematic agenda. This is what makes Rohatyn and Nixon anxious—and it brings us back to a question about the utility of the tactics discussed in this chapter.

Reliance on the market to produce more socially responsible behaviour on the part of the corporate sectors is permitted precisely because it affirms the essential goodness of the market. Thus, when organizers try to use economic boycotts to wage class struggle, as unions do when they employ secondary boycotts, their tactics (which were once branded as illegal) are tolerated only if they do no harm to wealth-owners' right to continue to trade. See *U.F.C.W., Local 1518 v. K Mart Canada Ltd.* (1999); and *R.W.D.S.U., Local 558 v. Pepsi-Cola Canada Beverages (West) Ltd.* (2002). For a fuller discussion, see Drache and Glasbeek, *Changing Workplace.*

13 Government in Their Own Image: Corporations and Political Power

p.229, The top six corporations together had more annual revenues: *Multinational Monitor,* June 1999.

p.229, A United Nations report found that: As reported in *Australian Financial Review,* April 4, 2001.

p.230, In one massive cross-border transaction: Du Boff and Herman, "Mergers, Concentration and the Erosion of Democracy," p.14.

p.230, William Stanbury's number crunching in the 1980s: Stanbury, "New Competition Act and Competition Tribunal Act."

p.231, These well-known phenomena have led to a series of arguments: Dahl, *Preface to Democratic Theory*; Dahl, *After the Revolution?*; Deetz, *Democracy in an Age of Corporate Colonization.*

p.231, As a study of corporate power and public policy pointed out: Beck, "Corporate Power and Public Policy," pp.82, 85.

p.231, M.V. Nadel has put it in a more scholarly fashion: Nadel, "Hidden Dimensions of Public Policy."

p.231, As an editorial in *Maclean's* pithily put it: *Maclean's,* Aug. 2, 1999.

p.232, The headline over a sports column is typical: *Toronto Star,* Aug. 12, 2000, p.C9.

p.232, This is presumably why the Quebec Federation of Labour accepted the support: Quebec Federation of Labour, "For Health, for Safety, for Jobs in Asbestos," 16th Constitutional Convention of the CTC, Toronto, 1986.

p.232, The Asbestos Institute is funded: "Chrysolite Asbestos—Asbestos Institute Financing Briefing Note, *Natural Resources Canada,* June 1999.

p.233, For instance, Patrick Herman and Annie Thibaud-Mony reported: Herman and Thibaud-Mony, "Canada v. France—WTO Rules."

p.233, In 113 dominant corporations, Clement found 1,848 interlocked positions: Clement, *Canadian Corporate Elite,* p.159.

p.234, In the mid-1980s John Fox and Michael Ornstein provided: Fox and Ornstein, "Canadian State and Corporate Elites," p.48.

p.234, They, and a host of well-funded industrial-sector lobby groups and business think-tanks: For fulsome accounts of their activities and successes, see Dobbin, *Myth of the Good Corporate Citizen*; and Clarke, *Silent Coup.*

p.235, Robert MacDermid has provided clear snapshots: MacDermid, "Funding the Common Sense Revolutionaries: Contributions to the Progressive Conservative Party of Ontario—1995–1997."

p.235, A former player, now a disenchanted critic: Hurtig, *Betrayal of Canada,* p.234.

p.235, There is a good deal of agitation: Rebick, *Imagine Democracy.*

p.235, Chantal Hebert notes: Hebert, "Money Talks in the World of Politics," p.A25.

p.237, Indeed, according to Stanbury the very feebleness of competition policy enforcement: Stanbury, "New Competition Act and Competition Tribunal Act." Stanbury's illuminating study goes on to analyse the nature of the new merger and monopoly provisions. This raises a stack of important issues, but they are not taken up here.

p.238, In a scholarly summary of the studies of the benefits and disadvantages: Du Boff and Herman, "Promotional-Finance Dynamic of Merger Movements," p.107.

p.238, This historical analysis is supported by a recent survey: "Mergers Not All Bad for Shareholders," *The Age*, April 30, 2001, p.B3.

p.239, Sometimes these losses are so great: See Winkler, "Lower Roller"; and Roll, "Empirical Evidence on Takeover Activity and Shareholder Wealth."

p.239, The corporations announced: *Toronto Star*, Sept. 5, 2001, p.E11.

p.239, In May 2001, Clairol's workers were left on tenterhooks: *Toronto Star*, May 22, 2001, p.C3.

p.239, Stock markets find this sort of thing to be very cheering: *Australian Financial Review*, Feb. 3–4, 2001; Toronto Star, June 19, 2001, p.D7, July 4, 2001, p.E3.

p.239, This vast miscalculation had led to the shedding: *Toronto Star*, July 27, 2001, p.F1.

p.239, The darling of Canadian stock exchanges: *Toronto Star*, June 16, 2001, p.E3.

p.240, Even this was not quite enough, and Trujillo also received: "U.S. West Execs Set Bonus for Trujillo, Others Get $18.5 Million," *Denver Post*, March 14, 2000.

p.240, An initial announcement of two thousand layoffs: *The Age*, Feb. 2, 2001, p.B2; *Too Much*, Winter 2000, p.9.

p.240, Vodaphone denies that it tried to bribe: *Toronto Star*, Aug. 23, 2001, p.C6.

p.242, As one senior chemical corporate executive put it: Quoted by Gunningham, "Chemical Industry"; see also Belanger, "Responsible Care"; Macdonald, *Politics of Pollution*.

p.242, Douglas Macdonald reports: Macdonald, "Voluntary Action or Elite Lobbying?"

p.242, But in the United States, the industry had been forced: Gunningham, "Chemical Industry."

p.243, The Royal Society of Canada, in response to a government request: Clark, "Contradictory Reports Baffle Public."

p.243, This is why Eyal Press and Jennifer Washburn: Press and Washburn, "Kept University." See also Buchbinder and Newson, *University Business*.

p.244, For instance, the U.S. General Accounting Office reported: Pianin, "Toxic Chemical Review Process Faulted," p.A02.

p.244, Things must be at a pretty pass: *Toronto Star*, Sept. 10, 2001, p.A2.

p.245, Her hospital not only did not support her but: Tittle, *Ethical Issues in Business*, p.86.

p.245, But these factors were all said to have played no part: "Why Was He Fired?" Editorial, *Toronto Star*, Sept. 9, 2001, p.A12; "Prozac Won't Help U of T's Credibility Blues," *Toronto Star*, Sept. 11, 2001, p.A2.

p.245, This is why universities are increasingly joining forces: Noble, "Digital Diploma Mills," p.38. See also Noble's book *Digital Diploma Mills*.

p.246, This reliance on non-enforceable regimes is referred to: See Yanz, Jeffcott, Ladd, and Atlin, *Policy Options to Improve Standards for Women Garment Workers*; Fudge, "Consumers to the Rescue?"; OECD, Corporate Responsibility; Canada , *Voluntary Codes*.

p.246, Even then, by 1999 *Business Week* had reported: "Global Business Ethics Code Unveiled," *Toronto Star*, Sept. 6, 1997, p.B2, reports another set of voluntary codes to which a handful of major corporations have become signatories.

p.246, In a slightly different setting, Laura Cram documented: Cram, "Calling the Tune without Paying the Piper?"

p.247, Eventually trade sanctions on the breaching party, or even a fine: Fudge and Glasbeek, "Challenge to the Inevitability of Globalization."

p.247, Once again, here was a major corporation insisting on its right: Barlow and Clarke, *Global Showdown*, have documented several other cases of this skewering of Canadian policy by corporate beneficiaries of hard, binding free-trade law.

p.247, It is meant to be enforceable as if it were hard law: Gwyn, "Hypocrisy Surrounds Bribery Issue."

p.248, In return for this largesse, EDS Corporation: "Nova Scotia Is Subsidy King," *Toronto Star*, Aug. 1, 2001, p.C11.

p.248, IBM, too, obtained $33 million for research and development: "Who Gets Handouts?" Editorial, *Toronto Star*, July 7, 1999, p.A18.

p.248, Even Nortel Networks Corp., the huge and for a while marvellously successful corporation: Dobbin, "Facts on Tax Cuts."

p.248, On average in the 1990s, $13 billion a year was doled out: Livesey, "Great Canadian Pig-Out."

In late 2001, *The Toronto Star* (Dec. 8, Dec. 9, 2001) published an investigative account of the rise and fall of Nortel. During its halcyon period, Nortel grew largely by acquisitions of existing corporations. The stated aim was to enter into arrangements that would yield benefits because of the synergy of the combined assets. As part of *The Toronto Star's* report, David Olive noted that, on average, Nortel paid 118 times the value of the net tangible assets of the corporations it acquired. This included a payment of $3.2 billion for a company that owned a mere $3 million worth of tangible assets. All in all, Nortel shelled out $19.7 billion for companies that, at the time of purchase and sale, had a combined total of $167 million in net tangible assets. Its supervisory board of directors consisted of the crème de la crème of the Canadian business establishment, including the chair of the Toronto Stock Exchange's blue ribbon Joint Committee on Corporate Governance, the president and CEO of Bombardier, the chairman of BCE, a senior executive at GlaxoSmith Kline, and even a former U.S. ambassador to Canada and the former Secretary of Defense in the Reagan administration. They were all paid handsomely to pay attention, but, apparently, were not perturbed by anything they saw.

At the head of the management team the directors were supervising—and himself also a director and a member of the Toronto Stock Exchange corporate governance oversight committee—was John Roth. During the acquisition phase he was celebrated and influential. For example, on Aug. 2, 1999, *Maclean's* ran an editorial bemoaning how "corporations call the shots." To prove this, it pointed out that because Roth had launched a campaign to have taxation rates lowered, there was nothing much that the Prime Minister could do but to give in, whether or not he thought it a wise thing to do. Giantism leads to prestige, celebrity status, and political influence. It does not matter all that much that it may be grounded in quicksand: size and the potential to menace harm to government will do the trick. A fawning business press will lend a patina of wisdom to government's concessions.

The force that speeds up giantism and gives CEOs and their immediate colleagues such great standing and power, the merger and acquisition movement, also threatens these managers' security. When investors make a bid to acquire control of a corporation, members of that targeted corporation may very well lose their jobs in the restructuring that is bound to follow. It is often in the target management's interest to convince their shareholders to resist the bid, even though it offers these shareholders a premium price for their shares. When managers determine to resist—always notionally in the interests of shareholders, never their own—the bid will become a hostile bid. A war begins, and the language of war is used to describe the tactics and ploys. The language itself reveals something of the mentality that rules the elite boards and management teams: it reflects a culture of machismo, of locker-room brawling, more like the World Wrestling Federation than the cool, deliberate world that high financial circles like to portray as the preserve of the sane and rational. Indeed, while this is not a point that can be documented, it is hard to see how anyone can believe that these people could be made socially sensitive.

An acquisition bid can be friendly, which means that the targeted corporation is happy to get it. Such a bid is seen as teddy bear hug; if the bidder is really saying, "Take it or leave it," the bid is known as an iron maiden hug. The target's managers may decide to resist a bid. They will set out to develop schemes to ward off the raider. They will be looking for shark repellents. Some onlookers see a bidder offering shareholders a premium as a raider or a shark. One defence mechanism in common use is to find another investor who will undertake to support the incumbent management team. Such an investor will be sold enough shares—usually on favourable terms—to stop the unwanted bidder from getting a controlling number of shares. This friendly investor is known as a white knight. The language of jousting, of hand-to-hand combat, of sexism, inheres in corporate culture.

Sometimes the defensive tactic will be a counterattack. The target corporation will make a bid to get control of the challenger. If successful, the target managers will be able to dislodge the management team that threatened it in the first place. Occasionally, this defence is called the Pac-Man defence, after a computer game in which the goal is to eat or be eaten. Another defensive strategy is to make the target corporation not worth having, or too expensive to buy. To make it not worth having, executives might sell off its best assets, making it unattractive to the bidder. This tactic is known as selling the crown jewels. Of course, once it is done and the bidder has gone away, the target corporation has less assets. Another way to make the bidder go away is to introduce a poison pill. The language is evocative, is it not? A poison pill is a set of rules that allow the target corporation to sell new shares to existing shareholders at bargain-rate prices. The kicker is that these cheap shares will not be available to the unwanted bidder. The technique of identifying who will not be entitled to cheap shares, and under what circumstances, is very complex and is the sort of problem that makes lawyers very rich. Managers frequently try to put these poison pills into the corporation's bylaws before there is a bid. Their argument is that, if they are there, for all to see, only bidders who really want to give the shareholders better value for their shares will make a bid for them because they know that they will be forced to buy a great number to get control. Shareholders, however, are afraid that, once a poison pill is there, there never will be a bid for control and they will never get the opportunity to get a better value for their shares than the stock markets provide. (Note that this argument rests on the proposition that the market for shares does not work as it should.) Inevitably, a small army of advisers has been spawned by these intraclass strains. They offer advice as to whether a managerial proposal to introduce a poison pill into a corporation's bylaws balances the corporation's need to have a stable business environment—one not conditioned by having to make decisions to keep up its share prices to ward off hostile bids—and the shareholders' interest in having their managers maximize their share values. One of the better known advisory groups is Fairvest Securities Corporation, which puts out a newsletter under the name of "Corporate Governance Review," which suggests quite a bit about what it is that motivates shareholders: profit-maximization. The newsletter also offers a glimpse of what the corporate sector believes corporate governance issues are about. To it, these disputations are about creating the best setting for profit-maximization, not about promoting social responsibility.

One other stratagem favoured by management teams faced with a bid for control by a new set of investors also says much about the interests to which these managers are paying most attention. Quite simply, they contract with their employer to be bought off. If the corporation wants managers to let a bidder do what comes naturally and to permit the shareholders to accept or not accept an offer for their shares, regardless of management's opinion and gyrations, it might be wise to give the managers the right to collect a handsome severance package. This provision for golden parachutes, as these devices for peace and quiet are known, are remarkable. After all, one of the most frequently given reasons for offering existing shareholders more than the market value of their shares is that the bidder believes that the existing management team is not doing as well as it should with the assets under its control. To pay these managers money to avoid having to fight them when the judgement has been made that they were doing a bad job makes sense only in a system in which merit has little meaning.

14 Outing the Captains of Industry, Finance, Retail, and Everything Else

p.252, Lewis Lapham, editor of *Harper's* magazine, wrote: Lapham, "Lights, Camera, Democracy!"

p.253, More, even the casual liberal: some recent newspaper headlines tell us this in no uncertain terms: "Indians Say They Need Food" (*Toronto Star*, June 26, 2001, p.A10); "Hunger a Fear for 3 Million Canadians" and "420,000 Children Live in 'Food Insecurity'" (*Toronto Star*, Aug. 16, 2001, p.A1— stories based on a Statistics Canada report).

p.253, Richard Gwyn has written, with echoes of Lapham: *Toronto Star*, Dec. 13, 2000, p.A33.

p.254, Pierre Bourdieu pointed out: Bourdieu (1977), *Outline of a Theory of Practice*.

p.254, As E.P. Thompson noted: Thompson, *Writings by Candlelight*.

p.254, As Sue Hickey, a speaker at a conference on citizenship in New Zealand, said: Hickey, "Citizenship and Disability."

p.255, As the bishops and superiors of religious orders in Brazil proclaimed: *Les Obistpos Latinoamericanos entre Medellin y Puebla* (San Salvador: Universidad Centroamericana, 1978), p.71.

p.255, These capitalists' interests, as protected by their laws: Fanto, "Role of Corporate Law in French Corporate Governance," p.32.

p.256, Profiteering, which still is prized: Clegg and Redding, *Capitalism in Contrasting Cultures*.

p.256, Researcher Douglas Branson, after reviewing the literature: Branson, "Very Uncertain Prospect of 'Global' Convergence."

p.256, According to Gordon Redding these firms have remained: Redding, *Spirit of Chinese Capitalism*.

p.256, In Indonesia major corporations are also family-based organizations: Robinson, *Indonesia*; see also Loveard, *Suharto*.

p.257, The intensity and effectiveness of these protests can be measured: See, for instance, "G8 Summit," *Globe and Mail*, June 24, 2001, pp.A6–A9: "By moving the G8 summit site to Kananaskis, Alta., officials have attempted to put leaders beyond the reach of potential terrorist threats and the violent protests that have shaken other gatherings."

p.257, Friedman's warning to such decent protestors is that they should be aware: As reprinted in *Toronto Star*, July 29, 2001, p.B2.

p.258, The much more scholarly Professor Paul Krugman—who once empirically proved: Krugman, *Age of Diminished Expectations*, p.104.

p.258, After the Quebec confrontations Krugman wrote: *New York Times*, Op-ed piece, April 22, 2001.

p.258, At Seattle William Tabb found groups ranging: Tabb, "World Trade Organization?"

p.259, Even as conservative a personage as the Chair of the London Stock Exchange: Quoted in Carroll, "Undoing the End of History," p.5.

p.259, Barbara Epstein has observed: Epstein (2001), "Anarchism and Anti-Globalization."

p.260, These values may inhibit their effectiveness as political agents: Gindin and Panitch, "Rekindling Socialist Imagination."

p.260, The political philosopher Gerald Cohen has made a powerful case: Cohen, *If You're an Egalitarian, How Come You're So Rich?*

p.261, As Tabb put it: Tabb, "World Trade Organization?" p.15.

p.261, At least a small part of this struggle: Gindin, "The Party's Over"; see also Gindin and Panitch, "Rekindling Socialist Imagination."

p.262, Even the most optimistic should expect a long period of transition: Nielson, "On Justifying Revolution," p.526, and "On the Choice between Reform and Revolution," p.271; Bay, "Civil Disobedience," p.6; Gonick, "Democratic Vision for the 21st Century."

p.263, For twenty-five years or so after World War II, the Canadian government: Mulvale, *Reimagining Social Welfare*, p.17

p.263, Most analysts would agree that in the past two decades: See Glasbeek, "Looking Back towards a Bleak Future for Lawyers," p.263.

p.263, President Roosevelt's radical proposals: Roosevelt and Balkin, *Why Market Socialism?*

p.264, Contemporary Canadian studies, as summarized by Jane Jenson: Jenson, "Mapping Social Cohesion."

p.264, Neil Brooks, too, has marshalled evidence: Brooks, "Role of the Voluntary Sector in a Modern Welfare State."

p.265, Indeed, there are many such claims: For a non-exhaustive set of globalization believers, see Dunning, *Globalization of Business and Multinational Enterprises and the Global Economy*; Thomas, *Capital beyond Borders*; and Ohmae, *Borderless World*.

p.265, Kenneth Ohmae summed up this mainstream literature: Ohmae, "Rise of the Regional State," p.72.

p.265, Many serious analysts and activists have gathered their own brand of empirical evidence: Teeple, *Globalization and the Decline of Social Reform*, pp.171–72, presents an outline of people with these views.

p.265, Indeed, some commentators say, this particular phase may not even be much more pronounced than previous such phases: For sources and data on global scepticism, see Gordon, "Global Economy," p.24; Hirst and Thompson, "'The Problem of Globalization'"; Ostry, "Domestic Domain," p.7; Henwood, "Post What?" p.1; Wichard and Lowe, "Ownership-Based Disaggregation of the U.S. Current Account," p.75; Tabb, *Amoral Elephant*; Jones, *World Turned Upside Down?*; Doremus et al., *Myth of the Global Corporation*; Gray, *False Dawn*.

p.265, . . . although impressive studies show that even this is not empirically true: Helleiner, "Post-Globalization"; UNCTAD, *World Investment Report 1995*.

p.265, Stephen Clarkson has shown how: Clarkson, "Constitutionalizing the Canadian-American Relationship." See also Fudge and Glasbeek, "Challenge to the Inevitability of Globalization."

p.266, According to Frances Fox Piven: Piven, "Is It Global Economics or Neo-Laissez-Faire?" p.107.

p.266, . . . and William Carroll provides an incisive analysis of what is significantly distinct: Carroll, "Undoing the End of History."

p.266, Aijaz Ahmad puts this clearly: Ahmad, "Issues of Class and Culture," p.10.

p.267, Frank Pearce and Laureen Snider record: Pearce and Snider, "Regulating Capitalism."

p.267, Michael Mandel calculated: Mandel, *Readings in Criminology*.

p.272, Following are a few possible steps: This represents a brief restatement of some of the measures that I have elaborated on elsewhere, in Glasbeek, "Why Corporate Deviance Is Not Treated as Crime."

p.273, For instance, Robert Waldrop . . . has published a list: www.justpeace.org.

p.273, Democracy Watch has made similar recommendations: Democracy Watch, *Corporate Citizenship and Social Responsibility*.

p.274, For instance: Wal-Mart is running advertisements that display its multi-ethnic staff: *In These Times*, April 1, 1996, p.10. See also Freeman, "World's Largest Retail Company Is a Neighbourhood Bully," pp.32–34; a sidebar item, "The Real Wal-Mart," provides a list of the company's wrongdoings with regards to the law.

p.277, As Jenson argues, this project would require measures: Jenson, "Mapping Social Cohesion."

p.278, In a context of a deepening appreciation of the corporate sectors' inimical impact: Brooks, "Role of the Voluntary Sector in a Modern Welfare State."

p.278, Of course, corporate employers represent the paradigm: Hyman, *Marxism and the Sociology of Trade Unionism*.

p.278, The corporation's political aspects remain unseen: Drache and Glasbeek, *Changing Workplace*.

p.279, A debate may open up around how sensible it is to further a system: Klein, *No Logo*; Glasbeek, "Occupational Health and Safety."

p.279, The push is to make it plausible for workers: Gindin and Panitch, "Rekindling Socialist Imagination."

p.279, But what is relevant here is that the litigation neatly illustrated: Kellman, "Public or Private?" p.3.

p.280, In this sense democracy is understood: Lummis, *Radical Democracy*.

p.280, Between 1945 and 1988 about 75 per cent of eligible voters participated: CAW, "Proportional Representation."

p.280, The number of people making themselves available as candidates: *Toronto Star*, Nov. 8, 2000, p.A34.

p.280, This skewing of the wishes of the supposed sovereign voters has led to calls for changes: Rebick, *Imagine Democracy*; Milner, *Making Every Vote Count*; Bradford, "Which Ideas Matter When?" See also the work of Fair Vote Canada.

p.281, Now, because the Supreme Court of Canada has acknowledged: *Gray v. Kerslake* (1968); see also Pesando and Rae, *Public and Private Pensions in Canada*.

p.281, Hence, many critics argue that it would make sense: Cornoy and Shearer, *Economic Democracy*.

p.281, A huge number of such schemes have been proposed: Mathews, *Age of Democracy*.

p.281, They include giving workers a way of becoming equity owners: Korpi, *Democratic Class Struggle*.

p.282, In 1983 Boris Frankel made a powerful case: Frankel, *Beyond the State?*

p.282, Only then could it become plausible to talk: Gonick, 2001, "A Democratic Vision for the 21st Century."

p.283, As Stanley Deetz noted when describing the effect: Deetz, *Democracy in an Age of Corporate Colonization*, p.15.

p.283, Only a few weeks after the devastating events of September 11, 2001: See Peter G. Gosselin and Warren Keith, "After the Attack the Recovery: As Markets Reopen, U.S. Seeks to Prop up Economy," *Los Angeles Times*, 17 September 2001; and for the text of President Bush's news conference, Associated Press, Oct. 11, 2001.

p.283, As C. Douglas Lummis argued: Lummis, *Radical Democracy*, p.22.

First, an acknowledgment is in order. I first got the idea that everyone should be a unionist as part of her/his birthright from Shalom Shachter. He is a lawyer/unionist, and he spoke and wrote about this notion during a political campaign in which both of us were involved. I have treasured this idea ever since.

The outline of proposed strategies that I present are not, for instance, directly pointed at the transnational conduct of corporations or at the democratic deficit that characterizes the fatal decision-making processes of the WTO, IMF, World Bank, and the like. Nor do the proposals take up many of the existing proposals and tactics already in use and that are similar to those discussed here. For instance, some environmentalists have propagated a non-costly, symbolically useful idea: they would have the "authorities" name natural disasters differently. Instead of having a flood or a hurricane named as "Hugo" or "Betty," they suggest names such as "Exxon" or "Weyerhauser" to denote the reality that these corporations' profit-chasing activities have much to do with the erosion of the ecology that leads to the increased occurrences of "natural" disasters.

I have also not discussed the very important work being done to curtail or terminate corporate funding of political parties and politicians. This private funding leads to such obvious distortions of electoral democracy that even the most staunch of status quo commentators have remarked regularly on the problem. Political parties rely on such funding, even as they deplore it. Campaigns to eliminate such overt assaults on liberal democracy are worthy of support, and my non-discussion of this tactic does not downgrade its importance.

I have also not mentioned a movement that has gained a lot of anti-corporate activists' support in the United States: the struggle to have governments and/or courts de-register corporations that act in socially unacceptable ways. The argument is that corporations are created by the state—which in U.S. parlance is said to be "We, the People"—and that, therefore, if they do not behave as the people want them to behave, they should lose their privileges. The work of David Korten (1999, 2001) has been theoretically influential, and groups such as the Program on Corporations, Law and Democracy provide a stream of information and organize legal and political actions around this issue. One of the means they use is to get municipalities to refuse to contract with bad corporate actors. This strategy has met with little success so far, but it is significant for its symbolism and its attempt to assert the sovereignty of individuals over inhuman collections of wealth.

Another worthy idea is that anti-corporate forces should organize to reverse the government's decision to let some very major economic decision-making be within the discretion of the unelected, unaccountable Reserve Bank of Canada. This movement to uncouple central banks from political control has occurred in most advanced industrialized nations and has given the corporate sector, whose influence with these institutions vastly outweighs that which they could exercise in the one person/one vote sphere, a nuclear-size weapon in respect of public policy-making. If evidence is needed, watch how the world waits with bated breath for the next announcement of Alan Greenspan (an Ayn Rand follower) or David Dodge.

There are many other such worthy ideas. The lacunae left by the proposals offered are evident and acknowledged.

References

Adams, Roy J., G. Betcherman, and B. Bilson. *Good Jobs, Bad Jobs, No Jobs: Tough Choices for Canadian Labour Law.* Toronto: C. D. Howe Institute, 1995.

Adams, Stanley. *Roche versus Adams.* London: Jonathan Cape, 1984.

Ahmad, Aijaz. "Issues of Class and Culture: An Interview with Aijaz Ahmad." Conducted by Ellen Meiksins Wood. *Monthly Review* 48,5 (1996).

Albanese, J. "Love Canal Six Years Later: The Legal Legacy." Federal Probation 48 (June 1984).

Amin, S. *Re-Reading the Postwar Period: An Intellectual Itinerary.* New York: Monthly Review Press, 1994.

Anderson, D. "The Curse of the Corporate Vampires." *Maclean's* 94 (March 1981).

Appen Report, *The Bhopal Tragedy: One Year After.* Penang: Sahabat Alam Malaysia, 1985.

Ashton, T.H. and C.H.E. Philpin, eds. *The Brenner Debate: Agrarian Class Structure and Economic Development in Pre-Industrial Europe.* Cambridge and New York: Cambridge University Press, 1985.

Ashworth, W. *The Late Great Lakes: An Environmental History.* Toronto: Collins Publishers, 1986.

Ayers, I. and J. Braithwaite. *Responsive Regulation.* Oxford: Oxford University Press, 1992.

Bagdikian, Ben H. *The Media Monopoly.* 6th ed. Boston: Beacon Press, 2000.

Bailey, Fenton, *Fall from Grace: The Untold Story of Michael Milken.* Foreword by Alan Dershowitz. New York: Carol Publishing Group, 1992.

Baistow, T. *Fourth-Rate Estate: An Anatomy of Fleet Street.* London: Comedia Publishing Group, 1985.

Baldasty, Gerald. *The Commercialization of News in the Nineteenth Century.* Madison: University of Wisconsin Press, 1992.

Baran, P. and P. Sweezy. *Monopoly Capital: An Essay on the American Economic and Social Order.* New York and London: Monthly Review Press, 1966.

Barlow, Maude and Bruce Campbell. *Straight through the Heart: How the Liberals Abandoned the Just Society.* Toronto: A Phyllis Bruce Book, HarperCollins Publishers, 1995.

Barlow, Maude and Tony Clarke. *Global Showdown: How the New Activists Are Fighting Global Corporate Rule.* Toronto: Stoddart Publishing, 2001.

Barnett, H. "Corporate Capitalism, Corporate Crime." *Crime and Delinquency* 27,1 (January 1981).

Barthes, Roland. *Mythologies.* St. Albans: Paladin Books, 1973.

Bartomole de las Casas. *A Short Account of the Destruction of the Indies.* Ed. and trans. by N. Griffin. Introduction by A. Pagden. London and New York: Penguin Books, 1992.

Bay, Christian. "Civil Disobedience: Prerequisite for Democracy in a Mass Society." *Our Generation* 5,4 (1971).

Beck, S. "Corporate Power and Public Policy." In *Consumer Protection, Environmental Law, and Corporate Power,* ed. I. Bernier and A. Lajoie, vol. 50, Studies for Royal Commission on the Economic Union and Development Prospects for Canada (McDonald Commission). Toronto: University of Toronto Press, 1985.

Becker, G. "Crime and Punishment: An Economic Approach." *Journal of Politics and Economics* 76 (1968).

Beier, A.L., C. Cannadine, and James M. Rosenheim, eds. *The First Modern Society: Essays in Honour of Lawrence Stone.* Cambridge and New York: Cambridge University Press, 1989.

Belanger, J. "Responsible Care: Delivering on a Promise." International Responsible Care Workshop, Rotterdam, April 9, 1991.

Bell, D. *The End of Ideology: On the Exhaustion of Political Ideas in the Fifties.* New York: Free Press, 1965.

Benson, M. "The Influence of Class Position on the Formal and Informal Sanctioning of White Collar Offenders." *Sociological Quarterly* 30, 3 (September 1989).

Bequai, A. *White Collar Crime: A 20th Century Crisis.* Toronto: Lexington Books, 1978.

Berle, A.A. *Power without Property: A New Development in American Political Economy.* New York: Harcourt, Brace, 1959.

————. "Modern Functions of the Corporate System." *Columbia Law Review,* 62 (1962).

————. Research Notes, 1929–30, Special Collections, Columbia University Law Library, New York.

Berle, A.A. and G.C. Means. *The Modern Corporation and Private Property.* New York: Commerce Clearing House, 1932.

Bernstein, A. "Sweatshop Reform: How to Solve the Standoff." *Business Week,* March 31, 1999.

Block, Alan A. and Frank R. Scarpatti. *Poisoning for Profit: The Mafia and Toxic Waste in America.* New York: William Morrow and Co., 1985.

Block, M. "Optimal Penalties, Criminal Law and the Control of Corporate Behaviour." *Buffalo University Law Review* 71 (1991).

Bobst, Elmer Holmes. *Bobst: The Autobiography of a Pharmaceutical Pioneer.* New York: McKay, 1973.

Boulton, D. *The Grease Machine.* New York: Harper and Row, 1978

Bourdieu, Pierre. *Outline of a Theory of Practice.* New York: Columbia University Press, 1977.

Box, Steven. *Power, Crime, and Mystification.* London and New York: Tavistock Publications,1983.

Bradford, Neil. "Which Ideas Matter When? From Technocratic Keynesianism to Neo-Liberalism." *Socialist Studies Bulletin* 54 (1998).

Braithwaite, J. *Inequality, Crime and Public Policy.* London: Routledge and Kegan Paul, 1979.

————. *Corporate Crime in the Pharmaceutical Industry.* London: Routledge and Kegan Paul, 1984.

————. *To Punish or Persuade: Enforcement of Coal Mine Safety.* Albany: State University of New York Press, 1985.

Branson, Douglas M. "The Very Uncertain Prospect of 'Global' Convergence in Corporate Governance." *Social Science Research Electronic Library,* 2001. papers.ssrn.com/sol3/papers.cfm

Bratton, Jr., W.W. "The Nexus of Contracts Corporation: A Critical Appraisal." *Cornell Law Review* 74 (1988).

————. "The New Economic Theory of the Firm: Critical Perspectives from History." *Stanford Law Review* 41 (1989).

Brenner, R. "Bourgeois Revolution and Transition to Capitalism." In *The Brenner Debate: Agrarian Class Structure and Economic Development in Pre-Industrial Europe,* ed. T.H. Ashton and C.H.E. Philpin. Cambridge: Cambridge University Press, 1985.

British Social Attitudes Survey. Aldershot, Eng.: Gower, 1984–88.

Broadbent, Edward. "Democracy and Corporations: What's Gone Wrong?" Corry Lecture, Queen's University, Kingston, 2000.

Brodeur, P. *Outrageous Misconduct: The Asbestos Industry on Trial.* New York: Pantheon Books, 1985.

Brooks, Neil. "The Role of the Voluntary Sector in a Modern Welfare State." In *Between State and Market: Essays on Charities Law and Policy in Canada,* ed. J. Phillips, B. Chapman, and D. Stevens. Toronto: McGill-Queen's University Press, 2001.

Brown, M. *Laying Waste: The Poisoning of America by Toxic Chemicals.* New York: Pantheon Books, 1979.

Brudney, Victor. "The Independent Director—Heavenly City or Potemkin Village?" *Harvard Law Review* 95 (1982).

Bruun, Kettil. "International Drug Control and the Pharmaceutical Industry." In *Social Aspects of the Medical Use of Psychotropic Drugs,* ed. R. Cooperstock. Toronto: Addiction Research Foundation, 1974.

Buchbinder, Howard and Janice Newson. *University Business: Universities, Corporations and Academic Work.* Toronto: Garamond Press, 1988.

Burnham, James. *The Managerial Revolution—What Is Happening in the World?* Westport, Conn.: Greenwood Press, 1972 [1941].

Cadman, John W. *The Corporation in New Jersey*. Cambridge, Mass.: Harvard University Press, 1949.

Calavita, K. and H. Pontell. "'Heads I Win, Tails You Lose': Deregulation, Crime and Crisis in the Savings and Loan Industry." *Crime and Delinquency* 36,1 (1990).

————. "'Other People's Money' Revisited: Collective Embezzlement in the Savings And Loan Insurance Industries." *Social Problems* 38,1 (1991).

————. "Saving the Savings and Loans? U.S. Government Response to Financial Crime." In *Corporate Crime: Contemporary Debates*, ed. F. Pearce and L. Snider. Toronto: University of Toronto Press, 1995.

CALURA. *Inter-Corporate Ownership*. Ottawa: Statistics Canada, Business Division, 1984.

Cameron, James M. *The Pictonian Colliers*. Halifax: Nova Scotia Museum, 1974.

Campbell, R.L., ed. *Control of Corporate Management*. North York, Ont.: Captus Press, 1992.

Canada. Task Force on Labour Relations. *Final Report* (H.D. Woods, chair). Ottawa: Privy Council, 1968.Canada.

————. Senate Special Committee on Mass Media. *Report of the Senate Special Committee on Mass Media* (Senator Davey, chair). Ottawa: Queen's Printer, 1970.

————. *Royal Commission on Corporate Concentration* (Bryce). Report of the Royal Commission on Corporate Concentration. Ottawa: The Commission, 1978.

————. *The State of Competition in the Canadian Petroleum Industry*. Ottawa: Department of Consumer and Corporate Affairs, 1981.

————. *Report of the Inquiry into the Collapse of the CCB and the Northland Bank* (Estey, Willard Z., Commissioner). Ottawa: Supply and Services Canada, 1986.

————. Royal Commission on Electoral Reform and Party Financing (Lortie). *Reforming Electoral Democracy: Final Report*. Ottawa: Minister of Supplies and Services Canada, 1991.

————. *Voluntary Codes—A Guide for the Development and Use*. Ottawa: Government of Canada, 1998.

Canadian Auto Workers (CAW). "Proportional Representation: Medicine for Canada's Ailing Democracy?" Toronto: CAW Research Department, April 2001.

Canadian Democracy and Corporate Accountability, *Final Report: the New Balance Sheet, Corporate Profits and Responsibility in the 21st Century*. Toronto, 2002.

Canadian Labour Congress (CLC). *Falling Behind: The State of Working Canada, 2000*. Ottawa, April 2000.

Carey, Alex. *Taking the Risk Out of Democracy: Propaganda in the US and Australia*. Ed. Andrew Lohrey, Foreword by Noam Chomsky. Sydney: University of New South Wales Press, 1995.

————. *7 Days*. Pilot Issue, Melbourne, June 20, 1986.

Carroll, William K. "Undoing the End of History: Canada-Centred Reflections on the Challenge of Globalization." *Socialist Studies Bulletin* 63–64 (January–June 2001).

Carson, Rachel. *Silent Spring*. New York: Fawcett World Library, 1962.

Carson, W.G. *The Other Price of Britain's Oil: Safety and Control in the North Sea*. New Brunswick, N.J.: Rutgers University Press, 1982.

Cassels, Jamie. *The Uncertain Promise of Law: Lessons from Bhopal.* Toronto and London: University of Toronto Press, 1993.

Cataldo, B. "Limited Liability with One-Man Companies and Subsidiary Corporations." *Law and Contemporary Problems* 18 (1953).

Cherniack, Martin. *The Hawk's Nest Incident: America's Worst Industrial Disaster.* New Haven, Conn. and London: Yale University Press, 1986.

Churchill, W. A *Little Matter of Genocide: Holocaust and Denial in the Americas, 1492 to the Present.* Winnipeg: Arbeiter Ring, 1998.

Cimino, M.T. "Workplace Safety Violations." *West Virginia Law Review* 94 (1992).

Clark, Ann. "Contradictory Reports Baffle Public." *The Toronto Star*, Aug. 29, 2001.

Clarke, M. *Business Crime: Its Nature and Control.* Cambridge: Polity Press, 1990.

Clarke, Tony. *Silent Coup: Confronting the Big Business Takeover of Canada.* Ottawa and Toronto: CCPA/James Lorimer, 1997.

Clarkson, Max. "In Praise of the Stakeholder Concept." *The Globe and Mail*, Dec. 28, 1990.

————, ed. *The Corporation and Its Stakeholders: Classic and Contemporary Readings.* Toronto and London: University of Toronto Press, 1998.

Clarkson, Stephen. "Constitutionalizing the Canadian-American Relationship." In *Canada under Free Trade*, ed. D. Cameron and M. Watkins. Toronto: Lorimer, 1993.

Clement, Wallace. *The Canadian Corporate Elite: An Analysis of Economic Power.* Toronto: McClelland and Stewart, 1975.

Clegg, Stewart and Gordon S. Redding, eds. *Capitalism in Contrasting Cultures.* Berlin and New York: W. de Gruyter, 1990.

Clinard, Marshall. Illegal Corporate Behaviour. Washington, D.C.: National Institute of Law Enforcement and Criminal Justice, 1979.

————. *Corporate Corruption: The Abuse of Power.* New York and Westport, Conn. and London: Praeger, 1990.

Clinard, Marshall B. and D. Yeager. *Corporate Crime.* New York: Free Press, 1980.

Coffee Jr., J. "'No Soul to Damn: No Body to Kick': An Unscandalized Enquiry into the Problem of Corporate Punishment." *Michigan Law Review* 79 (1981).

————. "Liquidity versus Control: The Institutional Investor as Corporate Monitor." *Yale Law Journal* 91 (1991).

Coffee Jr, J., Louis Lowenstein, and Rose Rose-Ackerman, eds. *Knights, Raiders and Targets: The Impact of the Hostile Takeover.* New York: Oxford University Press, 1988.

Cohen, Gerald. *If You're an Egalitarian, How Come You're So Rich?* Cambridge, Mass. and London: Harvard University Press, 2000.

Comish, S. *The Westray Tragedy.* Halifax: Fernwood Books, 1993.

Conklin, J.E. *Illegal but Not Criminal: Business Crime in America.* Englewood Cliffs, N.J.: Prentice-Hall, 1977.

Conference Board of Canada. *Market Explorers Survey of Canadians.* Ottawa, 2000.

Corcoran, Terence. "Disclosing the Great Stakeholder Hoax." *The Globe and Mail*, Dec. 15, 1990.

Cornoy, M. and D. Shearer. *Economic Democracy: The Challenge of the 1980s.* New York: M.E. Sharpe, 1980.

Cram, Laura. "Calling the Tune without Paying the Piper? Social Policy Regulation: The Role of the Commission in European Social Policy." *Policy and Politics* 21,2 (1993).

Crete, Raymonde. *The Proxy System in Canadian Corporations: A Critical Analysis.* Montreal: Wilson and Lafleur, 1986.

Crooks, H. *Dirty Business: The Inside Story of the New Garbage Agglomerates.* Toronto: Lorimer, 1983.

————. *Giants of Garbage: The Rise of the Global Waste Industry and the Politics of Pollution Control.* Toronto: Lorimer, 1993.

Cruise, David and Alison Griffiths. *Fleecing the Lamb: The Inside Story of the Vancouver Stock Exchange.* Vancouver and Toronto: Douglas and McIntyre, 1987.

Crystal, Graef S. *In Search of Excess: The Overcompensation of American Executives.* New York: W.W. Norton, 1991.

Cullen, F.T., W. Maakestad, and G. Cavender. *Corporate Crime under Attack: The Ford Pinto Case and Beyond.* Cincinnati: Anderson, 1987.

Curran, J. "Communications, Power and Social Order." In *Culture, Society and the Media,* ed. Michael Gurevitch et. al. London: Methuen, 1982.

Curran, J. and J. Seaton. *Power without Responsibility—The Press and Broadcasting.* London: Methuen, 1985.

Dahl, R.A. *Preface to Democratic Theory.* New Haven, Conn.: Yale University Press, 1966.

————. *After the Revolution? Authority in a Good Society.* Albany: State University of New York, 1970.

Daniels, Ronald J. "Must Boards Go Overboard? An Economic Analysis of the Effects of the Burgeoning Statutory Liability on the Role of Directors." In *Conference on Canadian Corporate Governance.* Vancouver: C.D. Howe Institute, February 1994.

Daniels, Ronald J. and Susan M. Hutton. "The Capricious Cushion: The Implications of the Directors' and Officers' Insurance Liability Crisis on Canadian Corporate Governance." *Canadian Business Law Journal* 22 (1993).

Deetz, Stanley. *Democracy in an Age of Corporate Colonization.* Albany: State University of New York Press, 1992.

Democracy and Corporate Accountability Commission (Avie Bennett and Edward Broadbent, co-chairs). *An Overview of Issues.* 2001.

Democracy Watch. *Corporate Citizenship and Social Responsibility: An Agenda for Raising the Standards in Canada,* Ottawa: Democracy Watch, 1994.

Devlin, Lord. *The Enforcement of Morals.* London: Oxford University Press, 1965.

Dobbin, Murray. *The Myth of the Good Corporate Citizen: Democracy under the Rule of Big Business.* Toronto: Stoddart, 1998.

————. "The Facts on Tax Cuts." *Canadian Perspectives,* Summer 2000.

Dodd, E.M. "For Whom Are Corporate Managers Trustees?" *Harvard Law Review* 45 (1932).

————. *American Business Corporations until 1860.* Cambridge, Mass.: Harvard University Press, 1934.

Domhoff, G.W. *Who Rules America?* Englewood Cliffs, N.J.: Prentice-Hall, 1967.

————. *The Higher Circles: The Governing Class in America.* New York: Random House, 1970.

Doremus, Paul N., William W. Keller, Louis W. Pauly, and Simon Reich. *The Myth of the Global Corporation*. Princeton, N.J.: Princeton University Press, 1998.

Dowie, M. "Pinto Madness." In *Crisis in American Institutions*, 4th ed., ed. J. Skolnick and E. Currie. Boston: Little, Brown, 1979.

Drache, Daniel and H.J. Glasbeek. *The Changing Workplace: Reshaping Canada's Industrial Relations System*. Toronto: Lorimer, 1992.

Drohan, Madelaine. "Into Africa." *The Globe and Mail Report on Business Magazine*, October 1999.

Du Boff, R. and E. Herman. "The Promotional-Finance Dynamic of Merger Movements: A Historical Perspective." *Journal of Economic Issues*, 23,1 (March 1989).

————. "Mergers, Concentration and the Erosion of Democracy." *Monthly Review* 53,1 (May 2001).

Duke, Daryl. "Exiles in Our Own Country." *Canadian Perspectives*, Spring 1999.

Dunning, J. *The Globalization of Business*. London: Routledge, 1993.

————. *Multinational Enterprises and the Global Economy*. Reading, Eng.: Addison-Wesley, 1993.

Durkheim, Emile. *The Division of Labor in Society*. New York: Free Press, 1949.

Easterbrook, F. and D. Fischel. "Limited Liability and the Corporation." *University of Chicago Law Review* 52 (1985).

EDK Associates, INC. "Corporate Irresponsibility: There Ought to be Some Laws." New York: EDK Associates, 1996.

Edwards, Cheryl A. and George Parris. "Regina v. Inco: Righting an Old Wrong." *OHS Canada*, September 2001.

Ellis, D. *The Wrong Stuff*. Toronto: Collier-Macmillan, 1986.

Ellmen, E. *How to Invest Your Money with a Clear Conscience*. Toronto: Lorimer, 1987.

Emerson, T. *The System of Freedom of Expression*. New York: Random House, 1970.

Entine, J. "The Queen of Bubble Bath." *BRAZZIL*, 1996.

Epstein, Barbara. "Anarchism and the Anti-Globalization Movement." *Monthly Review* 53,4 (September 2001).

Epstein, Samuel S. *The Politics of Cancer*. San Francisco: Sierra Club Books,1978.

Ermann, M. David and Richard J. Lundman. *Corporate and Governmental Deviance: Problems of Organizational Behaviour in Contemporary Society*. 2nd ed. New York and Oxford: Oxford University Press, 1982.

Ewen, Stuart. *Captains of Consciousness: Advertising and the Social Roots of the Consumer Culture*. New York and Toronto: McGraw-Hill, 1976.

Faberman, H.A. "A Criminogenic Market Structure: The Automobile Industry." *Sociology Quarterly* 16 (1975).

Fanto, J. "The Role of Corporate Law in French Corporate Governance." *Cornell International Law Journal* 31 (1998).

Fillmore, Nick. "The Big Oink: How Business Won the Free Trade Battle." *This Magazine* 22,8 (March–April1989).

Fisse, B. "The Use of Publicity as a Criminal Sanction against Business Corporations." *Melbourne University Law Review* 8 (1971).

Fisse, B. and J. Braithwaite. *The Impact of Publicity on Corporate Offenders*. Albany: State University of New York Press, 1983.

————. "Sanctions against Corporations: The Limitations of Fines and the Enterprise of Creating Alternatives." In *Corrigible Corporations and Unruly Law*, ed. B. Fisse and P. French. San Antonio: Trinity University Press, 1985.

————. "The Allocation of Responsibility to Corporate Crime: Individualism, Collectivism, and Accountability." *Sydney Law Review* 11,468 (1985).

Foster, John Bellamy. "Global Ecology and the Common Good." *Monthly Review* 46,1 (1995).

Fox, J. and M. Ornstein. "The Canadian State and Corporate Elites in the Post-War Period." *Canadian Review of Sociology and Anthropology* 23 (1986).

Francis, Diane. *Controlling Interest: Who Owns Canada?* Toronto: McClelland and Stewart, 1986.

————. *Contrepreneurs: Stock Market Fraud and Money Laundering in Canada.* Toronto: Macmillan of Canada, 1988.

Frank, Andre Gunder. *World Accumulation 1492–1789*. New York and London: Monthly Review Press, 1978.

Frankel, Boris, *Beyond the State? Dominant Theories and Socialist Strategies.* London: Macmillan, 1983.

Frederick, Gregory. "Prisoners Are Citizens." *Monthly Review* 53,3 (July–August 2001).

Freeman, Mike. "The World's Largest Retail Company Is a Neighbourhood Bully." *The CPPA Monitor* 8,7 (December 2001–January 2002).

French, P. *Collective and Corporate Responsibility.* New York: Columbia University Press, 1984.

Friedman, L. *A History of American Law.* New York: Simon and Schuster, 1973.

Friedman, Milton. *Capitalism and Freedom.* Chicago: Chicago University Press, 1962.

————. "The Social Responsibility of Business Is to Increase Its Profits." *The New York Times Magazine*, Sept. 13, 1979.

Friedman, William. "The Limits of Limited Liability: Fairness, Efficiency and the Courts." In *The Future of Corporation Law*, Queen's Annual Business Symposium. Toronto: Carswell, 1999.

Friedmann, W. *Legal Theory.* London: Stevens and Sons, 1944.

Fudge, Judy. "Consumers to the Rescue? Campaigning against Corporate Abuse of Labour." In *[Ab]Using Power: The Canadian Experience*, ed. Susan Boyd, Dorothy E. Chunn, and Robert Menzies. Halifax: Fernwood Publishing, 2001.

Fudge, J. and H.J. Glasbeek. "A Challenge to the Inevitability of Globalization: Repositioning the State as the Terrain of Contest." In *Global Justice, Global Democracy*, ed. Jay Drydyk and Peter Penz. Winnipeg and Halifax: Society for Socialist Studies/Fernwood Publishing, 1997.

Fukuyama, F. *The End of History and The Last Man*, New York: Avon, 1993.

Fuller, J. *The Gentlemen Conspirators: The Story of the Price-Fixers in the Electrical Industry.* New York: Grove Press, 1962.

Gabaldon, T. "The Lemonade Stand: Feminist and Other Reflections on the Limited Liability of Corporate Shareholders." *Vanderbilt Law Review* 45 (1992).

Galbraith, J. Kenneth. *The Age of Uncertainty.* Boston: Houghton Mifflin, 1977.

————. *The Culture of Contentment.* Boston and New York: Houghton Mifflin, 1992.

Gans, Herbert. *Deciding What's News: A Study of CBS Evening News, NBC Nightly News, Newsweek and Time.* New York: Vintage Books, 1980.

Gartner, H. "Institutional Investors and the New Financial Order." *Rutgers Law Review* 44 (1992).

Geis, G. "The Heavy Electrical Equipment Anti-Trust Cases of 1961." In *Criminal Behavior Systems,* ed. Marshall B. Clinard and R. Quinney. New York: Holt, Rinehart and Winston, 1967.

————. "Criminal Penalties for Corporate Crimes." *Criminal Bulletin* 8 (1972).

Geis, G. and R.F. Meier, eds. *White Collar Crime.* New York: Free Press, 1977.

Geis, G. and E. Stotland, eds. *White-Collar Crime: Theory and Research.* New York: Sage, 1980.

Gerbner, G. and L. Gross. "Living with Television: The Violence Profile." *Journal of Communications,* Spring 1976.

Gibbs, Lois M. *Love Canal: My Story, As Told to Murray Levine.* Albany: State University of New York Press, 1981.

Gierke, O. *Political Theories of the Middle Age.* Trans. and Introduction by F. W. Maitland. Boston: Beacon Press, 1958.

Gilchrist, J. *The Church and Economic Activity in the Middle Ages.* New York: St Martin's Press, 1969.

Gilson, R.J. and R. Kraakman. "Reinventing the Outside Director: An Agenda for Institutional Investors." *Stanford Law Review* 43 (1991).

Gindin, Sam. "The Party's Over." *This Magazine,* November/ December 1998.

Gindin, Sam and Leo Panitch. "Rekindling Socialist Imagination: Utopian Vision and Working-Class Capacities." *Monthly Review* 51,10 (March 2000); also in more formal form as "Necessary and Unnecessary Utopias," in *Socialist Register 2000,* ed. Leo Panitch and Colin Leys (London: Merlin, 1999).

Glasbeek, H.J. "Why Corporate Deviance Is Not Treated as Crime—The Need to Make 'Profits' a Dirty Word." *Osgoode Hall Law Journal* 22 (1984).

————. "Voluntarism, Liberalism and Fairness—Dream, Romance and Real Life." In *Essays in Labour Relations Law,* ed. G. England. Toronto: CCH, 1986.

————. "Entrenchment of Freedom of Speech for the Press—Fettering of Freedom of Speech of the People." In *Media and the Charter,* ed. P. Anisman and A.M. Linden. Toronto: Carswell, 1986.

————. "Labour Relations Law as a Mechanism of Adjustment."*Osgoode Hall Law Journal* 25 (1987).

————. "The Corporate Social Responsibility Movement—The Latest in Maginot Lines to Save Capitalism." *Dalhousie Law Journal* 11 (1988).

————. "A No-Frills Look at the Charter of Rights and Freedoms or How Politicians and Lawyers Hide Reality." *Access to Justice* 9 (1989).

————. "Commercial Morality through Capitalist Law—Limited Possibilities." *La revue juridique Themis* 27 (1993).

————. "More Direct Director Responsibility: Much Ado About . . .What?" *Canadian Business Law Journal* 25 (1995).

————. "Occupational Health and Safety: Criminal Law as a Political Tool." *Australian Journal of Labour Law* 11 (1998).

————. "Looking Back towards a Bleak Future for Lawyers." *Access to Justice* 19 (2001).

Glasbeek, H.J. and M. Mandel. "The Crime and Punishment of Jean-Claude Parrot." *Canadian Forum* 60,691 (1979).

Glasbeek, H.J. and S. Rowland. "Are Injuring and Killing at Work Crimes?" *Osgoode Hall Law Journal* 17 (1979).

Glasbeek, H.J. and E. Tucker. "Death by Consensus: The Westray Story." *New Solutions* 3, 4 (Summer 1993).

Glaser, D. "A Review of Crime-Causation Theory and Its Application." In *Crime and Justice*, vol.1, ed. Norval Morris and Michael Tonry. Chicago: University of Chicago Press, 1979.

Goff, C. and C. Reasons. *Corporate Crime in Canada.* Toronto: Prentice-Hall, 1978.

Golden, A. *Taking Responsibility for Homelessness: An Action Plan for Toronto.* Report of the Mayor's Homelessness Action Task Force. Toronto, 1999.

Gonick, Cy. "A Democratic Vision for the 21st Century." *Canadian Dimension* 34 (March/April 2000).

Goodrich, Carter, ed. *The Government and the Economy, 1783–1861.* Indianapolis: Bobbs-Merrill Co., 1967.

Gordon, David. "The Global Economy: New Edifice or Crumbling Foundations?" *New Left Review* 168 (1988).

Graves, F., B. Gauthier, and D. Jansen. *Rethinking Government 94: An Overview and Synthesis.* Ottawa: Ekos Research Associates, 1995.

Gray, John. *False Dawn: The Delusions of Global Capitalism.* London: Granta Books, 1998.

Greenwood, D. "Fictional Shareholders: For Whom Are Corporate Managers Trustees?" *Southern California Law Review* 69 (1996).

Greider, William. "Waking up the Global Elite." *The Nation*, Oct. 2, 2000.

Gross, E. "Organizations as Criminal Actors." In *Two Faces of Deviance*, ed. P. Wilson and J. Braithwaite. Brisbane, Aust.: University of Queensland Press, 1990.

Gunningham, Neil. "The Chemical Industry." In *Smart Regulation: Designing Environmental Policy*, ed. Neil Gunningham, P. Grabosky, and D. Sinclair. Oxford: Clarendon Press, 1998.

Gwyn, Richard. "Hypocrisy Surrounds Bribery Issue." *The Toronto Star*, July 18, 2001.

Hackett, Robert A. and Richard Gruneau, with D. Gutstein, A. Gibson, and Newswatch Canada. *The Missing News: Filters and Blind Spots in Canada's Press.* Ottawa and Aurora, Ont.: Canadian Centre of Policy Alternatives/ Garamond Press, 2000.

Hadden, T. *Company Law and Capitalism.* 2nd ed. London: Weidenfeld and Nicholson, 1981.

Halpern, P., M. Trebilcock, and S. Turnbull. "An Economic Analysis of Limited Liability in Corporation Law."*University of Toronto Law Journal* 30 (1980).

Handy, Charles. *The Hungry Spirit beyond Capitalism: A Quest for Purpose in the Modern World.* New York: Broadway Books, 1998.

Hansmann, H. and R. Kraakman. "Toward Unlimited Shareholder Liability for Corporate Torts." *Yale Law Journal* 100 (1991).

Harden, Blaine. "Pagers, Video Games and the Congo." *The Toronto Star*, Aug. 25, 2001.

Hasson, R.A. "How to Hand Weapons to Your Enemies—The Charter of Rights Fiasco." *Steelshots* 5 (June 1982).

Hart, H.L.A. "Immorality and Treason." *Listener* 62 (June 30, 1959).

Hartz, L. *Economic Policy and Democratic Thought: Pennsylvania, 1776–1860.* Cambridge, Mass.: Harvard University Press, 1948.

Hawken, Paul. *The Ecology of Commerce.* New York: HarperBusiness, 1993.

Hayden, Anders. "Capitalist Crunch." In *Ethical Issues in Business,* ed. Peg Tittle. Peterborough, Ont.: Broadview Press, 2000.

Hebert, Chantal. "Money Talks in the World of Politics." *The Toronto Star,* Sept. 7, 2001.

Heilbroner, Robert. *The Nature and Logic of Capitalism.* New York: Norton, 1985.

————. *The Making of Economic Society.* 7th ed. Englewood Cliffs, Cal.: Prentice-Hall, 1985.

Helleiner, E. "Post-Globalization: Is the Financial Liberalization Trend Likely to Be Reversed?" In *States against Markets: The Limits of Globalization,* ed. R. Boyer and D. Drache. London and New York: Routledge, 1996.

Heller, Tom. *Poor Health, Rich Profits: Multinational Drug Companies in the Third World.* London: Spokesman Books, 1977.

Henwood, Doug. "Post What?" *Monthly Review* 48 (1996).

————. *Wall Street: How It Works and for Whom.* London/ New York: Verso, 1998.

Herman, Edward S. and Noarm Chomsky. *Manufacturing Consent: The Political Economy of the Mass Media.* New York and Toronto: Pantheon Books/ Random House, 1988.

Herman, Patrick and Annie Thibaud-Mony. "Canada v. France—WTO Rules: The Asbestos Conspiracy." *Le Monde Diplomatique,* July 2000.

Hickey, Sue. "Citizenship and Disability: Invisibility Exists." Paper, "Revisioning Citizenship for the Twenty-First Century" conference, University of Waikato, Hamilton, New Zealand, 2000.

Hill, Jennifer. "Deconstructing Sunbeam—Contemporary Issues in Corporate Governance." *University of Cincinnati Law Review* 67 (1999).

Hills, Stuart L., ed. *Corporate Violence: Injury and Death for Profit.* Totowa, N.J.: Rowman and Littlefield, 1987.

Hirschi, Travis. *Causes of Delinquency.* Berkeley: University of California Press, 1969.

Hirschman, Albert O. *The Passions and the Interests.* Princeton, N.J.: Princeton University Press, 1977.

Hirst, P. and G. Thompson. "'The Problem of Globalization': International Economic Relations, National Economic Management and the Foundation of Trading Blocs." *Economy and Society* 21, 4 (1992).

Hodden, T., R. Forbes, and R. Simmonds. *Canadian Business Organizations Law.* Toronto: Butterworths, 1984.

Howse, R. and M. Trebilcock. "Protecting the Employment Bargain."*University of Toronto Law Journal* 43 (1993).

Hurst, J.W. *The Legitimacy of the Business Corporation in the Law of the United States, 1780– 1970.* Charlottesville: University of Virginia, 1970.

Hurtig, Mel. *The Betrayal of Canada.* Toronto: Stoddart, 1991.

Hutton,Will. *The State We're In.* London: Jonathan Cape, 1995.

Hyman, Richard. *Marxism and the Sociology of Trade Unionism.* London: Pluto Press, 1973.

Industry Canada. *Small Business Quarterly.* Ottawa: Entrepreneurship and Small Business Office, Fall 1997.

————. "Small Business in Canada: A Statistical Overview." Ottawa: Entrepreneurship and Small Business Office, March 1, 1996.

Ireland, P. "The Triumph of the Company Legal Form 1856–1914." In *Essays for Clive Schmitthoff,* ed. John Adams. Abingdon, Eng.: Professional Books, 1983.

————. "Capitalism without the Capitalist: The Joint Stock Company Share and the Modern Doctrine of Corporate Personality." *Legal History* 17 (1996).

————. "Corporate Governance, Stakeholding and the Company: Toward a Less Degenerate Capitalism?"*Journal of Law and Society* 23 (1996).

————. "Corporations and Citizenship." *Monthly Review,* May 1997.

Jackall, Robert. *Moral Mazes: The World of Corporate Managers.* New York: Oxford University Press, 1988.

Jackson, J., P. Weller, and the Waterloo Public Interest Research Group. *Chemical Nightmare: The Unnecessary Legacy of Toxic Wastes.* Toronto: Between the Lines, 1982.

Jenson, Jane. "Mapping Social Cohesion: The State of Canadian Research." CPRN Discussion Paper no. F03. Ottawa: Canadian Policy Research Network, 1998.

Jobb, D. *Calculated Risk.* Halifax: Nimbus Publishing, 1994.

Johnson, Arthur. *Breaking the Banks.* Toronto: General Publishing Paperbacks, 1986.

Jones, Barry J. *The World Turned Upside Down? Globalization and the Future of the State.* Manchester, Eng.: Manchester University Press, 2000.

Karliner, Joshua. *The Corporate Planet: Ecology and Politics in the Age of Globalization.* San Francisco: Sierra Club Books, 1997.

Kellman, Peter. "Public or Private?" *By What Authority,* Summer 2000.

Kesner, I., B. Victor, and B. Lamont. "Board Composition and the Commission of Illegal Acts: An Investigation of Fortune 500 Companies." *Academy of Management Journal,* December 1986.

Klein, Noami. *No Logo: Taking Aim at the Brand Bullies.* Toronto: Knopf Canada, 2000.

Kolko, Gabriel. *Wealth and Power in America: An Analysis of Social Class and Income Distribution.* New York: Praeger, 1962.

————. *The Roots of American Foreign Policy: An Analysis of Power and Purpose.* Boston: Beacon Press, 1969.

Koning, H. *The Conquest of America: How the Indian Nations Lost Their Continent.* New York: *Monthly Review* Press, 1993.

Korpi, W. *The Democratic Class Struggle.* London: Routledge and Kegan Paul, 1983.

Korten, David C. *The Post-Corporate World: Life after Capitalism.* San Francisco: Berrett-Koehler,1999.

————. *When Corporations Rule the World.* 2nd ed. San Francisco: Berrett-Koehler, 2001.

Krause and Lothian. "Measurement of Canada's Level of Corporate Concentration." *Canadian Economic Observer.* Ottawa: Statistics Canada, January 1989.

Kreisberg, S.M. "Decision Making Models and Control of Corporate Crime." *Yale Law Journal* 85 (1976).

Krugman, P. *The Age of Diminished Expectations: U.S. Economic Policy in the 1990s.* Cambridge: MIT Press, 1990.

————. *Accidental Tourist.* New York and London: W.W. Norton, 1998.

Kwitny, J. "The Great Transportation Conspiracy." *Harper's Magazine,* 1981.

Lapham, Lewis. "Lights, Camera, Democracy!" *Harper's Magazine,* August, 1996.

Lane, R.E. "Why Businessmen Violate the Law." In *White Collar Crime,* ed. G. Geis and R.F. Meier. New York: Free Press, 1977.

Law Reform Commission of Canada. *Our Criminal Law.* Ottawa: Information Canada, 1976.

————. *Crimes Against the Environment.* Ottawa: Law Reform Commission, 1985.

————. *Workplace Pollution.* Ottawa: Law reform Commission, 1986.

Leonard, W. and M. Weber. "Automakers and Dealers: A Study of Criminogenic Market Forces." *Law and Society Review* 4 (1969–70).

Levi, M. *Regulating Fraud: White Collar Crime and the Criminal Process.* London: Routledge, 1987.

—————. *Customer Confidentiality, Money Laundering and Police-Bank Relationships.* London: Police Foundation, 1991.

Levinson, Mark. "Wishful Thinking: A Response to 'Realizing Labor Standards.'" *Boston Review,* April 12, 2001.

Lexchin, Joel. *The Real Pushers: A Critical Analysis of the Canadian Drug Industry.* Vancouver: New Star Books, 1984.

Livesey, Bruce. "The Great Canadian Pig-Out." *Eye,* Nov. 11, 1999.

Locke, J. "Second Treatise on Civil Government: An Essay Concerning the True Original, Extent and End of Government." In *Social Contract: Essays by Locke, Hume and Rousseau,* Introduction by Sir Ernest Baker. London: Oxford University Press, 1946.

Lord, Miles. "The Dalkon Shield Litigation: Revised, Annotated Reprimand by Chief Justice Miles Lord." *Hamline Law Review* 9 (1986).

Louis, Arthur M. "Lessons from the Firestone Fracas." *Fortune,* Aug. 28, 1978.

Loveard, Keith. *Suharto: Indonesia's Last Sultan.* Singapore: Horizon Books, 1999.

Lummis, Douglas C. *Radical Democracy.* Ithaca, N.Y.: Cornell University Press, 1996.

Lux, K. *Adam Smith's Mistake: How a Moral Philosopher Invented Economics and Ended Morality.* Boston and London: Shambala Publications, 1990.

Maakestad, William J. "State v. Ford Motor Co.: Constitutional, Utilitarian and Moral Perspectives." *Saint Louis University Law Journal* 27 (1983).

MacDermid, Robert. "Funding the Common Sense Revolutionaries: Contributions to the Progressive Conservative Party of Ontario 1995–97." Scott Library, York University, Toronto.

Macdonald, Doug. *The Politics of Pollution.* Toronto: McClelland and Stewart, 1991.

————. "Voluntary Action or Elite Lobbying? The Canadian Chemical Industry and Environmental Policy." Paper, annual meeting, Canadian Political Science Association, University of Laval, Quebec, May 27, 2001.

Mace, Myles. *Directors: Myth and Reality.* Cambridge, Mass.: Harvard University Press, 1971.

————. "Directors: Myth and Reality—Ten Years Later." *Rutgers Law Review,* 1979.

Macey, J. "Agency Theory and the Criminal Liability of Organizations."*Buffalo University Law Review* 71 (1991).

McChesney, Robert W. *Corporate Media and the Threat to Democracy.* New York: Seven Stories Press, 1997.

McCormack, C., ed. *The Westray Chronicles.* Halifax: Fernwood Publishers, 1998.

McManus, John. *Market-Driven Journalism: Let The Citizen Beware!* Thousand Oaks, Cal.: Sage Publications, 1994.

McMullan, John. *Beyond the Limits of the Law: Corporate Crime and Law and Order.* Halifax: Fernwood Publishing, 1992.

McMurtry, John. *Unequal Freedoms: The Global Market as an Ethical System.* Toronto: Garamond Press, 1998.

Macpherson, C.B. "Elegant Tombstones: A Note on Friedman's Freedom." *Canadian Journal of Political Science* 1,8 (1968).

————. *Democratic Theory: Essays in Retrieval.* London: Clarendon Press, 1973.

Mandel, Harlan. "In Pursuit of the Missing Link: International Worker Rights and International Trade?" *Columbia Journal of Transitional Law* 27 (1989).

Mandel, Michael. *Readings in Criminology.* Toronto: Osgoode Hall Law School, York University, 1987.

————. *The Charter of Rights and the Legalization of Politics in Canada.* Rev. ed. Toronto: Thompson Educational Publishing, 1994.

Manteca Films. *Song of the Canary.* Franklin Lakes, N.J.: New Day Films, 1979.

Martin, Dianne. "Passing the Buck: Prosecution of Welfare Fraud." *Access to Justice* 12 (1992).

Mathews, J. "The Promotion of Press Diversity: Options Available to the Australian Government." Occasional Paper no. 4. Institute for Cultural Policy Studies, Griffith University, Queensland, Australia, 1988.

————. *Age of Democracy: The Politics of Post-Fordism.* Melbourne, Oxford, Auckland, and New York: Oxford University Press, 1989.

Mathieson, T. *The Viewer Society: On Media and Control in Modern Society.* Copenhagen: Socpol, 1987.

Mattson, Kevin. "Talking about My Generation (and the Left)." *Dissent,* Fall 1999.

Mazzocco, Dennis. *Networks of Power: Corporate TV's Threat to Democracy.* Foreword by Herbert I. Schiller, Boston, Mass.: South End Press, 1994.

Merton, R. *Social Theory and Social Structure.* New York: Free Press, 1957.

Michalowski, R. *Order, Law and Crime: An Introduction to Criminology.* New York: Random House, 1985.

Milner, Henry, ed. *Making Every Vote Count: Reassessing Canada's Electoral System.* Peterborough, Ont., and Orchard Park, N.Y.: Broadview Press, 1999.

Mintz, M. *At Any Cost: Corporate Greed, Women and the Dalkon Shield.* New York: Pantheon, 1985.

Mokhiber, R. *Corporate Crime and Violence: Big Business Power and Abuse of the Public Trust.* San Francisco: Sierra Club Books, 1988.

Mokhiber, R. and R. Weissman. *Corporate Predators: The Hunt for Mega-Profits and the Attack on Democracy.* Monroe, Me: Common Courage Press, 1999.

Monahan, Patrick. *Meech Lake: The Inside Story.* Toronto: University of Toronto Press, 1991.

Monroe, Arthur Eli, ed. *Early Economic Thought.* Cambridge, Mass.: Harvard University Press, 1930.

Morris, Jane Anne. "Help! I've Been Colonized and I Can't Get Up . . . : Take a Lawyer and an Expert to a Hearing and Call Me in a Decade." In *Defying Corporations, Defining Democracy*, ed. Dean Ritz. New York: Apex Press, for Program on Corporations, Law and Democracy (POCLAD), 2001.

Muller, M. *The Health of Nations*. London: Faber and Faber, 1982.

Mulvale, James P. *Reimagining Social Welfare: Beyond the Keynesian Welfare State*. Toronto: Garamond Press, 2001.

Nadel, M.V. "The Hidden Dimensions of Public Policy: Private Governments and the Policy-Making Process." *Journal of Politics* 37 (1975).

Nelson, Joyce. *Sultans of Sleaze: Public Relations and the Media*. Toronto: Between the Lines, 1989.

Nielson, Kai. "On Justifying Revolution." *Philosophy and Phenomenological Research* 37 (1976–77).

————. "On the Choice between Reform and Revolution." *Inquiry* 14 (1971).

Nitkin, David. "Socially Responsible Investing." *Corporate Ethics Monitor*, September-October 1993.

Noble, David. "Digital Diploma Mills: The Automation of Higher Education." *Monthly Review* 49,9 (1998).

————. *Digital Diploma Mills: The Automation of Higher Education*. Toronto: Between the Lines, 2002.

Novak, M. *Toward a Theology of the Corporation*. Washington and London: American Enterprise Institute for Policy Research, 1981.

Nova Scotia. *Report of the Commission of Public Inquiry: The Westray Story—A Predictable Path to Disaster* (Mr. Justice Peter Richard, Commissioner). Halifax, 1997.

Nove, A. *The Economics of Feasible Socialism*. London: Allen and Unwin, 1983.

O'Connor, James. *The Fiscal Crisis of the State*. New York: St. Martin's Press, 1973.

Ohmae, Kenneth. *The Borderless World: Power and Strategy in the Interlinked Economy*. New York: HarperBusiness, 1990.

————. "The Rise of the Regional State." *Foreign Affairs* 2 (1993).

Olive, David. *Just Rewards: The Case for Ethical Reform in Business*. Markham, Ont.: Penguin Books, 1987.

————. *White Knights and Poison Pills: A Cynic's Dictionary of Business Jargon*. Toronto: Key Porter Books, 1990.

Organization for Economic Cooperation and Development (OECD). *Corporate Responsibility—Private Initiatives and Public Goals*. Paris: OECD Publications, 2001.

Orhnial, T. ed. *Limited Liability and the Corporation*. London: Croom Helm, 1982.

Osberg, L., F. Wien, and J. Grude. *Vanishing Jobs: Canada's Changing Workplaces*. Toronto: James Lorimer, 1995.

Ostry, Sylvia. "The Domestic Domain: The New International Policy Arena." *Transnational Corporations*, 1,1 (1992).

————. "Will There Be Life after Seattle?" *The Globe and Mail*, Dec . 7, 1999.

Ouellet, Andre. *Misleading Advertising Bulletin*, 1975. Ottawa: Minister of Consumer and Corporate Affairs, 1975.

Packard, Vance O. *The Hidden Persuaders*. Harmondsworth, Eng.: Penguin Books, 1970.

Paltiel, Khayyam Z. *Party, Candidate and Election Finance: A Background Report.* Ottawa: Royal Commission on Corporate Concentration, no. 22, 1976.

Parenti, Michael. *Inventing Reality: The Politics of News Media.* 2nd ed. New York: St. Martin's Press, 1993.

————. *Make Believe Media: The Politics of Entertainment.* New York: St. Martin's Press, 1992.

Parker, Jeffrey S. "Criminal Sentencing Policy for Organizations: The Unifying Approach of Optimal Penalties." *American Criminal Law Review* 26,3 (Winter 1989).

Parkinson, J.E. *Corporate Power and Responsibility: Issues in the Theory of Company Law.* Oxford: Clarendon Press, 1993.

Patiel, K.Z. *Party, Candidate and Election Finance: A Background Report.* Toronto: Royal Commission on Corporate Concentration, 1977.

Pearce, F. *Crimes of the Powerful: Marxism, Crime and Deviance.* Foreword by Jock Young. London: Pluto Press, 1976.

Pearce, F. and S. Tombs. *Toxic Capitalism: Corporate Crime and the Chemical Industry.* Toronto: Canadian Scholars' Press, 1999.

Pearce, F. and L. Snider, eds. *Corporate Crime: Contemporary Debates.* Toronto and London: University of Toronto Press, 1995.

Pearce, F. and Snider, L. "Regulating Capitalism." In *Corporate Crime: Contemporary Debates,* ed. Pearce and Snider. Toronto and London: University of Toronto Press, 1995.

Pearce, F. and M. Woodiwiss, eds. *Global Crime Connections: Dynamics and Control.* Toronto: University of Toronto Press, 1993.

Pekkanen, John. *The American Connection: Profiteering and Politicking in the "Ethical" Drug Industry.* Chicago: Follett, 1973.

Pesando, J.E. and S. Rae. *Public and Private Pensions in Canada: An Economic Analysis.* Toronto: University of Toronto Press, 1977.

Pianin, Eric. "Toxic Chemical Review Process Faulted." *Washington Post,* July, 16, 2001.

Pickering, Murray A. "The Company as a Separate Legal Entity." *Modern Law Review* 31 (1968).

Pink, Daniel. "The Valdez Principles: Is What's Good for America Good for General Motors?" *Yale Law and Policy Review* 8 (1990).

Pirenne, H. *Medieval Cities: Their Origins and the Revival of Trade.* Princeton, N.J.: Princeton University Press, 1952.

Piven, Frances Fox. "Is It Global Economics or Neo-Laissez-Faire?" *New Left Review* 213 (1996).

Polanyi, K. *The Great Transformation: The Political and Economic Origins of Our Time.* Foreword by Joseph E. Stiglitz, Introduction by Fred Block. Boston, Mass.: Beacon Press, 2001.

Posner, Richard A. *The Economics of Justice.* Cambridge Mass.: Harvard University Press. 1981.

Postman, Neil. *Amusing Ourselves to Death.* London: Heinemann, 1985.

Press, Eyal and Jennifer Washburn. "The Kept University." *Atlantic Monthly* 285,3 (March 3, 2000).

Pring, George W. and Penelope Canan. *SLAPPS: Getting Sued for Speaking Out.* Philadelphia: Temple University Press, 1996.

Rand, A. *The Virtue of Selfishness: A New Concept of Egoism*. New York: New American Library, 1964.

Reasons, C., L. Ross, and C. Paterson. *Assault on the Worker: Occupational Health and Safety in Canada*. Toronto: Butterworths, 1981.

Rebick, Judy. *Imagine Democracy*. Toronto: Stoddart, 2000.

Redding, S. Gordon. *The Spirit of Chinese Capitalism*. New York: Walter de Gruyter, 1990.

Reiman, Jeffrey H. *The Rich Get Richer and the Poor Get Prison: Ideology, Class and Criminal Justice*. 2nd ed. New York: John Wiley and Sons, 1984.

Reynolds, D.D. Graham. "Observations on Sentencing in 'White Collar' and 'Blue Collar' Fraud Cases." Unpublished paper, Federal Prosecutors' Conference, Toronto, 1994.

Riches, G. *Food Banks and the Welfare Crisis*. Ottawa: Canadian Council on Social Development, 1986.

Ringleb, A. and S. Wiggins. "Liability and Large Scale, Long-Term Hazards." *Journal of Political Economy* 98 (1990).

Ripley, Don. *The Roos of Bay Street*. Halifax: Ripley Books, 1991.

Robinson, Richard. *Indonesia: The Rise of Capital*. Sydney and London: Allen and Unwin,1986.

Roe, Mark J. "Corporate Strategic Reaction to Mass Tort." *Virginia Law Review*, 1986.

Rohatyn, Felix G. "The Betrayal of Capitalism." *The New York Review of Books*, Feb. 28, 2002.

Roll, Richard. "Empirical Evidence on Takeover Activity and Shareholder Wealth." In *Knights, Raiders and Targets: The Impact of the Hostile Takeover*, ed. J. Coffee Jr., Louis Lowenstein, and Rose Rose-Ackerman. New York: Oxford University Press, 1988.

Roosevelt, F. and D. Balkin, eds. *Why Market Socialism?* Armonk, N.Y.: M.E. Sharpe, 1994.

Ross, E.A. *Sin and Society*. Boston: Houghton Mifflin, 1907.

Rubin, G.R. "Aron Salomon and His Circle." In *Essays for Clive Schmitthoff*, ed. J. Adams. Abingdon, Eng.: Professional Books, 1983.

Saltzburg, S. "The Control of Criminal Conduct in Organizations." *Buffalo University Law Review* 71 (1991).

Sampson, Anthony. *The Arms Bazaar*. New York: Viking Press, 1977.

Sargent, N. "Law, Ideology and Social Change: An Analysisof the Role of Law in the Construction of Corporate Crime." *Journal of Human Justice* 1,2 (1990).

Schmidt Jr., B. *Freedom of the Press vs. Public Access*. New York: Praeger, 1976.

Schlosser, Eric. *Fast Food Nation: The Dark Side of the All-American Meal*. New York: Houghton Mifflin, 2001.

Schor, J. *The Overworked American*. New York: Basic Books, 1991.

Sennett, Richard. *The Corrosion of Character: The Personal Consequences of Work in the New Capitalism*. New York: Norton, 1998.

Shapcott, Michael. "Government Fails the Homeless Again," *The Toronto Star*, Sept. 22, 2000.

Shapiro, Susan. *Wayward Capitalists: Targets of the Securities and Exchange Commission*. New Haven, Conn.: Yale University Press, 1984.

Sherrill, R. "Murder Inc: What Happens to Corporate Criminals?" *Utne Reader*, March–April 1987.

Shkilnyk, A. *A Poison Stronger Than Love: The Destruction of an Ojibwa Community*. New Haven, Conn.: Yale University Press, 1985.

Silverman, M. and P.R. Lee. *Pills, Profits and Politics*. Berkeley: University of California Press, 1974.

Sinclair, Upton. *The Jungle: The Lost First Edition*. Ed. and with an Introduction by Gene Degruson. Memphis and Atlanta: St. Lukes Press, 1988.

Slapper, G.A. "Corporate Killing." *New Law Journal* 144 (1994).

Smith, Adam. *The Theory of Moral Sentiments*. Indianapolis: Liberty Classics, 1976.

————. *An Inquiry into the Nature and Causes of the Wealth of Nations*. Ed. by Edwin Cannan. New York: Modern Library, 1994.

Snider, L. *Bad Business: Corporate Crime in Canada*. Toronto: Nelson Canada, 1993.

————. "Relocating Law: Making Corporate Crime Disappear." In *The Case for Penal Abolition*, ed. Gordon W. West and R. Morris. Toronto: Canadian Scholars' Press, 2000.

Soble, R.L. and R.E. Dallos. *The Impossible Dream: The Equity Funding Scandal*. New York: Putnam's, 1974.

Sobol, Richard B. *Bending the Law: The Story of the Dalkon Shield Bankruptcy*. Chicago and London: University of Chicago Press, 1991.

Sossin, Lorne. "Welfare State Crime in Canada: The Politics of Tax Evasion in the 1980s." *Access to Justice* 12 (1992).

Squires, James. *Read All About It! The Corporate Takeover of America's Newspapers*. New York: Times Books, 1997.

Stanbury, W. "Penalties and Remedies under the Combines Investigation Act 1899–1974." *Osgoode Hall Law Journal* 14 (1976).

————. "The New Competition Act and Competition Tribunal Act: 'Not with a Bang, but with a Whimper.'" *Canadian Business Law Journal* 12 (1986–87).

Stanford, Jim. *Paper Boom: Why Real Prosperity Requires a New Approach to Canada's Economy*. Toronto: James Lorimer, 1999.

Stapledon, G.P. and J. Lawrence. "Board Composition and Independence in Australia's Largest Companies." *Melbourne University Law Review* 21 (1997).

Statistics Canada. Small Business and Special Surveys Division. *Employment Dynamics, Business Size and Life Status*, 1993.

Sterngold, J. "California Justices Ban Suit against Gun Manufacturers." *The New York Times*, Aug. 7, 2001.

Stewart, James B. *Den of Thieves*. New York: Simon and Schuster, 1991.

Stewart, Walter, *Towers of Gold Feet of Clay*. Toronto: Totem Books, 1983.

Sutherland, E.H. "White Collar Crime." In *White Collar Crime*, ed. G. Geis and R.F. Meier. New York: Free Press, 1977.

Tabb, William K. "The World Trade Organization? Stop World Takeover." *Monthly Review* 51,8 (January 2000).

————. *The Amoral Elephant: Globalization and the Struggle for Social Justice in the Twenty-First Century*. New York: Monthly Review Press, 2001.

Teeple, Gary. *Globalization and the Decline of Social Reform into the Twenty-First Century*. Toronto: Garamond Press, 2000.

Thomas, Kenneth P. *Capital beyond Borders*. London: Macmillan, 1997.

Thompson, E.P. *Writings by Candlelight*. Cartoons by Gabriel. London: Merlin Press, 1980.

Tittle, Peg, ed. *Ethical Issues in Business: Inquiries, Cases, and Readings*. Peterborough, Ont.: Broadview Press, 2000.

Tollefson, C. "Corporate Constitutional Rights and the Supreme Court of Canada." *Queen's Law Journal* 19 (1993).

Toronto Stock Exchange, Committee on Corporate Governance in Canada. "Where Were the Directors?" Draft report (Dey, P., chair). Toronto, May 1994.

Troyer, Warner. *No Safe Place*. Toronto and Vancouver: Clarke, Irwin and Co., 1977.

Tucker, E. *Administering Danger in the Workplace*. Toronto: University of Toronto Press, 1990.

————. "The Westray Mine Disaster and Its Aftermath: The Politics of Causation." *Canadian Journal of Law and Society* 10,1 (Spring 1995).

————. "The Road from Westray: A Predictable Path to Disaster?" *Acadiensis* 28,1 (1998).

Tyler, Patrick. *Running Critical: The Silent War, Rickover and General Dynamics*. New York: Harper and Row, 1986.

UNCTAD. *World Investment Report 1995: Transnational Corporations and Competitiveness*. New York: United Nations, 1995.

United States. House of Representatives, Subcommittee on Oversight and Investigations of the Committee on Interstate and Foreign Commerce. *The Safety of Firestone 500 Steel-Belted Radial Tires*. 95th Congress, 2nd Session, Aug. 16, 1978.

United States. Sentencing Commission. "Sentencing Guidelines for Organizational Defendants." Preliminary draft, Nov. 1, 1989.

Varette, S.E., C. Meredith, P. Robinson, and D. Huffman. *White Collar Crime: Exploring the Issues*. Ottawa: Ministry of Justice, 1985.

Veblen, T. *The Theory of the Business Enterprise*. New York: Scribner's, 1904.

————. "The Theory of the Leisure Class." In *The Portable Veblen*, ed. and with an Introduction by Max Lerner. New York: Viking Press, 1948.

Veltmeyer, Harry. *Canadian Corporate Power*. Toronto: Garamond Press, 1987.

Waldman, M. and the Staff of Public Citizen's Congress Watch. *Who Robbed America? A Citizens' Guide to the S and L Scandal*. Introduction by Ralph Nader. New York and Toronto: Random House, 1990.

Wedderburn, Lord. "Trust, Corporation and the Worker." *Osgoode Hall Law Journal* 23 (1985).

Weedon Jr, D. "The Evolution of Sullivan Principle Compliance." *Business and Society*, Spring 1986.

Weiner, Tim. *Blank Check: The Pentagon's Black Budget*. New York: Warner Books, 1990.

Weir, David and Mark Schapiro. *Circle of Poison: Pesticides and People in a Hungry World*. San Francisco: Institute for Food and Development Policy, 1981.

Weissman, Robert. "Sixteen Years for a Snickers Bar." Focus on the Corporation web site. April 11, 2000. www.Corporate predators.org.

Welling, B. *Corporate Law in Canada: The Governing Principles*. 2nd ed. Toronto: Butterworths, 1991.

Wells, Celia. *Corporations and Criminal Responsibility*. Oxford: Clarendon Press, 1993.

Wells, Jennifer. "Ethics and Oil Brew up a Toxic Mixture in Sudan." *The Toronto Star*, Oct. 17, 2001.

Wichard, O. and J. Lowe. "An Ownership-Based Disaggregation of the U.S. Current Account." *Survey of Current Business*, October 1995.

Winkler, Matthew. "Lower Roller: Eurobond Market Sags, Crimping High Finance." *Wall Street Journal*, March 29, 1988.

Winslow, George. *Capital Crimes*. New York: Monthly Review Press, 1999.

Winter, John. *Democracy's Oxygen: How Corporations Control the Press*. Montreal: Black Rose Books, 1997.

Wolff, M. "On the Nature of Legal Persons." *Law Quarterly Review* 54 (1938).

Wolfgang, Marvin E. *National Survey of Crime Severity*. Washington, DC.: Bureau of Justice Statistics, 1985.

Wood, Ellen Meiksins. *Democracy against Capitalism: Renewing Historical Materialism*. Cambridge and New York: Cambridge University Press, 1995.

Wright, J.P. *On a Clear Day You Can See General Motors: John DeLorean's Look Inside the Automotive Giant*. New York: Avon, 1979.

Yalnizyan, Armine. *The Growing Gap: A Report on Growing Inequality between the Rich and Poor in Canada*. Toronto: Centre for Social Justice, 1998.

Yalnizyan, A., T. Ran Ide, and A.J. Cordell. *Shifting Times: Social Policy and the Future of Work*. Toronto: Between the Lines, 1994.

Yanz, L., B. Jeffcott, D. Ladd, and J. Atlin. *Policy Options to Improve Standards for Women Garment Workers in Canada and Internationally*. Ottawa: Status of Women, 1999.

Yates, Michael D. *Longer Hours, Fewer Jobs: Employment and Unemployment in the United States*. New York: Basic Books, 1991.

Yudkin, John S. "Wider-World Provision of Medicines in a Developing Country." *The Lancet*, April 15, 1978.

Ziegel, J. "Is Incorporation (with Limited Liability) Too Easily Available?" *Les Cahiers de Droit* 31 (1991).

Ziegel, Jacob, Jeffrey G. McIntosh, J. Daniels, and David L. Johnson. *Cases and Materials on Partnerships and Canadian Corporations*. 3rd ed. Toronto: Carswell, 1994.

Judicial Decisions

Abood v. Detroit Board of Education, 431 U.S. 209, (1977) (Sup. Ct. U.S.).

Anti-inflation Reference, [1976] 2 S.C. R. (Sup. Ct. Canada).

Attorney-General of Canada v. RJR-MacDonald, [1995] 3 S.C.R. 519 (Sup. Ct. Canada).

Attorney-General of Quebec v. Irwin Toy Ltd. (1989), 58 D.L.R. (4) 577 (Sup. Ct. Canada).

B.G. Preeco I (Pacific Coast) Ltd. v. Bon Street Holdings Ltd. (1989), 60 D.L.R. (4th) 30 (B.C.C.A.).

63502 British Columbia Limited v. Minister for National Revenue (1999), 248 N.R. 216 (Sup. Ct. Canada).

Brown (Henry) and Sons Ltd. v. Smith, [1964] 2 Lloyd's Rep. 477 (QB).

C.F.R. Holdings Ltd. v. Fundy Chemical International Ltd. (1980), 14 C.C.L.T. 87 (B. C.).

Canadian Dredge and Dock Co. Ltd. v. The Queen (1985), 19 C.C.C. (3d) 1 (Sup. Ct. Canada).

Consumer Education and Research Centre v. Union of India, [1995] All India Rep. 922 (Sup. Ct. India).

Covert et al. v. Nova Scotia, [1980] 2 S.C.R. 774 (Sup. Ct. Canada).

Daishowa Inc. v. Friends of the Lubicon (1998), 39 O.R. (3d) 620 (Ont. Sup. Ct.).

Einhorn v. Westmount Investments Ltd. (1969), 69 W.W.R. 31 (Sask. Q.B.).

Ford v. Quebec (Attorney-General) (1988), 54 D.L.R. (4th) 577 (Sup. Ct. Canada).

Gray v. Kerslake, [1968] S.C.R.3 (Sup. Ct. Canada).

Grimshaw v. Ford Motor Co., Cal. Sup. Ct. 1981.

Hunter v. Southam, [1984] 2 S.C.R. 145 (Sup. Ct. Canada).

Kosmopoulos v. Constitution Insurance Co. of Canada, [1987] 1 S.C.R. 2 (Sup. Ct. Canada).

Lennard's Carrying Co. Ltd. v. Asiatic Petroleum Co. Ltd., [1915] A.C. 705 (House of Lords).

Mesheau v. Campbell (1983), 39).R. (2d) 702 (Ont. Ct. App.).

Michaud v. National Bank of Canada and Royal Bank of Canada, [1997], R.J.Q. 547 (Quebec Sup. Ct.).

550551 Ontario Ltd. v. Framingham (1991), 4 O.R. (3d) 571 (Ont. Div. Ct.).

Pacific Coast Coin Exchange Ltd. v. Ontario Securities Commission, [1978] 2 S.C.R. 112 (Sup. Ct. Canada).

Parke v. Daily News, [1962] 1 Ch. 927 (U.K. Ct. Chancery).

People v. Pymm (1990), 563 N.E. (2d) 1.

Public Service Alliance of Canada v. Attorney-General Canada, [1987] 1 S.C.R. 424 (Sup. Ct. Canada).

R. v. Amway, unreported, Toronto, Sup. Ct. Ont. (Evans C.J.), Nov. 10, 1983.

R. v. Amway, [1989] 1 S.C.R. 21 (Sup. Ct. Canada).

R. v. Bata Industries (1992), 9 O.R. (3d) 329 (Ont. S. Ct.).

R. v. City of Sault Ste. Marie (1975), 85 D.L.R. (3d) 161 (Sup. Ct. Canada).

R. v. Ellis Don, [1992] 1 S.C.R. 840 (Sup. Ct. Canada).

R v. Fane Robinson Ltd., [1943] 3 D.L.R. 409 (Alta. S.C. App. Div.).

R. v. Inco Ltd. (2001), 155 C.C.C. (3d) 383 (Ont. Ct. App.).

R. v. Kite, Stoddard and OLL, unreported, Winchester Crown Court, U.K. (Ognall, J.), Dec. 9, 1994.

R. v. McKinley Transport Limited, [1990] 1 S.C.R. 627 (Sup. Ct. Canada).

R v. Sears Canada Inc., March 23, 1990 (unreported), (Ont. District Ct., Peterborough).

R. v. The Great North of England Railway Company (1846), 115 E. R. 1294 (Eng. Q. B.).

R. v. Vasil (1981), 35 N.R. 451 (Sup. Ct. Canada).

R. v. Wholesale Travel Group Inc., [1991] 3 S.C.R. 154 (Sup. Ct. Canada).

R. v. Zundel (1992), and 5 C.C.C. (3d) 449 (Sup. Ct. Canada).

Re Public Service Employee Relations Act, [1987] 1 S.C.R. 313 (Sup. Ct. Canada).

Retail, Wholesale and Department Store Union, Locals 544, 496, 635 and 955 v. Government of Saskatchewan, [1987] 1 S.C.R. 460 (Sup. Ct. Canada).

Rockwell Developments Ltd. v. Newtonbrook Plaza Ltd., [1972] 3 O.R. 199 (C.A.).

R.W.D.S.U., Local 558 v. Pepsi-Cola Canada Beverages (West) Ltd. (2002) SCC8/ File no. 27060 (Sup. Ct. Canada).

Salomon v. Salomon and Co., [1897] A.C. 22 (H.L.).

Teck Corporation Ltd. v. Millar, [1973] 2 W.W.R. (B.C.).

Thomson Newspapers v. Director of Investigations and Research, [1990] 1 S.C.R. 420 (Sup. Ct. Canada).

U.F.C.W., Local 1518 v. K Mart Canada Ltd., [1999] 2 S.C.R. 1083 (Sup. Ct. Canada).

Valentine v. Chrestensen, 316 U.S. 52 (1942) (Sup. Ct. U.S.).

Virginia State Board of Pharmacy v. Virginia Citizens Council, 425 U.S. 748 (1976), (Sup. Ct. U.S.).

Walkovsky v. Carlton, 223 N.E. 2d 6 (N.Y. C.A. 1966).

Westinghouse Canada Limited, [1980] O.L.R.B. Rep. 577 (Ont. Labour Relations Board).

Selected Statutes

Canada Business Corporations Act, R.S.C. 1985, c. C-44, as am.

Charter of Rights and Freedoms, Part I of the *Constitution Act*, 1982, being Schedule B to the Canada Act 1982 (United Kingdom).

Competition Act.

Employment Standards Act, R.S.O. 1980, c.137, as am.

Securities Act, R.S.O. 1980, c.466, as am.

Index